D1565948

THE
STRUGGLE FOR
POWER

RUSSIA IN 1923

RUSSIAN STUDIES SERIES

Valery Kuvakin, General Editor

GENERAL INTEREST

History of Russian Philosophy, 2 volumes, edited by Valery Kuvakin

The Basic Bakunin: Writings 1869–1871, translated and edited by Robert M. Cutler

Anton Chekhov: Stories of Women, edited and translated by Paula Ross

FROM THE SECRET ARCHIVES
OF THE FORMER SOVIET UNION

Out of the Red Shadows: Anti-Semitism in Stalin's Russia, by Gennadi V. Kostyrchenko

Lenin's Will: Falsified and Forbidden, by Yuri Buranov

The Red Army and the Wehrmacht: How the Soviets Militarized Germany in 1922–1933, and Paved the Way for Fascism, by Yuri L. Dyakov and Tatyana S. Bushuyeva

The Struggle for Power: Russia in 1923, by Valentina P. Vilkova

THE
STRUGGLE FOR
POWER

RUSSIA IN 1923

VALENTINA VILKOVA

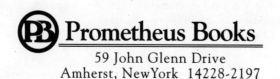 Prometheus Books

59 John Glenn Drive
Amherst, NewYork 14228-2197

Published 1996 by Prometheus Books

00 99 98 97 96   5 4 3 2 1

Library of Congress Cataloging-in-Publication Data

Vilkova, Valentina P.
    [Rossiia v 1923 godu. English]
    The struggle for power—Russia in 1923 : from the secret archives of the former Soviet Union / Valentina Vilkova.
        p.   cm.
    Includes bibliographical references.
    ISBN 1–57392–026–6 (alk. paper)
    1. Soviet Union—Politics and government—1917–1936—Sources. 2. Kommunis-ticheskaia partiia Sovetskogo Soiuza—History—Sources. I. Title.
DK266.5.V5513   1996
947.084—dc20   95–26143
                                                                              CIP

Printed in the United States of America on acid-free paper

Contents

---

*NOTE: The transliterated Russian abbreviations TsK, TSKK, and RKP(b) are used respectively for TsK (Central Committee), TSKK (Central Control Commission) and RKP(b) (Russian Communist Party of Bolsheviks, which was the name of the Communist Party of Russia up to December 1925).

5

List of Abbreviations

Glavkom (Glavnokomanduyuschii)—Commander-in-Chief.

Gosplan (Gosudarstvennyi Planovyi Komitet)—State Planning Committee.

GPU (Gosudarstvennoe Politicheskoe Upravlenie)—State Political Directorate (SPD).

Gubkom (Gubernskii Komitet)—Guberniya (Provincial) Committee.

Komintern (Kommunisticheskii Internatsional)—Communist International, Comintern.

KPG (Kommunisticheskaya Partiya Germanii)—The Communist Party of Germany (CPG).

MK (Moskovskii Komitet)—Moscow Committee (MC).

Narkomfin (Narodnyi Kommissar Finansov)—People's Commissar of Finance.

Narkomindel (Narodnyi Kommissar Inostrannykh Del)—People's Commissar of Foreign Affairs.

Narkomprod (Narodnyi Kommissar Prodovolstviya)—People's Commissar of Foodstuffs.

Narkomput (Narodnyi Kommissar Putei Soobscheniya)—People's Commissar of Communications.

NEP (Novaya Ekonomicheskaya Politika)—New Economic Policy.

NKID (Narodnyi Kommissariat Inostrannykh Del)—The People's Commissariat for Foreign Affairs (PCFA).

NK RKI (Narodnyi Kommissariat Raboche-Krestyanskoi Inspektsii)—The People's Commissariat of the Workers' and Peasants' Inspections (PC WPI).

NKVD (Narodnyi Kommissariat Vnutrennikh Del)—The People's Commissariat for Internal Affairs (PCIA).

OGPU (Obyedinennoye Gosudarstvennoye Politicheskoye Upravleniye)—Unified State Political Directorate.

Orgburo (Orgbyuro)—Organizational Bureau (OB).

Politburo (Politbyuro)—Political Bureau (PB).

RKP(b) (Rossiiskaya Kommunisticheskaya Partya [Bolshevikov])—Russian Communist Party (of Bolsheviks) RKP(b).

RSFSR (Rossiiskaya Sovetskaya Federativnaya Sotsialisticheskaya Respublika)—Russian Soviet Federal Socialist Republic (RSFSR).

RCChIDNI (Vserossiiskii Tsentr Khraneniya I Izucheniya Dokumentov Noveishei Istorii)—The Russian Center for Keeping and Study of the Documents of Modern History (RCKSDMH).

RVS, Revvoensovet (Revolyutsionnyi Voyennyi Sovet)—Revolutionary War Council (RMC).

RVSR (Revolyutsionnyi Voyennyi Sovet Respubliki)—Revolutionary War Council of the Republic.

SNK, Sovnarkom (Sovet Narodnykh Kommissarov)—Council of People's Commissars.

STO (Sovet Truda i Oborony)—Council of Labor and Defense (CLD).

TsK (Tsentralnyi Komitet)—Central Committee (CC).

TSKK (Tsentralnaya Kontrolnaya Komissiya)—Central Control Commission (CCC).

Ukom (Uyezdnyi Komitet)—Uyezd (District) Committee.

VSNKh (Vysshii Sovet Narodnogo Khozyaistva)—Supreme Council of People's Economy (SCPE).

VTsIK (Vserossiiskii Tsentralnyi Ispolnitelnyi Komitet)—the All-Russian Central Executive Committee (RCEC).

Preface

In the autumn and winter months of 1923 a political drama was taking place in the Russian Communist Party (Bolsheviks) (RKP[b])—the Party that was the monopolist ruler in the country—the consequences of which not only predetermined the tragic outcome in the personal fate of many of its participants, but also, to a considerable extent, stipulated the character and orientation of the subsequent events in the Party and in the country as a whole.

The point in question is the All-Party discussion that was under way at the time in the RKP(b), which can scarcely be considered a manifestation of democracy, since behind the official discussion and under its guise one could see the first stage of tough inner-Party struggle developing in the top echelons of the Party leadership at the time of V. I. Lenin's illness (1922–1923).

This present collection of archival materials is, in fact, the first attempt to give a more or less integral, scientific, and documentary presentation of the struggle at that stage. We hope that these documents—mainly unknown or little known even in Russia—will enrich the source material available to researchers dealing with the history of the Russian Communist Party of the 1920s. Possibly they will lead to certain modifications in historical concepts of that period and methodological principles in the study of the roots and stages of the formation of Stalinism.

The documents presented actually cover the period from September 1923 to January 1924. Space did not permit the inclusion of a large number of documents dealing with the struggle in the "top echelons" of the Party on the problem concerning the formation of the USSR and the so-called Georgian affair[1]; the documents of great interest dealing with the history of the publication of the last notes and articles by V. I. Lenin, known as the "political testament"; and materials concerning the preparation and carrying out of the Twelfth Congress of the RKP(b), as well as the correspondence between the members of the Political Bureau in the summer of 1923.[2] Clearly, all these documents help shed light on the prehistory of the discussion and the political, inner-Party situation which served as background.

The documents included here are a revealing record of a critical point within the Party during the struggle for power of 1923. That struggle became the dominating idea influencing and determining not only the solution to all remaining problems, but also the attitude of the members of the Party leadership to their ailing leader and his last works.

The starting point of the struggle for power in the Bolshevik Party was the moment when V. I. Lenin hung between life and death following a stroke on May 25, 1922, and the question about his official successor became a practical necessity. All the theoretical and political discussions were reduced to the personality factor. From the point of view of Lenin[3] himself, the only person in the leadership who could pretend to the post of the Chairman of the Sovnarkom,* was L. D. Trotsky. According to the tradition established when Lenin was still alive, the head of the Soviet government automatically became the chairman at the meetings of the Political Bureau of the TsK RKP(b).†

However, the possibility of such a variant did not suit certain members of the Politburo of the TsK, primarily those in whose hands were concentrated the levers of the Party-and-state power and whose ambitious pretensions to leadership in the Party were known enough well. The person in question was G. E. Zinovyev, who by that time held the post of Chairman of the Executive Committee of the Communist International and headed its Petrograd Soviet. The advent of Trotsky to power could considerably shake the positions of L. B. Kamenev, who in Lenin's absence replaced him in the Council of People's Commissars (Sovnarkom) and the Council of Labor

---

*See the List of Abbreviations. (Ed.)
†Ibid. (Ed.)

and Defense, and who also presided over the meetings of the Politburo of the Central Committee.

J. V. Stalin could not accept the possibility of Trotsky's being nominated for that post. Their relations remained strained from the days before the revolution and the differences between them intensified during the period of the civil war. But that was not the only point. Then Stalin was appointed to the post of General Secretary of the TsK RKP(b) in April 1922, he resolutely started to form the system of "hierarchy of secretaries," which would become the support of the General Secretary in the Party and ensure the majority of his camp over potential opponents in his struggle for power.

In spite of certain difference of opinion and far-reaching plans of every member of the "troika" (three-man commission) mentioned at that stage they were mostly united by the common cause—to preserve their own monopoly of power, and, therefore, not allow Trotsky to become the leader; to block his initiative and retaliatory actions, to discredit and, as a result, to isolate him from the process of political struggle. For the realization of these plans, on the basis of the personal agreements, the "troika" became, in fact, a non-statute leading group existing alongside the Politburo of the Central Committee. With the aim of isolating Trotsky, most questions of principle to be discussed at the Politburo were considered and solved in advance at the sessions of the "troika." The other members and candidates to be members of the Politburo—A. I. Rykov, M. P. Tomsky, and N. I. Bukharin—were gradually being involved in apparatus intrigues.

Within the Party circles close to the leadership it was evident to everybody who, in fact, ruled the Party and the country. The members of the old Party guard working side by side with Lenin for many years and the Party intelligentsia as a whole who had been watching the maneuvers of the "troika" began to understand more and more that the mechanism created by Lenin and in accordance with Lenin's political line would not work the same way without him; that neither "troika" nor "pyatyorka" (five persons) could replace the leader. This was openly declared by some delegates of the Twelfth Party Congress in April 1923.

Nevertheless, the members of the "main leading body" (as the members of the "troika" named themselves), zealously protecting their monopoly for power, consciously supported the illusion that all their actions were agreed to with Lenin. With just this aim in mind, the official propaganda of 1922–1923) had been constantly maintaining the myth about the rapid recovery of Lenin's health.

At the beginning of October 1922 Lenin did return to work. However, at that time, without knowing it himself, he actually became the hostage of the confrontation occurring within the Party leadership. As a result of the efforts exerted by the members of the "troika" and, first and foremost, by Kamenev and Stalin, who visited the ailing leader most often, Lenin was removed not only from performing his functions but also from receiving any objective political information. Strictly dosed and thoroughly selected information supplied by them would, according to their plans, "prepare" Lenin for taking certain decisions with respect to Trotsky.

Lenin wrote a message to Kamenev, first published in 1991, concerning the latter's proposal—a proposal apparently suggested on behalf of the "troika."—to expel Trotsky from the Central Committee. The message reads: "To throw Trotsky overboard—this is what you are making hints about. There cannot be another interpretation—it should be the height of absurdity. If you do not consider me to be hopelessly stupefied, how can you think so! . . . "[4]

Lenin considered difference of opinion and conflicts among the Party leadership to be a natural phenomenon and rarely he tried to bring these differences to the front and make them irreconcilable. However, returning to the leadership after a half-year absence, he was deeply disappointed with his nearest comrades-in-arms who had turned the Central Committee of the Party into a scene of an unprincipled and immoral struggle for power. N. K. Krupskaya wrote later that Lenin had been indignant and perturbed by the morals and manners being formed among the "top men" in his absence.[5] It did not take Lenin much time to realize that he was within a political vacuum, that the "troika" had once and for all openly taken a position differing from his own on a whole range of current political issues important in principle!

Besides, Lenin could not but pay attention to the fact that rather serious qualitative changes had taken place in the Central Committee of the Party: when Stalin became the General Secretary, he managed to transform the Secretariat of the Central Committee from an organizational-technical body into a political one, while his own post was changed into a supreme administrative one in the system of apparatus "hierarchy of secretaries," which, according to Lenin, allowed him to concentrate unbounded power in his hands. Lenin was realistic enough to understand that, possessing such power, Stalin could go to the end in his struggle against Trotsky right up to the split in the ranks of the Central Committee, which would threaten the stability of Bolshevik power as a whole.

The circumstances made Lenin seek for political counterbalance to the power of the "troika." As Trotsky later recalled, Lenin, during a long debate with him,* suggested concluding an alliance to struggle against bureaucracy in general and against the Orgburo (i.e., against Stalin) in particular.[6] The similarity of their positions has been strengthened by the unity of their views on other important problems.

As was illustrated by the events that followed, and as documentarily confirmed in the letters of Trotsky to the Central Committee[7] published in this collection, the Lenin and Trotsky bloc was based on the principal coincidence of their views and positions on cardinal problems in the political life of those times. The case in point was the preservation of the monopoly of foreign trade, the principles of the national policy, and the "Georgian affair,"[8] about stimulating the activity of the State Planning Committee (Gosplan), and the necessity to reorganize the supreme bodies of Party power. Judging from the documents the "Lenin-Trotsky" bloc could become the real political force capable of withstanding the "troika" and changing radically the course of events.

However, Lenin was not back at work for long. In mid-December 1922, he was obliged to leave the Kremlin again owing to abrupt deterioration of his health. Time became for Lenin the decisive factor, and he insisted that the doctors allow him to dictate (since he could no longer write) what he considered necessary to declare at the regular Twelfth Congress of the RKP(b).

On December 23, Lenin started to dictate the well-known "Letter to the Congress." He began with what worried him most of all at that moment: the proposed political reform of Party power which, in his opinion, would prevent the split of the leadership. However, the struggle for power that had begun with new force testified to the fact that Lenin was late with his proposals. The split in the top echelons of the Party, which was the point of his hypothetical reflections in the "letter to the Congress," had become a reality by the end of 1922. Lenin's "political testament" can be spoken about only in this context. Taken separately, without due attention given to the inner-Party struggle, it loses its genuine sense and concrete historic meaning.

It should be said that we are not going to study or appraise the last works by Lenin. For seventy years of its history the "political testament" as a political phenomenon and an object of research has gathered a rather

---

*The debate took place on October 11, 1922. (Ed.)

abundant harvest from the field of scientific researches which reflects a wide spectrum of approaches and estimates—from sweet panegyrics to frank disparagement.

From our point of view, the main thing is that Lenin, as a realist and pragmatist in politics, as well as a sociologist, understood fairly well that the mechanism of power created by him (an authoritarian paradigm with a charismatic leader at the top), in conditions of undeveloped Party democracy and bureaucratic centralism, would inevitably elevate the so-called apparatus leader to the levers of power, regardless of his personal traits. It happened just as we said. By the end of 1922 Stalin had the real power in the Party, since over half of the Party secretaries of the regional committees obtained their posts from his hands.

Lenin suggested breaking up such a system, replacing it with an oligarchic one (they called it collective leadership at those times), and putting it under the control of rank-and-file Party members. He thought out the mechanism of control presented by a unified body of the Party and State inspection (PC RCI-TSKK),* not subordinated to the leadership of the Party. Obviously it was the best but—in conditions of the growing struggle for power—the least possible of all the variants.

Note that nobody among the ruling circles at that time wanted the appearance of a sole leader similar to Lenin, and nobody from the members of the Politburo could expect to receive that post. The oligarchic principle of the "leading collective" could be acceptable, then, for all its members, including Trotsky, while the mechanism of an inevitable group struggle would compensate for the defects in democratic levers of government and the different interests being presented at the top of Party power. The alternative of a power organization suggested by Lenin could be convenient to the leadership, but the main point was: whether the Party leadership would agree to be controlled by the Party masses, i.e., to create the conditions which, according to Lenin, could not allow a group struggle to result in a split of the Party in its "top echelons."

However, there was nobody in the Party leadership who could carry out this reform. It was the political will of Lenin himself and his accomplices that was needed to put it into practice. But the "main leading body" of the Central Committee was, in truth, objectively not ready to accept Lenin's innovations, at the same time, having acquired a taste for power,

---

*See the List of Abbreviations. (Ed.)

they were not going to be controlled by the Party "masses" and did not want anything to be changed in essence. Lenin's "political testament" actually remained a doctrine without those who could realize it, without power. Moreover, it was turned into a weapon in the political struggle with Trotsky via manipulation of the text of Lenin's notes and articles (i.e., through different deletions and additions).[9]

We have deliberately drawn the attention of readers to the events preceding the appearance of Lenin's "Testament." These events, as well as the chronicle of those one hundred winter days, during which Lenin was dictating his last notes and trying hard to overcome the toughening isolation, as well as all the subsequent events—all this is not merely a history of the struggle with serious illness, nor only the Bolshevik leader's great human tragedy. The documents published in recent years testify to the fact that this is also the history of an acute and persistent political struggle that was being consciously carried out from both sides, in which the opponents of Lenin representing the "main leading body" allowed themselves to use methods that were beyond normal bounds of legality and common decency. Thus, for instance, Lenin begged his secretaries to keep secret the "Letters to the Congress" as well as other confidential notes and instructions dictated by him. He could not even imagine that the same day he dictated them they would become known to those against whom they were directed, as a result of which many of his initiatives and requests were blocked under the pretense of care about his health, or else simply ignored.

Nevertheless, Lenin managed to get the objective information on the question that worried him no less than the split in the Central Committee— the materials on the "Georgian affair." Having studied the matter, Lenin came to the conclusion that he had made gross political mistakes in his decision, which could strike an irreparable blow against the principles of federalism—equality and sovereignty of the republics—just at the moment when the foundations for the creation of the future Union were being laid. Proceeding from that, Lenin, according to Kamenev,[10] was going to make certain organizational rearrangement in the leadership at the upcoming Twelfth Party Congress and, first and foremost, relieve Stalin of the post of General Secretary of the Central Committee.

The preparation to the Twelfth Congress, planned for March 1923, was underway in the Central Committee of the Party as well. At the Plenum of the TsK they were supposed to discuss the theses of the resolution on the question of relations between nationalities written by Stalin and the theses of the report by Trotsky on industry. The text prepared by Stalin testified to the fact that he was not going to abandon his own views on the principles of creation of the unitary state, and that the concessions made to Lenin's plan (unification of equal and sovereign republics on the basis of federation) were a formal compromise.

Having received the text of Stalin's theses, Trotsky considered it necessary to include these important amendments, reflecting his own as well as Lenin's position on the problem of international relations. The point is that up to that time he was the only member of the Politburo who had the text of Lenin's dictated notes to the "Question of Nationalities or 'Autonomization,' " which were the draft of Lenin's speech to the Twelfth Party Congress. Lenin directed those materials to Trotsky after he found out that they both were at one with the appraisal of Stalin's group actions in the "Georgian affair." Stalin adopted the amendments. In the situation formed by the beginning of March 1923 he could not have behaved otherwise.

The situation in the Politburo of the Central Committee remained tense, while Stalin's position was critical. He knew, and not only from Kamenev, that Lenin "was preparing a bomb for him" at the Congress. Moreover, Stalin understood from Lenin's note of March 5 sent to him regarding his rude attitude to N. K. Krupskaya, that Lenin was ready to break his personal relations too. On the same day he decided to take a desperate step—he submitted a proposal about postponing the date of the Twelfth Congress.

Actually, this was a measure taken to isolate Lenin from the Twelfth Congress: having objective information on the state of Lenin's health, the "troika" hoped to win time. The proposal was supported unanimously by all the members of the Politburo.

On the night of March 6 to 7, and later on March 10, Lenin's condition abruptly worsened, which led to paralysis and loss of speech. From that moment on to his death, Lenin remained beyond political life and struggle.

Power remained in the hands of the "troika." Stalin was saved: he escaped the threat of the failure of his political career. The changed situation allowed the members of the "main leading body" to concentrate on the further struggle against Trotsky. Now any occasion could be used for his political discrediting. Such an attempt was made during the discussion of Trotsky's theses on industry, as well as in connection with the fact that on April 16 Trotsky sent materials concerning the "Georgian affair" to the members of the Central Committee. Yet the "troika" did not dare to come out against him openly. As shown at the Twelfth Congress, the authority of Trotsky in the Party was too high,

Many historians used to ask: Why didn't Trotsky speak at the Twelfth Congress on the problems of the national policy? For instance, an American researcher and biographer of Trotsky, J. Deutscher, believed that Trotsky and the "troika" made an agreement, according to which Trotsky, in return for his promise not to speak on the question of relation between nationalities, was given the right to state his position on the problems of economy.[11]

In our opinion, there could be another logical explanation of the situation. First, Trotsky knew that Stalin had adopted the amendments on the question of relations between nationalities and could believe that the resolution adopted at the Congress would correspond to Lenin's directives; second, he knew about the decision to inform the delegations about Lenin's dictations on "The Question of Nationalities or 'Autonomization.' " Therefore he could consider it necessary for himself to speak at the Congress on the problems of economic policy, the more so since serious differences of opinion concerning the solution of those problems had been revealed in the Party leadership.

However, the ruling echelons of the Party betrayed Lenin's position concerning the question of relations between nationalities, they gave him up when he was still alive, and deviated from his heritage just in the practice of national and state construction. The Union, as it was planned and pictured by Lenin, was never created. A month later, after the Twelfth Party Congress, Stalin convened the Fourth Conference with the leaders of the National Republics where the decisions of the Congress on the question of relations between nationalities were in fact repudiated and the struggle with local nationalism was determined as the main task. Thus they gave sanctions to take repressive measures against the leading national cadres, who opposed Stalin's imperial line. Soon after they dissolved the Ukrainian government headed by Kh. G. Rakovsky, they summoned the Georgian leaders to the Central Committee, fabricated the case, and arranged the trial over M. Sultan Galiev. All this further complicated the country's political situation, which was already intricate enough.

Focusing on the problem of their struggle for power, the "main leading body" was primarily interested in the further aggravation of the situation, and, therefore could not pay due attention to the urgent political and economic problems required by the objective situation.

' The first symptoms of the economic crisis appeared as early as spring of 1923, which was marked by difficulties in the sales of industrial products. It was necessary to promptly work out the mechanism of state regulation of the economy, to determine the line and methods of closer coordination between different economic sectors, and to solve the problems of priorities in the economic policy. These economic questions and different approaches to them were the main point of the differences between the majority of the Central Committee and Trotsky, who was supported by G. L. Pyatakov, E. A. Preobrazhensky, and other representatives of the "Left Wing."

Without considering both points of view as the absolutes,we may say that there were grains of truth both in the position of the "Left Wing" ("the dictatorship of industry") and in that of the majority of the Central Committee ("the dictatorship of finances"). In the present state of affairs it was necessary that the Party leadership come to a constructive correlation of positions and the working out of optimum decisions beforehand (peculiar symbiosis of economic, as well as planning and administrative measures) which, if it could not stop the approaching crisis of sales, could at least cushion its shocks. There was a real possibility for a dialogue and mutual search for solutions, since, first, in early 1923 Trotsky corrected his initial anti-market position, and, second, by the end of December 1922 the members of the Politburo knew the transformed position of Lenin, his support of Trotsky in principle on the problem of Gosplan.

However, it is precisely this circumstance that has determined the fate of Lenin's notes on Gosplan* and the theses of Trotsky on industry containing a number of constructive proposals for the stabilization of the economic situation.

In September the crisis had become a reality. The absence of the mechanism of state regulation of prices allowed the industrial trusts and trade syndicates that were monopolizing the home market to bloat prices. Besides, the peasantry, who for the first time had received the right to pay tax in kind not only by trade but also in cash, preferred to do the latter. In order to gain money, the peasants threw a great amount of grain on the market, as a result of which the price of grain abruptly dropped. On October 1 the difference in prices was 320 percent, and in some districts the figure was even higher.

The crisis struck the working class first. Industrial enterprises were

---

*They were first published in the USSR only in 1956. (Ed.)

closing, the number of unemployed exceeded a million, and the delay of payment to those who continued to work at the factories amounted to several months. In September and October a wave of strikes swept the biggest industrial centers in the country.

However, the growing dissatisfaction of the people with the Bolshevik power had not only economic roots. In addition to the market economy, social inequalities between workers and the Party dictatorship inevitably acquired the political character. Many reports of the GPU* of that period marked the growth of "hostility and antagonism" between the workers and administration of enterprises, consisting mostly of the Party members. The Party broke contact with the working masses which were considered to be its social support; the growing "opposition" sentiments turned out to be a serious threat to the Bolshevik power.

The threat came not from the working class alone. The introduction of the NEP† inevitably demanded definite democratic reforms in the political superstructure corresponding to the conditions of a "civil peace." The peasants striving for political activity, the petite bourgeoisie in towns declared that they should be represented in executive bodies. However, the Bolshevik leadership sought a way out not through the search for a compromise between certain social forces, but through the strengthening of the Party monopoly of power.

The socioeconomic and political crisis of the autumn of 1923 could not but have an impact on the ruling Party, on its inner-Party life. By this time the confrontation of the two tendencies had been determined quite definitely in the RKP(b); on the one hand, there was a bureaucratic tendency represented by the "hierarchy of the secretaries" already monolithic enough, united by common political and economic interests; and on the other hand, there was a democratic tendency represented by the "left-wing" opposition that was ideologically and organizationally disunited, that included all the different-minded persons in the Party whose leader would inevitably become Trotsky. The views of the representatives of the opposition on many problems were quite different, and in the autumn of 1923, the only thing that united them ideologically was the very fact of their opposition to the economic, political, and inner-Party course and an openly sharp criticism of that course. The only constructive political de-

---

*See the List of Abbreviations. (Ed.)
†Ibid. (Ed.)

mand common to all of them was the introduction of the elements of inner-Party democracy.

It was in such conditions that the inner-Party discussion of 1923 started. It was the continuation of the struggle for power which was imposed by the "troika" during the foregoing period. It is only natural that the crises in the economy, the social sphere, policy and inner-Party life demanded that necessary decisions be taken by the ruling majority; but the ways and methods for the solution of contradictions were beyond the search for constructive and businesslike approaches. According to the documents published in the present collection, all the actions of the "main leading body" of the Central Committee were subordinated to only one task—to politically smear the reputation of Trotsky and to ideologically destroy the opposition.

In our opinion, it is not necessary that we give a detailed chronological description of all the documents. We will dwell upon the most important stages in the discussion and analysis of the mechanism of tactional struggle created by the ruling majority headed by the "troika" which had served Stalin faultlessly for twenty years in his struggle against the opposition and any nonconformism.

It is not by chance that the decision of the September Plenum of the Central Committee concerning the staff of the Revvoensovet* is placed at the beginning of this collection. This was the first Plenum attended by Trotsky after his four months' absence (because of his poor state of health). The decision prepared without coordinating it with Trotsky who still was the Chairman of the RVSR,† was, in fact, of a provocative character. It was an occasion for a new aggravation of the struggle. The "troika" correctly calculated the direction of the main stroke—Trotsky would not permit the members of the Central Committee and the executive body created at RVSR to control his actions. The aim had been achieved—realizing the true sense of that decision, Trotsky "had risen against the Central Committee" and later he was accused of this during the discussion.

The first stage of the discussion that was going on during the whole of October, was characterized in the main by the correspondence between Trotsky and the members of the Politburo of the Central Committee and the Presidium of the TSKK.‡ The analysis of these documents shows that if the

---

*See the List of Abbreviations. (Ed.)
†Ibid. (Ed.)
‡Ibid. (Ed.)

leadership of the Central Committee was not going to discuss the problems of the economic crisis with the opposition, Trotsky and other members of the opposition were trying to make precisely those problems the main point of the discussion. In his letter to the Central Committee and the TSKK of October 8 (Document No. 4), Trotsky gave an account of his point of view on the causes of the crisis and the ways out of it.

The conviction of Trotsky that the "chaos was spreading from the top," that the crisis was provoked to a considerable degree by subjective reasons, was shared by many directors of economic departments and organizations. This was indicated by the Statement of the 46, received by the Politburo of the TsK on October 15, 1923 (Document No. 12). The fact that the document was signed mainly by non-Party officials[12] was not an accidental occasion. They were the representatives of the Party intelligentsia, occupying the leading posts in economic, administrative, and financial bodies in the Soviet departments and military establishments, as well as in the cultural sphere and the publishing industry. Their opposition to the leadership of the Central Committee meant their protest against the growing political dictates of the "hierarchy of secretaries." They were mainly members of the Party with the pre-Revolutionary length of Party membership. They tried to prevent the Party from slipping down from the positions of a political organization to the road of its etatization, by overcoming the unity ensured through implementation of directing and developing inner-Party democracy.

In this document the reader will undoubtedly feel that its authors were sincerely perturbed by the situation in the Party, and were ready for mutual dialogue with the Party leadership.

However, judging by the following documents, all the efforts Trotsky and the opposition exerted to correct the economic policy of the Central Committee were futile. The tasks of the inner-Party struggle and of the defeat of the opposition put forward by the "troika" greatly narrowed the range of the choice of anti-crisis economic decisions.

Trotsky's letter of October 8 was not unexpected by the "troika," since it was the result of their own provocative steps, and, moreover, any retaliatory measures by Trotsky could be blocked within the frames of the Politburo. The statement of the 46 testified to the serious situation, to the undesirability of the Central Committee turn of events. But it was impossible for the "troika" to simply turn their backs on the document either. Trotsky, as well as the opposition, suggested in the name of the 46, that the

Party should promptly discuss the economic and inner-Party problems in their unity and interrelation, since they believed that the artificially supported "regime of the factional dictatorship has outlived itself."

This, however, was the very thing that the majority of the main leading body was not interested in. In order to disavow the essence of the opposition's requirements and to parry the criticism directed against the ruling majority, at the "top" levels of the discussion, which was concealed from the rank-and-file Party members, the "troika" was already changing the subject of the discussion: attention was being concentrated on the inner-Party problems instead of the economic ones. Those were the minority's most vulnerable spots—Trotsky could be "beaten" for his "non-Bolshevism," while the opposition, and especially the members of the former group of the "democratic centralism," could be upbraided for their past mistakes.

In this respect, the most interesting documents of the first stage of the discussion are "The Answer" of the eight members and alternate members of the Politburo of October 19 (Document No. 17), and the materials of the October joint Plenary Meeting of the Central Committee and the TSKK, that completed this stage of the discussion (Documents 21, I–V). As a matter of fact, those majority documents predetermined the further course of the discussion and its final results.

Before "The Answer" of the eight had been sent to the members of the Central Committee and the TSKK, Trotsky's letter was, by way of apparatus manipulations, presented as a factional platform, a fact denied by the author (Documents Nos. 6, 8, 9, 10, et al.). The content and the form of "The Answer" is a vivid illustration of the methods used by the majority when carrying out the discussion. Most probably that document has been written by Stalin, since the argumentation and the style of presentation almost coincided with that of the speech of the General Secretary at the October Plenary Meeting of the Central Committee. The letter contained seriously strained interpretations, sheer lies, and the falsification of both the historical facts and the appraisal of the situation in the Party and in the country as a whole. For the first time the authors of "The Answer" allowed the name of Lenin, who was still alive, to be drawn into their unscrupulous game, falsifying his views and actions in the interests of the inner-Party struggle. And, finally, in their battery of charges against Trotsky they openly alluded to the Statement of the 46 and jumped to the conclusion that Trotsky had become the center uniting the opponents to the Party leadership.

On October 25–27, 1923, the joint Plenary meeting of the Central Committee and the TSKK took place with the participation of the representatives of the ten largest proletarian Party organizations (the organizations and their representatives were chosen directly by the Secretariat of the Central Committee). At the Plenary Meeting Trotsky openly declared that there existed the "troika" in the Politburo and that the TSKK had become an instrument of the Secretariat of the Central Committee in the inner-Party struggle; he repeated his arguments on the problem of the State Planning Committee and on the lack of democratic principles in the Party; he repudiated once again all the incriminating charges of factionalism and Bonapartism. In his speech Stalin, repeating in fact the appraisals given earlier by the Politburo, TSKK, and in "The Answer" of the Eight, declared that the "heart of the problem" was that Trotsky had addressed the members of the Party "over the head" of the Central Committee, thus stimulating the struggle between factions; he appealed to the Plenary Meeting to condemn Trotsky's behavior. Thus, from the formal point of view, the demand by Trotsky and the 46 to convoke the conference has been honored. However, there was no any discussion concerning the essence of the economic and inner-Party problems stated by the opposition. Everything came down to the denouncing of Trotsky and the opposition for their factional activities.

The atmosphere at the October Plenary meeting and the methods used by the majority in their struggle for power is eloquently demonstrated by the letter of N. K. Krupskaya, who was present at some sessions of the Plenary Meeting, to G. Ye. Zinovyev (Document No. 22). She openly accused the "troika" of being able but not desiring to overcome the differences with Trotsky within the bounds of comradely Party spirit and stated that it was precisely the Politburo that had been responsible for the general orientation of the discussion.

The second stage of the discussion embraces the period from the publication of Zinovyev's article "New tasks of the Party" in the November 7 issue of *Pravda* newspaper, which officially opened the All-Party discussion, to the adoption on December 5 of the resolution of the Politburo of the Central Committee and the Presidium of the TSKK "About Party Building" (See the Supplement to Document No. 24). The documents of this stage (these were mainly the materials of the Party press) have not been included in the present collection, since, as stated, our intention was to publish unknown or little-known archival documents having a direct relation to the problem of the inner-Party struggle for power.

An analysis of the November materials appearing in the press leads us to conclude that their appraisal of inner-Party life completely coincided with the opposition's point of view, as reflected in the documents. As we see it, it was precisely that circumstance that had made the "troika" unite with Trotsky in working out the resolution "About Party Building"—a document the historians were well enough familiar with. Trotsky, however, very quickly realized that the compromise turned out to be "corrupt," and that the "troika," while supporting the apparatus resolution of the October Plenary Meeting, was proceeding with its own factional activity (Documents No. 23–25).

It is necessary to note the beginning of November as the date of birth of the so-called factional "semyorka" (seven Party leaders) within the staff of the Party leadership. Besides Stalin, Zinovyev, and Kamenev it included Bukharin, Rykov, Tomsky, and Kuibyshev, Chairman of the Presidium of the TSKK (Document No. 29).

In the circumstances Trotsky ventured to take a step—correct in principle but too late—to address the Party masses. On December 8 he wrote "The Letter to the Party Conference" titled "A New Course" (Document No. 30). It was published in *Pravda* on December 11.

Exaggerating and absurdly misinterpreting quite a number of controversial problems declared by Trotsky, the main leading body of the Party immediately used "A New Course" to accuse him of violating the Party discipline, factional activity, and an attempt to split the Party. On December 13 an editorial by Bukharin was published in *Pravda*, in terms that could only have been formulated earlier in secret documents.

The struggle entered a new, final stage. It was of such a destructive character, that at many Party meetings the Communists expressed their apprehension over the split of the Party. As was stated in quite a number of information reports, many debatable problems were seen by rank-and-file Communists "as caused by the personality of Trotsky." In order to conceal the true causes of the struggle, Bukharin, speaking at the courses of the secretaries of the District Committee on December 14, declared that "such an incredible idea as to imagine Comrade Trotsky beyond our Party or beyond our Politburo—has never occurred to any of the members of the Politburo or the Central Committee" (Document No. 36-1). Then, on December 17 the Politburo adopted a resolution where that deliberate lie was confirmed (Document No. 38).

For a whole month, from the middle of December to the middle of January, two or three pages in *Pravda* were occupied by articles, materials, and resolutions of the Party organizations devoted to the discussion. How those resolutions serving the interests of the Central Committee were fabricated was demonstrated clearly enough by Documents Nos. 37, 40, 45, 46.

It seems that the Plenary Meeting of the Central Committee, which took place on January 14–15, 1924, with the participation of the members and alternate members of the Central Committee immediately preceding the 13th Party Conference, had summed up the results of the discussion; but, in fact, it was a mere formality (Document No. 48). In the statements of the speakers there was almost nothing new on the discussion compared with what was mentioned in the resolutions and letters of the Politburo and the Presidium of the TSKK, known to the majority of the participants of the Plenary Meeting. Only the charges against the opposition became more severe; as a matter of fact, they were transformed into the labels.

The fear of democracy experienced by the leading majority and their intolerance of any of its manifestations were distinctly heard in Bukharin's speech at the Plenary Meeting. In particular, he declared that the opposition, in its attention to the bureaucratic danger, was unable to make out the political democratic danger; it could not realize the fact, "that in order to support the dictatorship of the proletariat, it was necessary to support the Dictatorship of the Party, which was impossible without the dictatorship of the 'old guard,' which, in turn, was impossible without the leading role of the Central Committee as a ruling institution." In those arguments Bukharin appeared just as a Party apparatus member. An active advocate of the majority did gain the upper hand in him a theorist of the Party who was, according to Lenin, its most valuable and outstanding. Strictly speaking, one step alone was enough to justify the dictatorship of the leader, who would inevitably occupy the place at the head of the hierarchic pyramid of power outlined by Bukharin.

What the situation was at the Plenary meeting as a whole can be judged from the words of Pyatakov, who, explaining his refusal to speak on the results of the discussion, said that "today it is impossible to carry on a controversy in the Central Committee, when from the very beginning many of us, sometimes even me, are pictured as Mensheviks . . . , when the word Menshevik is equivalent to White Guard . . . , it is impossible to debate essential problems." Next he has given a precise appraisal of the situation: "It was a definite course aimed at the organizational defeat of the opposition."[13]

That course was confirmed at the same Plenary Meeting by the exam-

ination of the case of V. A. Antonov-Ovseenko, chief of the PUR, characterized by long discussions of insignificant facts. That "case" testified to
the fact that even then, by the end of the discussion, the leaders of the
"Left" opposition, experiencing the unfailing action of the mechanism of
the factional struggle created by the "troika," understood fairly well the
danger pernicious for the Party.

In our opinion, V. A. Antonov-Ovseenko, who was relieved of all his
posts at the Plenary Meeting of the Central Committee, suffered not only
because he had signed the Statement of the 46 and was among the closest
Trotsky's supporters. In his letter to the Central Committee of December
27, 1923 (Document No. 44-1), he dared to openly tell the truth about the
methods of the inner-Party struggle and to call the "leaders who went too
far" to order. In retaliation, the "troika" behaved quite indecently, like political charlatans, making short work of Antonov-Ovseenko, Radek, and
Pyatakov at the Plenary Meeting.

The final results of the discussion were summed up at the Thirteenth
All-Union Party conference, which took place from January 16 to January
18, 1924. An extended resolution was adopted which condemned the opposition and qualified its actions as a petit bourgeois deviation. The opposition was charged with unleashing petit bourgeois forces and with having
put the demands of political democracy outside the Party. It is obvious that
the discussion itself favored the development of the centrifugal forces in
the country and was the legal form of expression of the dissatisfaction of
various social strata of society with the Bolshevik power. But, first, it was
the "main leading body" of the Central Committee that was responsible for
the discussion provoked by the leadership; and, second, the causes and the
roots of the process were, first and foremost, to be sought in the objective
contradiction existing between multiform economy and single-Party political system.

As regards Trotsky, no decisions were taken at the conference. However, the discussion staged for him personally meant the prologue of his
own tragedy. He could have never recovered from that stroke. His prestige
was undoubtedly undermined by the incriminating charges of factional activities, anti-Bolshevism, and revision of Leninism; as a result, the "troika"
could plot further steps that would finally lead to the isolation of Trotsky
from political leadership.

As is known from N. K. Krupskaya's reminiscences, Lenin knew about
the discussion being carried out within the Party and acquainted himself

with its important materials. On January 19 and 20 the resolution of the Thirteenth Party Conference on economic problems was read. Lenin had no time to read the resolution on the results of the discussion, since it was published in *Pravda* only on January 26. There is good reason to believe that Lenin's agitation at that time and the sharp deterioration of his health were provoked by the fact that he grasped the real danger for the Party in connection with the victory of the Stalin-Zinovyev bloc and realized his own inability to influence the course of events.

Unofficial results or the discussion, truly fatal for the Party, were as follows: At the moment when, according to Lenin, the proletarian policy of the Party was being determined by the efforts and the authority of a very thin layer of the old Party guard, by their unity, the leading Group of the Central Committee managed to rather quickly split them into "faithful" and "unfaithful" Leninists. Practically everybody who signed the Statement of the 46, who supported the opposition in the course of the discussion, would be reckoned among the Trotskyites, and up to the tragic end of their lives would retain that despicable political label. The remaining, greater part of the old Bolsheviks, supported Stalin and Zinovyev in the leadership of the Central Committee in the name of strengthening the directive unity of the Party. As a consequence, the opportunity for the Party to be turned toward democracy was missed. The tendency of bureaucratic degeneration was gaining strength. In his book *The Conscience of the Revolution*, R. Daniels, an American historian, justly calls the results of the discussion of 1923 "the triumph of the Party apparatus."[14]

In the course of the discussion the "troika" elaborated the effectively acting mechanism of the struggle between factions. One of the key factors of that mechanism was deliberately carried out forgery of the points of contention and final aims during the discussion. Here also belonged the falsification of the opponents' views and ascribing to them demands never put forward by them, which could serve the point of their political discrediting in a concrete situation. The mechanism that was tested during the discussion and that safeguarded the victory of the "troika" would later be used by Stalin in his struggle for autocracy.

For the first time at that stage of the inner-Party struggle, the Party found itself involved in quite a new form of discussion approved by Stalin, which was based on principles of repression. From that time on, the creation of an antagonistic image of those who, in the "troika's" opinion, were, or could be, ideological opponents to power, became an inalienable accompanying factor of the ideal. The personality of Stalin perfectly suited the proposed model. Stalin's personal features as distinguished from Lenin's, such as his rudeness, disloyalty, and animosity in politics, became the model for a qualitatively new style of inner-Party relations; moreover, aggressive, militant ignorance, fear, intolerance, and group struggle for room in the Party hierarchy were encouraged and cultivated. The victory of the "troika" at that stage of the struggle for power considerably strengthened Stalin's position in the leadership, which was an important step along the road to absolute rule in the Party. Bolshevism as a political organization of the working class ceased to exist, giving way to a new social stratum—the growing Party and state nomenclature.

*   *   *

Most of the documents included into the present collection refer to 1923. for almost seventy years they were preserved in special, secret Party archives and were inaccessible to researchers. For many years Soviet historiographers were forced to study the history of the inner-Party struggle of the 1920s based on a very limited number of the sources, and the position of the defeated minority (Mensheviks) was given mainly in conformity with Stalin's version. The interpretation of the sources available to the researchers was, as a rule, within the scope of political appraisals, fixed in official documents of the triumphant majority (Bolsheviks).

The American, English, and French researchers studying the history of political oppositions in the USSR were in a better position, since they had an opportunity to work with the archival materials brought by Trotsky after he had been exiled from the Soviet Union, as well as his numerous published works. This led to the rapid development of historical research which nowadays has its traditions, schools, etc. In addition, their provision with the sources allowed Western historiographers to cover a problem of the inner-Party struggle broadly, in all its interrelations with the other problems of political history of the USSR. But, above all, the acquaintance with and the study of the documents written by the opposition allowed Western historians to work out all those research approaches to the problem, which helped restore the genuine picture and goals of the inner-Party struggle. The Russian researchers have received the opportunity to do this only recently.

Even so, a true historical researcher is always happy to enrich the arsenal of the sources on the problem he is interested in. Many documents included in this collection have been suggested to scientific researchers for the first time. Some of the documents were published in 1990–1991 by the *Izvestiya TsK KPSS* magazine. It present the greater part of the original texts of these documents are being kept in the archives of the President of the Russian Federation, while another part (in the original form or their copies) is in RCChIDNI.* All the information is given in the legends to the documents and in the notes. The titles of the documents are, as a rule, given by the editor.

In preparing the texts of the foreword and the notes, special attention has been paid to the research development of the appropriate problems in the scientific works of well-known Western Sovietologists E. Karr and I. Deutscher, J. Boff, P. Bruet, Sh. Fitzpatrick, S. Cohen, R. Thaker, and M. Kuhn. A special place in this list is occupied by the researches of R. Daniels, *The Conscience of the Revolution: Communist Opposition in Soviet Russia.* Operating with a wealth of factual material and using correct methods, the author could publish the second edition of his book thirty years after the first with practically no changes.

We were guided by the critical experience accumulated by the Soviet historiographers, especially by the critique on the works of G. Bordyugov, V. Kozlov, M. Gorinov, A. Nenarokov, V. Zhuravlyov, A. Pantsov, V. Rogovin, S. Tsakunov, and N. Simonov.

The editor acknowledges the valuable contribution of those who rendered their assistance in preparing this book for publication.

NOTES

1. The conflict between the Transcaucasian Territorial Committee of the Party headed by G. K. Ordzhonikidze and the group of the Party and state leaders of Georgia has developed into a confrontation between the TsK RKP(b) and the TsK of the CPG (See the List of Abbreviations) and which, as a matter of fact, reflected the two principally different approaches—the Leninist and the Stalinist ones—to the unification of Soviet Republics in a single Union. (These documents have been published nowadays in the collection *The Jubilee That Was Never Held: Why Has the USSR Not Celebrated Its 70th Anniversary?* [Moscow: Terra, 1992].)

---

*See the List of Abbreviations. (Ed.)

2. They have been published in the magazine *Izvestiya TsK KPSS,* 1989, No. 11; 1990, Nos. 1 and 9; 1991, Nos. 3, 4, 5. See also the collection *Na perekryostke mnenij. Diskussii po natsionalnomu voprosu v 20-ye godi* (Moscow: Nauka, 1993).

3. This is proved by the fact that in September 1922, at Lenin's personal request, the Politburo of the Central Committee suggested that Trotsky should occupy the post of the Deputy Chairman of the SNK. (See the List of Abbreviations.)

4. See *Kommunist,* 1991, No. 5, p. 36.

5. See Document No. 22 of the present collection.

6. See Trotsky, *Moya zhizn'. Opyt biografii* (Moscow, 1991), p. 455.

7. See, for example, Document No. 20.

8. The latest researches of the Russian historians have documentally shattered a myth according to which Trotsky supposedly refused Lenin's offer "to be the one who would defend the Georgian affair." The given subject has been studied in detail in the publications on the national policy problems by A. P. Nenarokov.

9. See this in detail in the notes to the texts of the documents.

10. See *Izvestiya TsK KPSS,* 1990, No. 9, pp. 151, 158.

11. See: J. Deutscher, *The Prophet Unarmed* (Oxford, 1987), pp. 92, 98–99.

12. In the Name Index to the Collection for the first time in the seventy-year history of this document, the posts held by all the forty-six persons who signed the Statement, have been listed and deciphered.

13. RTsKhIDNI, f.17, op.2, d.108, 1.12 ob.

14. R. V. Daniels, *The Conscience of the Revolution: Communist Opposition in Soviet Russia* (Westview Press, 1988), p. 230.

1

On the Composition of the RVSR.[1] *The Resolution of the Plenum of the Tsk of the RKP(b)*

September 25, 1923

a) The TsK establishes that Comrade Trotsky, having left the Plenary meeting in connection with Comrade Komarov's speech, in which the TsK does not see anything offensive to Comrade Trotsky, has thereby put the TsK in an awkward position.[2]

b) The TsK thinks that having refused to fulfill the request of the TsK for his return to the meeting, Comrade Trotsky acted wrongly and thereby compelled the Plenum to discuss the issue on the composition of the RVSR in his absence.

c) The TsK resolves:

1) to approve the actual drawing of next forces into the RVSR and the increase of its membership with the representatives of the major nationalities forming the Union and, in view of the tremendous importance of the role fallen to the lot of the RVSR with regard to the new prospects,[3] to reinforce the composition of the RVSR with new member-Tsekists: Comrades Piatakov, Lashevich, Ordzhonikidze, Voroshilov, Stalin and Muralov. The Soviet legalization of this resolution should be postponed[4] till the beginning of the mobilization[5]; however, one or two of the latter six comrades shall right now be introduced formally into the RVSR by a de-

cision of the Politburo,[6] their mission being the supervision of the war industry.

2) The TsK suggests that the RVSR should organize an executive body under the chairman of the RVSR, with its composition being approximately as follows: the chairman—Trotsky, the members—Comrades Kamenev S., Sklyansky, Lebedev, Pyatakov, Lashevich, Stalin, Muralov.

The Politburo shall be in charge of conducting the final confirmation of the members of the RVSR executive body after the Soviet registration is through.

3) Since the absolutely single will is of more vital necessity in the military job than in any other field, no disagreements between the RVSR Party members, especially between the members and the chairman of the board, shall be revealed at Plenums of the RVSR or its Presidium. Therefore, the TsK Plenum suggests that such disagreements are to be settled beforehand at the sessions of the Revsovet Party members or at its Presidium. (Carried unanimously).

RTsKhIDNI, f. 17, op. 2, d. 103, l. 2–3; typewritten copy. First publication.

NOTES

1. See List of Abbreviations in the end of manuscript. Revolutsionnii Voyennyi Sovet Respubliki (RVSR)—see the List of Abbreviations. The first chairman of the RVSR from the moment of its establishment until January 26, 1925, was L.D. Trotsky, who at the same time had headed the Narkomat po Voyennym i Morskim Delam since April 1918.

During the civil war of 1918–1920 a rigid centralization of authoritative structures took place,. as a result of which the staff changes of higher officials, including those in the RVSR, were discussed and predetermined at the TsK RKP(b) sessions, whereupon they were confirmed by the Sovet Narodnykh Komissarov (SNK) or the VTsIK Presidium. However, after the end of the civil war, especially after the complete defeat of the petit-bourgeois parties, the monopoly of power held by one Party—the RKP(b)—caused further proliferation of the bureaucratic tendency. This resulted in an extreme growth of the role played by the Secretariat headed by I. V. Stalin and its subordinate Registration and Distribution Department that handled all nomenclature appointments. This is also supported by the above document.

At the same time, the given resolution should be considered first of all within the context of the inner-Party struggle that raged against L. D. Trotsky in the top Party echelons.

Taking advantage of Lenin's illness and trying to break the political bloc of Lenin and Trotsky taking shape, the TsK leading core (Zinovyev, Kamenev, Stalin) launched a vigorous campaign for Trotsky's political isolation, purging "Trotskyists" from the RVSR and "surrounding" its chairman with Stalin and Zinovyev's people.

It was this very document coming from the TsK but not Trotsky's letter of October 8, 1923 (see document No. 4), as it was considered by the Soviet and foreign historiography, that provoked the aggravated struggle and started the first, "top echelon," stage of the 1923 discussion within the Party, a dramatic page in the history of the struggle for power already raging in Lenin's lifetime.

2. B. Bazhanov, the then assistant of Stalin, wrote later about the incident at the Plenum and the reasons for Trotsky's withdrawal from the meeting: "Trotsky saw the meaning of this measure [the increase of the RVSR membership] quite clearly. He made a crushing speech: the proposed measure was a new link in the chain of the backstage manipulations directed against him, with their ultimate goal being his removal from the revolutionary leadership" (Boris Bazhanov, *The Memoirs of Stalin's Former Secretary* [France: The Third Wave, 1980], p. 7).

3. It refers to the new wave of strikes in Germany in summer and autumn of 1923.

4. The confirmation of the given appointments by the top Soviet authorities (SNK, VTsIK, Presidium of VTsK).

5. It refers.to the callup and mobilization of Communists to the Red Army carried out at the most difficult moments of the Civil War.

6. On October 27, K.E. Voroshilov and M.M. Lashevich were introduced into the RVSR by the decision of the TsK RKP(b) Politburo, the first being from I.V. Stalin's environment, the second, from G.E. Zinovyev's (RTsKhIDNI, f. 17, op. 3, d. 384, 1. 3).

The Politburo of the TsK RKP(b) was the leading organ of the TsK, elected by the TsK to guide the Party work in the periods between Plenums of the TsK. It was first established in October 1917 for political leadership of the armed uprising. In 1919 it became a permanent acting body. In 1923 the Politburo consisted of the following members: G. E. Zinovyev, L. B. Kamenev, V. I. Lenin, A. I. Rykov, I. V. Stalin, M. P. Tomsky, and L. D. Trotsky; the candidates were N. I. Bukharin, M. I. Kalinin, V. I. Molotov, and Ya. E. Rudzutak.

2

L. D. Trotsky's Letter to the Members of the TsK and the TSKK of the RKP(b)

October 4, 1923

TO ALL MEMBERS OF TSK AND TSKK[1]

The Plenum resolution of September 25 says:

"The TsK establishes that Comrade Trotsky, having left the Plenary meeting in connection with Comrade Komarov's speech, in which the TsK sees nothing offensive (!) to Comrade Trotsky, has thereby put the TsK in an awkward position."[2]

The statement is based on obvious misunderstanding: I said nothing about "offensiveness" of Comrade Komarov's speech, and what's more, I would not have left the plenary meeting for such reason. I motivated my withdrawal in approximately the following words:

"I have advanced the following arguments against the proposed RVS enlargement:

"1) In the next months the preparation center will be not in the RVSR but in the war industry, so workers should be sent there; (2) a new large RVSR will be understood by whole world as the beginning of our aggressive policy; (3) a day-after-day work on the Board presupposes uniformity of working methods; it is not so in this case, and I for one, based on my former experience, would not be able to bear the responsibility for directing military jobs as I should as chairman of the RVSR.

"The proposal of a new board, as anyone here can see, has been prompted by quite definite combinations inside the Party.

"These inner-Party 'combinations,' occupying more and more place in the policy of the TsK leading core,[3] are threatened with the most harmful consequences in military work, and there have already been quite a lot of them in other areas. Comrade Komarov has just answered my concrete arguments in a vague official wording, deliberately not giving the real reasons for the proposal on the RVS. I consider it to be unworthy to conduct debates in such a way. It should be said openly, at least to the TsK, that this is a matter of a continuing inner-Party struggle, which is systematically being carried on from the top, behind the Party's back."

I am not citing my speech literally as it was not recorded, but its essence was exactly the same. When Comrades Kuibyshev and Pyatakov came to me on the instruction of the TsK,[4] I pointed out to Comrade Kuibyshev the impossibility of such a policy when appointments, discharges, reshuffles, and so on are made according to definite inner-Party considerations, ignoring direct harm caused to the deed, while formally being motivated by the Party for quite other reasons. After Comrade Pyatakov had left, Comrade Kuibyshev answered me literally as follows: "You should understand the difficulty of the situation: we cannot denounce you as an enemy but we think that it is in the Party interests to struggle against you. This is where the necessity for such methods comes from."

As the TsK Plenum considered it necessary to record this episode in a special resolution, which was distributed in dozens of copies[5] and became widely known that very day, I, on my part, decided to circulate the present explanation. Should any points of the letter meet objections, I am ready to give necessary factual explanations, quite exact and concrete ones, orally or in written form, before any Party authority.

It is high time we put an end to today's regime of a double-entry bookkeeping in the Party, which has already done great harm and is fraught with grave new consequences: the last Plenum has summed up the results of the half-year work,[6] briefly described above; these results have proved to be negative.

L. Trotsky

RTsKhIDNI, f. 17, op. 2.
d. 685, 1. 48–49;
certified copy. First publication.

NOTES

1. Tsentralnaya Kontrolnaya Komissiya (TSKK),—the highest control organ of the Party in 1920–1934. It was established on V. I. Lenin's initiative as an organization "reporting only to Party congresses" (V. I. Lenin, *Complete Works*, vol. 45, p. 200). However, in the course of inner-Party struggle, the TSKK, then headed by V. V. Kuibyshev and E. M. Yaroslavsky, for the sake of the directive "monolithic unity" of the Party, rendered active support to leading "the three," and thus actually became a weapon of the TsK Secretariat in its struggle against the opposition.

2. See document No. 1.

3. L. D. Trotsky gave a correct characteristic of the situation in the Party leadership. However, at that time he still did not know the main thing: already during V. I. Lenin's illness, "the leading core of the TsK" (G. E. Zinovyev, L. B. Kamenev, I. V. Stalin), ignoring Party rules and ethical standards, based on private agreement and secretly from the majority of the TsK, created a real factional center, with its main objects being strengthening of "the troika's" power, isolation of the ailing Lenin, and struggle against Trotsky. By the end of 1922 the split in the Politburo became a fact. During the 1923 discussion, "the troika" were joined by N. I. Bukharin, A. I. Rykov, M. P. Tomsky, and V. V. Kuibyshev and turned into an openly factional leading group inside the TsK ("the seven"), its main target being to exclude Trotsky from the political struggle for power as a possible successor to Lenin.

4. After Trotsky left the session of the TsK Plenum on October 25, V. V. Kuibyshev and G.L. Pyatakov were sent to him "to persuade Comrade Trotsky to return." Trotsky refused, stating his position in the above letter.

5. Resolutions of TsK Plenums, along with closed informative or circular letters under corresponding marks (indicating different types of secrecy), were sent to members and candidates of the TsK; members of the TSKK, and the Revision Committee; heads of TsK departments; TsK secretaries of the Communist Parties of the Union Republics; secretaries of territorial, district, regional Party committees; district committees of Moscow and Petrograd; and editors of central newspapers, and some others.

6. Apart from the composition of the Revvoensovet, the September Plenum of the TsK discussed the problems of cooperative development, wage policy, and the situation in the Party.

3

V.V. Kuibyshev's Memo to the Members of the TsK and the TSKK of the RKP(b)

October 7, 1923

Top Secret
TO ALL MEMBERS OF THE TsK AND TSKK

In his letter to all members of the TsK and TSKK, circulated on October 4,[1] Comrade Trotsky cited the conversation I had with him during the break of the TsK Plenary meeting on September 25, when I and Comrade Pyatakov were sent to ask Comrade Trotsky so come back to the Plenary meeting: "You should understand the difficulty of the situation: We cannot denounce you as an enemy but we think that it is in the Party interests to struggle against you. This is where the necessity for such methods comes from."

When I first read this, I could have sworn that I had never said it, so much doe it contradict the spirit, tone, and the contents of the statement I made to Comrade Trotsky in the conversation on September 25. It contradicts my sincere desire to accomplish the mission of the Plenum and to persuade Comrade Trotsky to come back, and, finally it contradicts the mood I was in when I returned to the Plenum and, in spite of Comrade Trotsky's behavior being obviously insulting to the Plenum, suggested a compromise in the form of putting off the enforcement of the Resolution on the composition or the Revvoensovet. The Trotsky quotation contains my words but not the phrase I used. The sense of my words was perverted beyond recognition, specifically because they were removed from the context of the en-

43

tire conversation. I would not have allowed myself to capture the attention of the TsK and TSKK members by analyzing my *private** talk with Comrade Trotsky (I insist that it was my private talk, as the TsK delegation had already left—Pyatakov had gone and Kuibyshev stayed to speak with Comrade Trotsky on subjects beyond the mission of the delegation), if Comrade Trotsky had not tried to back up his wrong political conclusions by imparting a sort of official character to my words. Therefore I think that the elucidation of the exact meaning of my words acquires sone common interest, and I would allow myself to make the following remarks and corrections:

1) The main essence of my conversation after Comrade Pyatakov's departure was that I tried to convince Comrade Trotsky that he had formed a wrong notion of the TsK attitude to him (as it seemed to me). Judging by the irritation with which Comrade Trotsky left the TsK[2] and by some of his statements during the talk with me and Comrade Pyatakov, I thought that Trotsky detected some intentional hostility in the Plenum's attitude to him and its decisions. I wanted to say to Comrade Trotsky that both in cases where the TsK disagreed with him and when the TsK thought it necessary to safeguard itself from Trotsky's explosive temperament, his risky wide-ranging entrepreneurship in important issues, it was not easy for the majority of the Plenum to make this or that decision; that respect for Trotsky and liking for him excluded every possibility of enmity and that the revolutionary expediency made [the Plenum] take this or that decision despite Comrade Trotsky's categorical protest (as it was with the issue of the Revvoensovet). This is what I told Comrade Trotsky.

2) During our conversation, I repeated several times (twice that I clearly remember) approximately the following: "Nobody has authorized me to tell you what I want to. I am speaking for myself, though *it seems to me†* that I am expressing the opinion of the majority." Thus, the word we, which sounds in the Trotsky citation as if I were speaking on somebody's behalf, was either not pronounced or, being said after my above-mentioned introductory words, could not be understood by Comrade Trotsky other than conditionally, i.e., conditioned by the correctness of my personal supposition that my opinion actually coincided with that of the majority of the Plenum.

3) "We cannot denounce you as an enemy." Having read this phrase, anyone understands it in the following way: Kuibyshev told Trotsky: "You

*Emphasis in original. (Ed.)
†Emphasis in original. (Ed.)

are our enemy but we cannot denounce you as one, much as we should like to; do understand the difficulty of our position." With all I have said above, it is needless to prove that I could not have said it. I would only quote one of my phrases as I remember it. While I am not sure of its complete accuracy, I can guarantee the sense. "Comrade Trotsky, do understand that there is no hostile attitude to you on the part of the TsK members, it is not enmity that makes us vote against you in spite of your protests. Your position in the Party and the attitude of the TsK members to you exclude the possibility of openly contrasting you with the TsK majority. Personally I have and will oppose you since my revolutionary conscience makes me do so, because your temperament often leads you far astray. But it is not a reason for denouncing you as an enemy and beginning a public discussion with you."

There is some similarity with the quotation of Trotsky but the sense is quite different. And I insist on its identity with the essence of our conversation.

4) I talked with Comrade Trotsky only about himself and the attitude of the Plenum participants to him. In my private conversation with Comrade Trotsky nothing was said about "appointments" or "discharges and reshuffles." Comrade Trotsky says that he drew my attention to abnormalities in this field in the presence of Pyatakov and alleges that he got an answer when we were alone together. When we were alone together, I said what I have stated above.[3]

7/X

V. Kuibyshev
RTsKhIDNI, f. 17, op. 2,
d. 685, l. 50–52.
Certified copy. First publication.

NOTES

1. See the previous document.
2. It refers to the meeting of the TsK Plenum.
3. Verbose in its form and casuistic in essence, full of contradictory and dubious arguments, the explanatory note of the chairman of the TSKK simply showed the regime of "double-entry bookkeeping" firmly established in the TsK, and the clear-cut political hypocrisy. On October 10, in reply to the note of V. V. Kuibyshev, L. D. Trotsky addressed the members of the TsK and TSKK in a new letter (see document No. 5).

4

L. D. Trotsky's Letter to the Members of the TsK and the TSKK of the RKP(b)

October 8, 1923

Top Secret
TO THE MEMBERS OF THE TsK AND TSKK.[1]

1. One of the proposals made by Dzerzhinsky's committee[2] (concerning the strikes,[3] etc.) says that it is necessary to oblige the Party members aware of factions in the Party to inform immediately the GPU,[4] TsK, and TSKK.

Reporting to a Party organization about hostile elements taking advantage of their Party membership is seemingly so elementary a duty of every Party member that there is no need to pass a special resolution six years after the October Revolution. The need for such a resolution is an extremely alarming symptom along with some other not less impressive ones. It means the following: (a) illegal oppositional groups[5] have been formed in the Party and may jeopardize revolution, and (b) the atmosphere in the Party makes it possible that comrades who know of such factions do not report them to Party organizations. Both facts show the extreme worsening of the inner-Party situation after the Twelfth Congress,[6] when the TsK reports established a complete unanimity of 90 percent of the Party. However, the estimate was too optimistic even then. Many Party members, by no means the worst, were very anxious about methods used for calling the Twelfth Congress.[7] Most of the Congress delegates shared the anxiety. It is indisputable that the overwhelming majority of the Party, considering both the international situation and especially Lenin's illness, was firmly resolved to support the new TsK. It was this desire to ensure a possibility of unanimous and successful work by the Party, mainly in the field of economy, that smoothed Party groups, and made many people suppress their discontent and conceal their natural anxiety from the Congress. However, the half-year work of the new TsK intensified the methods used for calling the Twelfth Congress, as a result of which openly hostile and aggressive groups were formed inside the Party and there appeared a great number of elements who were aware of the danger but did not bring information about it. Here we see both a dramatic worsening of the inner-Party situation and the increased isolation of the TsK from the Party.

2. The utmost worsening of the situation in the Party was caused by two reasons: (a) the absolutely abnormal and unhealthy inner-Party regime and (b) workers' and peasants' discontent with the critical economic situation resulting from not only real difficulties but also obvious fundamental mistakes in economic policy. As will be made clear later, the two reasons are closely connected with each other.

3. The Twelfth Congress was held under the slogan of "smychka"[8] (alliance). As the author of the main theses on industry,[9] I indicated to the TsK that it was extremely dangerous that our economic targets were presented at the Twelfth Congress again in an abstract propaganda form, while the task was to "turn the attention and will of the Party" to specific targets of life in order to cut production costs in the state sector. I can only recommend that all TsK members familiarize themselves with the then correspondence in the Politburo on the matter.[10] I was trying to prove that with a purely propaganda interpretation and use of the "smychka" slogan, without consideration of its real economic essence (planned economy, rigid concentration of industry, strict reduction of overhead expenses in industry and trade), the report on organizational targets of economy would lose its practical importance. However, on the insistence of the Plenum, I made the report in order not to hamper, on my part, the work of the new TsK first elected without Comrade Lenin.

4. The resolution on industry[11] requires Gosplan strengthening[12] and reinforcement as the main planning organ. It is very important that after the Twelfth Congress, the TsK had at its disposal the notice Lenin had written after he was already ill, in which he expressed the idea of the necessity to confer even legislative (or rather administrative and practical) rights[13] upon Gosplan. However, after the Congress, Gosplan was in fact rele-

gated. Its work on reaching individual targets is useful and necessary, but has nothing in common with the planned regulation of the economy as it was passed by the Twelfth Congress. The lack of coordination in planning is especially trying in the work of central and, in general, major state economic bodies. To an even greater extent than before the Twelfth Congress, the most important economic issues are being solved in a hurry, without due preparation, regardless of their planning connections. Comrades Rykov and Pyatakov, responsible for management of the state industry, with Comrade Rykov being responsible for the economy as a whole, submitted a report to the TsK, in which they mildly wrote that "some decisions of the Politburo compel us to draw your attention to the fact that the current situation makes it extremely difficult for us to direct the state industry we are in charge of." Admittedly, the named comrades gave up circulating their letter as they believed it unreasonable to arose debates on the matter at the Plenum. But this formal circumstance (refusal to distribute the letter) does not change a bit in the fact that the leaders of the economy have characterized the economic policy of the Politburo as a policy of accidental, unsystematic decisions, which make any planned management of economy "extremely difficult." This assessment becomes far more categorical in private talks. There is no Party or Soviet body, where economic subject are considered and settled with regard to their interrelationships and the proper perspective. To be completely accurate, one should say: there is no management in the economy, the chaos originates at the top.

5. In this letter. I shall not dwell upon the specific characteristic of our policy in finance, industry, bread purchasing, bread export, and taxes because it would have required presentation of very complicated argument and vast material. Now there can be no doubt that one of the main reasons for today's trade and industrial crisis is the self-sufficing, i.e., not subordinate to the general economic plan, character of our financial policy. Occasional great advances in industry are being upset or are at risk of being upset by the lack of coordination between the main elements of the state economy and, what is more, due to its very NEP (New Economic Policy) nature, every failure in state industry or state trade means the growth of private capitalism at the expense of the state. The key characteristic of the moment is that the enormously increased disproportion between the prices for industrial and agricultural products equals to liquidation of NEP as it makes no difference for a peasant, the base of NEP, why he is not able to buy: because trade is prohibited by decrees or because two boxes of

matches cost as much as a *pood* of bread (16.38 kg). I shall not describe how the concentration, a matter of life and death for industry, is constantly confronting "political" (i.e., local) interests and is developing much more slowly than prices for industrial goods are growing. But it is necessary to touch upon a part of the problem, which, however, illuminates the problem as a whole by showing what the Party's leadership of economy degenerates into given no plan, system, or correct Party line.

The Twelfth Congress demonstrated an outrageous abuse of industrial and trade announcements by some Party organizations.[14] What is the essence of the abuse? It is that some Party organizations, which should administer economic organs by means of accustoming them to a higher conscientiousness, accuracy, economy, and sense of responsibility actually demoralize them, resorting to the most rough and wasteful way of cheating the state: instead of simply direct imposing taxes on industrial enterprises in favor of Party organizations, which would have been illegal though at least it would have made a real sense, they turn to a compulsory gathering of senseless advertisements, with the ensuing waste of paper, printer's labor, etc. The most outrageous in this is that business managers dare not resist the depredation and demoralization by submissively paying for a half-page or a page advertisement of some *Sputnik Kommunista*[15] in accordance with the instruction of a "gubkom"* secretary. If any business manager dared contradict, i.e., had in fact shown understanding of his Party duty, he would be immediately numbered among those who do not acknowledge the "Party leadership," with all ensuing consequences. The Twelfth Congress has not brought about any progress in this aspect, not to mention some minor individual cases. One should have no notion of what the proper economic work and sense of responsibility are, in order to turn a blind eye to such kind of "running" economy, or to consider this matter to be of no great importance.

6. There is no doubt that the Twelfth Congress, together with all the Party, sought to increase the leading and controlling influence of the Party on managerial organs, chiefly with the aim of making business managers really responsible for methods and results of their performance. However, the progress in this very matter (initiative, economy, responsibility, etc.) is minimal. Public discontent is caused mainly by wasteful and uncontrolled

---

*Gubernskii Party Committee. Guberniya (province)—the then main administrative-territorial unit in Russia. See the List of Abbreviations. (Ed.)

activity of a great many managerial bodies, whose administrators the more willingly obey the so-called Party "leadership" (in the form of senseless advertisements and other extortion), so that all their major activity remains out of real leadership and control.

7. The last Plenum of the TsK set up an extraordinary committee for reduction of overhead expenses and prices.[16] This fact itself is bitter evidence of our mistakes in the economic work. All price elements were analyzed in due time and the decisions of the Twelfth Congress on reduction of production costs and trade expenses were carried unanimously.[17] The organizations to implement these decisions are well known. They are VSNH, Gosplan, STO[18] and the Politburo as the leading political organ. Given all this, what does the establishment of the extraordinary committee mean? It means that the permanent acting bodies that should ensure production at a minimal possible cost failed to achieve the desired effect. What innovation can be introduced by the extraordinary committee? Acting independently, it can remind, prompt, insist, and, finally, order administratively to cut these or those prices. But it is quite clear that a mechanical price reduction by state organs under some political pressure will in most cases only enrich middlemen and will hardly influence the peasant market. Easing of price discrepancies,[19] i.e., an approach to a real economic "smychka" (alliance, link—translator's note), may be achieved by routine systematic work: strict concentration, not a raid-like but fundamental reduction of overhead and ensuring real responsibility of business managers for methods and results of their management. The establishment of the committee for price reduction itself is an eloquent and at the same time devastating proof of the fact that a policy which ignores the importance of planned flexible regulation, affected by its own inevitable consequences, is returning to the attempts of the War Communism command of prices. Supplementing each other, they ruin economy but not normalize it.

8. Absurd price disproportions together with the burden of the single tax, being heavy mainly because of the lack of its coordination with the real economic relations, again stirred up extreme discontent among peasants. This discontent directly and indirectly affected the feelings of workers, and finally, the changed state of workers' opinion spread among the Party masses. Oppositional factions came back to life and increased. Their discontent grew acute. Thus, the "smychka" from the peasant through the worker to the Party did not turn out as we intended. Those who did not see it earlier or turned a blind eye to it till the last days, have learned an object

lesson. General propaganda slogans of "smychka" give quite opposite results leaving unsolved the key problem—rationalization of state industry and easing of price imbalance. This was the essence of the sharp discussion in the Politburo on the eve of the Twelfth Congress. Life has given an irrefutable answer to this dispute. This consequences of this bitter lesson could have been avoided, at least by half, if not three quarters, given consideration of economic factors' interaction and a planning approach to key economic problems that were correct in any way.

9. The Twelfth Congress indicated that one of the main targets of the near TsK is a thorough personal selection of managerial personnel.[20] The Orgburo,[21] however, applied quite different criteria to the candidates. For appointments, discharges, and transfers, Party members were assessed from the point of view of their ability to support or oppose the inner-Party regime, which is being secretly though no less actually established by the Orgburo and the Secretariat,[22] At the Twelfth Congress it was said that the TsK needed "Independent"[23] members.This statement needs no comment. Later, the General Secretariat[24] began to apply the "independence" criterion to appointments of "gubkom" secretaries and further, from top to bottom, up to the last cell. Selection of Party hierarchy from those comrades whom the Secretariat considered to be "independent" in the above meaning of the word acquired a prodigiously strenuous character. There is no need to list individual examples now, as all Party members know and discuss hundreds of the most outstanding cases. I will only mention the Ukraine, where the grave consequences of this truly disorganizing work will show themselves in the next few months.[25]

10. In the most severe time of War Communism, such practice of appointments[26] was not spread at one-tenth of its present scale. Appointments of "gubkom" secretaries have become a rule. It makes a secretary actually independent from the local organization. In case of opposition, criticism, or discontent, the secretary applies for a transfer with the help of the Center. It was stated with satisfaction at a Politburo meeting that the only question of interest for the amalgamating organizations in the process of "gubernia" (province) amalgamation was the following: who would be the secretary of the united "gubkom"? Appointed by the Center and thus almost independent from the local organization, the secretary, in his turn, is a source of future appointments and discharges within the "gubernia." Selected from top to bottom, the secretary's apparatus becomes more and more self-sufficient and concentrates all authority. Participation of Party

masses in the actual formation of a Party organization becomes more and more transparent.* In the last year or year and a half a specific secretary's psychology has been formed, its main feature being the conviction that a secretary is able to solve any problem without familiarizing himself with the gist of the matter. At every step we see how comrades who showed no organizational, administrative, or other skills while heading Soviet establishments, begin to authoritatively solve economic, military, and other questions as soon as they become secretaries. Such practice is all the more harmful in that it disperses and kills the sense of responsibility.

11. The Tenth Party Congress was held under the sign of worker's democracy.[27] Many speeches of that time made in favor of workers' democracy seemed larger than life to me, quite demagogic in view of the incompatibility of complete, highly developed worker's democracy with dictatorship. But it was perfectly clear that the pressure of the War Communism epoch was bound to give up its place to broader and more lively Party circles. However, the regime that had already developed on the whole before the Twelfth Congress, and was only finally consolidated and legalized after it, was much farther from workers' democracy than the regime of the toughest periods of War Communism. The selection of secretaries resulted in an unprecedented bureaucratization of the Party apparatus. While in the most critical hours of the Civil War we were discussing, even in the press, the drawing of specialists,[28] guerrilla and regular armies, discipline and so on and so forth, now there is no trace of such open exchange of opinion on matters of true importance to the Party. In state and Party bodies there has appeared a large stratum of Party functionaries who completely give up their own opinion on Party problems; at least they do not express it openly, as if considering the secretary's hierarchy to be that very apparatus that forms Party opinion and decisions. Under the stratum of those refraining from expressing their own opinion there is a broad stratum of Party members who receive any decision already in the form of an appeal or an order. Here, in the midst of the Party, there is a lot of discontent, both quite natural and caused by incidental reasons. This discontent does not disperse through an open exchange of opinions at Party meetings or through the possibility of influencing Party organizations (elections of Party committees, secretaries, etc.), but accumulates secretly and then leads to abscesses. While the official, i.e., Party secretary's, apparatus

---

*In the document this is probably a misprint. It obviously should be "illusory." (Ed.)

more and more resembles an organization that has achieved an almost automatic uniformity, the most acute and pressing problems are being considered and discussed outside the official Party apparatus, thus creating conditions for illegal factions inside the Party.

12. The Twelfth Congress has officially adopted a policy oriented to the old Bolsheviks.[29] It is obvious that the ranks of the old, underground Bolsheviks are the revolutionary stock of the Party, its organizational backbone. Appointment of old Bolsheviks to leading Party posts, of course, if they have other necessary qualities, may and should be encouraged with any normal Party measures. But the way the selection is being carried out—direct appointment from top to bottom—is all the more dangerous in that it splits the old Bolsheviks into two groups with the help of the "independence" criterion. In the Party's opinion, the responsibility for all specific features of today's inner-Party regime and its blunders in the economy is being shifted to the Old Bolshevism as such. One should not forget that the overwhelming majority of the Party members are the young revolutionaries hawing no underground experience or coming from other parties. Today's growing discontent with the self-sufficient secretary's apparatus, which identifies itself with the old Bolshevism, may have the most grave consequences for the ideological hegemony and organizational leadership of old Bolsheviks in our half-million-member Party.

13. The attempt by the Politburo to base the budget on vodka sales,[30] i.e., to make the revenues of the worker's state independent from its economic development, was a formidable sign. Only a resolute protest inside and outside the TsK held up the attempt, which could have dealt us a severe blow not only in the economic work but in the Party itself. Nevertheless, the TsK has not yet given up the idea of vodka legalization in future. There is no doubt of the existing link between the self-sufficient character of the secretary's organization becoming more and more independent from the Party, and the tendency toward drawing up the budget to be as independent from the success or failure of collective Party work as possible. The attempt to present a negative attitude to vodka legalization as nearly a crime against the Party, and the removal of a comrade who demanded free discussion of this pernicious plan from the editorial board of the central organ, will forever remain among the most unworthy moments in the Party history.[31]

14. The army suffered and still suffers from both unsystematic management of the economy and the above-described inner-Party regime. The

decisions of the Politburo concerning the army are always of an episodic, incidental character. The key matters dealing with the structure of the army, its preparation for a military deployment have never been considered by the Politburo, because the latter, buried in an avalanche of individual questions, has no opportunity to consider in full even one of them. Under the pressure of economic or international developments, the Politburo makes directly contrary decisions regarding the army within a very short period of time. Not going into details, I would say that by the time of Curzon's ultimatum,[32] the Politburo had discussed the question of boosting the strength of the army by 100,000 to 200,000 people twice and it took a great effort to rebuff this proposal. In July, when I was on my vacation, the TsK charged Revvoensovet with working out a plan for army reduction by fifty or a hundred thousand people. During July and August the headquarters were working hard at the problem. At the end of August the assignment was canceled because of the events in Germany[33] and substituted with another: to work out a plan of army reinforcement. Every decision of this kind, requiring complicated and hard work, entails a number of corresponding proposals, resolutions, and inquiries from the Center to districts. The latter get an impression that Revvoensovet has no leading idea in its work. One of the Tsekists,* who might have been able to know where the pressure came from, found it possible to formulate in the press a conclusion about the contradictory character of the resolutions of Revvoensovet. It was published in a military magazine of the Ukraine military district.[34]

As to the Party selection, carried out under the protection of official Party establishments, its effect on the moral solidarity in the army is no less detrimental. A systematic work perfectly similar to that, carried out from the top, say, against the old Ukrainian Sovnarkom,[35] was conducted and continues now against Revvoensovet of the Republic. In the latter case, the work is being done somewhat more slowly, in a more careful and disguised way. But in fact, being appointed again are mainly those functionaries who are ready to help isolate the leading organ of the army. Duality is introduced from the top into the internal relations in the military apparatus. By different roundabout ways, and sometimes quite openly, Revvoensovet is being opposed to the Party. However, there is hardly another Soviet establishment that would so accurately, observing the essence and the letter, fulfill not only resolutions of the Party presented by its congresses, but also

---

*A member of the Tsk RKP(b). (Ed.)

all decisions of the Politburo, permitting no criticism or even discussion of these decisions within its precincts, although, as was said, they are not always reasonable and coordinated. The simplest thing would be to replace Revvoensovet. However, not deciding on this step now, the Orgburo pursues such organizational policy in the military field, which makes all serious army workers ask themselves with anxiety: Where will the work stop and what results will it bring about?

15. Today, nine-tenths of the fighting efficiency of the army depends on industry rather than on the military department. The general lack of an economic system has certainly affected in full measure the industry working for the army. So quickly was the replacement of executives according to the "independence" criterion carried out that in the current period of paramount importance the war industry, which should work with a ten-fold energy, has been left without a real leader for almost three months.

Instead of concentrating its attention on industry as a whole, especially on the war industry, the last Plenum tried to include a group of Tsekists, with Comrade Stalin at the head, in Revvoensovet.[36] Regardless of the inner-Party sense of the measure, which needs no explanation, the very declaration of a new Revvoensovet could not have been understood by our neighbors otherwise than as turning toward a new, i.e., aggressive, policy. Only my protest, expressed in the most resolute form, prevented the Plenum from carrying out the above measure. The Plenum put off the creation of a new Revvoensovet "till mobilization." At first sight, it seems to be unclear why one would pass such a resolution beforehand and distribute it in dozens of copies, while nobody knows the time and terms of mobilization, if any takes place, and whom the Party will be able to send to military work at that moment. In reality, this seemingly vague resolution is one of those indirect preparatory steps often practiced by the majority of the Politburo for achieving a chosen aim. Moreover, the Plenum decided to introduce immediately one or two TsK members into Revvoensovet "especially to supervise the war industry," which is not at all subordinate to Revvoensovet and has remained without a leader for three months. Based on the resolution, the Politburo introduced Comrades Lashevich and Voroshilov into Revvoensovet, with Comrade Voroshilov appointed "especially to supervise the war industry," staying in Rostov.[37] In reality, this measure also has the above-stated preparatory character. It was not by chance that when I told Comrade Kuibyshev that the real reasons for the proposed changes in Revvoensovet had nothing in common with those officially claimed, he, without denying this contradiction—how could he—told me openly, "We consider it necessary to struggle against you but we cannot denounce you as our enemy, which is why we have to use such methods."

16. Today's quickly growing crisis in the Party cannot be overcome by repressive measures, be they reasonable or not in each separate case. The objective difficulties of development are great. And they are not eased but grow as a result of the basically wrong Party regime, with attention being paid to inner-Party grouping rather than to creative targets, artificial selection of workers regardless of their Party and Soviet weight, and the substitution of authoritative and competent leadership with formal orders to be passively executed by each and every person. Undermining the economic progress, the inner-Party regime was and remains an immediate reason for the growing discontent of some, the apathy and passivity of others, and the actual removal from work of still others. The Party could resort temporarily to today's painful inner-Party regime if it secured economic progress. But that is not the case, which is why the regime cannot hold for a long time. It must be changed.

17. While the lack of a system in economic policy and the secretary's bureaucratism in Party policy had already caused anxiety before the Twelfth Congress, probably no one expected this policy to reveal its insolvency so soon. The Party is entering perhaps the most crucial epoch of its history, encumbered with the blunders of its leading organs. The Party's activity is cramped. With great anxiety the Party observes the tragic contradictions of its economic work with all their consequences. Perhaps with an even greater anxiety the Party observes the dissension sown from the top which is weakening the leading Party and Soviet bodies. The Party knows that the officially claimed motivation behind appointments, discharges, transfers, and reshuffles is far from being always true and seldom coincides with the real interest of the case. As a result, the Party has been enfeebled. On the sixth anniversary of the October Revolution and on the eve of a revolution in Germany, the Politburo has to discuss a draft resolution saying that every Party member shall inform Party establishments and the GPU of illegal groups in the Party.

It is clear that such a regime and such Party health are incompatible with the challenges that may and, judging by all evidence, will arise for the Party from the very fact of the German revolution. We must put an end to the secretary's bureaucratism. Party democracy, at least within limits guaranteeing the Party a buffer against intransigency and degradation, must be enforced. Party masses should speak out within the Party about what troubles them and must be afforded a real opportunity to form its organizational apparatus according to the Party rules and, what is more, according to the spirit of our Party. The Party forces should be regrouped with regard to the real necessities of work, primarily in industry, particularly the war industry. Without actual implementation of the Twelfth Congress decisions concerning industry, it is impossible to maintain any stable wage level and to increase it systematically. The least painful and the shortest way out of the situation would be the realization by the leading group of all the consequences of the regime it artificially supports, and a sincere willingness to improve inner-Party life. In such a case, methods and organizational forms for the change of course would be easily found. The Party would draw a sigh of relief. This is the way I propose to the TsK.

18. Members of the TsK and TSKK know that, struggling resolutely and definitely inside the TsK against its wrong policy, especially in matters of economy and inner-Party strategy, I consistently shunned any discussions of this struggle in the TsK with even a very small circle of comrades, including those who would have occupied prominent places in the Central Committee or TSKK if the inner-Party line had been in any way correct. I must say that my one-and-a-half-year efforts[38] in this direction were fruitless. This threatens the Party with a sudden and extremely acute crisis. And in such a case the Party would have a right to blame everyone who saw the danger but did not openly name it, for rating the form above the contents.

In view of the current situation, I consider it to be my right and duty to give my opinion on the matter to every Party member whom I regard as adequately prepared, mature, consistent, and therefore able to help the Party emerge from the deadlock without factional convulsions and shocks.

L. Trotsky
October 8, 1923

RTsKhIDNl, f. 17, op. 2, d. 685,
l. 53–68, certified copy.First published
in *Izvestia TsK KPSS* , 1990, pp. 165–173.

NOTES

1. This letter of L. D. Trotsky is a logical continuation of all previous documents: the resolution of the September Plenum on the composition of the RVSR; the way it was presented to the Party, i.e., concealment of true reasons, which were mainly connected with the inner-Party struggle, became an immediate ground for Trotsky's giving a detailed explanation of his position concerning the main problems of the TsK internal policy.

As G. E. Zinovyev admitted later (1926), that in order to isolate Trotsky, the factional "leading core" met on the eve of the TsK Politburo meetings to solve beforehand all issues on the agenda. That is why the very form of this appeal—a written address by Trotsky to the organs, whose member he was—reflects the then situation in the Party leadership, which excluded any other form of posing and discussing acute economic, social and political problems.

Some quotations from the letter first appeared in the *Sotsialistichesky Vestnik* magazine (Berlin), no. 11 (81) of May 24, 1924. In the Soviet press, the letter was published in full in the *Izvestiya TsK KPSS* magazine, 1990, no. 5, pp. 165–173.

2. The reference is to the committee which included F.E. Dzerzhinsky. G.E. Zinovyev, V. M. Molotov, A. I. Rykov, I. V. Stalin, and M. P. Tomsky. It was established by the TsK Politburo on September 18, 1923, its task being to analyze the economic and inner-Party situation. The results of its work were reported at the extended meeting of the Politburo on September 20 and at the TsK Plenum on September 23. No materials of the committee have been found. The committee was liquidated by the Politburo on December 24, 1923.

3. One of the factors of the economic crisis that had erupted by autumn 1923 was a sharp decrease of industrial output. The number of unemployed was twice that of 1922 and exceeded one million people. Those enterprises that were still working often had to defer wages for several months. In autumn, the country saw a wave of strikes (in Moscow, Tula, Kharkov and elsewhere). In October there were 217 strikes, with 165 000 workers taking part.

4. Gosudarstvennoye Politicheskoye Upravleniye (GPU)—(see the List of Abbreviations). The chairman of the GPU was F. E. Dzerzhinsky.

The proposal made by Dzerzhinsky's committee and cited by Trotsky obliged Communists to denounce the oppositional groups not only to the Party organs (TsK and TSKK) but also to the GPU. This fact shows the intention by the Party leadership to guard the "monolithic unity" of the Party and their own power, delegating the functions of inner-Party detection to the GPU.

5. This concerns Rabochaya pravda (Worker's Truth) and Rabochaya gruppa RKP (Worker's Group of the Russian Communist Party). Rabochaya pravda (the central group "Rabochaya pravda") was an illegal faction in RKP(b) formed in spring 1921. Its members considered that turning to NEP RKP(b) was irrevocably losing its touch and community the with proletariat. Rabochaya pravda set a goal "to make things clear from the class point of view to the ranks of the working class." In some of its illegal publications, it stated that "high-ranking Party functionaries are the new bourgeoisie against which a proper struggle should be waged." Therefore, its major task was to establish a new Worker's Party.

Rabochaya gruppa RKP was formed in spring–summer 1923. One of its founders was G.I. Myasnikov, a member of the former "worker's opposition," who was expelled from the

Party in 1922. The group was joined by some old Bolsheviks who did not obey the decisions of the Tenth and Eleventh Congress of RKP(b), prohibiting any inner-Party groups. Rabochaya gruppa deemed that it was necessary to organize Soviets of People's Deputies at all factories and plants; to elect the boards of directors of trusts and syndicates at Congresses of the Soviets; to apply the principle of "proletarian democracy" to economic management; to turn trade unions into control organs; to close down Sovnarkom; and "to remove the Party leading group" that "has totally lost touch with the working class."

The existence of illegal worker's organizations testified to the growing oppositional mood in RKP(b). That is why the September 1923 Plenum had to put the item of "worker's democracy" on the agenda. At the same time, it stated that it Rabochaya pravda and Rabochaya gruppa were conducting "anti-Communist and anti-Soviet work" and declared participation in the groups incompatible with the membership of RKP(b). In December 1923 active members of the group were expelled from the Party according to the decision of the TSKK.

6. The Twelfth Congress of RKP(b) was held in Moscow, on April 17–25, 1923.

7. By saying "methods used for calling the Twelfth Congress," Trotsky means that on the eve of the Congress, many provincial Party conferences elected delegates to the Congress on the nonalternative basis, with candidates being recommended by gubkom secretaries who, in their turn, beginning from summer 1922, were elected on recommendation of the TsK, i.e., were actually appointed by the TsK Secretariat.

8. Literally: union, alliance, linking. The word implies establishment of ties between state industry and the petty peasant economy by use of market relations, and trade and market development, i.e., on an economic basis. One of the key elements of the new economic policy (NEP) formulated in Lenin's reports and adopted by the Tenth Congress of the Party in March 1921 was "smychka."

Unlike the economic policy of War Communism (1918–1920), with its rigid planned centralization of production and distribution, food surplus requisitioning (prodrazviorstka), and complete prohibition of private trade, the new economic policy, applying economic mechanisms (substitution of prodrazviorstka with a food tax; development of private trade; cooperation; the permitting of some elements of state capitalism in the form of concessions, leasing, and so on; introduction of cost-accounting; substitution of payment in kind with money payment and other economic steps), facilitated the recovery of the country's productive forces.

In the matter of politics, NEP strengthened the confidence of peasants in the ruling Party and eliminated the power crisis of the Bolshevik dictatorship caused by the peasants' discontent with the policy of "War Communism."

9. A part of Trotsky's theses was published in the book *Dvenadtsatyi syezd RKP(b). Stenografichesky otchet* (The Twelfth Congress of the Russian Communist Party [b]): Shorthand Report (Moscow, 1968), pp. 810–815.

10. A part of this correspondence was published ibid. pp. 316–320.

11. Ibid., pp. 675–688. See also the publication: *Kommunisticheskaya partia Sovetskogo Soyuza v rezolutsiakh i resheniakh syezdov, konferentsii i plenumov TsK* (The Communist Party of the Soviet Union in Resolutions and Decisions of Congresses, Conferences, and Plenums of the Central Committee) (Further referred to as "CPSU in resolutions . . . "). vol. 3, Moscow, 1984, pp. 57–75.

12. Gosudarstvennaya planovaya komissia (Gosplan). See the List of Abbreviations. The chairman of Gosplan was G. M. Krzhizhanovsky.

13. The reference is to Lenin's work "O pridanii zakonodatelnykh funktsii Gosplanu" ("On Imparting Legislative Functions to Gosplan"). See *Complete Works,* vol. 45, pp. 349–53. First published in the USSR in 1956.

14. See *Dvenadtsatyi syezd RKP(b). Stenografichesky otchet.*

15. It was the name of rather small magazines published by local Party committees.

16. The reference is to the September Plenum of the TsK RSP(b) in 1923.

17. See *Dvenadtsatyi syezd RKP(b). Stenografichesky otchet,* pp. 680–681.

18. VSNH (Vysshii sovet narodnogo hozyaistva) and STO (Sovet truda i oborony). See the List of Abbreviations. In 1923 the chairman of VSNH was A.I. Rykov, STO— V.I. Lenin.

19. "Price discrepancies": an increasing gap between high prices for industrial goods and low prices for agricultural products. In early October 1923 the price disproportion was 320 percent (*Ekonomicheskaya zhizň* [*The Life of Economy*], 1923, October 1).

20. See *Dvenadtsatyi syezd RKP(b). Stenografichesky otchet,* p. 673.

21. Organizational Bureau of the TsK RKP(b) (Orgburo), the executive body of the TsK RKP(b), elected by the TsK to administer organizational work, mainly in selection and placement of personnel. It was first elected in 1919. In 1923, the activity of the Orgburo was completely controlled by the TsK Secretariat and personally by I. V. Stalin and V. M. Molotov. Since 1921 the latter had been the TsK Secretary on organizational matters. The other members of the Orgburo were A. A. Andreyev, F. E. Dzerzhinsky, Ya. E. Rudzutak, A. I. Rykov, and M. P. Tomsky.

22. Secretariat TsK RKP(b) was first established in August 1917 to ensure communication between the TsK and local Party organizations. By 1929 it had developed into the leading board of TsK secretaries. Its functions included supervision over everyday work, especially regarding personnel selection and control over execution of TsK resolutions. In 1923, the TsK Secretariat included I. V. Stalin (General Secretary), V. M. Molotov, and Ya. E. Rudzutak.

23. By this was meant the following: Independently thinking persons, having their own opinion and being not afraid of expressing it (See *Dvenadtsatyí syezd RKP[b]. Stenografichesky otchet,* p. 68, 200–201; see also note 7 to the present document).

24. The reference is to the Secretariat of the TsK RKP(b).

25. Trotsky means the discharge of Chairman of the Ukrainian Sovnarkom H.G. Rakovsky and many other Soviet officials in the republic after the June (1923) Plenum of the TsK KP(b) of the Ukraine.

26. The reference is to the practice of appointing Party functionaries by higher authorities to posts elective under the Party rules.

27. The Tenth Congress of RKP(b) was held in Moscow on March 8–16, 1921. Among other things, it passed the resolution "On the Problems of Party Build-Up," speaking about the necessity of democratization for the inner-Party life. See *Desiatyi syezd RKP(b). Stenografichesky otchet (The Tenth Congress of RKP[b]: Shorthand Report)* (Moscow, 1963, pp. 559–571). A year later, however, G. E. Zinovyev had to admit at the Eleventh Party Congress that the decisions of the Tenth Congress on Party democracy were

not being implemented. See *Odinadtsatyi syezd RKP(b). Stenografichesky otchet* (Moscow, 1961, pp. 408, 427).

28. By this is meant the drawing of military specialists of the former tsar's army into work for Soviet military establishments and service in the Red Army.

29. See *Dvenadtsatyi syezd RKP(b). Stenografichesky otchet*, pp. 705–706. In this and a number of other documents by "underground Bolsheviks," "underground political workers," and "old Bolsheviks" are meant the members of the Bolshevik Party who had joined it before 1917 and had acquired certain experience in illegal work.

30. The TsK RKP(b) Plenum held on June 26–27, 1923, again discussed establishing a state monopoly on vodka sales. In his letters of that period, in particular that to the TsK and TSKK of June 29, Trotsky categorically protested against holding a state monopoly on vodka sale for fiscal purposes.

31. By this Trotsky meant the staff changes in the editorial board of the central Party press organ newspaper *Pravda* and the removal of E. A. Preobrazhensky by I. V. Stalin in July 1923 (in the absence of *Pravda* editor-in-chief N. I. Bukharin). E. A. Preobrazhensky's "fault" was that, sharing Trotsky's views on vodka sales, he had expressed his disagreement with the decision of the TsK Politburo according to which any debatable publications in *Pravda* on the matter were prohibited.

32. The reference is to the memorandum of the British Government prepared by Minister of Foreign Affairs G. N. Curzon. It was handed over to the Soviet government on May 8, 1923. The memorandum included the following demand: the recall of Soviet diplomats from Iran and Afghanistan and an apology for those actions which they saw as wrong, being directed against the British Empire, and reduction of the Soviet coastal zone along the Kola Peninsula. The English government threatened to renounce the English-Soviet trade treaty of 1921. In its answer of May 11, 1923, the Soviet government rejected the claims, having, however, satisfied some minor wishes of the English side. In June 1923, both sides declared the conflict settled.

33. The reference is to increasing revolutionary events in Germany from the late summer of 1923.

34. Trotsky probably means M.V. Frunze, who was Commander-in-Chief of the Ukraine and Crimea armed forces.In 1921 he was elected a member of the TsK RKP(b).

35. See note 25 to this document.

36. See document 1.

37. In Rostov were the military headquarters of Northern Caucasia, headed by K.E. Voroshilov. In 1924, Stalin appointed Voroshilov Commander of the Moscow Military district instead of the "Trotskyist" N. I. Muralov.

38. In this case, Trotsky refers to the period starting from the first acute worsening of Lenin's health (May 25–27, 1922) and including his following four-month absence. The period concurred with activation of the apparatus intrigues against Trotsky on the part of G. E. Zinovyev, L. B. Kamenev, and I. V. Stalin.

5

L.D. Trotsky's Letter to the Members of the TsK and the TSKK of the RKP(b)

October 10, 1923

TO THE MEMBERS OF THE TsK AND TSKK

Comrade Kuibyshev's refutation[1] to my letter is an attempt to put the question again on the plane of those conventional and imaginary arguments that are offered to the outside world, though all the insider, most of all Comrade Kuibyshev himself, know the real arguments.

1. I said to Comrade Kuibyshev: "It is possible to understand why you do not inform the Party of the real reasons of Comrade Rakovsky's banishment to London[2] and other similar measures, interpreting them differently in a way more acceptable to the Party, though not answering the real situation. But isn't it monstrous that you insist on my participation in the discussion [of the RVS membership]; and nobody gives real arguments, though they are known to everyone, even to you, Comrade Kuibyshev. To this Comrade Kuibyshev answered with the words which I quoted in my first declaration.[3] Comrade Kuibyshev did not dispute that the arguments at the Plenum did not meet the real reasons of the reform suggested by Comrade Kuibyshev himself,[4] on the contrary, he proceeded from this as if it had been quite clear for both of us.

2. The point was not at all that in both cases the TsK voted against me. And Comrade Kuibyshev knows it quite well. The point was the systematic, everyday inner-Party policy aiming at isolation and blockading of a num-

ber of persons, their only fault being that they do not consider this kind of the inner-Party policy to be a healthy and proper one. While Comrade Kuibyshev, being the TsK Chairman, did not (and does not) protest against the disorganizing work of removals, displacements, and appointments caused by the needs of our present inner-Party policy, he (Comrade Kuibyshev) is, at any rate, well enough informed about these conditions. The thing is not these or those political decisions, where I am a minority (Comrade Kuibyshev knows it well enough), but the policy systematically implemented within the Party, which I thought and still believe to be pernicious.

3. It is quite clear that Comrade Kuibyshev's declaration quoted by me was not official and was not connected with any instructions. But even so, his declaration does not lose its fundamental sense. It corresponds to the reality utterly and completely. Its text needs no verification, as every day and every hour in the course of a year and a half,[5] and especially during the last six months, it has tallied with the facts.

4. It is not true that I left the Plenum in irritation. Quite the contrary, I asked the Plenum not to consider my leaving as a demonstration against the Plenum, but only as my inability to discuss the most important questions on the plane of conventional and imaginary, i.e. false, arguments, as was clear to all the participants.

5. As to my "being energetic" (Comrade Kuibyshev's words), I think that my fault is rather the want of it, i.e., it took me too long to answer energetically enough to the policy, which is now a very great danger to the Party successes.

6. As to "the risky solution of the important questions in a big way" (Comrade Kuibyshev's words), I do not think it necessary to carry on incidental polemics in this connection with Comrade Kuibyshev. The important questions of our disagreement both before and after the Twelfth Congress are the following:[6]

1. The establishment of industry and the planned management of the economy.

2. the correlation of financial and economic policies.

3. the monopoly over foreign trade.[7]

4. the nation (Comrade Lenin's letters).[8]

5. the TSKK (Comrade Lenin's letters).[9]

6. the correlation of military and economic plans.

7. the establishment of a vodka system for fiscal purposes.

8. some crucial questions in connection with the German revolution.

9. our Present foreign policy methods.

I am ready to have a talk on any of these questions with the Party concerned at any moment. These vexed questions are clarified enough by the facts now.

10/X-23.

L. D. Trotsky
RTsKhIDNI, f. 17, op. 2, d. 685,
1. 69–71; the attested copy
first publication.

NOTES

1. See Document No. 3.
2. See Note 25 to Document No.4. Kh. G. Rakovsky, the Chairman of the Council of People's Commissars of Ukraine, charged with confederalism and national deviationism after the Ukrainian government had been broken up, was sent as a political representative to England.
3. See Document No. 2.
4. The question of the Revolutionary Military Council membership was examined at the September Plenum according V.V. Kuibyshev's report (see Document No. 1).
5. See note 38 to Document No. 4.
6. Trotsky described the disagreements on items 1, 2, 6, 7, 8, and 9 at rather great length in his letter to the TsK and TSKK dated October 8 (see Document No. 4). The disagreements on other questions he would discuss in his letter dated October 23 (see Document No. 18).
7. In the autumn of 1922 there arose severe disagreements on the question of the state monopoly over foreign trade in the Party TsK. On October 6 the TsK Plenum (V. I. Lenin was absent) adopted the resolution on the report of G.Ya. Sokolnikov, People's Commissar for Finances, which allowed temporary "import and export of some articles." Lenin disagreed with this decision, as he believed that it led to the disruption of the monopoly. Sokolnikov's opinion on the possibility of slackening of the foreign trade policy was shared by N. I. Bukharin, G. E. Zinovyev, I. V. Stalin, and G. L. Pyatakov. Lenin's position on the necessity to maintain and improve the monopoly of foreign trade was energetically supported by Trotsky, People's Commissar for Foreign Trade L. B. Krasin, and others. The TsK Plenum, held in December 1922, which had been preceded with the rigorous political pressure on Lenin's side against the TsK members, disavowed the decision of October 6 and approved the "absolute necessity of maintenance and organized improvement of the monopoly over foreign trade."
8. Trotsky refers to the sharp political struggle that took place in the Party leadership

on the question of the principles of national and state construction in the period of the USSR's establishment (October–December 1922). As is known, Lenin's attitude to the "Draft Resolution on Mutual Relations of the RSFSR and Independent Republics" proposed by Stalin, which was later known as Stalin's project of autonomization, was a critical one. Greatly besides agitated with manifestations of a Great-Russian, chauvinist frame of mind on the part of a number of leaders (I. V. Stalin, F. E. Dzerzhinsky, and G. K. Ordzhonikidze) in the so-called Georgian incident (the conflict between the Communist Party of Georgia TsK and the Transcaucasian Krai Party Committee, with G. K. Ordzhonikidze at the head), on December 30–31, 1922, Lenin dictated his article (or, rather, notes or a letter) "K voprosu o natsionalnostyakh ili ob 'avtonomizatsii' " ("The Question of Nationalities or 'Autonomization' ") (see V. I. Lenin, *Poln. sobr. soch.*, v. 45, pp. 356–362). In it Lenin expressed his own attitude to the problem of establishing the USSR and international relations (the establishment of a voluntary union of nations enjoying equal rights)— an idea fundamentally different from Stalin's project of autonomization, which intended the entry of the other republics into the RSFSR on the principle of autonomy, thus limiting their sovereignty.

Having learned that Trotsky was at one with him in his evaluation of "the Georgian conflict," on March 5, 1923, Lenin sent his article to him alone, with the request "to undertake the defense of the Georgian case in the Party TsK." For a long time historians maintained the myth that Trotsky, pleading illness, refused to carry out Lenin's request. But recent documental publications provide evidence that Trotsky made some fundamental corrections to Stalin's theses on the national question, which the latter was preparing to the Twelfth Party Congress, along the lines of Lenin's article, and the author of the theses agreed with them (see *Izvestiya TsK KPSS*, 1989, No. 9, pp. 191–215; 1990, No. 9, pp. 147–163).

At the same time, the fact that Lenin's article was kept by Trotsky for some time and that he did not inform the Politburo members about it (indeed, it had been sent by Lenin marked "secret" and "personal") was used by "the troika" (the three-man commission) for the purpose of the inner-Party struggle. Trotsky was condemned by Stalin for having hidden Lenin's article, which supposedly was the origin of rumors and legends in the Party. In his letters to the TsK members and personally to Stalin, Trotsky proposed to investigate the case by the conflict commission of the Twelfth Party Congress. Fearing that the unattractive details of the apparatus games would become known to the delegates of the Congress, the TsK "steering nucleus" passed the decision through the Congress Presidium, which agreed to consider all the rumors about temporizing over Lenin's article to be a calumny (see *Dvenadtsatyi syezd RKP(b). Stenograficheskii otchet* (The Twelfth RKP(b) Congress: A Stenographic Report), p. 821). For documents referring to the problem of the USSR establishment, see *Nesostoyavshiisya yubilei. Pochemu SSSR ne otprazdnoval svoego 70-letiya?* (The Anniversary Celebrations Which Never Took Place. Why Didn't the USSR Celebrate Its 70th Anniversary?) (Moscow, 1992, part III, 1–6.

9. Trotsky refers to Lenin's article "Kak nam reorganizovat' Rabkrin (Predlozhenie XII syezdu partii)" ("How We Should Reorganize the Workers' and Peasants' Inspection [Recommendation to the Twelfth Party Congress]"), where he suggested reorganizing central executive and control Party organs, as well as the People's Commissariat of the Workers' and Peasants' Inspection (NK RKI). (See V.I. Lenin, *Poln. sobr. soch.*, v. 45, pp. 383–388).

Lenin's recommendations to amalgamate the TsK and RKI into the People's Commissariat independent of the TsK, its reinforcement with representatives of workers and peasants who had no training in apparatus service, aimed to provide more efficient control of the TsK activity for rank-and-file Party members. These measures, Lenin thought, were to guarantee unity and stability of the TsK, to keep it from disintegration. Lenin demanded immediate publication of his work.

The article provoked a stormy discussion in the TsK Politburo. Its members understood well enough the essence of the reform proposed by Lenin, i.e., to limit to a certain extent their freedom from TsK control. Opinions were voiced not to publish the article or (according Trotsky, V.V. Kuibyshev suggested) to print one issue of *Pravda* with the article to calm Lenin. Trotsky was for immediate publication of Lenin's work; he also supported its crucial ideas.

On January 25, 1923, *Pravda* was published with Lenin's article. But from the following passage " . . . anybody's authority, without exception, neither that of the General Secretary [of the TsK], nor any other member of the Central Committee, to prevent them from putting questions . . . " the words in italics were withdrawn. They were first printed in: Poln. sobr. soch., v. 45, p. 387. It is still not known when and by whom this falsification was made. At least it is possible to suppose that on January 24 at the Politburo session (on the eve of publication), Trotsky read the "improved" text, because later he just could not miss this defending Stalin's manipulation of Lenin's article.

At the same time Trotsky, like other Politburo members, feared the response unwanted for them, which the article could find in the Party masses. So, in favor of maintenance of "the stability" of the Party he made the unscrupulous compromise with "the majority" to become an author and a subscriber, like other TsK Politburo and Orgburo members, of the secret instructions for "guberniva" and oblast Party committees, which assured Communists that there were no signs of a split in the TsK and which in fact disavowed the reform suggested by Lenin.

But Lenin's suggestions referring to the reform of the TsK and TSKK were too late in any case. The split, about which the article spoke only hypothetically, had become a reality by that time. Moreover, the reform suggested by Lenin by no means limited the Bolshevik Party monopoly of power. The problem of the expansion of political democracy in the country, being the objective basis of the relevant political superstructure of the NEP, was not even considered.

For the document referring to the history of the publication of Lenin's article "How We Should Reorganize the Workers' and Peasants' Inspection." See *Izvestiya TsK KPSS*, 1989, No. 11, pp. 179–192.

6

The Extract from the Minutes of the Politburo of the TsK of the RKP(b) Session

October 11, 1923

An Extract from the Minutes of the Politburo Session of the Tsk of the RKP of 11/X-23. No. 39

AGENDA

Comrade Trotsky's letter[1]

DECISION

a) To consider Comrade Trotsky's declaration that the contents of the letter which he sent to the TsK Secretariat for delivery to all the TsK and TSKK members, are let known to a narrow circle of officials, who are not TsK and TSKK members.

b) To consider Comrade Trotsky's declaration about his consent to comply with the request of the Politburo majority to temporize with the delivery of his letter until the next Politburo session.

The TsK Secretary—Molotov
RTsKhIDNI, f. 17, op. 2, d. 685, 1. 72
Typescript attested copy
First published in
Izvestiya TsK KPSS,
1990, No. 5, p. 175.

NOTE

1. The reference is to Trotsky's letter dated October 8 (see Document No. 4).

7

R. P. Rein's Letter to the TsK of the RKP(b)

October 13, 1923

TO THE RKP TSK

Dear Comrades,

Being called from the province and having gotten into the "Moscow" maelstrom, I was greatly surprised with the atmosphere in the center of the proletarian state, not only in Soviet bureau offices, but in the Party milieu as well; i.e., the lack of friendly union and solidarity, intrigues, egging on, and, finally, a contest for "the chair," starting from the Soviet subdivision and a Party cell and ending with the guiding "elite" of the Soviet and Party hierarchy. Being an old Party member and therefore unused to all these strange, sometimes disgraceful, phenomena, I could do only this: watch what was going on and determine whether it was really so or only my imagination.

Watching the events in the course of six weeks, I became certain that if the future revolution in Germany comes about, it will not be well in our Party milicu—not only in primary cells, but also in the Central Committee itself: there is no unity, which is wanted in the existing situation. Some persons are withdrawn from immediate participation in the activity of the TsK, others, though secretly, are contesting for the leadership, etc. All

69

these conditions cause dismay and the stagnation of Soviet and Party activity as well as a ferment in the Party "bottom" and "top," which, in turn, spreads to workers' districts and infects the atmosphere there, which has already become unhealthy; Party and non-Party factions are organized, which have always been and still are skillfully used by our enemies. Illegal conferences, factions within the Party, echoes of "the incident" at the TsK Plenum,[1] and echoes of Comrade Trotsky's letter to the TsK,[2] etc., are now known to masses and are interpreted in various ways, while the Party mass, the group of old members of underground organizations,[3] for example, keep aloof; the TsK does not take any measures to improve relations at least between themselves.

Dear Comrades, I do not belong to any factions, I do not recognize any "palace" coups, nor do I recognize any "workers' democracy" acting in an underhanded way, all the more so now, on the eve of great world events; nonetheless, the actual situation is intolerable and the RKP TsK should take urgent measures to eliminate these abnormalities.

On my part I think that the best way to improve the existing atmosphere to call the extraordinary conference of all the members of underground organizations.

With comradely greetings
R. Rein

Party member from 1904

Moscow—the Kremlin
13/X-23

RTsKhIDNI, f. 17, op. 2, d. 685, 1. 100–101
the typescript attested copy. The first publication.

NOTES

1. The reference is to the September TsK Plenum (see Document No. 1).
2. The reference is to Trotsky's letter dated September 8 (see Document No. 4).
3. In the Party milieu those who had joined the Party before 1917 were so called.

8

The Minutes of the Meeting of the Moscow Committee Bureau of the RKP(b)

October 14, 1923

Minutes No. 22 of the Session of the MK Bureau from October 14, 1923

Those Present: MK Bureau members: Comrades Zelensky, Mikhailov, Ivanov, Likhachyov, Zemlyachka, Belenky, Kotov, Karrvai, Melnichansky; Bureau candidates: Comrades Zakharov, Giber, Aronshtam; MKK members: Comrade Filler, the Secretary of Khamovniki district Comrade Malinovsky.

Agenda:

1. Comrade Trotsky's letter to the TsK and TSKK members

Resolution:

The MK Bureau, having familiarized itself with Comrade Trotsky's letter to the TsK and TSKK members and having examined the incident which took place at the TsK Plenum,[1] *considers that*:

1) Comrade Trotsky's letter, distributed among Moscow organization members, is in its essence the platform for energetic attempts to form a fac-

tion (the distribution of the letter, visiting officials, collecting subscriptions, demand to call the Congress). The MK Bureau decisively condemns all these attempts to form a faction.

Note 1: the item is adopted with the majority of seven against two. Three candidates voted "FOR."

Note 2: the amendment was made for the item, i.e;: instead of " . . . is in its essence the platform for . . . " it was suggested to insert: "some of them are trying to use as a platform for their . . . " four voted for the amendment, four were against it, and one abstained.

2) To form a faction within the RKP now is fraught with numerous dangers for the Party, the country, and the cause of the world revolution, so the Party cannot let the faction be formed. (Adopted unanimously)

3) To present Comrade Trotsky's document for a broad discussion means the elimination of the possibility for the Party to carry out the most important tasks of the present moment: activization of Party opinion, that of the broad workers' and peasants' masses in connection with the developing German revolution. The Party cannot be ready itself and cannot train the working class and peasantry for revolutionary fights, if its will is not unified, if its attention is distracted by inner-Party discussion and by factional struggle. (Adopted unanimously)

4) The disorder in the RKP ranks will cause the greatest blow to the GKP[2] and German proletariat, who are going to take power. (Adopted unanimously)

5) The MK Bureau considers the TsK policy to be quite right and thinks that the actual task is the unity of the Party ranks around the TsK. (Adopted unanimously)

6) The MK Bureau considers it necessary to offer the question raised in Comrade Trotsky's letter to be discussed at the TsK Plenum. (Adopted unanimously)

7) For the purpose of eliminating the existing situation as soon as possible, the MK Bureau insists on the necessity to call the extraordinary MK Plenum with representatives of the most numerous proletarian Party organizations. As the document is widely known among Party members of

Moscow organization, its discussion should be offered to the TsK Plenum, which should be called next week.

NOTE 1: the item as a whole is adopted unanimously.

NOTE 2: the amendment "with representatives of the most numerous proletarian Party organizations had six "FOR" and three "AGAINST."

8) The resolution should be brought to the TsK Politburo notice *immediately.*

MK Secretary — Zelensky

RTsKhIDNI f. 17, op. 2, d. 685, 1. 93–95; the attested copy. First published in *Izvestiya TsK KPSS*, 1990, No. 5, pp. 175–177.

NOTES

1. Here and further on the reference is to Trotsky's letter dated October 8 and to the September TsK Plenum (see Documents Nos. 1–4).

2. The reference is to the Communist Party of Germany (KPG).

9

V. M. Molotov and M. P. Tomsky's Letter to the Members of the Politburo of the TsK of the RKP(b) with L. D. Trotsky's and N. I. Bukharin's Remarks and with the Extract from the Minutes of the Politburo of the TsK of the RKP(b)

October 15, 1923

Top secret
15/X-23

To the TsK Politburo members

From the accompanying resolution of MK Bureau[1] it is clear that Comrade Trotsky's letter[2] spread much wider than the TsK Politburo could have supposed (on October 11),[3] in discussing this question, and it is very soon going to become an object of discussion in Moscow organization districts. So, we suggest that the Politburo should adopt the following resolution and deliver Comrade Trotsky's letter immediately, as his wish was, to all the TsK and the TSKK members.

We suggest the adoption of the following resolution:

As Comrade Trotsky's letter-platform turns out to have already penetrated broad Party circles, despite the Politburo's wish to solve the question only within the Tseka,* the Politburo considers it to be disloyal with regard to the TsK and TSKK members to temporize with the delivery of Trotsky's letter and to place the whole responsibility on Comrade Trotsky;

---

*The Central Committee.

therefore, the Politburo considers itself compelled to deliver his letter immediately to all the TsK and the TSKK members.

Tomsky, Molotov

"FOR"—M. Kalinin

"FOR"—A.I.Rykov

According the agreement at the last Politburo session, I took measures immediately, so that the letter would not be distributed before the Politburo session. If it is being distributed by someone, it is being done against my will (Could it pass through the technical apparatus of the TsK Secretariat?—I ask someone to check). I do not object, of course, to the delivering of my letter to the TsK members.[4]

L. Trotsky.

P.S. I consider it impossible to distribute my letter within the Moscow organization by those comrades who have familiarized themselves with it (more so for signatures).

"FOR"—N. Bukharin. It is also necessary to check up on the Secretariat (Comrade Trotsky's request) against every eventuality. I know also that the contents of the latter were known to broad Party circles independently of the secretariat.

N. Bukharin.

The Extract from the Minutes No. 40 of the TsK Politburo Session from 15/X-23

AGENDA:

Comrades Molotov's and Tomsky's suggestion from 15/X-23 in connection with Comrade Trotsky's letters [*sic*] dated 8/X-23 and the resolution of the PB from 11/X-23, minutes No. 39

RESOLUTION:

To adopt

The Tseka Secretary—V. Molotov.
RTsKhIDNI, f. 17, op. 2, d. 685, 1. 91–92
the attested copy. First published in *Izvestiya TsK KPSS*, 1990, No. 5, pp. 177–178.

NOTES

1. For the resolution of the Bureau of Moscow Party committee see Document No. 8.

2. For Trotsky's letter dated October 8, 1923, see Document No. 4.

3. For the extract from the minutes of the TsK Politburo session from October 11, see Document No. 6.

4. The question of actual sources and channels of the distribution of Trotsky's letter needs additional study. The contents of the letter could have been distributed by Trotsky's supporters. But one should also note that, first, the text of the letter, as is clear from the previous document had already been examined by the Bureau of Moscow Party committee, and, second, the discussion of the letter at the TSKK Presidium, as Document No. 11 shows, took place on October 15, 1923, i.e., on the day of the TsK Politburo session, which adopted the resolution about the delivery of Trotsky's letter to the TsK and TSKK members.

10

A. M. Nazaretyan's Memo to V. M. Molotov

October 15, 1923

TO THE TsK SECRETARY COMRADE MOLOTOV

Top secret

According to your order I am delivering the draft resolution about the delivery of Comrade Trotsky's letter to the TsK and TSKK members around to the PB members to vote on.[1] On the draft PB resolution handed back by Comrade Trotsky there is Comrade Trotsky's remark, where he supposes that the distribution of his letter among Moscow organization members could be done through the apparatus of the TsK Secretariat.

As to Comrade Trotsky's remark I should report the following:

1. According your order we have made 125 copies of Comrade Trotsky's letter to be delivered to the TsK and the TSKK members. (The first offprint was made on stencil with the paper duplicate for proofreading on October 8 of this year; on October 9 of this year multiple copies were made with the duplicating machine.)

2. In October 10 of this year, also, according your order twelve copies were transmitted to the PB and the TSKK Presidium members (the troika),[2] three copies were given to the secret archive, and 110 copies were put into the safe.

3. In addition, on the day of the delivery to Comrade Stalin, 9/X-23, one copy was typed, with my supervision, for Comrade Stalin.

To check up these facts and to clarify that the TsK apparatus was not privy to the distribution of the above-mentioned documents in Moscow both orally and in written form, I ask that the commission be appointed with the participation of the TSKK representative.

With Communist greeting: NAZARETYAN

15/X-23.

RTsKhIDNI, f. 17, op. 2, d.685, 1. 99
the attested copy
The first publication

NOTES

1. The reference is to the draft TsK Politburo resolution suggested by V. M. Molotov and M.P. Tomsky (see Document No. 9).

2. Apparently the reference is to the leading "troika" within the TSKK Presidium: V. V. Kuibyshev (the TSKK chairman), E.M. Yaroslavsky (the TSKK Party Collegium secretary), and S. I. Gusev (the TSKK secretary).

11

The Resolution of the Presidium of the TsK of the RKP(b)

October 13, 1923

Secret

The Resolution adopted by the TSKK Presidium[1] on 15/X-23.

1. Having discussed Comrade Trotsky's letter dated October 8 of this year to all the TsK and TSKK members, the TSKK Presidium ascertains that in this letter the Party faces the suggestion of a certain platform by one of the TsK members which is opposed to the policy being carried out now by our Party as represented by its Central Committee, and the attempt to form a faction on this platform, which both in its form and in its essence contradicts the resolutions of our Party Tenth Congress.[2]

2. Also, the TSKK Presidium ascertains that this letter became known to broad circles of Party comrades before being delivered to the TsK and TSKK members, which considerably hampered the quiet solution of the questions put by Comrade Trotsky, within the TsK and TSKK.

3. At the same time the TSKK Presidium cannot keep from remarking that Comrade Trotsky's difference of opinion with those of the Central Committee, mentioned by him, is not the total sum of Comrade Trotsky's opinions opposed to those of other Politburo members or the whole TsK membership. Within the TsK there were various combinations of votes on these questions. So Comrade Trotsky has no grounds for opposing the policy carried out by the Central Committee on the basis of the resolutions of the Twelfth Con-

gress. Comrade Trotsky is responsible for this policy like other TsK members, as he did not suggest his own platform at the Twelfth Congress.

4. The TSKK Presidium considers Comrade Trotsky's letter to be lacking concrete suggestions, which, having been formulated, could probably provide for easy agreement in a businesslike way about all the vexed points. It also thinks that the difference of opinions itself mentioned by Comrade Trotsky is to a great extent artificial and farfetched, and that Comrade Trotsky has no grounds for sharp differences of opinions on matters concerning everyday collegial work. All this assures the TSKK Presidium that at the present stage the difference of opinions can (and should) be overcome within the TsK and TSKK.

5. The TSKK Presidium, being quite solidly in agreement with the TsK policy as a whole, is absolutely convinced that in the present historical epoch, when our Party shoulders extremely difficult tasks connected with the future revolution in Germany, the maximal unity of the Party and the union of all its members around the Central Committee is necessary, and that suggestions, similar to those of Comrade Trotsky, threaten to ruin this unity and to be fatal for the revolution. The existence of the proletarian state and the Party itself depends now literally on the maintenance of the unity within the Party. So the TSKK Presidium considers it necessary to evade at all costs the broad Party discussion, which under present conditions could damage the Party greatly, and to eliminate the emerging difference of opinions within the TsK and TSKK.

6. The TSKK Presidium, keeping in mind its great responsibility before the revolution, calls on all TsK and TSKK members to put aside differences of opinions at the next TsK and TSKK Plenum and not let the resolutions adopted at this Plenum be broken until the next congress.

7. The TSKK Presidium confiders it necessary to call as soon as possible the TsK and TSKK plenum, where the questions raised by Comrade Trotsky should be put. Before the resolution of the TsK Plenum is adopted, the TSKK Presidium considers it quite impossible to go on publicizing and distributing the letter and the documents on these questions, and it asks the Politburo to pass the decision obligating all the TsK and TSKK members to keep the emerging difference of opinions within the TsK and TSKK only.

RTsKhIDNI, f. 17, op. 2, d. 685, l. 96–97
the attested copy
First published in *Izvestiya TsK KPSS*, 1990, No. 5, pp. 178–179.

NOTES

1. The TSKK Presidium: the steering organ of the RKP(b) Central Control Commission, elected at the TsK Plenum.

2. The Tenth RKP(b) Congress was held on March 8–16, 1921. The reference is to the congress's resolution on Party unity, adopted by V.I. Lenin's suggestion and banning every faction for the purpose of maintenance of Party unity (see *KPSS v rezolyutsiyakh* [*The CPSU in Resolutions*], vol. 2, pp. 334–337). Like other documents of the congress, this resolution was the result of sharp political struggle, which developed in the steering Party in 1920–1921. In general it reflected Lenin's evaluation of the inner-Party crisis (the existence of several factions with their platforms), caused by the necessity to elaborate novel forms of the inner-Party life and methods of political leadership under that the conditions of transition from wartime to peacetime conditions. In the years that followed, Lenin's resolution on Party unity became in its essence a political baton in Stalin's hands in his contest for power and suppression of heterodoxy within the Party.

12

"The Declaration of the 46"
to the Politburo of the TsK of the RKP(b)

*October 15, 1923**

Top secret
TO THE RKP TsK POLITBURO[1]

The extremely aggravated situation makes us (in the interests of our Party, in the interests of the working class) tell you outright that the continuation of the policy of the Politburo majority is fraught with severe troubles for the whole Party. The economic and financial crisis which began in late July of this year with all its political consequences, the inner-Party struggle among them, graphically showed that Party policy, both in economics and in inner-Party relationships, is unsatisfactory.

The TsK resolutions, being casual, precipitate, and unsystematic, which cannot make both ends meet in the economy, resulted in this situation. When having great successes in the spheres of industry, agriculture, finances, and transport, which had been achieved by the economy of the country spontaneously but despite the unsatisfactory guidance—or rather lack thereof—we are facing not just the prospect of a halt in these successes, but a serious general economic crisis as well.

We are facing the approaching fall of the chervonets,[2] which became the main currency spontaneously before the elimination of the budget

---

*Dating by the contents of the RKP(b) Tsk Politburo resolution from October 18, 1923. (Ed.)

deficit; we are facing a credit crisis, when the State Bank cannot finance not only industry and commerce with manufactured goods, but also the purchase of grain for export without the risk of severe shock; we are facing the halt of the sale of manufactured goods due to high prices, which are caused, on the one hand, by the absence of systematic organizational guides in industry, and on the other by an incorrect credit policy; we are facing impossibility of carrying out the grain export program as a result of the impossibility of purchasing grain; we are facing extremely low prices for food, which is ruinous for the peasantry and threatens a mass reduction of agriculture; we are facing interruptions in payments, causing a natural indignation among workers; we are facing budget chaos, followed by chaos in the state apparatus; "revolutionary" methods which consist of budget reductions and new actual reductions during its realization stopped being a transitional measure and became a constant phenomenon, which continuously shakes the state apparatus and as a result of the absence of reduction plans does it casually and spontaneously.

All these are some elements of the emerging economic, credit, and financial crisis. If some broad, considered, planned, and energetic measures are not undertaken, if the present absence of guidance continues, we are facing the possibility of extremely sharp economic shock, inevitably connected with domestic political aggravations and with the full paralysis of our foreign activity and capability. It is clear that we now need the latter more than ever; the future of the world revolution and of the working class of all the countries depend on it.

In the sphere of inner-Party relations as well, we see the same wrong policy paralyzing and breaking down the Party, which is especially clear in the course of the present crisis.

We believe that the cause of this is not the political incapability of the present Party leaders; on the contrary, no matter what the differences of our evaluation of the situation and of our selection of measures for its change are, we believe that our present leaders in any case cannot be appointed by the Party to the advanced posts of dictatorship of the proletariat. Rather, we believe that the cause lies under the cover of exterior official unity; indeed, we have a one-sided selection of people and policy adaptable to the views and sympathies of a narrow circle. As a result of the Party leadership's perversion by these narrow views, the Party is to a great extent ceasing to be a living independent body sensitive to the present reality, and being connected with this reality through thousands of bonds. Instead we see the progressing and almost undisguised split of the Party into a hierarchy of secretaries[3] and "laymen," into professional Party officials, selected from above, and other rank-and-file members who do not participate in social life.

This is a fact known to every Party member. Those who are not content with this or that order of the TsK or even of a gubernia committee, who harbor certain doubts or privately note various mistakes and disorders, are yet afraid to speak at Party meetings; moreover, they are afraid to talk to each other, even if the other Party is quite a secure person, i.e., a "nontalkative" one. In fact, free discussion in the Party has disappeared, Party social opinion has died away. At the present time it is not the Party nor its broad masses that advance and elect gubernia conferences and Party congresses, which in turn, advance and elect gubernia committees and the RKP TsK. To the contrary, the secretary hierarchy and Party hierarchy more often select the participants of conferences and congresses, which to a great extent become organizing conferences of this hierarchy. The regime inside the Party is quite intolerant; it kills Party independence, substituting the Party with a selected apparatus of officials, which usually runs smoothly, but which inevitably misfires during crises and which threatens to be quite inefficient in facing the approaching important events.

The cause of the existing situation is that the regime of the factional dictatorship in the Party, naturally constituted after the Tenth Party Congress, has become obsolete. There are many of us who consciously agreed not to resist this regime. The turning point of 1921,[4] and then Comrade Lenin's illness demanded, as some of us thought, the dictatorship within the Party as a temporary measure. Other comrades from the very beginning took it either skeptically or negatively. Be that as it may, by the Twelfth Party Congress this regime became obsolete. It began to show its reverse side. Inner-Party bonds became weak. The Party began to die. The extremely oppositional, clearly abnormal trends within the Party began to acquire an anti-Party character, as there was no inner-Party comradely discussion of questions of the day in it. Such a discussion could easily show the abnormal character of these trends to both the Party mass and to the majority of their participants. It resulted in illegal factions,[5] leading Party members out of the Party, and in the Party's isolation from the working masses.

The economic crisis in Soviet Russia and the crisis of the factional dictatorship within the Party will strike a severe blow both to the dictatorship of the proletariat in Russia and to the Russian Communist Party, if the existing situation is not crucially changed in the very near future. Having this load on its shoulders the dictatorship of the proletariat in Russia and its leader (RKP) can enter the period of approaching world troubles with only the prospect of failure along the whole front of proletarian struggle. Of course, at first sight it would be so simple to solve the problem by accepting that with having the whole existing situation before us, it is untimely to discuss the possibility of changing the Party policy, to put complicated new tasks into the agenda, and so on. But it is quite clear that this opinion would be the position of a bureaucratic turning of a blind eye to the existing situation, as the whole danger is that there is no real ideological and efficient unity in the face of the extremely complicated internal and external situation. The contest within the Party is the more embittered the more secret it is. It is for the purpose of leaving behind the controversies tearing the Party apart of placing the Party immediately on healthy ground that we are posing this problem to the TsK. We need real unity of opinions and actions. The approaching ordeal demands unanimous, fraternal, quite conscious, absolutely active, and absolutely united action by all our Party members.

The factional regime should be eliminated and it should be done first of all by its initiators, it should be substituted by a regime of comradely unity and inner-Party democracy.

To realize the foregoing and to adopt the necessary measures to exit the economic, political, and Party crises, we suggest that the TsK call the conference of the TsK members, including the most outstanding and active members, as a first and urgent step, provided that the list of those invited include a number of comrades with opinions of the situation different from those of the TsK majority.

E. Preobrazhensky
S.V. Breslav
L. Serebryakov

While disagreeing with some points of this letter, interpreting the causes of the existing situation, believing that the Party is in real earnest with regard to the questions, which cannot be solved with the methods used up to now, I concur with the conclusion of this letter.

A.Beloborodov
11/X.23.

I agree with the suggestion wholly, though deviating from some points of the justification.

A.Rosengoltz

M. Alsky

In general I agree with the thoughts of this appeal. The need for the direct and frank attention to all our defects is so great that I wholly support the suggestion to call the said conference for the purpose of elaborating practical ways that can lead us out of accumulated difficulties.

Antonov-Ovseyenko

A. Venediktov
I. N. Smirnov
G. Pyatakov
V. Obolensky (Osinsky)
N. Muralov
T. Sapronov
A. Goltsman

The Party situation and the international situation are such that they demand the extreme efforts and unity of Party forces more than ever. Joining the declaration, I consider it to be the only way to recreate the unity of the Party and its readiness for approaching events. Naturally, at the present moment there is no question about the inner-Party struggle in any form. It is necessary that the TsK evaluate the situation soberly and take urgent measures to eliminate the discontent within the Party and the non-Party masses as well.

A.Goltsman*
11/X.23.

V. Maximovsky
L. Sosnovsky
Danishevsky

---

*Having subscribed "The Declaration of 46" A. Goltsman enclosed also a note on a separate sheet of paper with it. (Ed.)

P. Mesystsev
G. Khorechko

I do not agree with a number of assessments in the first Part of the declaration; I do not agree with a number of evaluations of the inner-Party situation. At the same time I am deeply convinced that the Party condition demands to the undertaking of crucial measures, since at the present time the situation in the Party is not safe. I wholly share the practical suggestion.

A. Bubnov
11/X.23.

A. Voronsky
V. Smirnov
E. Bosh
I. Byk
V. Kassior
F. Lokatskov

I agree with the evaluation of the economic situation. At the present moment I consider the weakening of the political dictatorship to be dangerous, but some renovations are necessary. I consider the conference to be quite necessary.

Koganovich

Drobnis
P. Kovalenko
A. E. Minkin
B. Yakovlev

I quite agree with the practical suggestions.

B. Eltsin

I share Comrade Bubnov's reservations.

M. Levitin

I likewise share Bubnov's reservations, while not sharing either the form or the tone, and it convinces me, moreover, to agree with the practical part of this declaration.

I. Poliudov.

O. Shmidel
V. Vaganyan
I. Stukov
A. Lobanov
Rafail
S. Vasilchenko
Mikh. Zhakov
A. Fuzakov
N. Mikolayev

Since I have recently kept somewhat aloof from the work of the Party centers, I am abstaining from the statements of the first two paragraphs of the introduction; I agree with the rest.

Averin

I agree with the exposition in the part about the economic and political situation of the country. I think that in the part on the inner-Party situation it is laid on thick. It is quite necessary to take measures to maintain the unity of the Party.

I. Boguslavsky

I do not quite agree with the first part, about the economic situation of the country; the latter is really very hard and demands an extremely careful attitude, but up to now the Party has not advanced any persons who could be better leaders than those who are leaders now.

As to the question of the inner-Party situation, I think that there is a considerable share of truth in the foregoing and I consider it necessary to take urgent measures.

F. Dudnik
Printed by the original text,[6] published in
Izvestiya TsK KPSS, 1990, No. 6, pp. 189–193.

NOTES

1. The document was first published, with some errors, in English, in E. H. Carr, *The Interregnum, 1923–1924* (London, 1954), pp. 367–373. Some fragments were published in *Diskussiya 1923 goda. Materialy i dokumenty* (The 1923 Discussion: Materials and Documents) (Moscow/Leningrad, 1927), pp. 9–10. The first complete Russian publication was by V. Chalidze Publishing rouse (USA) in *Kommunisticheskaya oppozitsiya v SSSR. 1923–1927. Iz arkhiva Lva Trotskogo* (*The Communist Opposition in the USSR, 1923–1927: From Leo Trotsky's Archive*), 4 vols. vol. 1, "1923–1926." Ed. Yu. Felshtinsky (Benson, Vermont, 1988), pp. 83–88. The documents published in this book have some variant readings, which, however, do not change the meaning of the original text.

2. Chervonets—from 1922 the banknote, that the State Bank launched to issue in the course of the money reform (1922–1924). Unlike widely dispersed paper money, which was not backed by gold (Sovznaks), 25 percent of the nominal value of the issued chervonets was backed by gold, other precious metals, and stable foreign currency, and the rest by easily realized goods and short-term bills of exchange.

3. "The hierarchy of secretaries, secretary apparatus." The main backbone of the Party nomenclature was so called in the documents of the opposition, formed under the conditions of rigorous bureaucratic centralization of inner-Party life and established not as a result of elections, but by appointing secretaries from top to bottom. In 1923–1924 the process of establishing of the secretarial hierarchy system was in general accomplished. By the time of the discussion of 1923, about a half of all the secretaries of Gubernia Party committees ("gubkoms") were appointed or "recommended" by the TsK. This let the Secretariat of the TsK, with I. V. Stalin at the head, in the course of the discussion, control the whole apparatus of the secretarial hierarchy system, which, naturally, provided the carrying out of the relevant policy (see, for example, Documents Nos. 40, 41, and 44).

4. The reference is to the resolutions of the Tenth RKP(b) Congress, which was held in March of 1921, on the transition to NEP.

5. See note 5 to Document No. 4.

6. At the present time the original of the document kept in the Archive of the President of the Russian Federation, is represented with the two original typescript texts with some variant readings, which do not change the meaning of the text. The first text contains 54 signatures, the second contains 12. Its typescript and printed duplicates are kept in RTsKhIDNI (f. 51, op. 1, d. 21, l. 50–50ob.).

13

A. G. Beloborodov's Letter to the Politburo of the TsK of the RKP(b)

October 15, 1923

Top secret
TO THE POLITBURO OF THE RKP(b) CENTRAL COMMITTEE

On October 11 together with other comrades I signed the letter to the Politburo[1] concerning the question of inner-Party relations and TsK activity. I signed it with the reservation about my disagreement with some points of the letter, declaring at the same time that the Party is now facing such problems that it cannot solve them with the methods used before. In my opinion, this was made especially clear at the All-Russian conference on September 26 and at Moscow conference on October 3.[2]

Formally it is considered that both these conferences worked to solve greatly important questions of an inter-Party* nature. But one would be a blind optimist not to reach, following these conferences, the most depressing conclusions about the nature of the Party's attitude toward the solution of the most complicated questions. It is not accidental that it seems to have been only one (Comrade Sosnovsky) or two persons who spoke at the All-Russian conference on Comrade Zinovyev's report; there were "none registered" at Moscow conference. Can it testify to the striking unanimity with which the Party is beginning to solve the international problems it is facing? It is, perhaps, only half true. There is no doubt that the

---

*Should be read "inner-Party." (Ed.)

Party is aware of its liabilities in connection with the events in Germany,[3] but there is also the other aspect of the task; i.e., the question of those inner preconditions, which could let it face these liabilities (the situation in the country and in the Party itself is meant). It would be naïve to think that everything is clear here, everything is solved, and that there are no questions and no resolutions are needed. The TsK speaker construed these tasks as agitation and, being agitation, they, of course, hardly needed discussion. But the situation of the country and of the Party demands not only the development of agitation (even if it, to the opinion of the reporters, is superior to the forces of our agitprops),* but also earnestly considering the question of relationships between the peasantry and the state, the working class and the Party, the Party and its leading elite.

Did the Party pay attention to these questions? Have they been thoroughly thought through? Are all the conclusions made and are the necessary measures planned? No, these questions were only mentioned in passing. But they are unquestionably of decisive importance in the training for an active role in European events. The fact that these questions were not mentioned, that the conferences concluded with rare "unanimity," quickly and smoothly, does not reveal at all a well-being in the Party and in the country. Everybody knows that this "unanimity" only shows the passivity of Party thought: the absolute agreement with what "the superiors" say, the readiness to accept and to realize any directive in accordance with Party discipline.

If matters in the country and in the Party were different, one could not demand for better, it would be quite natural for our Party. Take, for example, the relationship of the Party with the working class. Do you think, comrades, that our Party organizations, despite organizing successes in establishing the apparatus, marked at the Twelfth Congress,[4] despite the Party apparatus acting wonderfully from top to bottom, overlooked the strike movement?[5] Of course, the fact that they overlooked it does not mean that they did not see it, but that they learned about the strikes only after they broke out. The same refers, of course, to the trade union organizations. We have a very expensive, absorbing great apparatus of forces represented in factory committees, responsible and technical secretaries of cells, group organizers,[6] etc.; and it turns out that it is face to face with the strike movement, but it does not know about it, to say nothing of its preventing this movement.

---

*Agitation and propaganda departments of Party committees. (Ed.)

The TSKK had prepared the letter on the struggle with excesses by the Party conference.[9] Very well, the case of Krasnoshchekov[8] should be excised, there is no doubt about it; but are these excesses up to now the latest in TSKK wisdom? The tasks of the TSKK Party sector[9] grew long ago out of both this struggle with excesses and throwing out of the Party tens and hundreds of scoundrels who were its members.

Recently at the public session of a cell I was a witness of such a scene: a non-Party woman worker, having heard of the events in Germany and of the necessity to help German workers, said: "How long will it take? What is it? We are barefoot, our salary is not enough to buy boots." When she was leaving, the secretary of the cell asked her to visit him the next day for a talk. This secretary wanted to explain to her in detail why her attitude to the German events was wrong. But the woman worker answered: "Perhaps you will arrest me there." The workers on strike might have had the same attitude to cells. Why does the woman worker associate her visit to the cell with arrest? And may I ask all the KK[10], which is more dangerous: the Krasnoshchekovs (whether their interviews are available or not)[11] or the fear of the woman worker?

The Party TsK and TSKK pay attention to the case of Krasnoshchekov. But are they steadfast enough to discuss what to do in order that the woman worker not fear being arrested in the cell?

About these very arrests being the method of elimination of some inner-Party cases: has the analysis of a typical phenomenon of the Party life (Myasnikov's case) been carried out?[12]

The Party has evidence for this "case," testifying that Myasnikov, after being expelled from the Party, did not break off his relations with it, i.e., he went on, successfully working, organizing an inner-Party faction. Myasnikov has been banished to Germany, but his group remains in Russia, and is discovered and arrested by GPU. The members of Myasnikov's group discuss in their own confused and illiterate way a number of questions of the day for the working class; they are a success among the Party members, confusing those who doubt and uniting the discontented around themselves. There is only one weapon in the Party arsenal, i.e., arrest and banishment. There appear fabricated martyrs of Myasnikov's group, and the whole movement is lavished with the aura of martyrdom in the eyes of workers and Party members. The TsK turns to the Party members for help in finding the criminals and to be a member of "The Workers' Group" is declared incompatible with being a Party member. But it is quite clear that all the acts of repressions whip the shaft but not the horse, because the Party hesitates to strike the hardest (i.e., ideological) blow and the repressions leave no place for this blow.

Party organs lack both information about the situation within the organization and the decisiveness to scatter and shake out Myasnikovites, and it goes on corroding and breaking down the Party organism.

A typical analogy: Party organizations are overlooking the strike movement, Party organs are overlooking Myasnikov's case, and the TSKK should demand the Party members to inform about the factions; otherwise the TsK and TSKK will overlook them.

The sense of all this is that we overlook the events that the Party apparatus at large runs "idle," as well as our agitation about the link between the town and the countryside. The difference in the evaluation of the causes of these events between the authors of the declaration mentioned at the beginning of this letter and myself is that they consider the cause to be the TsK and Politburo policy, while I am quite sure that here the whole Party as a part of the working class experiences the deepest crisis. The Party can reproach the steering organs by charging that the phenomena of this crisis are not taken into consideration fully enough and in every aspect, and the questions of the struggle with its consequences are solved in such a way that it leaves no confidence in success.

At last it is (and it will be) impossible to hide these phenomena from the Party which are taking place at the top stratum of the Party atmosphere.[13] I think these Phenomena are in direct logical and historical connection with the TsK and TSKK attitude to the inner-Party situation, discussed above.

These phenomena cannot be ignored, they create a tense situation of factional struggle within the Party and, developing under the cover of outer unity, they threaten our ranks with demoralization and aggravation.

A. Beloborodov

This letter had been written before Comrade Zinovyev spoke on October 12 and Comrade Molotov on October 13.[14] One can judge by Comrade Molotov's speech that since the Party conference the TsK opinions on some questions have changed. I judge it by some moments of Comrade Molotov's speech in the Zamoskvorechye Club ("we underestimated the Workers' Group; the Workers' Group did not receive due ideological rebuttal," "too strong pressure on the working class," etc.). The heart of the matter, I think, is now not to acknowledge past mistakes, but the fact that the struggle with the Workers' Group is now put into a condition created by repressions of the Party members from the Workers' Group. Only the politically blind man cannot see that.

I think that all the questions put to the Party with the latest events, should be discussed in a businesslike manner, but the precondition for their businesslike discussion should be a retreat from constant threats of expel from the Party. The Party as a whole faces the task to make the Workers' Party members not leave it, but the Party will not manage the expulsion of those who should be expelled, believe me.

A[leksandr] B[eloborodov]

15.X-23.

RTsKhIDNI, f. 17, op. 2, d. 685, 1.85–90
the attested copy
Published for the first time.

NOTES

1. A. G. Beloborodov appointed People's Commissar for Internal Affairs of the RSFSR in July 1923, signed "The Declaration of 46" among others (see Document No. 12).

2. The reference is to the meeting called by the TsK All-Russian conference of the heads of agitation and propaganda departments of Party committees (agitprops), agitators and propagandists. A similar conference with ideological workers of Moscow was also held by the agitprop of the Moscow Party committee. These conferences, as a rule, would be conducted by the Party every year and timed for the beginning of Communist studies in the political education system. At the meetings mentioned they spoke about the tasks of the Party in connection with the events in Germany.

3. In the autumn of 1923 there rose another wave of the workers movement in Germany. In Saxony and Thuringia workers' governments were established, in a number of regions of Germany armed "proletarian hundreds" appeared. The events in Germany, the culmination of which was in late October of 1923, raised hopes for the continuation of the world revolution in the leadership of the RKP(b) and the Comintern. Thus, following the Bolshevik concept of internationalism, the Party leadership thought it their duty to make both the Party and the army ready to render revolutionary assistance to the German proletariat.

4. The Twelfth RKP(b) Congress which was held in April 1923, in the resolutions on the TsK report and on the organizing question, marked the improvement of the whole or-

ganizing work of the TsK and charged it with the task of improving the role of the Counting and Distribution Department managing the staff "for the purpose of providing an actual steering role for the Party in absolutely all spheres of administration" (see *KPSS v rezolyutsiyakh* (The CPSU in Resolutions), vol. 3, pp. 54–55).

5. The reference is to the wave of workers' strikes in the summer and autumn of 1923, covering major industrial regions of the country.

6. The reference is to the trade union apparatus: factory committees ("zavkoms"), secretariats of the primary trade union organizations, and group organizers in shop cells ("grouporgs").

7. The inevitable sequence of NEP, like every market economy, was the social stratification of society, which could only concern the steering Party. The question of the material inequality of the "elite" and "lower classes" was very acute in the RKP(b). Every fact of so-called "excesses" (personal cars, the best lodgings, servants in the families of Party superiors, hard drinking, etc.) made rank-and-file Communists and non-Party persons discontent. That is why the social inequality of the "elite" and "lower classes" of the Party under the condition of the RKP(b) dictatorship inevitably acquired a political character, threatening the stability of power.

In this connection the appearance of the letter mentioned by A.G. Beloborodov and taken as the basis of the Party instruction No. 58 dated October 19, 1923, "On the Struggle with Excesses and with the Criminal Use of the Official Post by Party Members" was quite natural. The instruction established a great difference between the material position of the officials of the Party and of the state apparatus and that of rank-and-file masses. The struggle with "excesses," it said, should not, however, take the form of a struggle between the "lower classes" and "the elite" (see *Spravochnik partiinogo rabotnika* (The Handbook of the Party Official), issue IV, (Moscow, 1924), pp. 277–279).

8. Under the conditions of the sharply aggravated problem of material inequality between the Party "elite" and "lower classes" which the previous note refers to, the RKP(b) leadership should have quickly shown the proofs of its own struggle with "excesses" to bring down the wave of rising discontent. In the autumn of 1925 the famous case of the director of the All-Russian Trade and Industrial Bank of the USSR (Prombank), and Party member from 1917, A. M. Krasnoshchekov ("Krasnoshchekov's case"), sued for using his official position for the purpose of his own enrichment, was offered to the public opinion as the uncompromising Party struggle with the demoralizing influence of NEP (see also note 11).

9. The reference is to the TsK Party Collegium (Partcollegia), whose task it was to consider the cases of the breach of Party ethics, and RKP(b) Rules and Program.

10. Control commissions (KK), elected by local Party organizations (republic, oblast, gubernia, and district), whose aim, like that of the Central Control Commission (TSKK), it was to improve Party unity by drawing new members into its ranks, to struggle with the breach of Party ethics and the RKP(b) Program and Rules by Communists, etc.

11. The reference is to the interview granted to *Pravda* by the TSKK Chairman, People's Commissar of the Workers' and Peasants' Inspection (RKI), V. V. Kuibyshev, in connection with the arrest of A. M. Krasnoshchekov. The interview emphasized that the revision did not find any serious violations in the bank's operations and financial activity;

revealed facts of the violation of financial discipline were connected with the work of the economic department of the bank and with the lack of control by the director over his clerks' work.

The interview also marked that Krasnoshchekov was being additionally accused of "criminal use of the means of the Prombank economic department for personal purposes," which, in V.V. Kuibyshev's opinion, was "an ugly manifestation of NEP" (see *Pravda*, October 3, 1923).

Krasnoshchekov himself, who had degrees in law and economics from the University of Chicago, considered the facts revealed by the revision to be inconsequential and caused by the inevitable costs of organizing the Bank. Accused of enriching himself and indulging in a grand lifestyle, he pleaded not guilty. In the trial that took place in March of 1924, Krasnoshchekov was sentenced to six years' imprisonment. Rut six months later (at first due to his bad health) he was in fact set free, which was officially affirmed by VTsIK in January 1925. Starting in 1926 he worked in the system of the People's Commissariat for Agriculture. In 1937 he was repressed illegally as "a Trotskyist" and rehabilitated in 1956.

12. It was called by the surname of one of the leaders of The RKP Workers' Group, G. I. Myasnikov (see note 5 to Document No.4 and note 6 to Document No. 20).

13. The reference is to the group factional struggle developed in the Party TsK on the initiative of the "troika" (G. E. Zinovyev, L. B. Kamenev, and I. V. Stalin) against Trotsky. A. G. Beloborodov justly has this phenomenon as being directly dependent on the methods (repressions of the heterodoxies) the RKP(b) TsK and TSKK used to manage formal Party unity.

14. G. E. Zinovyev spoke on October 12, 1923, at the session in honor of the thirtieth anniversary of the Moscow Party organization (*Rabochaya Moskva,* October 14, 1923). I did not manage to find out where and when V. M. Molotov spoke.

14

V. M. Molotov's Memo to the Members and Candidates Members of the Politburo of the TsK of the RKP(b)

October 17, 1923

To all Politburo members and candidates

In connection with Comrade Trotsky's suggestion, supported by Comrade Bukharin, I ask you to check on whether the distribution of Comrade Trotsky's letter was carried out through the technical apparatus of the TsK Secretariat;[1] I am informed that my checkup did not confirm this (Comrade Nazaretyan's information is enclosed).[2]

The confirmation of the fact that Comrade Trotsky's letter was distributed independently of the TsK apparatus comes Comrade Zelensky, who familiarized himself with Comrade Trotsky's letter (October 12–13) in the copy received by him from Comrade Stukov. He was also informed that Comrades Sapronov and I.N. Smirnov had Comrade Trotsky's letter.

Here is an extract from a letter by Comrade Rein, who works in the Presidium of the VTsIK, received today in the TsK (dated October 13).[3] Comrade Rein writes: ". . . echoes of the 'incident' at the TsK Plenum and echoes of Comrade Trotsky's letter to the TsK, etc., are now known to the masses and are interpreted in various ways."

Comrade Rein's letter will be delivered to the Politburo members.

I do not object the checkup of the TsK technical apparatus by a special commission, according to Comrade Nazaretyan's proposition.[4]

TsK Secretary—V. M. Molotov

17/X-23.

RTsKhIDNI, f. 17, op. 2, d. 685, 1. 98
the attested copy. Published for the first time.

NOTES

1. See Document No. 9.
2. For A. M. Nazaretyan's memo, see Document No. 10.
3. For R. P. Rein's letter, see Document No. 7.
4. There is no information about the setting up of this commission and its action.

15

The Extract from the Minutes of the Politburo of the TsK of the RKP(b) Session

October 18, 1923

AGENDA:
i.11. The TSKK resolution
(Kuibyshev)[1]

RESOLUTION:
a) To call, on October 25 of this year, an urgent Plenum of the Central Committee, and to add to the agenda of the Plenum the question of the inner-Party situation. To predetermine that the session of the TsK Plenum will be held together with the TSKK Plenum.

b) To take into account the TSKK suggestion about the halt of the distribution of Comrade Trotsky's letter, confirming that this suggestion cannot be realized.

c) To invite representatives (2 from each) of the most numerous proletarian Party organizations (10–15) to the joint session of the TsK and TSKK Plenum, charging the TsK Secretariat to register them and deliver their list to all the Politburo members.

RTsKhIDNI, f. 17, op. 3, d. 388, 1. 4; typescript duplicate
First published in *Izvestiya TsK KPSS,* 1990, No. 6, p. 194.

NOTE

1. The reference is to the resolution of the RKP(b) TSKK Presidium dating October 15, 1923 (see Document No. 11).

16

L. D. Trotsky's Letter to the Presidium of the TSKK of the RKP(b) and the Politburo of the TsK of the RKP(b)

October 19, 1923

To the TsK Presidium. To the TsK Politburo

Top Secret

1. The TSKK Presidium resolution concerning my letter[1] is carried out without inviting me to the session of the Presidium, without listening to the actual explanation of mine, i.e., without observing elementary guarantees of correctness and impartiality of the resolution referring to every Party member.

2. The TSKK Presidium characterizes my letter as the platform for setting up a faction. In this evaluation I can see but the continuation of the very struggle about which Comrade Kuibyshev had told me before my letter and independently of it.[2]

3. In my letter I tell about its aims. On the ground of my behavior in the TsK and the TSKK Presidium one can but acknowledge that I mostly avoided such steps, which outwardly, at any rate, could bring to mind an attempt to set up a faction. While the discussions withing the Central Committee became known immediately to the broad Party circles (in the form directed against me), I always abstained from making explanations about the vexed questions to those who were not members of the Central Committee.

4. I always kept hoping that the objective experience together with the criticism in the TsK would provide in the end the correct policy for the vexed questions.

5. On my return from Kislovodsk after being under lengthy treatment,[3] I found the situation in the country and in the Party suddenly changed for the worse. I must say that this change became clear to me only at the TsK Plenum,[4] since during my stay in Kislovodsk I did not get any information from anybody about it. The general course of the Plenum work was, however, completely unchanged. No measures in any way relevant to the existing situation were planned.

6. At the Politburo session after the Plenum I described the actual severe situation and pointed to the necessity of extraordinary measures in both the economic and inner-Party spheres for the purpose of providing a real possibility of unanimous Party work.

7. The answer to my speech was Comrade Rykov's suggestion to call a private conference of the Politburo members. This private conference did not take place due to a series of my misunderstandings, which were nobody's fault. Only on October 15 did I get Comrade Rykov's explanatory memo, which opens with the word: "I feel very sorry that I did not answer your memo, which you sent me in response to the invitation to call a conference with some TsK members."

8. Not receiving an answer to my note, I had every right to believe that the Politburo members rejected the discussion of the most important questions of the inner crisis suggested by me. Only after that did I write my letter, whose task, mentioned in it, was to urge the TsK, in accordance with the whole existing situation, to put and to solve the most acute and morbid questions of the inner life of the Party in a different way.

To check up on my own evaluation of the existing situation, I showed my letter to fewer than a dozen responsible comrades, who were quite aware that the question is about an inner-Party top secret document, which in no way can be widely distributed due to international reasons, and consequently it cannot be a platform

9. When some Politburo members raised the question of not distributing the letter to the TsK and TSKK members in order to prepare the solution of the question of the Politburo,[5] I agreed to this, while warning that some comrades who were not the TsK members had familiarized themselves with my letter. Having learned that some copies of my letter had been made, I not only insisted, after the Politburo session,[6] that they should

not be distributed, but that they should be given back to me. The whole manner of their actions is rather unlike the distribution of the platform.

10. The TSKK Presidium said that the question should be solved with the TsK and the TSKK.[7] The Politburo rejected this point of view on the ground that my letter had supposedly bee distributed to the masses.[8] I cannot check whether this is true, i.e., whether, to the extent the letter is known now, it was delivered to all the TsK and TSKK members. But we are all aware of the fact that Comrade Lenin's letter on the national question was known to a relatively wide circle of Party members and at the same time, according to the common consent, it was not widely circulated.[9] It is quite clear to me that, if I so desire, my letter, addressed by its very essence (and due to the international situation) to a very limited circle of persons, could not leave these limits, if there were any resoluteness to consider the questions without factional convulsions and shocks.

11. The Politburo's refusal to join the relevant part of the TSKK resolution can be understood only as permission to put the letter into wide circulation. It is in this way that the character of a factional platform can be attached to it, which it does not have now.

12. Absolutely rejecting the TSKK evaluation of my letter, I restore the main facts in this declaration, which I could not expose before the TSKK Presidium in time.

L. Trotsky

October 19, 1923.

N 373

The original from L.D. Trotsky's facsimile.[10]
Published according to the text of the first publication
in *Izvestiya TsK KPSS*, 1990, No. 7, pp. 174-175.

NOTES

1. Reference to the RKP(b) TSKK Presidium resolution dated October 15, 1923 (see Document No. 11).

2. See Documents Nos. 2, 3, and 5.

3. Trotsky was on sick leave from June 15 to September 7, 1923.

4. The reference is to the September RKP(b) TsK Plenum (see Document No. 1).

5. The reference is to the RKP(b) TsK Politburo session on October 11, 1923 (see Document No. 6).

6. The reference is to the TsK Politburo session on October 15, 1923 (see Document No. 9). As A. M. Nazaretyan testifies, on October 8 and 9, according to V. M. Molotov's order, 125 xerox copies were made of L. D. Trotsky's letter; one of them (especially for I. V. Staling) was typed. On October 19, thirteen copies of the letter were sent to the Politburo and TSKK Presidium members (see Document No. 10).

7. The reference is to the points 2 and 5 of the RKP(b) TSKK Presidium resolution dated October 15 (see Document No. 11).

8. The reference is to the TsK Politburo session which took place on October 18, 1923 (see Document No. 15).

9. The reference is to the publicizing of Lenin's letter "The Question of Nationalities or 'Autonomization' " (see *Lenin V.I. Poln. sobr. soch.*, vol. 45, pp. 356-362, 594-596) at the Senioren-Convent (the conference of the representatives of the delegations) of the Twelfth RKP(b) Congress.

10. At the present time the original of the document is kept in the archive of the President of the Russian Federation. There is a typescript copy of the document in the RTsHIDNI (f. 17, op. 2, d. 658, 1. 108-109).

17

The Politburo of the TsK of the RKP(b) Members' Reply to L. D. Trotsky's Letter of October 8, 1923

October 19, 1923

Strictly confidential
To be kept as a cipher
Subject to return

TO TsK and TSKK Members[1]

I. WHY A DETAILED REPLY TO COMRADE TROTSKY'S LETTER OF OCTOBER 8 IS NECESSARY.

Many of the TsK and TSKK members are aware of the fact that cooperation between Comrade Trotsky and the majority of Politburo members has already been going on for a number of years, mainly in the form of Comrade Trotsky's sending in letters and declarations in which he invariably subjects to criticism practically entire activity of the TsK. In the main the majority of Politburo members has refrained from replying to these documents in writing. Only occasionally, in exclusive cases, Lenin gave a written explanation to one or another of Trotsky's most erroneous statements.[2] However, shortly before the RKP Twelfth Congress the undersigned were obliged to reply in writing to several such declarations of Comrade Trotsky,[3] for it became clear that he was going to make two grave political mistakes: (1) on the question of union with peasantry Comrade Trotsky took at that time an obviously erroneous stand, tending to underestimate the peasantry's role; (2) on the question of the Party's role in controlling state and economic bodies Comrade Trotsky took then an attitude similar to that of Comrade Osinsky.[4]

Since then we have no once replied to Comrade Trotsky's written declarations and statements, which on termination of the Twelfth Congress became more frequent. Nevertheless, Comrade Trotsky's letter of October 8 is a document which ought not to be left without a reply. First, in this letter Comrade Trotsky, *starting an attack against the Party TsK*, acts as an instigator of struggle against the TsK, as an initiator putting forward a slogan of attacking the TsK at a difficult moment from the viewpoint of international situation, on account of which the Politburo simply hasn't the right to leave Comrade Trotsky's letter unanswered. Second, in this letter which was justly characterized by the TSKK Presidium and Moscow Gubkom* Bureau[5] as a "letter-platform" and undisguised attempt at creating factionalism, Comrade Trotsky is making *a number of mistakes* which may prove more perilous to the Party than even his "pamphlet-platform," issued before the Tenth Congress of the RKP,[6] and which (mistakes) may bring about a real crisis in the Party and a split between the Party and the working class. If our Party fails in making Comrade Trotsky retrieve the monstrous mistakes he is perpetrating by his demonstration in the "letter-platform" of October 8, 1923, great damage will be caused not only to the RKP and USSR, but also to the German revolution.

II. ECONOMIC QUESTIONS

Naturally, we are by no means inclined to overlook huge difficulties and dangers facing our Union of Republics on the path of its economic development. However, when Comrade Trotsky and his nearest confederates, lavishly laying it on thick, talk of our economic bankruptcy, we regard it as either panic, as it was in 1921, when Comrade Trotsky predicted our im-

---

*Guberniya (Provincial) Committee. (Ed.)

minent—in a few months or even weeks—"going bust," or ignorance of the actual state of affairs, or else deliberate exaggeration actuated by factional motives. Already at the very beginning of Comrade Trotsky's "economic" demonstrations against the TsK majority two to three years ago, none other than Lenin explained to Comrade Trotsky dozens of times that in economic questions speedy successes were impossible and years and years of patient and stubborn effort were required to attain serious results. Comrade Lenin repeatedly pointed out that in the sphere of restoration of our economy, nothing serious could be achieved all in a rush, by a sudden attack or strong language and still less by panicky exaggerations.

Comrade Trotsky reminds us in his letter of the contents of his report on industry at the RKP's Twelfth Congress. Whatever was sound in this report was, at the proposal of the TsK majority, accepted by the congress and is now gradually being put into practice; whereas all that was artificial and farfetched in it, was refuted at that very congress by most prominent industrial executives irrespective of "trends." It is enough to recall here Comrades Bogdanov, Chubar, Smilga, and others' speeches against Comrade Trotsky's report.[7]

Comrade Trotsky's phrases on importance of "planned, maneuverable regulation" have not got any real content and strongly resemble the phrase of the "production atmosphere"[8] used by him before the RKP's Tenth Congress and ridiculed by Comrade Lenin. For the purpose of ensuring adequate management of the economic life of the country from one center and introducing a maximally systematic character into this management, the TsK reorganized in the summer of 1923 the STO,* having introduced into it a number of most prominent industrial executives of the Republic. Comrade Trotsky was also introduced into the STO. However, Comrade Trotsky would not deign to attend the STO sessions, in the same way as he ignored for a number of years Sovnarkom† sessions and declined Comrade Lenin's proposal about appointing Comrade Trotsky one of Sovnarkom vice chairmen.[9] Comrade Trotsky quotes Comrade Lenin's note, already written at the time of Lenin's disease and devoted to the Gosplan. Everybody who has read this letter of Comrade Lenin knows that its essence is in Lenin's *opposing* the idea of Comrade Trotsky being appointed Gosplan

---

*Council of Labor and Defense. See List of Abbreviations. (Ed.)

†Sovnarkom (SNK)—Council of People's Commissars. See List of Abbreviations. (Ed.)

chairman. Lenin advises to retaining Comrade Krzhizhanovsky at the post of Gosplan chairman, having given to him as assistant one of our prominent administrators.[10] And it was this way exactly that the Politburo acted: it appointed to that post first Comrade Pyatakov and later on Comrade Smilga. Still, the Gosplan's work is not yet satisfactory and needs improvement. But this improvement can *never* be achieved by haste or by *phrases* about "planned, maneuverable regulation."

The TsK advanced at the congress the idea of a single agricultural tax.[11] That this decision was correct and improved peasants' position is now beyond any doubt.

The Republic's financial position has doubtlessly become more stable. Extra-tax state income is increasing, the national currency situation is improving. But half a year ago Comrade Trotsky predicted a failure of our currency and the inevitability of passing over to work payment in kind. Now it is clear that he was in the wrong. The chervonet banknote is quite viable, and nobody is even breathing a work of work payment in kind.

In the sphere of grain export we have passed from words to deeds. We have exported over 40 million *poods* of grain. We contemplate (if the international situation allows it) exporting 200 million *poods*—and with a good certainty of success. We have achieved our passive trade balance and changed it into an active, favorable one.

Large-scale industry is gradually but steadily reviving. The fuel problem (coal, oil) has been satisfactorily solved. The railway department is seriously developing in the direction of self-sufficiency.

All these are results testifying not to a "crisis," but to improvement—gradual, that's true, but improvement.

However, in regard to the stability of tchervonet currency, in the sphere of credits, budget, and industry the position is doubtlessly extremely difficult. Serious anxiety is being caused by the so-called "discrepancies in prices,"[12] the importance of which was justly stressed by Comrade Lenin and Politburo majority long before theTwelfth Congress as well as at the Twelfth Congress. The TSK duly started working up measures on this question before the September (1923) Plenum, long before Comrade Trotsky's letters, at the time when he was busy with questions of literature, art, and private life,[13] etc. Nevertheless, only those who regard the Party work as somebody else's duty can qualify this phenomenon as a sign of bankruptcy of the TsK's economic policy. The NEP is surely going to bring us dozens of such "crises." Only people fully ignorant of the pace and nature of economic development can be blind to the fact that stable and serious results in this field are achieved only as a result of years' effort. Since the RKP's Twelfth Congress Comrade Trotsky has not put forward—we are stating this quite definitely—a *single* practical suggestion in this field.[14] To speak of the liquidation of NEP is a gross exaggeration. The TsK has already worked up a number of measures which are gradually bringing and have already brought certain results (industrial products' prices are coming down).

Concentration of industry, reduction of overhead expenses in the industry and trade—all this is beyond doubt indispensable. In both spheres noticeable results have been achieved. Of special importance is concentration of industry, for the reduction of overhead expenses, which is in general possible, has not got decisive importance for the future of industry. But only a doctrinaire can, in the process of industrial concentration, disregard political considerations (Comrade Trotsky puts the words in disdainful inverted commas and calls these considerations "localistic"). The economic-rational concentration of industry is in the final analysis also advantageous politically—as a general algebraic formula it is correct. However, a good number of deviations are here unavoidable. Comrade Trotsky argues, without openly stating it, against the Politburo's decision on not closing down the Putilovsky plant in Petrograd[15] (and earlier Bryansk and some other plants), which is one of the Republic's unprofitable plants. The Politburo decided—on political considerations—not to close down these plants, and the immediate leaders of our industrial policy—Comrades Rykov and Pyatakov—had in the end to agree with it. The decision was and remains absolutely sound. Closing down such plants as Putilovsky or Bryansk would have been a political defeat for the entire Republic. Anybody approaching the question with the least bit of objectivity will realize it. Concentration is indispensable, and we shall go on with it, but if Comrade Trotsky at the end of his "letter-platform" speaks of working-class democracy to some purpose and not for nothing, he will easily understand that the blind, "rigid" concentration, on which he is insisting in a doctrinaire fashion, is among other things hardly compatible with working-class democracy.

Comrade Trotsky does not want to understand a small point": that we are a working-class state, that we cannot come up against the workers' main body for the reason of closing down such plants, that estrangement from workers in this is fraught with both political and economic complications. "Rigid concentration" in Comrade Trotsky's fashion would have surely led to strikes, to estrangement of the Party from workers, and to still more serious conflicts with workers. We are not going to embark on this road which is pernicious for the country.

That the Politburo has and still disagrees with Comrade Trotsky on the question of personal appointments to the high industrial posts, is true. We think it necessary to openly tell the Party that the basis of Comrade Trotsky's entire discontent; of all his irritation; of all his attacks against the TsK, continuing already for several years; of his determination to shake the Party, is that Comrade Trotsky wants the TsK to appoint him and Comrade Kolegayev to the highest posts in the economy's administration. This appointment was for a long time opposed by Comrade Lenin, and we think that Comrade Lenin was quite right in opposing it.[16] We believe that there is no evidence at all that Comrade Trotsky would be able to effectively head the Republic' s highest industrial bodies under the present hard conditions. Quite the contrary, experience with the Narkomput* showed the opposite. On top of everything it led to a serious conflict with trade unions.[17] Despite all the caution of the TsK, which was unwilling to agree to Comrade Trotsky's dictatorship in the field of people's economy and armed forces, it took a number of steps that could help Comrade Trotsky achieve the desired goal. Comrade Trotsky is a Sovnarkom member, a reorganized STO member. Comrade Lenin offered him the post of Sovnarkom vice-chairman. Had Comrade Trotsky wanted it, he could have proved indeed, by his work at all these posts in the face of the entire Party, that the Party could entrust him with the virtually unlimited powers in the sphere of industry and armed forces he is striving for. However, Comrade Trotsky preferred another course of action, in our opinions incompatible with a Party member's duties as they are commonly understood. He has never attended sessions of Sovnarkom—either those led by Comrade Lenin or those held after his retirement on account of illness—or sessions of STO (old or reorganized); nor has he ever advanced a proposal on economic, financial, budget, or any other questions to Sovnarkom, STO, or Gosplan.[18] He has flatly declined the offer of the post of Comrade Lenin's assistant. Evidently, he considers it to be beneath his dignity. He behaves according to the formula: "either all or nothing." In fact, Comrade Trotsky has put himself in the following position in relation to the Party: either the Party confers on him practically dictatorial powers in the sphere of people's economy and armed forces, or he actually refuses to do any work in the

---

*People's Commissariat of Ways of Communication. (Ed.)

fields of economics and industry, retaining only the right of systematically disorganizing the TsK in its difficult everyday work. We declare that today, as before, the Politburo cannot take upon itself responsibility for satisfying Comrade Trotsky's claim on dictatorship in the economic and industrial management in addition to the powers he has already got as Predrevvoyensoveta.* We think it our duty to say: we cannot take upon ourselves responsibility for a risky experiment in this sphere.

III. GENERAL POLITICAL SITUATION IN THE COUNTRY

There are a number of signs showing a certain growth of discontent among peasants. The reasons for this discontent are apparently two: (1) a single agricultural tax and (2) "scissors of prices." According to information received by the TsK, the single agricultural tax is collected on the whole significantly more easily than taxes in 1922.[19] Of course, the very form of tax, as is the case in any *direct* tax, causes and will cause a certain discontent among the peasants. The Party's task for the next few years (if there is no war)[20] will consist in gradually abandoning direct taxes and passing over to levying corresponding sums from peasants through the system of state credit, cooperation, etc. Abandoning the direct tax would essentially improve the peasants' political attitude of mind, but it will become possible only after establishment of appropriate cooperation between the urban industry and agriculture.

Discrepancy of prices ("scissors") at present cannot but engender in the countryside some discontent, which to a certain extent affected also the layers of workers connected with the countryside. This was stressed at the TsK Plenum, and in this relation what Comrade Trotsky repeats following the TSK Plenum, does not represent anything new. The struggle for a reduction in prices has already begun and will go on more successfully the less this question will be complicated by outside circumstances.

Past irregularities in payment of wages (golden state loan, inaccurate payment of wages, etc.) caused ferment among workers in some towns. Naturally, the Party ought to pay most close attention to these phenomena.

---

*Revolutionary War Council (RWC) Chairman.

But if there was among TsK members a man who made doctrinaire mistakes also in this field, it is Comrade Trotsky, who here, too, insisted on exerting excessive pressure and motivated it by abstract-rationalistic reasons (self-financing). Time and again we stressed in the TsK of our Party that workers would never permit us to go back on the question of real wages. Comrade Trotsky was among those who regarded such a statement as "agitation," whereas it was just stating a fact, not agitation at all. Comrade Trotsky's and his side's present letters may, as they trickle downward, cause only new ferment among workers.

However, on the whole, the working class' attitude is quite sound,[21] and with the Party's sufficiently close attention to the questions of wages (Narkomfin* should receive the TsK's direct order to most accurately pay wages in all worker districts) and prices, there are ample grounds to hope that the attitude of the working class and peasantry will be quite satisfactory.

IV. QUESTIONS OF FOREIGN POLICY

In another letter, that of October 10, 1923,[22] written in reply to Comrade Kuybyshev's letter, Comrade Trotsky states that he does not fully agree with the majority of the Politburo on the question of foreign policy. Indeed, since the RKP's Twelfth Congress there have been two cases of serious disagreement with Comrade Trotsky in this sphere. We shall briefly state them here and request TsK and TSKK members to form their own judgment as to who was right in this argument.

This spring when Gurzon delivered his well-known ultimatum, Comrade Trotsky at the beginning really took a stand different from that of the majority of the Politburo. He argued that we should *not* concede, for breaking off was all the same unavoidable. The Politburo majority started and pursued to the end another line of policy. Breaking off did not occur. The course of events showed, we believe, that our state, not Comrade Trotsky's, was right. Lather Comrade Trotsky stopped insisting on his erroneous standpoint.

The second disagreement concerns our relations with Poland. For nearly

---

*Narkomfin—People's Commissar of Finance (at that time it was G. Ya. Sokolnikov). (Ed.)

a month already, Comrade Trotsky has been insisting on Narkomindel making an open demonstrative proposal to the Polish government for concluding an agreement (in connection with German events) on mutual noninterference in Germany's affairs. Comrade Trotsky reasons that in both cases, whether the Polish government accepts the proposal or flatly declines it, we shall ostensibly be sure winners: in the first case it will be a certain advantage to us, and in the second we shall have good material for agitation. Already in September 1923, Comrade Trotsky drew up an army order of the day on the Polish question. Publication of such an order would have been at that time highly dangerous and would have doubtlessly worsened the situation. By a Politburo majority's decision, publication of this order was put off. The Politburo majority thinks such course of action at present extremely dangerous. An "agitator" approach, indeed. We cannot presently advance proposals which may make us out as inspirers of breaking off and initiators of war with Poland, and lead us to breaking off or half-breaking off *before the commencement of the German revolution*. Such a policy, which might afford workers and peasants even the slightest grounds for suspecting the Party in thoughtlessly provocating war, would be a virtual disaster. The majority of Politburo members thinks the policy of "violational impulses" especially dangerous in the sphere of foreign policy, and that at such a moment fraught with terrible consequences as the present one. The Politburo majority considers Comrade Trotsky's attacks against Comrade Chicherin, who has been for a number of years leading, under the Politburo's guidance, our foreign policy on the whole rightly and cautiously, to be inappropriate.

These two serious mistakes by Comrade Trotsky very clearly show how easy it is to expose the Republic to dangers and ordeals, if Comrade Trotsky's erroneous schemes are not repulsed.

It's noteworthy, by the way, that the Politburo's difference of opinion with Comrade Trotsky on the Polish question proved sufficient for Comrade Trotsky's—according to his numerous declarations in the Politburo—having refrained from public statements on the question of German revolution because of the Party's allegedly not having got "a general line." Every TsK and TSKK member is well aware that the Party's line on the question of German revolution does not at all consist in whether Narkomindel* is going to send today or tomorrow a demonstrative declaration of the aforesaid kind to the Polish government.[23]

---

*People's Commissar of Foreign Affairs (at that time G.V. Chicherin). (Ed.)

V. QUESTIONS OF THE GERMAN REVOLUTION

In the same letter, that of October 10, Comrade Trotsky also mentions among radically disputable issues "cardinal questions,connected with German revolution."

This question is now a central one. To withhold any facts relating to it would be a crime. We, therefore, think it our duty to inform comrades of the following.

In August, when the Politburo summoned Comrades Trotsky, Zinovyev, and Bukharin for the first discussion of the question connected with the German revolution, Comrade Zinovyev proposed to the Politburo theses on this question, which in September served as a basis for the decisions unanimously taken by the TsK Plenary session. Comrade Trotsky then only strongly emphasized the necessity of drawing up "a calendar program" of preparation and carrying out of German revolution, considering it to be alpha and omega of the entire problem. According to his statement, the German Party's foremost task was already not political but just military-technical preparation for an uprising. In this latter statement the Politburo saw a mistake, or rather, which is usual for Comrade Trotsky, exaggerations. But in the main there was not any difference of opinion. All the resolutions were passed by the Politburo unanimously.[24] For looking to the practical side of the matter, a commission, headed by Comrade Zinovyev and including also Comrades Trotsky, Radek, Stalin (later on Bukharin), and Chicherin, was appointed. All the decisions were at that time taken unanimously. Before the September Plenary session the TsK formed a special commission for drawing up theses for the forthcoming Plenum and discussing a number of other practical questions connected with the German revolution. Besides the above mentioned comrades, Pyatakov, Sokolnikov and Dzerzhinsky were also delegated to the commission. The commission unanimously approved (with some alterations) Comrade Zinovyev's theses. Comrade Trotsky also voted for them. All the preparatory negotiations with the German Communist Party as well as negotiations after the Tsk Plenary Session were conducted by this commission. All the decisions, except one on an insignificant question (relating to leaving Comrade Rut Fischerr in the Berlin organization), were also taken unanimously. The theses themselves, as is well-known to the TsK members who were present at the Plenary session, were unanimously approved by the Plenum. Only at the very end of the session, after the questions connected with the German revolution had been long since considered, when the well-known incident with the composition of Revvoensovet* arose,[25] Comrade Trotsky, before leaving the hall the TsK meeting was held in, delivered a speech that deeply upset all the TsK members. He said that the German Communist Party's leadership was good for nothing, that its Central Committee was imbued with fatalism, heedlessness, etc., and, in view of this, the German revolution was doomed to failure.This speech made a dispiriting impression on all those present, but the great majority of comrades thought the philippic was occasioned by an extraneous episode disconnected with the German revolution, and did not accord with the real state of affairs.

However, at present, if there is any point in the questions of the German revolution on which we and Comrade Trotsky are at variance, it is that of the calendar schedule pattern of preparation for the uprising. The protocol of the German Communist Party Central Committee session of October 12, 1923, reads: "Comrade *Brandler* reports of negotiations with Russian comrades in Moscow on the questions of general situation and opposition. No disagreement was there—except that of the so-called fixing of the date of action with Comrade Leo (Trotsky). Thus, Comrade Brandler also states complete unanimity—except the disagreement with Comrade Trotsky.

All the members of the Politburo and TsK, who are regular workers of the Komintern,[26] are fully aware of the crucial importance of the situation and have been doing all in their power to ensure harmoniousness and collectivity all throughout the preparatory activities. At all the stages of work Comrade Trotsky has been taking a most active part, and, therefore, all the talking about "cardinal differences," connected with the German revolution are exaggerated, far-fetched, and at the very least premature. Comrade Trotsky just cannot be unaware of the fact that discord and disagreement in our TsK and our Party at the present moment will be a most severe blow to the German Communist Party, holding now the outposts of the world revolution.

---

*Revolutionary War Council. See the List of Abbreviations. (Ed.)

VI. THE REVVOENSOVET OF THE REPUBLIC

The object of special attacks on the part of Comrade Trotsky is the well-known unanimous (including Comrade Pyatakov) decision of the TsK Plenum concerning inclusion in the Revvoensovet of the Republic of a group of TsK members of the military profession.[27] Supporting Comrade Kuibyshev's suggestion on reinforcing the RVSR,* we were guided by the following considerations.

Comrade Trotsky himself has been of late giving quite insufficient attention to the army. The main work in the Revvoensovet—in the hands of Comrade Sklyansky and a group of non-Party specialists,† including the Glavkom,‡ Kamenev, Shanposhnikov, and Lebedev. These latter men are very conscientious, assiduous, and competent workers. However, at the moment when the TsK decided to double or treble the army and when there is certainty that the time is drawing near when the army will decide the fate of the Republic, we have naturally arrived at a conclusion that one ought not to entrust the fate of the army to the aforementioned group. Organization of the army's economic management is hopelessly bad. The entire supplies business in the army is managed by Ardzhanov, whom almost all of our high military workers consider to be an unreliable man. The necessity of Ardzhanov's removal from office has been repeatedly pointed out to the RVSR by the Party secretary.§

In view of all this and of the tasks which the Revvoensovet is going to face in the near future, it was, in our opinion, quite opportune to raise the question of reinforcing it. It was suggested to include in the Revvoensovet as its rank-and-file members Moscow Military District Commander Comrade Muralov and the entire group of the TsK's military members (Voroshilov, Lashevich, Stalin, Pyatakov, and Ordzhonikidze).

At the same time it was specified that Comrade Trotsky's majority in the RVSR Presidium would be guaranteed and that disagreements between the TsK members and the RVSR would not be discussed.[28] Hardly anybody would venture to disprove the statement that such a reinforcement will be

---

*Revolutionary War Council of the Republic. (Ed.)
†Military Specialists of the former czarist army, military professionals. (Ed.)
‡Commander-in-chief of the country's armed forces. (Ed.)
§So it is in the test. Apparently, one ought to read "Part Tsk Secretary." (Ed.)

of great benefit to our cause and will raise the authority of RVSR in the eyes of the army, Party, and the entire country.

And this decision, taken by the Plenum—we repeat—unanimously, Comrade Trotsky declared to be a factious step, although Comrade Trotsky's direct supporter Comrade Pyatakov had also voted for it. In his speech Comrade Trotsky rejected candidatures of military TsK members and declared that with such a RVSR membership he would be declining responsibility for the armed forces. When the TsK member Comrade Komarov reminded Comrade Trotsky of the inadmissability of this sort of rejection and giving up the work at such a moment, Comrade Trotsky declared that he was not inclined to listen to preliminarily prepared speeches and left the hall. Despite the Plenum's unanimous request, sent to Comrade Trotsky through a special delegation, he did not return to the Plenum, having as a result put the TsK in a very difficult situation. Such an unprecedented mode of action by Comrade Trotsky did not unfortunately remain a secret to wider circles (including the army) and gave rise to various rumors and legends.

We affirm that the immediate motive of Comrade Trotsky's present attack against the TsK is namely the expansion of the RVSR and not imaginary economic and other "crises," of which Comrade Trotsky did not breathe a word at the Plenum itself at the end of September of this year.

VII. THE QUESTION OF SELLING VODKA

The most far-fetched point of Comrade Trotsky's "letter-platform" is point 13, devoted to the question of selling vodka. Here Comrade Trotsky spares no rhetorical colors. In view of the singular vividness of the point, we reproduce it in full:

The Politburo's attempt at forming the budget on the basis of selling vodka, i.e., at making a working class state's incomes independent of successes of industrial construction, was a threatening symptom. Only a decisive protest within as well as outside the TsK stopped this attempt, which would have been a severe blow not only to the industrial work but also to the Party itself. However, the idea of further legalization of selling vodka has not been discarded by the TsK up to now. Beyond all doubt, between the self-sufficing nature of the secretarial organization becoming more and more independent of the Party and the tendency toward creating a budget as far as possible independent of successes and failures of the Party's collective construction effort, there is some inner connection.[29]

This citation deserves the Party's memorizing it and having a good laugh at it. Lo and behold. The Politburo wants to make the working-class state's incomes "independent" of successes, and failures of the industrial construction. Who can still doubt that "between the self-sufficing nature of the secretarial organization becoming more and more independent of the Party and the tendency toward creating a budget, most possibly independent of successes and failures of collective construction effort, there is some inner connection"? Is not Comrade Trotsky ashamed of talking such nonsense with a serious air?

What actually happened, however?

As far back as the time when the question of granting concessions to Urkart[30] was considered, Comrade Lenin repeatedly stated that we might find ourselves facing the question which is better: granting concessions of Urkart's type or, if the worst comes to the worst, legalization under certain conditions of sale of vodka for the purpose of improving state finances? Comrade Lenin stated without hesitation that the latter was better.[31] Before Comrade Lenin's having fallen ill, more than once the question was raised of appointing a competent commission which would study the question in a businesslike manner, and thoroughly weigh all the pros and cons. Nothing new was decided also by the Party's TsK. At the moment of hard financial difficulties the TsK only appointed a secret commission for *considering* the question. The change in the situation (possibility of war, etc.) removed the question from the order of the day.

What, then, is there in it "unworthy" of the Party? Unworthy only is the behavior of people who deliberately exaggerated and continue exaggerating this question.

VIII. SITUATION IN THE PARTY

That we are going through a "quickly escalating Party crisis,"[32] Comrade Trotsky considers to be something self-evident, needing no proofs.

What is this assertion based on?

In his "platform-letter" of October 8, 1923, Comrade Trotsky twice mentions "methods and modes" by which the RKP(b) Twelfth Congress was called. In other words, Comrade Trotsky is seeking now to discredit the Twelfth Congress although it took place almost half a year ago. The Party has long age gotten out of the habit of talking about "methods and modes"—approximately at the time of our finally parting from the Mensheviks.[33]

Neither before the Congress, nor at the Congress itself or after it did Comrade Trotsky adduce a single fact discrediting the composition of the Twelfth Congress. What right has he got to repeat such accusations against our Party? The entire Soviet apparatus sees and must see in the RKP a source of governmental power. When one of the Politburo members declare that the Twelfth Congress membership was ostensibly being juggled with—how will it influence the Soviet apparatus? Yes, it is clear. It is nothing else but preparation of the ground for *separating the Soviet apparatus from the Party*. Comrade Trotsky with the most serious air tells that "secretarial bureaucratism has done away with any life in the Party," that "secretaries of provincial Party committees and further downward to the lowest Party cell are appointed by the TsK General Secretariat," that "in the most severe periods of war communism, the appointment method within the Party was not spread even to one tenth the extent it is spread now," that the "entire [!] Party now talks of unjust appointments" that, in a word, the Party has turned into a callous machine.

We do not know to what such statements by Comrade Trotsky can be more just ascribed—to his absolute ignorance of the actual state of affairs in our local Party organizations or his special attitude toward the Party TsK. Before the Party Twelfth Congress Comrade Trotsky let fly his winged expression on the "gubkom oblomovshchina,"[34] and now he crowns the matter with a good number of characteristics, depicting the inner-Party situation in the same hues that are used by Mensheviks and Myasnikov's group.[35]

We are, of course, by no means inclined to color the truth also in this sphere and assert that everything is perfectly all right. However, only people completely unacquainted with the inner life of our Party can fail to notice the new positive elements which are appearing in it. For over a year already no fewer than twenty-five thousand of the best young members of our Party are diligently studying in communist universities and Soviet-

Party schools.[36] A great deal of hard work that is going to yield good results in the very near future is being done by Komsomol. A new generation of active workers, getting from the Party all it can give to them, is being molded. Party cells at factories and plants in both capitals* have during the last half year at least doubled their membership—at the expense of lathe workers.[37] Workers' eagerness to join the Party is rather significant. The general cultural level of Party members is steadily rising. The Party press has doubtlessly improved. Secretaries and organizers, spoken of in a broad sense, consist to a great extent of active young workers. Talks of the "upper and lower strata," which formerly sometimes assumed an utterly unwholesome and disagreeable character, have almost ceased.[38] Liquidation of Socialist-revolutionary and Menshevik parties is in process.[39] Only a man isolated from active Party work can be ignorant of all this.

Absence of Party discussions? Not true at all. When a burning topical question—a national one—arose, the TsK called the well-known all-Russian Conference devoted to the problem, which passed with rather a good degree of animation.[40] True, in the last half year, especially in the summer months, the Party was passing through some period of calm. Important and urgent questions seemed to have been temporarily removed from the order of the day, and we got busy with positive construction work, each one at his own place, with all kinds of "small" tasks, etc., which was in accordance with the situation. Now, when in connection with the German revolution great political prospects are reopening before the Party, the political life in our organizations will certainly become more brisk. Notorious "discussions on platforms" are no more, that's true. But they are, in our opinion, just what the Party can do without. And to invent them would be harmful.

That the principles of "broad democracy" are not being fully and sufficiently implemented in our Party, is true. But Comrade Trotsky must have forgotten that some decisions of the Eleventh and Twelfth Congresses deliberately limit broad democracy. Thus, for instance, the Eleventh Congress made a decision on, and the Twelfth Congress confirmed, the necessity of "gubkom" secretaries having prerevolutionary Party membership and "ukom"† secretaries—three year Party membership length, with approval

---

*Moscow and Petrograd. (Ed.)

†Uyezd committees (Ukoms)—Uyezd Party Committees. Uyezd is an administrative-territorial unit, a part of Guberniya. (Ed.)

of a higher Party institution required in both cases.[41] This, naturally, significantly limits "broad democracy," but it is absolutely indispensable in order to guard the Party from the influence of the new economic policy. The same ought to be said of the Party purge, of restriction of admission to the Party,[42] etc. Does Comrade Trotsky suggest cancelling all this?

One can hardly doubt that Comrade Trotsky's attempt to play with the idea of "broad democracy" will be met in the entire Party with a smile.

As regards "appointment of 'gubkom' secretaries," in this respect, as in many others, Comrade Trotsky is gravely mistaken. With rare exceptions present-day "gubkom" secretaries enjoy the full support of local organizations. Not a single "appointee" in the bad sense of the word will, in any "guberniya," hold out even a few months. We are certain Comrade Trotsky will not find a single "gubkom" secretary who does not enjoy full confidence of the majority of organization. "Gubkom" secretaries, recommended by the TsK, have in a majority of cases already been reelected two or three times by their "guberniyas" and won full comradely confidence and support.

Comrade Trotsky is surprised at our being obliged in the sixth year of the proletarian dictatorship to pass special resolutions, demanding that Party members knowing of anti-Party groups should immediately inform the TsK and TSKK. We, in our turn, are surprised at Comrade Trotsky's naivete. Comrade Trotsky knows perfectly well what Party members are meant here—such as Ryazanov,[43] for example, who has long been maintaining a half-hostile stance in relation to our Party.

About Myasnikov's group and confederates Comrade Trotsky speaks as thought it were an occurrence of the last few days or weeks and as if the group had been called into being by Politburo "mistakes," whereas all the Party knows that Myasnikov's group was formed as far back as 1921, that Myasnikov was expelled from the Party with the consent of Comrade Lenin and without objections on Comrade Trotsky's part, that the TsK did its best to make Myasnikov and others change their minds, and that Myasnikov and his cohorts long ago turned into openly inveterate enemies of our Party.[44] We advanced a proposal, and the TsK September Plenum took a number of practical measures for localization and elimination of this evil.

We admit that such a group as Myasnikov's creates certain difficulties for the Party. However, is it right for a TsK member to make use of difficulties arising in the Party's activity, in order to aggravate and deepen these difficulties? Positively, it looks as if Comrade Trotsky wanted to declare to the TsK: yield to *my demands*, lest *they* (the Myasnikovists) should start fighting against the Party.

IX. STATEMENT OF COMRADE TROTSKY'S FORTY-SIX SUPPORTERS

Comrade Trotsky has more than once declared in the Politburo that he has up to now been "too loyal" in relation to the TsK and that now he is going to untie his hands. His letter of October 8, 1923, finishes with the words: "in view of the situation that has arisen at present, I think it my duty to tell the truth to every Party member whom I consider to be sufficiently advanced, mature, self-restrained and, consequently, capable of helping the Party find a way out of the impasse without factional convulsions and shocks."*

In our opinion, it is a statement, unprecedented in our Bolshevik environment. A TsK member, a Politburo member has not got the right, simply *cannot* make such statements. This is really too much. A Politburo member of our Party thinks that his hands are fully untied and he is entitled to carry on propaganda when talking with each sufficiently "advanced, mature, and self-restrained" Party member. And these latter Party members will be apparently entitled, in their turn, to carry on the same kind of propaganda when speaking with less "advanced, mature, and self-restrained" Party members. No TsK worthy of respect will ever put with such a state of affairs.

Comrade Trotsky's above-mentioned "letter platform" (dated October 8) was brought to the TsK of our Party on October 9, and on October 15 came a "petition" representing a rehash of Comrade Trotsky's letter, bearing about fifty signatures, including a number of signatories with various reservations.[45] Clearly, there is a close connection between the two documents. It is beyond doubt, a sample of "planned," "coordinated," "maneuverable" action.[46] Even the style of both documents ("secretarial hierarchy," etc.) points to a common origin.[47] The document, signed by forty-six comrades, in some paragraphs is putting into words what was held back by

---

*The quotation is not accurately cited. See Document No. 4. (Ed.)

Comrade Trotsky. The economic and financial crisis has ostensibly "mercilessly exposed the unsatisfactory direction of the Party." But what the document of forty-six has actually "mercilessly exposed," is detachment from the Party and political unscrupulousness of its main initiators. When the memo's authors write that the "regime, established within the Party, is quite intolerable, it kills any spontaneous and independent activity of the Party, substituting for it a specially selected bureaucratic apparatus," they are apparently unaware that they are thereby plagiarizing from Myasnikov's works. When the memo's authors write: "the present situation is accounted for by the regime of factional dictatorship within the Party after the *RKP Tenth Congress*, "they are just putting into words what Comrade Trotsky's held back." "The regime which formed after the Tenth Congress," was, as is generally known, established with *Comrade Lenin's direct participation*. Hence, the "petition's authors" think that the regime of factional dictatorship was headed by Lenin. And they accordingly write: "many of us consciously chose non resistance to such a regime—a political turning point in 1921 and subsequently Lenin's illness, in some comrades' opinion, called for dictatorship in the Party as a temporary measure."*

Will many people in our Party agree with the assertion that Comrade Lenin headed only a faction and not the entire Party?

Comrade Trotsky in his "letter-platform" is more diplomatic. Outwardly he is carrying on controversy only with the present Politburo majority, whereas his near supporters are perfectly well aware that the same accusations, which are being brought against us now, were brought by Trotsky against the majority of the Politburo, headed by Lenin, a year ago and earlier. More than once these burning questions were discussed by the Politburo in the period of Comrade Lenin's work in it. And none other than Comrade Lenin passed through the Politburo by the end of 1921, a decision appointing Comrade Trotsky a plenipotentiary representative of Narkomprod† in the Ukraine—a decision afterward duly cancelled, but at the time necessitated by the intolerable situation which arose as a result of Comrade Trotsky's repeated declarations against the TsK majority.[48]

The analysis of the signatures under the document shows that the following two groups have reached understanding: (1) a notorious "democratic centralism" group,[49] politically bankrupt and repeatedly rejected by

---

*All quotations inaccurately cited. See Document No. 12, pp. 82–89. (Ed.)
†People's Commissar of Foodstuffs. (Ed.)

the entire Party. In the document of Forty-Six this faction is represented by: Osinsky, Sapronov, Maksimovsky, V. Smirnov, Drobnis, Rafail, Boguslavsky, etc.; (2) Comrade Trotsky's group, represented in the document, signed by forty-six persons, by the following comrades: Preobrazhensky, Serebryakov, I. N. Smirnov, Pyatakov, Beloborodov, V. L. Kassior, Eltsin, Alsky, Danishevsky, etc.

The essence of the document is namely in the joining up of two small groups whose policy was more than once condemned by our Party.

The agreement between these two groups—the "democratic centralists" and Comrade Trotsky's —has given rise to a document which is hardly destined to occupy an especially honorable place in RKP history.

We are regrettably induced to state that Comrade Trotsky has become a center around which all the opponents of the Party's main cadres are gathering.

X. CONCLUSION

At the end of September of 1923 took place the TsK Plenary meeting in which Comrade Trotsky also took part. The questions, considered at the Plenary meeting, were as follows: (1) The international situation, (2) workers' position and wages, and (3) the inner-Party situation (Myasnikovshchina). At the Plenary meeting Comrade Trotsky did not say anything definite against the decisions of the TsK majority on all these questions. There was no hint of any "crises."

The Plenary meeting completed its work. Two weeks passed, and lo and behold—Comrade Trotsky comes forward with a platform on all these questions. What does it all mean? Why did Comrade Trotsky keep silent at the Plenum?

What has happened during these two weeks?

Only reinforcement of the Revvoensovet by a group of TsK members. To start an argument against reinforcing the RVSR with the most tried and tested military workers obviously seemed awkward. It was necessary to look for some other, more suitable "platform." Now it has been found. At once three "crises"—economic, general-political, and inner-Party—have been invented.

In Comrade Trotsky's declarations there are many imaginary, far-fetched "disagreements" However, as regards (most importantly) the genuine differences of opinion, they consist in the following:

1. In the sphere of *economic questions* Comrade Trotsky has not got a natural discernment for the adequate rate of development in this sphere. He is continually harassing the Party, insisting on straight-forward "rigid concentration," embodied in Comrades Trotsky-Kolegayev dictatorship, which would have led to the Party's breaking off from the working-class nucleus.

2. In the sphere of *foreign policy* Comrade Trotsky is imposing on us the policy of "volitional impulses," which may plunge the country into a military venture, fraught with our complete lack of political credibility with the peasantry.

3. In the sphere of *inner-Party policy* Comrade Trotsky becomes the focus around which all the elements struggling against the main cadres of our Party are gathering.

4. Comrade Trotsky *does not know* the Party, its inner life, and, apparently, is not able to comprehend it. Hence his "lapidary" characteristics like "gubkom oblomovshchina," his lack of confidence in local Party organizations, and his dangerous mistakes on the question of the Party and state's interrelations—mistakes, that are playing fully into the hands of the political enemies of our Party.

5. On the question of *peasantry* Comrade Trotsky, has more than once made essential mistakes. Before the Tenth and Twelfth RKP Congresses Comrade Trotsky's mistakes consisted in the main of underestimating the peasantry's role. In such a country as ours this is fraught with most dangerous complications.

6. In the sphere of *military work* Comrade Trotsky, rejecting the best possible group of military professionals—TsK members—is weakening the Revvoensovet and is isolating it from the Party.

7. And the most important—Comrade Trotsky is shaking Party unity at a crucial moment for the Republic and world revolution.

Such are our actual differences of opinion. They are, of course, not all unimportant. However, they will not in the slightest shake the unity of our Party, if the Party displays a sufficient degree of firmness.

To the comrades who are sincerely aggrieved by what has happened we say: there were also times when the situation was much worse. Collective work without differences of opinion is impossible. Only one ought not to exaggerate the differences. The Party will successfully pass through this episode as well and overcome the present difficulties. Let all of us be more firm than at any time before, and the unanimous rebuff on the side of the Party will make sincere revolutionaries acknowledge their mistake and leave the disastrous path of splitting the Party.

Members and alternative members of the Politburo:

N. Bukharin[50]
G. Zinovyev
M. Kalinin
L. Kamenev
V. Molotov
A. Rykov
J. Stalin
M. Tomsky
(Absent: Comrades Lenin, Rudzutak)
      October 19, 1923

Original.[51]
Printed according to the text of
the first publication in the magazine
Izvestiya TsK KPSS, 1990, No. 7, str.176-189.

NOTES

1. On the first page of the document there is a note, written by I.V. Stalin's assistant, A. M. Nazaretyan: "Typewritten in 2 (two) copies. 19/X.23. A.N. 300 copies to be printed. A. N." In the text of the document in Stalin's handwriting notes, corrections, and addenda have been made. Apparently, the document's main author is Stalin. The supposition is borne out not only by the style, form of exposition, and pejorative manner of address to political opponents, which N. I. Bukharin called "signs of a newspaper feuilleton," but also by what is perhaps the main point—argumentation, brought up in the document, which in essence and form coincides with what Stalin said at the Central Committee and Central Control Commission's October Plenum (see document No. 21-1).

2. Apparently, reference to Lenin's works of the beginning of 1921: "Krizis partii" (Party Crisis) and "Yeshche raz o profsoyuzakh o tekushchem momente i ob oshibkakh tt.

Trotskogo i Bukharina" (Once More on Trade Unions, on the Current Moment, and Comrades Trotsky and Bukharin's Mistakes) (V.I. Lenin, *Complete Works*, vol. 42, pp. 234–244 and 264–304).

3. A part of the correspondence has been published in the book *Dvenadtsatyi syezd RKP(b). Stenograficheskii otchet* (RKP(b) Twelfth Congress: Stenographical Account), str. 816–820.

4. In essence, Trotsky's position on the question of Party guidance in industrial construction was at that time closer to the Central Committee majority (Party dictatorship) than to the "democratic centralism" group, one of whose leaders was N. Osinsky (see note 49 to the present document and note 8 to document No. 35). As the leaders of "democratic centralism" group, forbidden by the Tenth Party Congress, signed the "Statement of 46," the TsK's "leading nucleus" had to maximally "identify" positions of their political opponents in order to accuse Trotsky of creating a faction.

5. Gubkom = Guberniya (Provincial) Committee. See documents Nos. 8 and 11.

6. Trotsky's pamphlet "Rol i zadachi professionalnykh soyuzov" (The Role and Tasks of Trade Unions) was published in December 1920, in the course of the All-Party discussion on the role and tasks of trade unions. The essence of the discussion consisted in determination of principles of organization and administration of the workers' mass under the conditions of peaceful construction. Trotsky, consistently, developing the principles of war communism on the basis of logics, advanced the idea of "transforming trade unions into state organization." Lenin criticized Trotsky's pamphlets' propositions as erroneous in a number of his works and speeches (see Lenin, *Complete Works*, vol. 42, pp. 234–244, 264–304, etc.). The discussion on trade unions was an organic part of the general crisis of the war-communism system, which began at the termination of the civil war. The discussion played an important role in transition to the new economic policy.

7. At the RKP(b) Twelfth Congress P. A. Bogdanov, I. T. Smilga, and V. Ya. Chubar, agreeing in principle with Trotsky's theses on the whole, disagreed with him in some particular questions (see *RKP[b] Twelfth Congress: Stenographical Account*, pp. 353–358, 360–365, 372–376).

8. Apparently, this expression was used by Trotsky in the period of discussion on trade unions (see V. I. Lenin, *Complete Works*, vol. 42, pp. 277–278).

9. In September 1922 Lenin placed before the TsK Politburo a proposal about appointing Trotsky as his assistant in the Soviet government, i.e., to the post of Council of People's Commissars vice chairman. However, Trotsky declined the offer. The same offer, repeated in January 1923 by Stalin, was also declined. (See *RKP[b] Twelfth Congress: Stenographical Account*, pp. 198–199; as well as Trotsky's speech at the RKP(b) TsK and TSKK October Plenum, document No. 21-II.)

10. In this case the "reply's" authors committed an obvious falsification of the essence of Lenin's article "O pridanii zakonodatelnykh funktsiy Gosplanu" (On Imparting Legislative Functions to Gosplan), which at that time, by the Politburo's decision, was not published. Substantiating the idea of upraising the Gosplan's role in the economic life of the country, Lenin expressed support in essence for Trotsky's position on the given question: "In this respect, we can and must, I think, meet Comrade Trotsky's wishes, but not in the sense of chairmanship in Gosplan, or special political leadership, or chairmanship in the

Supreme Council of People's Economy, etc." Thus, Lenin did not advance any proposals as to the appointment or nonappointment of Trotsky to the post of Gosplan chairman (see Lenin, *Complete Works*, vol. 45, pp. 349–353).

11. Reference to the RKP(b) Twelfth Congress's resolution "On the Tax Policy in the Countryside" (see *RKP[b] Twelfth Congress: Stenographical Account,* pp. 688–691).

12. "Scissors of prices"—discrepancy between the prices of industrial and agricultural goods (see note 19 to Document no. 4).

13. Reference to the pamphlets "Literatura i revolutsiya" (Literature and Revolution) and "Voprosi byta. Epokha kulturnichestva i yeye zadachi" (Questions of Private Life. Epoch of Culturalism and Its Tasks), written by Trotsky in the period of his sick leave (June 10 through September 7, 1923) and published in Moscow in 1923, as well as three articles on the same subject, published in *Pravda* in September of the same year.

14. Here and further the authors of the "reply" are not accurate in stating appraisals and conclusions made by Trotsky in his letter (see points 7 and 8 of Document No. 4).

15. In summer of 1923 the VSNKH (Supreme Council of People's Economy) Presidium, on the basis of a proposal advanced by a group of high industrial executives, took a decision on temporary closing down the Petrograd "Krasnyi (Putilovskyi) Putilovets" (Putilovsky) plant because of its being unprofitable. The decisions caused serious discontent among workers. On August 31 the STO (Council of Labor and Defense), by the Politburo's proposal, cancelled the SCPE Presidium's decision on closing down the plant, having assigned to the plant the sum of 2,200 roubles for covering the deficit.

16. The present assertion contradicts the facts, adduced by the "reply's" authors themselves, in particular, Lenin's proposal about appointing Trotsky SNK (Council of People's Commissars) vice chairman.

17. Reference to Trotsky's activity at the post of People's Commissar of Ways of Communication in spring of 1920. For the purpose of overcoming the extremely grave situation which arose at the railway transport, Trotsky issued in May of that year order No. 1042, according to which a strict schedule of repairs of faulty locomotives was introduced. The order was positively appraised by Lenin, N. I. Bukharin, and F. E. Dzerzhinsky. The carrying out of the schedule was ensured by severe administrative measures which were necessitated by the acuteness of the transport crisis and had at first a positive effect. However, Trotsky also tried to transfer military command methods of work to the activity of transport workers' trade union. "Having shaken up" trade union cadres, he formed—by means of appointments—the Central Committee of Trade Unions of Transport Workers (Tsektran) and effected "coalescence" of its personnel with the People's Commissariat of Ways of Communication. Before long a part of Tsektran officials came out against the trade union leadership, which resulted in the organization's splitting.

18. For Trotsky's explanation on this question, see Document No. 21-II.

19. The present assertion is at variance with the information the Party leadership had at its disposal. According to summary reports of OGPU (Unified State Political Administration), which were sent to the Party Central Committee and can be considered most trustworthy, in the autumn of 1923 in many "guberniyas" (provinces) of the country there was a famine: "Condition of peasantry of the majority of 'guberniyas' is virtually disastrous . . . In Nemkommuna, Pribaikalsky 'guberniya,' Chuvash region, Novgorod 'guberniya,' a significant portion of the peasants is on the verge of famine. In Buryat region people, after pay-

ing taxes, will go hungry. The same is expected in Vitebsk, Tambov, Samara, and many other 'guberniyas.' In the rest of the 'guberniyas' peasants will not have a surplus for further restoration of their farmsteads ... Famine starts assuming great proportions in the Siberia and Far East (RTsHIDNI, f. 17, op. 87, d. 178, 1. 28, etc.).

20. The point here was of potential war between the USSR and Poland in the case of rendering armed assistance to German workers.

21. The given assertion is also at variance with the documentary data. According to OGPU (Unified State Political Administration) summary reports, the condition of workers in autumn of 1923 was continually worsening, unemployment was growing, and the delay in payment of wages reached several months. In October there were in all 217 strikes with the participation of 165 thousand workers, which was the maximum figure for 1923. In the September-October OGPU summary report it was stated that the political attitude of mind of workers was unsatisfactory. (RTsHIDNI, f. 17, op. 84, d. 468, 1. 16; op. 87, d. 178, 1. 20). See also note 3 to Document No. 4.

22. See Document No. 5.

23. At the outset of revolutionary events in Germany, Trotsky insisted on the TsK and Soviet government's taking a firm stand in regard to Poland, consisting of concluding with Poland an agreement on mutual non interference in Germany's affairs and taking all necessary measures for precluding war with Poland. Trotsky repeatedly stated his position not only in the Central Committee, but also in his public speeches. Thus, on October 20, 1923, while making a report on the international situation at the Moscow 'guberniya' Congress of Metallurgists' Trade Unions, he said: "I have already pointed out some comrades who are certain that war with Poland is unavoidable. It would not be right, if our government caught such a mood. We must carry on our current work on restoring the economy, we must strengthen the army, strengthen aviation, which, of course, does not at all mean that we are carried away with warlike plans. . . . We must take every possible measure to ward off war, and this means first of all that we must redouble, increase by tenfold our current everyday effort (*Pravda*, October 21, 1923).

24. On the question of the nature and prospects of revolutionary events in Germany, which were in rather full swing by October 1923, in essence there were no cardinal differences of opinion between Trotsky and the TsK Politburo. On the whole the leadership of the RKP(b) and Communist International (G. Ye. Zinovyev, N. I. Bukharin, Stalin, Trotsky, etc.), proceeding from the Bolshevist concept of world revolution and orientating German communists toward a socialist revolution in the very near future, had obviously overestimated the ripeness of the revolutionary situation in the country. The Hamburg uprising (October 23 through 25), which was the high point of revolutionary upsurge, did not get necessary support on the country's scales. The Germany's Communist Party Central Committee cancelled the decision made earlier on an all-Germany uprising. Finding themselves in isolation, the leaders of the Hamburg uprising were obliged to issue an order to stop the struggle.

25. See Document No. 1.

26. Komintern—See List of Abbreviations. The leading political body of the Komintern was the Executive Committee (CIEC) which in 1923 included the following RKP(b) representatives: G. Ye. Zinovyev (chairman), N. I. Bukharin, Lenin, K. B. Radek, and Trotsky.

27. See Document No. 1.

28. The resolution in not quite accurately expounded (see Document No. 1). Be-

sides, it is not mentioned that a recommendation was made to form in the RVS Chairman's office an executive body, which would place the work of Revvoensovet and its chairman under full control of the TsK.

29. The quotation is not accurately cited (see Document No. 4 C).

30. Reference to the negotiations about granting concessions on working and extraction of minerals in Siberia and Urals to the English industrialist and financier L. Urkart, which were conducted starting in summer of 1921.

31. Documentary data of V. I. Lenin's such statements not found.

32. See Document No. 4 C.

33. Bolsheviks and Mensheviks, existing since 1903 as independent factions within the Russian Social-Democratic Workers Party (RSDWP) finally parted in the period of revolutionary upsurge in 1917. For more detail see note 37 to the present document.

34. "Oblomovshchina": a collective expression (after the name of the hero in the prominent Russian I.A. Goncharov's novel *Oblomov)* meaning laziness, lack of will, or apathy. By the expression, given in the text, Trotsky meant sluggishness, inertness in the work of provincial Party organizations, which was by the way also touched upon in G.E. Zinovyev's article "Party New Tasks," published in *Pravda* on November 7, 1923; the article officially opened an inner-Party discussion.

35. Reference to the "RKP(b) Rabochaya Gruppa" (Workers' Group), headed by G.I. Myasnikov (see note 5 to Document No. 4 and note 6 to Document No. 20).

36. Communist universities and Soviet-Party schools: educational institutions for training managing Party and Soviet cadres.

37. The data of the quantitative growth of factory-plant Party cells on account of industrial workers (from the lathe) are significantly overstated. The greatest addition to their membership occurred in the last three months of 1923, when in Petrograd, the Urals, and other Party organizations, a mass admission to the Party on the occasion of the sixth anniversary of the October Revolution was announced.

38. The question of the "upper and lower strata of people" was at the time quite urgent. So, F. E. Dzerzhinsky, in his speech at the Party TsK Conference at the end of September, 1923, said in particular: "We see that the main reason causing workers' discontent, finding a certain expression namely in opposition to the Soviet state, is our isolation from the lower Party cells and isolation of lower Party cells from the masses. (RTsHIDNI, f. 76, op. 3, d. 296, 1.41). The problem was especially sharply felt in the course of the inner-Party discussion that began at that time.

39. Menshevism, Mensheviks: a faction side by side with Bolsheviks in the Russian Social-Democratic Workers Party (RSDWP). The faction was formed in 1903, at the Party's Second Congress, at which Mensheviks differed with Bolsheviks on the questions of the organizational structure of the RSDWP, thinking that rigid centralism would inevitably lead to bureaucratization of the Party. There were also serious differences of opinion on the questions of strategy and tactics of the Russian revolutionary movement. True to the Marxist doctrine of gradual and stage-by-stage development of the revolutionary process Mensheviks did not accept Lenin's April theses (1917), which proclaimed the course for a socialist revolution in Russia, and final Party split took place. In the revolutionary events of 1917, Mensheviks were for unifying all democratic forces, and forming a revolutionary government on a multi-Party basis. In 1920–1921 many Menshevik leaders had to emigrate. In

1921 they started in Berlin the publication of *Sotsialisticheskyi Vestnik* (Socialist Bulletin) magazine. In the inner-Party struggle, calling dissidents "Mensheviks" and later "Trotsky-ists" became a most serious political accusation in the Bolshevik Party (see note 33 to Document No. 36).

Socialist-Revolutionaries: the biggest political Party in Russia, which expressed the interests of a considerable part of the peasantry, who wished to have farmsteads of their own. It came into being in 1901-1902. Its main demands were: a democratic republic, political freedom, working-class legislation, socialization of land; its main tactical means were individual terror. In November 1917, the Party's left wing broke off as an independent Party of leftist Socialist-Revolutionaries, which up to the middle of 1918 acted in a political bloc with Bolsheviks. By a GPU (State Political Administration) decision in 1921, the most active members of the Socialist-Revolutionary Party were brought to trial by the War-Revolutionary Tribunal for counter revolutionary terrorist struggle against the Soviet power. The trial took place in the summer of 1921. Out of thirty-four Socialist-Revolutionary Party leaders tried, twelve were sentenced to capital punishment, which was later changed to ten years of prison. A number of defendants repented and were acquitted.

40. The Fourth Conference of the RKP(b) Central Committee with responsible workers of national republics and regions took place in Moscow on June 9-12, 1923. It marked, in essence, a turning moment in reevaluation and digression of the Stalinist leadership from the Party's Twelfth Congress's decisions on the national question, taken in the spirit of Lenin's article "To the Question of Nationalities or Autonomization."

41. See: *RKP(b) Eleventh Congress. Stenographical Account* (Moscow, 1961), Str. 555; *RKP(b) Twelfth Congress. Stenographical Account*, p. 705.

42. Preferential terms of admission to the Party were only for industrial workers: by the Twelfth Congress' decision, they were required to present two recommendations of Communists with a two-year Party membership length; for other people, wishing to join the Party admission requirements were much more strict: five recommendations of Communists with a five-year Party membership length.

43. Apparently, a reference to D. B. Ryazanov's temporarily leaving the Party at the beginning of 1918 because of difference of opinion with Lenin over the question of the Brest peace treaty, and his coming out against Lenin's standpoint in the period of discussion on trade unions.

44. Such a sharp wording of statements and pinning on political labels was caused by the acuteness of the factional struggle. As distinct from the "reply's" authors, for instance, A. G. Beloborodov's approach to G. I. Myasnikov and Myasnikovism is more cautious; he regards them as an expression of attitudes of mind among certain layers of the working class (see Document No. 13).

45. Reference to the "Statement of the Forty-Six" (see Document No. 12).

46. Trotsky's expressions, said by him on a completely different occasion (see Document No. 4 C.).

47. Evidence of Trotsky's taking any part in writing the "Statement of the Forty-Six," ot of its signatories' having been acquainted with Trotsky's letter of October 8, 1923, has not been found.

48. According to the documents, available in the RTsHIDNI, this episode is as follows. At the meeting of the RKP(b) Politburo on July 16, 1921, there was considered

Lenin's proposal on appointing Trotsky the Ukraine's People's Commissar of Foodstuffs. The proposal was accepted, but, in view of Trotsky's protest, the Politburo agreed to suspend the decision until the RKP(b) TsK Plenum. The Plenum, which took place on August 9, 1921, cancelled the decision and resolved that "in view of aggravation of the international situation, Comrade Trotsky is to pay more attention to the military work."

49. The group of "democratic centralism" came forward with its platform on the questions of Party and Soviet construction at the RKP(b) Eighth, Ninth, and Tenth Congresses. After 1921 the group ceased to exist, though some of its representatives (T. V. Sapronov, V. M. Sminov, and others) continued expressing disagreement with the majority line. The traditional approach to the appraisal of the group as a factional and anti-Party one today appears untenable and requires objective investigation.

50. N. I. Bukharin, at the time of preparation of the "reply," was in Petrograd and sent from there to the TsK Secretariat a telephone message (see Document No. 18).

51. The original of the present document is being kept in the archives of the Russian Federation President. In the RTsHIDNI there are typewritten and typographical copies (f. 51, op. 1, d. 21, 1. 51-54).

18

N. I. Bukharin's Telephone Message from Petrograd to the Secretariat of TsK of the RKP(b)

October 20, 1923

To Secretariat
To Stalin
To Tomsky
I flatly insist on the following amendments to be introduced into the text:[1]
I)—In the first place, it is absolutely necessary to include and to further develop the point dealing with inner-Party democracy;—in the second place, it is impossible to depict the economical crisis by looking at it through such rose-colored spectacles;—in the third place, it is necessary to use the note on the Party unity to a much greater extent;—in the fourth place, it is necessary to abolish all signs of the newspaper satire. The document should be strict and correct in its form to the greatest extent.

BUKHARIN
The original[2]
Printed according to the text published for the
first time in the journal *Izvestiya TsK KPSS,* 1990,
No. 7, p. 190.

NOTES

1. Meant here is the answer of the members of the Political Bureau of Central Committee (Politburo TSK), dated October 19, given in reply to Trotsky's letter, dated October 8, 1923 (refer to Document No. 17 above). But, as is seen from the "answer's" text, neither Stalin nor M. P. Tomsky, to whom the telephone message had been addressed, introduced into it those amendments which Bukharin flatly insisted on.

2. The original copy of the document is kept at present at the archives of the President of the Russian Federation.

19

V. V. Kuibyshev and Ye. M. Yaroslavsky's Letter to the TsK and TSKK of the RKP(b)

October 20, 1923

To All Members and Candidate Members of TsK and TSKK

In connection with the letter sent by Comrade Trotsky on October 19[1] and addressed by him to the Presidium of the TSKK and to the Politburo, and simultaneously distributed among all members and alternate members of the TsK and TSKK, the Presidium of the TsK considers it necessary to ascertain the following:

1. Comrade Trotsky, before and instead of applying to the Central Control Commission (TSKK) to solve the problems raised in his known letter,[2] since the Central Control Commission is the highest Party Department, designed to preserve peace in the Party, as Comrade Lenin had thought of it and the Twelfth Party Congress had resolved, has addressed a group of comrades who are neither in the TsK nor in the TSKK.[3] Having done so, he has given rise to a mobilization of public opinion of one part of Party members against the TsK (the group of Preobrazhensky, Serebryakov, Smirnov, and others who have handed in their application to the TSKK).[4]

2. The resolution of the Presidium of the TSKK[5] was intended for discussion at the plenary meeting of the TSKK, and Comrade Trotsky and other members of the Politburo were supposed to be invited to take part in it, as is seen from the resolution adopted at the meeting of the Presidium

of the TSKK, held with the presence of the available members and alternate members of the TSKK* on October 17 of the present year.[6]

3. The Presidium of the TSKK discussed the letter of Comrade Trotsky in his absence; the other remaining members of the Politburo were absent as well. It was done simply because it was necessary to discuss the letter.under calm conditions, without any heated arguments Comrade Trotsky might got into with the majority of the members of the Politburo, and to provide some guarantee of an impartial appraisal of this letter by members of the TSKK themselves, independent of any argumentation by Comrade Trotsky or other members of the Politburo.

4. Comrade Trotsky's letter is so clear in its contents, and the fact of its appearance is in such vivid contrast with the present situation and the Party's tasks,that no additional explanations were engendered in any way.

5. The preventive measures (withdrawal of its copies and secondary copies) to interrupt the distribution of the letter among the Party's members not in the TsK and TSKK,were taken by Comrade Trotsky at a moment when it was too late to take them, and so they could not turn to be actual.†

6. As to the occasion and purpose of writing such a letter by Comrade Trotsky, the Presidium of the TSKK has already appraised the objective importance of this document, but not the subjective resolutions of Comrade Trotsky, about which the Presidium might have no idea. The appearance of a collective letter of 46 comrades (Preobrazhenskyt Serebryakov, Smirnov, and others), expressing their solidarity with the letter of Comrade Trotsky, has in full measure justified our appraisal of this letter as a platform for a discussion outside of the TsK and TSKK.[7]

On a commission from the Presidium of the TSKK

V. Kuibyshev
Ye. Yaroslavsky

---

*The members and alternate members of the TSKK, who were in Moscow at that moment, are meant here. (Ed.).

†It has been written in the text in this way. But it is apparently necessary to read "effective." (Ed.).

October, 20, 1923.

RTsKhIDNI (Rossiiskii Tsentr aneniya i Izucheniya Dokumentov Noveishei Istorii—Russian Center for the Preservation and Study of Documents of Recent History, RCPSDMH). f. I8, op. 2, d. 685t 1. 11O—111, attested copy.[8] It was published for the first time in the journal of *Izvestiya TsK KPSS*, 1990, No. 7, pp. 190–191.

NOTES

1. The letter of Trotsky, sent to the Presidium of the TSKK and to the Politburo of the TsK of the RKP(b), is presented in Document No. 16.

2. Here Trotsky's letter sent to the members of the TSK and TSKK and dated October 8, 1923, is meant. (Refer to Document No. 4).

3. With regard to this application, refer to the extract from the minutes of the conference of the Politburo of the TsK held on October 11 (Document No. 16 above) and to Trotsky's explanation as presented in his letter dated October 19 (Document No. 16, Points 8 and 9).

4. Here the Declaration of the Forty-Six is meant (refer to Document No. 12 above).

5. Here the resolution of the Presidium of the TSKK of the RKP(b), dated October 15, is meant (refer to Document No. 11 above).

6. The conference held by the Presidium of the TSKK together with the "present-in-Moscow" members of the TSKK, took place on October 17. The arguments cited by V.V.Kuibyshev to explain the reasons why Trotsky had not been invited to take part in the conference of the Presidium of the TSKK, held on October 15 and 17, when his letter to the TSK, dated October 8, was under discussion, look rather unconvincing. The Presidium of the TSKK needed to receive as soon as possible an approval of its resolution, dated October 15 (Document No. 11), by the remaining members of the TSKK, even if by those members of the TSKK who were in Moscow at that moment. The conference, held on October 17, in the presence of only twenty-six members and alternate members of the TSKK (out of sixty, elected at the Seventh Party Congress), adopted the following resolution: "Without discussing point after point of the resolution of the Presidium of the TSKK, the conference has agreed in the main with the appraisal of the incident, given by the Presidium of the TSKK, and it has supported the line taken by it in the given situation." The results of the vote were as follows: out of twenty-six present, eighteen voted for, four voted against, and four abstained (RTsKhIDNI, f. 17, op. 29 d. 68591. 102).

7. In essence, the given point of the letter by V.V.Kuibyshev and Y.M.Yaroslavsky reconsiders the resolution of the Presidium of the TSKK, dated October 15, according to which it was suggested to limit settlement of the differences to within the confines of the TsK and TSKK. Such an unscrupulous correction of the position of the leaders of the Central Control Commission, which, according to the V. I. Lenin's conception (so far as V. V.

Kuibyshev refers to it), should be independent and answerable to the Congress only, had been made in accordance with the decision adopted by the Politburo of the TsK on October 18, which, as a matter of fact, gave permission to place Trotsky's letter of October 8 into wide circulation (refer to Document No. 15 above). Because of it, as himself stated, his letter had been "lent a character of a factional platform," but it would have had nothing of the kind, if it had been discussed and considered within the confines of the TsK and TSKK (refer to Document No. 16, points 10 and 11 above).

8. The archives of the President of the Russian Federation contains a manuscript text of the given document, written by V. V. Kuibyshev. There is no signature by Ye. M. Yaroslavsky on the autograph. The text published here has been printed in accordance with the typewritten copy kept at the RTsKhIDNI; it has been collated with the autograph of V. V. Kuibyshev.

20

L. D. Trotsky's Letter to the Members of the TsK and the TSKK of the RKP(b), to the Plenum of the TsK of the RKP(b)

October 23, 1923

To Members of TsK
To Members of TSKK
To Plenary Meeting October 24, 1923[1]

The answer of the members of the Politburo[2] to my letter has such a character, as if the authors of the letter had considered it impossible to provide any chance and possibility for introducing some serious alterations into the Party and economical policy pursued at present; as if they had completely rejected any conception of a necessity to create some normal conditions for a healthy and collective work of the Party leading bodies. And just this circumstance arouses the greatest anxiety.

I. INNER-PARTY REGIME

1. First of all, it is necessary to state that the document shifts the whole problem of the Party crisis onto the plane of bringing a formal accusation of setting up a platform, factionalism, and the like. But such an accusation is a flagrant abuse of the resolutions of the Tenth Congress.[3] The

fact of the existence of factions, i.e., of organized unions of members having identical opinions, inside the Party, is in itself an extreme danger. There is no disputing that. But it is a very long way from here to declaring as a "faction" any attempt by a single Party member or group of Party members to draw the attention of the TsK to the irregularities and mistakes in the policy being pursued by the TsK. There is nothing more dangerous than carrying to a bureaucratic absurdity the decision prohibiting any creation of factional organizations inside the Party. Really no-factional regime in the Party can in practice remain inviolable only in such cases, where the Party itself, from its bottom to its top, remains to function as an active and independently acting Party collective; where any elaboration of a Party opinion is not dashed against unwarranted, far-fetched obstacles; where the leading bodies themselves do not pursue a policy of an ulterior factional selection of personnel; where they regard the voice of inner-Party criticism with the greatest attentions making no attempts to liquidate any independent thought in the Party by accusing it of factionalism.

2. At the conference of the Politburo, held on October 11,[4] comrade Dzerzhinsky accused the Moscow Committee of the fact that the Party common members of the Moscow organization did not consider it possible to openly express their opinion within the confines of their Party organization, and therefore they did it behind its back. Comrade Zelensky, the Secretary of the Moscow provincial committee, said the following in response, and I quote word for word: "You have said that there is no life in the Party nuclei, that all members refuse to open their mouths. Was it actually any different in Germany at the Party conference held to discuss the events? And no one present said one word."

Comrade Bukharin said the following, when opposing the proposal that the new resolution of the Politburo should oblige the Party members to inform on any groups organized in the Party: "It is purely pernicious. It will be understood as another police regulation; we have too many at present without that one. It is necessary for us to sharply turn the helm to the side of the Party democracy." Comrade Molotov declared that he, for his part, had no objections; and in answer to my question what Comrade Molotov had no objection to, he continued that he had no objections "against the truisms having been formulated by Comrade Bukharin," i.e., against the necessity to sharply turn the helm to the side of the Party democracy. Statements given above are presented word for word, since, owing to the utmost importance of the problem under discussion, I have recorded all the most crucial wording just at the moment it was given. Nobody was against the statement that our movement forward should be connected with a sharp turn of the helm to the side of the Party democracy, and not with the redoubling of threats, repressions, pressure, or, as it was put by Comrade Bukharin, further intensification of police regulations in the Party.

But in the letter by the members of the Politburo there is no longer any hint of such a statement of the problem. The inner-Party regime is declared normal.

The letter describes in more detail the Party teaching and educational work, training of the personnel and so on. It is beyond any doubt that the Party machinery has widely expanded, including its teaching and educational machinery; there is no doubt the study has been organized on a broad scale, and it is, of course, the greatest achievement. But even this fact does not exclude and does not refute by the slightest degree an extreme decrease of the Party political and critical activities, relaxation of its inner-Party life as a Party, and a parallel increase of purely mechanical organizational measures taken to ensure a pursuit of the line of the leading Party organs.

3. My mention of unhealthy methods, used at the time of preparations for the Twelfth Party Congress with the aim of setting off one part of the leading comrades to the other[5]—without sufficient or, at least, strongly pronounced ideological reasons—makes the authors of the answer bring yet again a radically groundless formal accusation against me as though I have "defamed" the rightness of theTwelfth Party Congress composition. In my letter there is not a single hint of it. It is at least irrelevant to raise a formal question of the competence or authoritativeness of theTwelfth Congress. But it is quite appropriate and right to raise the question of a necessity to ensure such an inner-Party regime that provides a possibility for the Party to formulate its conception of the most important problems day by day; and in doing so, the Party would be able to determine its will through the instrumentality of its congresses in the best possible way.

The "answer" of the members of the Politburo has ascribed to me the claim to set up some absolute "large-scale" democracy, and it puts a question to me whether I demand that all those Party resolutions, which limit the employment of the "large-scale" democratic methods, should be abolished. But in reality, my letter says that at that time (i.e., the Tenth Party Congress) it seemed to me that many of the speeches for the defense of the working-class democracy were overstated and demagogic in "view of incompatibility of a full-scale working-class democracy with the regime of a dictatorship." So, all the arguments of the "answer" dealing with this problem are a misunderstanding of the most complete kind. I would yet never have demanded "a sharp turn of the helm to the side of the working-class democracy," as was done by Comrade Bukharin at the conference of the Politburo on October 11, and there were no sides at the conference which raised any objection to what he had said. It is quite enough if such a turn is a sincere and conscientious one, not a sharp, but a prudent one, in compliance with the whole situation. If only this turn were really accomplished.Those limitations the Party has set up should be preserved, up to the moment when experience discovers their irregularity. But within the confines of these limitations, the Party should live a genuine life of a leading and ruling organization and not keep silent. That is what the whole problem comes to.

5. The fact that the Myasnikovshchina is not yesterday's phenomenon, as the "answer" has put it, is indisputable.[6] But it was the Politburo itself that had raised the alarm, a quite valid alarm, in connection with some growth of the Myasnikovshchina, in connection with some increase in the number of illegal nuclei within the Party, in connection with the participation of some Party members in strikes, and in connection with a passive attitude toward such phenomena on the part of a great number of Party members who are not members of these illegal nuclei. That.was the full implication of the conclusions the commission of Comrade Dzerzhinsky had arrived at.[7] This is the essence of the problem. It seems it was no secret to anybody that such a situation was dangerous. Having just proceeded from it, Comrade Dzerzhinsky demanded that the Moscow Committee be renewed since it had become too bureaucratic, as he characterized it. And just because of it Comrade Bukharin demanded that the helm be sharply turned to the side of Party democracy, while Comrade Molotov recognized all this as "truism." And now all this is proclaimed to be nonexistent, and the whole affair comes to expelling Myasnikov and . . . to Comrade Ryazanov. Such a striking volte-face represents in itself a very great danger which threatens the Party with an aggravation of antagonisms within it.

II. THE ATTEMPT TO DRAW THE NAME OF COMRADE LENIN INTO OUR DISCORD

The letter by the members of the Politburo has made an attempt to draw in the name of Comrade Lenin into our vexed questions, presenting the whole problem so that, on one side, there is allegedly a continuation of the policy of Comrade Lenin, and, on the other, a struggle against this policy. Attempts to depict our discords in such a way, but in more wary and concealed forms, have been made many times; it was done during our preparations for the Twelfth Party Congress, and especially, after the Congress. And because these attempts took the form of hints and innuendos, there was no possibility of responding to them. And these hints were being made simply because some people had deliberately counted my pass them over in silence. And the present "answer" of those members of the Politburo, trying to formulate these hints more concretely, reveals, by doing so, as we shall see now, their complete unfoundedness and, and with that, offers an opportunity to vividly and properly refute them. Here I consider the vexed questions point after point, presenting the exact quotations and references to the documents which are easily verified.

1. One of the central vexed questions in the field of the economy was and is at present the question of the role of the planned leadership, i.e., a systematic combination of the basic elements of the state economy in the process of their adaptation to the growing market. I have and still maintain the point of view that the lack of a proper, uniform regulation of the economy from the top is one of the most important causes of our economical crises and of their peculiar acuteness and destructiveness. It is quite true that there were some differences of opinion between me and Comrade Lenin with regard to the problem of organization of the planned leadership. The authority of Comrade Lenin was of no less significance to me than it was to any other member of the TsK. But I have considered and consider now that the Party elects members of the TsK to enable them to uphold in the Central Committee (TsK) those ideas considered by them to be right in every given case. How was the problem solved on the side of Comrade Lenin himself? On June 2 of this year the Politburo received from N. Krupskaya a special note of Comrade Lenin titled: "Concerning the Imposition of the Legislative Duties upon the Gosplan (Gosudarstvennyi Planovyi Komitet—

State Planning Committee)" which was dictated by him on December 27, 1922. In this document Comrade Lenin has written the following:

"It seems that this idea was suggested by Comrade Trotsky long ago. I came out against it since I considered then that in such a case there would be a basic discrepancy in the system of our legislative institutions. But on attentive consideration of the matter, I find that here there is a quite sensible idea, that is: the Gosplan stands a little aside from our legislative institutions, although it virtually possesses the most indispensable grounds to properly judge the state of affairs, since it represents an assembly of well-versed persons, experts, representatives of science and engineering. . . .

"I think, in this regard, that it is possible and necessary to meet Comrade Trotsky halfway, but not in the matter of appointing to the presidency of Gosplan either a special candidate from our political leadership or the chairman of the VSNKH (Vysshii Sovet Narodnogo Yhozyaistva—the Supreme Council of National Economy, SCNE) and the like."[8]

And in the conclusion, Comrade Lenin opposes such a character of the work of Gosplan, when the latter considers individual missions, and he is in favor of such functioning of Gosplan, when the latter is able "to systematically solve the whole sum of the problems that are under its authority.[9] As we can see, here the problem has been put quite clearly and completely.

The problem of combining the role of the chairman of the VSNKh with that of the Gosplan is a subordinate technical problem. At present in our case according to the decision of the TSK, the role of the vice-chairman of the STO (Soviet Truda i Oborony—Council of Labor and Defense, CLD) has been combined with that of the VSNKh, which leads much further than my suggestions in this respect. I have, time and again, said and written to the TsK that the combinations of such a kind are, of course, conditional and not the point of the matter. The essence of the matter lies in the necessity to organize the competent authoritative economic headquarters, so that there will be no economic problem that could pass it by. The moment Comrade Lenin was at the head of economic activities, he himself was, to a greatest extent, his own headquarters, and the question of the role of the Gosplan could not have had that decisive importance which it has acquired after Comrade Lenin fell ill. And now, estimating the management of the economy in its present state following his retirement, Comrade Lenin declares that there was a healthy idea in my main suggestion. A long-term leave by Comrade Lenin from his leading post may be, to some extent, compensated for only by a practicable and proper organization of the management of our economy. Meanwhile,we have made a step in this direction, but backward not forward. Nowadays the economic problems are being worked out in haste, in the order of improvisation, and not of systematic management, and it happens at a greater extent than ever before.

2. The other economic problem, where there were some differences of opinion at the plenary meeting of the TsK, with Comrade Lenin taking part, was connected with the monopoly of foreign trade,[10] i.e., the problem that I cited at the Twelfth Congress, without there being objections from any side, as being one of the foundations of the socialistic dictatorship in the conditions of the capitalist encirclement.As to this problem, I have a quite voluminous correspondence with Comrade Lenin. Here I present in full only one letter of Comrade Lenin, dated December 13, 1922. It throws a vivid light upon the way the problem has been stated by him:

Comrade Trotsky,

I have got your response to the letter of Krestinsky and to the plan of Avanesov. There appears to me to be a very great mutual agreement between me and you, and I think that the question about the Gosplan in the way it has been stated excludes (or puts off) any argumentation about the necessity for the Gosplan to possess administrative functions.*

In any case, I would entreat you take it upon yourself to advocate at the forthcoming plenary meeting our common standpoint on the unconditional need to maintain and consolidate the foreign trade monopoly. Since the previous plenary meeting adopted the decision, to be completely against the foreign trade monopoly, and since it is impossible to make any concession in this respect, I think, as I have written in my letter to Frumkin and Stomonyakov, that in case of our failure in persisting in our statement in this respect, we will be obliged to put this question on the agenda of the Party Congress. With this purpose in view, it will be necessary for us to briefly set forth our differences of opinion to the Party faction of the forthcoming Congress of Soviets. If I have time, I will write it, and I would be very glad if you would act in a similar way. Any vacillations in this respect will do unprecedented harm to us, and all the reasons against the monopoly come down to accusations of imperfection in our state machinery. But in our case the state machinery is notable here, there, and everywhere for its imperfection, and if we repudiate the

---

*As we have already seen, two weeks later (on December 27), Comrade Lenin recognized as necessary the concession of administrative functions to the Gosplan, and on a much wider scale than I have proposed.

monopoly just because of the imperfection of our state machinery, we shall throw out the child together with the bathwater.

December 13, 1922.

Lenin[11]

So, with respect to one of the most important problems of our economic policy, Comrade Lenin demanded that if the plenary meeting did not annul its obviously erroneous decision, I should openly speak at the faction of the Congress of Soviets to state the differences of opinion.[12] It quite dramatically proves, first of all, what kind of importance has been attached by Comrade Lenin to the mistake made by the plenary meeting,[13] and, second, it proves that he, understanding quite well the importance of a formal discipline, considered the content to be more important in the given case than the form.

3. The most important difference of opinion during the last year, with Comrade Lenin participating in the discussions, was connected with the national question.[14] And here, yet again, all the facts and documents are available. What kind of importance has been attached by Comrade Lenin to the national question and to the mistakes made in this respect, is quite vividly seen from that letter of his (dated December 30, 1922). which begins with the following words: "It seems to me that I stand guilty before the workers of Russia for the fact that I have not energetically and sharply enough stepped in. . . ."[15] And on coming to know (without my knowledge), what stand I took on the national question at the plenary meeting of the TsK, Comrade Lenin sent me the following note:

Strictly confidential.

Dear Comrade Trotsky,

I would ask you to take it upon yourself to advocate the Georgian cause at the TsK of the Party. Nowadays this cause is under the "prosecution" of Stalin and Dzerzhinsky, and I cannot rely on their impartiality. If you agreed to advocate it, I could be calm. In case you do not agree to do so for some reason or other, please return to me the whole dossier. I shall consider it as the sign of your nonagreement.

With best comrade greetings, Lenin.
Written by M.V. on March 5, 1923.

It has been exactly copied.

M.Volodicheva[16]

When I suggested to Comrade Lenin, via his secretary (Comrade Lenin was then already seriously ill, and he was barred from any personal appointments), showing this note of his and his article, dated December 30, which had been secretly sent to me by him, to the members of the Politburo in order to attain a change in the policy on the national question in the smoothest way, Comrade Lenin formally forbade me to do so for the reason that I have already been compelled to cite once at the sitting of the Presidium of the Twelfth Congress. Here it is: "On no account," V. I.* communicated it to me via his secretary. "He (Comrade Kamenev was meant here, who was going to leave for Georgia) will tell everything to Stalin, and Stalin will make a rotten compromise and then he will deceive us."

Here I could not but note that the letter of Comrade Lenin, about which it had been said, at the "senioren-convention,"[17] of the Twelfth Congress, that it should be published as a matter of course (perhaps, with the exception of some strongly worded personal remarks, as was suggested by some of those present), has remained unpublished to this day.[18]

4. One of the central questions of the Twelfth Congress was that raised by Comrade Lenin on reorganization of the Workers' and Peasants' Inspection (Rabkrin—Raboche-Krestyanskaya Inspektsiya) and TSKK.[19] It is remarkable that even this question has been and continues to be time and again represented as a contentious issue between Comrade Lenin and me, when, in reality, this question, like the national question, presents the groupings within the Politburo in exactly the opposite light. It is absolutely true that I had a very negative attitude toward the old Rabkrin. But Comrade Lenin, in his article titled "Better Fewer, But Better," gave a very negative evaluation of the Rabkrin, which I would never bring myself to do: "The People's Commissariat of the Workers' and Peasants' Inspection (Rabkrin) does not at present enjoy any vestige of the slightest authority. Everybody knows well that there are no other institutions more poorly organized than those of our Rabkrin, and that under the present conditions nothing can be expected from this People's Commissariat."[20] And if we recall now who was at the head of the Rabkrin for the longest period of time,[21] it will be not difficult to understand whom this assessment, together with the article on the national question, was aimed at.

And what was the reaction of the Politburo to the proposal of Comrade Lenin that the Rabkrin should be reorganized? Comrade Bukharin would

---

*V. I.—Vladimir Illich. (Ed.)

not dare publish the article of Comrade Lenin in the newspaper, whereas
Comrade Lenin, for his part, insisted that the article be published immediately. N. K. Krupskaya informed me of this article by telephone and requested that I intercede in order to hasten the publication of the article. At
the session of the Politburo that was immediately convened by my request,
all those present, namely, Comrades Stalin, Molotov, Kuibyshev, Rykov,
Kalinin, and Bukharin, were not only against the plan of Comrade Lenin,
but also against the article's publication. And the objections by the members of the Secretariat were particularly sharp and categorical.[22] Since
Comrade Lenin persistently demanded that he should be shown the article
in print, Comrade Kuibyshev, the future People's Commissar of the
Rabkrin, proposed at the session of the Politburo mentioned above that a
single copy of a special issue of *Pravda,* carrying the article of Comrade
Lenin, should be printed in order to satisfy his aspiration, while, at the same
time, the article itself should be concealed from the Party as a whole. I tried
to demonstrate that the radical reform suggested by Comrade Lenin was
progressive in itself, that is, under the condition of its proper realization; but
even if there was a negative attitude toward this suggestion, it would be
simply ridiculous and unreasonable to keep the Party from knowing Comrade Lenin's suggestions. In reply I heard arguments in the spirit of the
same formalism, such as: "We are the TsK, we bear full responsibility, we
decide." It was only Comrade Kamenev who was the seconder of my proposal, although he appeared at the Politburo session almost an hour late.
The main argument tilting the balance in favor of publishing the letter consisted of the fact that Lenin's article could not be concealed from the Party.
Later the given letter turned up in the hands of those who had not wanted
to publish it, a kind of special banner to be used . . . against me. Comrade
Kuibyshev, a former member of the Secretariat, was appointed to be the
head of the TSKK.[23] And so, in place of a struggle against the plan of Comrade Lenin, they embarked on the path of rendering this plan "harmless."[24]
Did the TsK thereby acquire the attribute of an independent, impartial
Party institution, upholding and maintaining the cornerstone of the Party's
legal standing and Party unity in its struggle against any Party administrative excesses? I will not get into a discussion of this point here, because I
suppose that the question and the answer to it are quite clear already.

   5. Such are the most instructive episodes of the recent period with regard to my "struggle" against the policies of Comrade Lenin. Does it not
seem startling that the "answer" of the members of the Politburo, over-

stepping these quite clear and undeniable facts of the previous year, considers it necessary to adduce the suggestion of Comrade Lenin dating from 1921 (!), which concerned my being sent on a mission to the Ukraine in the capacity of "an empowered representative of the Narkomprod (Narodnyi Komissariat po Prodovolstviyu—People's Commissariat for Food Supply)." But the given fact has been set forth in the wrong way and it has been misinterpreted. In the autumn of 1921, Comrade Lenin feared that the Ukrainians would fail to display sufficient energy in the course of collecting the tax in kind* (and at that period of time it was a problem of great importance); therefore, he suggested that I be sent there (and not from the Narkomprod, but from the TsK) "in order to pull strings" accordingly. During the first three or four years I have gone out on various missions of such a kind more than once—and not only to the fronts, but also to the Donbas, to the Urals (twice), and to Petrograd. None of these missions had anything to do with inner-Party differences of opinion at the Politburo; they were all occasioned by urgent and vital business requirements. Since after my previous mission to the Ukraine I had received the impression that the Ukrainian comrades would be able to do themselves what was necessary, I considered my mission there unnecessary. This difference of opinion had a pure practical character. The proposition of Comrade Lenin was adopted. Then I suggested, to avoid any confusion over the interrelations, that I be provisionally nominated (since it was a question of four to six weeks) to the post of Narkomprod of the Ukraine. And it was adopted (of course, without my being release from my other duties). But the next day Comrade Lenin himself, having received more reassuring news from Kharkov, came to me at the Military Registration and Enlistment Office to suggest reversing the decision adopted the day before, which was, it goes without saying, met by me with sympathy, since I considered the adopted decision to be inexpedient.[25] Such is this minor episode, which has nothing to do with the problems besetting the Party. That the Party's attention has been drawn to this petty and forgotten episode is in itself utterly glaring evidence of the absence of more convincing and solid facts and materials to feed and support the legend about my nearly anti-Leninist line. But there are not, and may never be, any fact or material of such a kind. For any malicious legend, even if painstakingly elaborated, remains but a legend.

---

*The tax in kind was imposed in 1921 instead of the surplus-appropriation system. (Ed.)

"UNDERESTIMATING THE ROLE OF THE PEASANTRY"*

One of the fantastic "accusations" formerly stated time and again either indirectly or behind my back, and now being formulated openly, is my alleged "underestimation" of the role of the peasantry in our revolution. In the authors' letter there is no hint of any attempt to prove this statement, but in reality there may not exist evidence of any kind. It would be too inappropriate here to consider the differences of opinion over the inner forces of the revolutions in the period of, let us say, 1905 to 1914. Since that time we have all learned so much that current estimations might be merely formally inferred from the differences of opinion of those times. The most important publications in principle, written by me (like "Summaries and Perspectives," "Our Differences of Opinion"), were republished long ago. Everything that was erroneous in my point of view of those times, I acknowledged and stated long ago both by word and deed. But in any case my old attitudes toward the problem not only did not interfere, but helped me to take as a matter of course the April (1917) theses of Comrade Lenin, while so many self-styled Leninists renounced them[26]; in addition, and more importantly, they did not prevent me from marching shoulder to shoulder with Comrade Lenin through the pre-October period and through the October Revolution. And if ever the analysis of the forces and estimation of the classes are subjected to the most thorough examination, it will take place precisely in the period of the greatest revolution. That is why I find it unnecessary—at least, within the framework of the present letter— to return to analyzing the pre-October period.

And in what way was my "underestimation" of the peasantry expressed after October? During the first three years of the revolution I was busy almost solely with formation of the peasant regiments with the help of the front-rank workers.[27] This work alone was more than enough to make anybody understand the role of the peasantry and the interrelations between the main classes in our revolution. And it was just my military experience that made me always be on the lookout with respect to everything that bore a relation to peasantry. In order to prove it—since in general it is in need of some proofs—I shall present below some facts of varying importance, but they carry equal weight with respect to the given question.[28]

---

*Further sections in the letter are titled but not numbered. (Ed.)

1. When, after the death of Ya. M. Sverdlov, Comrade V. I. Lenin suggested nominating Comrade Kamenev to the post of Chairman of the VTsIK (Vsesoyuznyi Tsentralnyi Ispolnitelnyi Komitet—All-Union Central Executive Committee), I expressed my opinion that the post should be occupied by an outstanding figure capable of winning the peasantry over to his side. And when Comrade Lenin, and, following him, the Politburo accepted this plan, I put forward Comrade Kalinin's candidacy.

2. In March 1919, in my report to the TsK, I upheld the necessity of more vigorously pursuing a policy aimed at the middle peasantry, and against the inattentive or superficial attitude still current in the Party with respect to this question. In a report prompted by a discussion in the Sengileievo organization,[29] I wrote the following: "The political situation, which, although temporary, may last for a long period of time, is a much more profound social and economical reality, for even if the proletarian revolution triumphs in the West, we will have to base ourselves in large measure, in the construction of Socialism, upon the middle peasants and draw them into the socialist economy."

3. On the basis of my observations of the state of mind of the army and my experience gained during my economic inspection trip to Urals, I wrote the following to the TsK in February 1920: "The present policies of requisitioning the food products according to the norm of consumption on the equalizing principle, of joint responsibility for the delivery of these products to the grain-collecting points*, and of equal distribution of the industrial products are directed toward lowering the agricultural production and bringing about the atomization of the industrial proletariat, and all this threatens to completely disorganize the economic life of the country."

As a fundamental practical measure, I proposed "replacing the requisitioning of surpluses† by a levy proportionate to the quantity of the products (a sort of a progressive income tax in kind), set up in such a way that it is more profitable to increase the acreage or to cultivate it better."

It is, of course possible, to consider that the given suggestion was pre-

---

*Delivery of grain to the state graineries. Meant here is the direct dependence (mutual guarantee) of the quantity of, for instance, manufactured goods allotted to the given village on the quantity of grain delivered to the state graineries by all the peasants of the given village (and not by an individual peasant household). (Ed.).

†The surplus-requisitioning system ("prodrazverstka") obliged the peasants to deliver to the state all their surpluses (in excess of the established norms determined for their personal and economical needs) of grain and other products. (Ed.)

mature in 1920,[30] but in any case it cannot be in any way interpreted as a deficiency of attention to the role and importance of the peasantry.

4. The essence of the debates that took place in the TsK on the eve of the Congress with respect to the question of "smychka" (linking of town and country) consisted in my attempt to prove, in full accord with the whole implication of the main speech of Comrade Lenin at the Eleventh Congress, that the "smychka," at its basis, was now becoming the question of correlation of prices ("scissors"),[31] and that the key to this "smychka" did not lie in agitated rhetoric or in political subversive activities, but in lowering the prices of the state industry products by means of the proper state industry organization. But even if this thinking was wrong, it did not imply any "underestimation" of the role of the peasantry. But in reality this thought turned out to be eminently correct. And now we have turned on the problem completely.

5. At the Twelfth Congress Comrade Kamenev confirmed that the initiative to state the question about a proper purchase and export of grain belonged to me. This fact may be easily confirmed by the respective documents.[32]

And thus, I sweep aside all unsubstantiated, obviously far-fetched statements about some erroneous line of mine on the question of peasantry. I consider them an artificially created legend, elaborated with the aim of justifying the partitions that are being erected inside the Party.

THE PARTY AND THE STATE

One more equally untenable fabrication is the statement that I am ostensibly trying to weaken the dependence of the state machinery on the Party. But the fact is that all my efforts have been and are now being directed toward ensuring actual, real, true Party leadership in solving all major questions, but not toward simple and occasional interference. In order not to make unsubstantiated statements, I present here an extract (one of a great number) from my letter sent to the members of the TsK on March 22 of the current year:

"1. The characteristic of our state machinery as a socially heterogenous, revolutionary, instable, and highly liable to the influence of the looks hostile to our course. It is very dangerous for us under the NEP conditions.

"2. The state machinery in its present state has been formed over the course of these five years, in spite of the fact that the whole preceding era was filled with the efforts of our Party organizations, groups, and cells to direct state activities during these whole five years. Primitive methods and means, for the most part episodically, to exert Party influence on the state machinery, lay at the bottom of such a state of affairs. We are in need of a radical change in this respect. And this change should begin at the level of activities of the TsK and its Politburo.

"3. The Politburo should work up the basic questions with the departments in a planned order to determine their functioning, i.e., to determine the program of their activities for a long period of time, and, in connection with it, to form the main staff of their personnel.

"4. The Politburo should periodically subject to consideration the accounts and reports of the departments from the viewpoint of the virtual fulfillment of their programs.

"5. The Politburo should constantly exert pressure upon and check the work of all the departments to make them establish and elaborate planned methods of their personnel renomination and education. The Politburo should abandon the policy of considering the numberless departmental and interdepartmental conflicts and financial appeals, and leave this job to be carried out by the Soviet organs.

"6. The Politburo and the Orgburo (organizatsionnoye Buro, Orgburo— Organization Bureau) should abandon the prevailing system which replaces the Party leadership and distribution with the secretaries' pulling-outs."

To the above extract, which convincingly enough disproves this senseless legend, I cannot add anything more in principle.[33]

After the Twelfth Congress the Politburo adopted a special resolution on the planned functioning of the Politburo, as if it were eager to make an attempt to take the path I had suggested. But the given resolution has not been enforced. A chaotic procedure for solving problems still remains to be identified with the Party dictatorship. And any attempt to introduce some plan and system into the methods and forms of the Party dictatorship are called attempts to shake the basis of the dictatorship itself.

ON PLANNED LEADERSHIP

We have seen already from everything said above, in what way Comrade Lenin raised the question of the leadership of our economy in his note dealing with the Gosplan (Gosudarstvennyi Planovyi Komitet—State Planning Committee). The authors of the letter repeat more than once that in the field of our economy quick successes are inconceivable, that there is no need to hurry up, to feel nervous, and so on. But all these considerations have no content whatsoever in light of the fact that we have entered an acute crisis, one of the main reasons for which, both in my estimate and according to the statement made by much more responsible economic executives,[34] is the lack of coordination between the main elements of our economy; first of all, between our finances on the one hand, and our industry and trade on the other hand. And if it is true that quick successes in the field of our economy are impossible to attain, then it is also true that quick failures, crises, obstructions, and partial catastrophes are quite likely to occur, when there is no circumspection and planned leadership. I have already quoted in my letter the recent statement of comrades Rykov and Pyatakov: "Some of the decisions by the Politburo made us focus our attention on the fact that under the emerging situation it becomes extremely difficult for us to direct the state industrial branches we have been entrusted with." Comrade Rykov's signature below the answer of the members of the Politburo does not mitigate, but, rather, reinforces the importance of his signature beneath the words quoted above. Comrade Pyatakov, a member of the Tsk, who, on the instructions of the Politburo, first worked at the Gosplan, and then at the head of the VSKNh (Vysshii Sovet Narodnogo Khozyaistva—the Supreme Council of National Economy), signed the note pointing out a complete absence of a planned leadership over our economy as one of the most important causes of our crises and frustrations.

On October 11 the representatives of the most important syndicates signed the note, the principal conclusions of which read as follows: "Adequate measures must be taken to coordinate the main conditions for the functioning of our industry and exert a great, often overwhelming, influence on the cost of its products; in addition, everyone of them pursues its own autonomous policy and its own "self-supporting policy, without any overall picture of the demands of the country's product-trade turnover."

One of the most responsible leaders of our industry, Comrade Bogdanov, wrote in his note, submitted on October 14, the following: "Such events taking place at present, when the program of reduction in credits announced by the state bank in July was completely unknown to the industry, are inadmissible; and they only raise a panic and entail disorganization of the market."

The number of such indisputable illustrations may be multiplied endlessly. All this we have seen in the seven months since the Twelfth Congress. And it is the lack of a really planned leadership, which inevitably entails improvisations and ad hoc decisions, that is the true and main evil. Meanwhile, in the light of this indisputable fact, the "answer" of the Politburo members states that speeches about "a planned flexible (maneuvering) regulation" have no real content, they only represent "phrases" (!) and are worthy of "derision" (!) only.

Here I must assert that the authors of the letter have dropped the resolutions of the Twelfth Party Congress from their memory. And the following is said there: "The planned principle under the economic policy conditions differs little in its scope from war communism conditions. But it radically differs with regard to the methods of its implementation. The central board-o-cratic* administration is being replaced with an economical maneuvering."[35] And so, my statement concerning the necessity of a planned maneuvering regulation is in itself just a petition of the text of the Party Congress resolution. And the Party Congress resolutions are subjects for fulfillment, not for "derision."

"It is necessary," the resolution of the same Party Congress continues, "to yield a more definite position to the Gosplan (State Planning Commission), to make it much better and more firmly organized, to make its rights and, especially, its responsibilities and duties clearer and more undeniable. It must be determined as a firm basis, that there should be no state economic problem that can be implemented by the highest organs of the Republic without the knowledge of the Gosplan."[36] Has it been carried out? No, not in the least!

And, finally, "It is necessary to fight via the Gosplan," says the resolution of the Twelfth Party Congress; "against the organization and formation of temporary and casual commissions of any kind, whose job is to

---

*It is a kind of government and management, which is based on the order of bureaucratic commands issued by various leading authorities, such as central boards, central departments, and so on. (Ed.).

study, guide, direct, check, prepare, and so on, all of them being the greatest evil of our state activities. It is necessary to ensure proper functioning of the state machinery through its normal and permanent organs. This is the only way to improve these organs and to develop their resourcefulness, so necessary now, and all this should be achieved by means of their comprehensive adaptation to fulfillment of the missions assigned to them, with adaptation being attained in the course of their continuous functioning."[37]

This last quotation from the resolution of the Twelfth Party Congress is especially striking and persuasive in light of the recent facts, especially in light of the formation of a number of special commissions to deal with the problems of wages, salaries, prices, and so on. "The fight in favor of price reductions has already begun," says the letter of the members of the Politburo as if it were just a matter of some independent, unrelated task. Price is the derivative of all our economic activity, including its planned maneuvering control. This fact itself, when a special commission has been formed with the aim of taking some measures for a price reduction, means that the normally existing organs are functioning in the wrong way, which is, according to the estimations of the Twelfth Party Congress, "the greatest evil of our state activities."

It is necessary to carry out, at any cost, the requirements of the resolution of the Twelfth Party Congress in regard to the Gosplan. It is necessary to make it the leading headquarters of our economy. It is necessary to ensure the rights of the Gosplan in full accord with Lenin's suggestions, already quoted above.

FOREIGN POLICY QUESTIONS

1. The representation of the course of the diplomatic negotiations given in the "answer," in connection with the Curzon Ultimatum, is fundamentally incorrect.[38]

Here the author of the letter, most probably, counted on his memory, and none of those who signed the letter made any inquiries as to the document. It would have forced me to overload the letter too much with references and quotations in order to correct obviously wrong statements grouped in several lines of the "answer." I am ready to do it in case of necessity at any time and anywhere. But I shall limit myself here now by reminding you that out of our four notes connected with the ultimatum, the first one was written by Comrade Litvinov and by me, the second by me, the third by Comrade Chicherin, and the fourth by me.

2. No comments are yet really required with regard to the policy in respect to Poland. The shift in policy, I insisted on a month ago,[39] has been mainly achieved. Our relations with Poland are no longer among the unimportant formal questions, but now stand at the same level of importance as our negotiations about the transit problems and military noninterference. This is the only right, realistic, businesslike way to pose the question which will ensure already known, perhaps even essential, practical results and create for us, at the same time, a clear position in the eyes of the masses of our country. For now, nothing more can be said about this issue.

I do not fully know why and for what purpose the Politburo in passing takes Comrade Chicherin under its wing to protect him from my allegedly "irrelevant" attacks. I have criticized certain suggestions of his, just as I have done in respect of the policy pursued by the majority of the Politburo, since I considered them incorrect. But there were no "irrelevant attacks" in this respect.

ON THE QUESTION OF THE GERMAN REVOLUTION

Depicted unilaterally, and wrongfully, in the letter were differences of opinion on the question of the German Revolution.[40] I consider that these differences have been in general settled by the resolutions and the practical decisions adopted later, which were achieved after a very serious and acute struggle. The fighting went on with respect to three questions, namely:

1) importance and determination of the date
2) Soviets of Deputies* and Soviets of Industries (Committees at Factories and Mills)†
3) interrelations between the TsK of the German Communist Party and the Berlin opposition.

---

*Sov. Dep. (Ed.).
†Fabzavcom. Committees at Factories and Mills. (Ed.)

We have adopted a resolution, in which (after a serious inner-Party struggle among us) we have pointed out that the greatest danger for the German revolution would be the lack of a quite decisive orientation among the leading circles of the German Communist Party on the side of the armed insurrection, which presupposed a plan and a set date for it. It is quite enough to recall our own pre-October experience in order to understand how necessary it was to have a clear and distinct position. The essential differences in opinion among us were presented in my article "About the Dates," published in *Pravda*.[41] In the course of the discussions on the resolution I was fighting with all resoluteness against allegedly Marxist wisdom, saying that "the revolution" (indeed, the seizure of power) cannot be scheduled for a certain date and so on. If we had no clear and distinct statement of this question, we would be facing the greatest danger that events in Germany would follow the Bulgarian model.[42] On the basis of all the data, in particular, the reports from Comrade Milyutin, the representative of the Komintern (Kommunist Internatsional—Communist International), we lost the revolution in Bulgaria just because we failed to timely treat the armed insurrection as an art. Nowadays we are entering a period of the greatest was and revolutionary political commotions, and the question of the armed insurrection in all its details is becoming one of the most important of our Communist policy.

As to the second question, an attempt has been made to press the German Communist Party in order to make it adopt a task of formation of the Soviets of Deputies alongside with the already existing industrial Soviets.[43] After very acute fighting, the given plan, which might have been too much for the German Communist Party, was given up.

It is a monstrously wrong statement that I allegedly spoke with disdain about the German TsK. On the contrary, in all my work I insisted, and already longer than during the first month, on the necessity to firmly support the German TsK against the mean-minded leaders of the Berlin left.[44] But I did not keep secret from the whole German delegation on the whole, that it was very dangerous for them to continue pursuing a temporizing policy with regard to the armed insurrection. Here the most decisive assistance and influence were demanded. Here the slightest inadvertence or imperfection was absolutely inadmissible. Since the time the last plenary meeting was held, very much has been done in the stated direction.

Private Information Contained in the Letter of the Members of the Politburo

In the "answer" there is a great number of private issues and accusations I would have been very glad not to consider, if it were only possible. But my refusal to do so would amount to a tacit capitulation to the authors of the letter who are allegedly eager to make the collective work impossible on the basis of principle. But I cannot compromise and I do not want to do so. Therefore, I consider it necessary to demonstrate that the authors of the letter are fundamentally in the wrong when they try to use private information to illustrate the impossibility of correct and healthy work, which would have been carried out in full on the basis of correcting the obviously erroneous and harmful sides of our present Party and economic regime. The general idea of the respective passages in the "answer" amounts to their saying that my understanding of the role of the planned leadership, of the Party bureaucratic machinery, and the like are neither more nor less than the product of my personal pretensions: "We declare," the authors of the letter are saying, "that, just as before, the Politburo cannot assume responsibility for satisfying Trotsky's pretensions to this dictatorship of his in the leadership of our economy, in addition to those powers he has already acquired as chairman of the Revolutionary War Council. Our duty is to say the following: it is impossible for us to assume the responsibility for a speculative experiment in this field."*

Such representation of the matter seems to be utterly incredible in the light of the facts previously mentioned. Here I shall list the most indisputable and obvious of them.

[1.] On January 6 of this year, in a special letter sent by Comrade Stalin to all the members of the TsK, Comrade Stalin suggested the following measures to be taken in addition to the others:

"a) It is necessary to appoint Comrade Pyatakov to be the head of the VSNKh and to make Comrade Bogdanov one of his deputies (it is quite clear to me that Comrade Bogdanov has failed and will continue to fail to gather the recalcitrant elements under his command).

---

*For some unknown reason the name of Comrade Kolegajec has been drawn in in connection with the question of my pretensions to the dictatorship in our economy. I am completely perplexed as to whence and for what purpose it has been done.

"b) It is necessary to appoint Comrade Trotsky to be the Deputy Chairman of the Council of People's Commissars (it was a suggestion of Comrade Lenin), putting the VSNKh under his special care.

"c) I think that these charges might make our work in eliminating the chaos much easier."

It is quite obvious that Comrade Stalin was making all these written suggestions with the knowledge of the other members of the Politburo.

On January 17 in his other circulated letter, Comrade Stalin wrote the following: "I would have no objections against simultaneous appointment of Comrade Trotsky as either the Deputy Chairman of the Council of the People's Commissars and the Chairman of the VSNKh, or the Deputy Chairman of the Council of the People's Commissars and the Chairman of the Gosplan (State Planning Committee)." My verbal and written objections to these suggestions were of a purely businesslike character, partially organizational and partially personal. There is no need to repeat them now, particularly since the respective correspondence is available for inspection. But it was just I who was trying to prove that combining the job of the Chairman of the VSNKh and that of the leader of the War Department is too difficult a task to fulfill. Comrade Stalin was trying to prove a it a possibility. In any case, as we see, the case was not that, on one side, there were "personal pretensions" to take the post of the chairman of the VSNKh and the like, and, on the other, the refusal by the P/byuro* to take upon itself the responsibility for "the speculative experiment." In reality Comrade Stalin, with the unanimous consent of the other members of the Politburo, insistently suggested this experiment, thinking that it would help us to "eliminate chaos." I myself was trying to avoid any additional responsibility, for fear, in addition to everything else, of squandering my energies in conflicting directions and of the negative impact of holding of more than one office. At the Twelfth Party Congress Comrade Stalin even considered it necessary to state in public that I was not inclined to carry out work of a broader character.[45] How is it possible to reconcile all these facts and statements with everything that the "answer" has now attributed to me, i.e., my alleged striving to become the Chairman of the VSNKh? In this case my striving for this post counts for so much, that because of it I am putting forward these or other questions of principle or organizational suggestions. It really is monstrous, isn't it?

---

*Politburo. (Ed.)

It was already after the Twelfth Congress (on April 25, 1923), when Comrade Rykov, refusing to take the post of the Chairman of the VSNKh, wrote the following to the TsK:

> In one of his suggestions, distributed among the members of the TsK, Comrade Stalin suggested that Comrade Trotsky should become become the leader of the VSNKh. I see no reasons to dispute this, since Comrade Trotsky has returned to study our industry and economy several times during the last few years, and he is well acquainted with both the main problems of the current economical practice, and the machinery controlling our industry.
>
> That exceptional success of Comrade Trotsky reported at the Congress, provides a full guarantee that the Party will entirely approve this appointment.
>
> It will be necessary to combine the work of Comrade Trotsky at the VSNKh with his participation in the general work of our government, using that reorganization of the CTO (Council of Labor and Defense) that has been suggested by Comrade Stalin in his letter.

Now how I ask, did it become possible to amend all the preceding historical events *ex post facto*? How is it possible to reconcile Comrade Stalin's suggestions, quoted above, with his signature under the last "answer"? How is it possible to combine Comrade Rykov's statement, presented above, with the rebuff with which he meets my alleged pretensions to seize power in the VSNKh now? Whence is it? For what purpose is all this done? I refuse to grapple with it.

And is it not monstrous to say that some dozens of the old unstained Party workers allegedly formulate their points of view and their demands in the letter to the TsK with only the purpose . . . of ensuring me the post of Chairman of the VSNKh? And when is it done? At such a moment when the combination of the work in the War Department with that in the economic agencies is the least realizable both from the economic agencies' and the War Department's points of view?

2.* I must present one more episode, which demonstrates how history is being made and how it is being written. At the Politburo session dealing with elaboration of the order of the day for the forthcoming Twelfth Congress, Comrade Stalin, with the support of comrades Kamenev, Kalinin,

---

*Trotsky has placed the numbers 2 and 3 at the subsections of the given section of his letter, omitting number 1; his numbering and indentation are preserved here. (Ed.).

and, if I am not mistaken, Tomsky (Comrade Zinoviev was not present), suggested that I undertake the political report of the TsK. This problem was being discussed at the Politburo session in very businesslike and calm tones. I replied that if somebody decided to address the congress it would only worsen the Party's depressed state, caused by the illness of Vladimir Ilyich. Therefore, it would be better to limit ourselves to a political account, which could be combined by Comrade Stalin with the practical account. As to the main questions, they should be examined under the respective points of the order of the day. Besides, I added, there were some substantial differences in opinion among us with regard to the economic problems. Comrade Kalinin, raising an objection to my last note, said: "These were your suggestions, most of which had passed the Politburo, and you had no reason to refuse to make a political report." I continued, however, to insist on adopting my suggestion. The question was not settled at that session, and then, as it is known, quite a different turn was given to the whole affair. Isn't it clear that the fact just now presented by me, which, of course, could not be blotted out of the memory of those who took part in the Politburo session of the mentioned above, flagrantly contradicts that general picture, the "answer" of the members of the Politburo have given now my using an ex post facto method in order to explain and justify the system of artificial partitions within the Party?

3. A quite incomprehensible character has accused me of "paying utterly inadequate attention to the army" during the last years. I do not know how to interpret this accusation: does it mean that I have too short a working day or that I fill up my working day with extraneous matters? In carrying out the numerous missions I was charged with by the TsK, I had to point out more than once that these missions distracted me from my military work. It has taken me, for instance, about two months of some strenuous work to prepare the report and theses on our industry. It takes me a very considerable amount of time to take part in the activities of the Comintern (Communist International). The only work that I am doing without any mission from the Politburo is my participation in the Moskust (Moscow Combined Group),[46] but that takes me hardly more than two to three hours per month. In the "answer" there is, true, a hint of "elaboration of the problems of literature, art, way of life, and the like" given as a reason for my inadequate attention to the army. But this hint is lent an indirect credence just because the authors know well that I was taking up these questions during the time I was undergoing a course of medical

treatment, when no strenuous mental work was allowed to me. I do not, by any means, see any reasons to excuse myself before the Party because I used two summer holidays not only for medical treatment, but also for writing books on literature and way of life.[47] I can only express my astonishment that they would try to use this fact in order to accuse me.*

It is quite true, however, that there was almost no creative work done in the area of our army due to an extremely difficult welfare standards of the army, the complete instability of its budget, permanent reductions and amendments of its staff organization, and very frequent personnel appointments and dismissals, completely inexpedient, according to my estimation, from the point of view of our national interests. All this created an extremely difficult situation for doing the job, in addition to introducing into the army, from the top down, that special "policy," examples of which are nowadays known by the majority of the Party and army executives. The "answer" of the Politburo members is the further development of the same policy, the purport of which is quite clear.

UNBELIEF IN THE PARTY

The accusation that would have been the heaviest, if it had not been so slight, is that of my unbelief in the Party and my disability to understand it. Adduced as proof of this is my expression of the "provincial committees oblomovshchina,"† which was once used by me somewhere, but there are no explanations of the connection and the sense with which these words have been said. Finally, my statement about the fact that I consider myself, due to an extremely crucial situation, to be obliged to place the essence of the matter higher than its form and to draw the attention of the most important Party executives to the situation was interpreted by the "answer" in the following way: "We consider it to be the completely unprecedented statement that has ever been made among our Bolsheviks."

---

*By the way, Comrade Lenin, with whom I spoke about the articles I planned to write about the "proletarian culture" about a year and a half ago, insisted on my stepping up this work. I managed to carry it out only this summer.

†Sluggishness, inertness, apathy, as illustrated by Oblomov, the Goncharoff character in the novel Oblomov, written by one of the outstanding Russian writers, I. A. Goncharoff.

The strict sense and tone of the "answer" in the given part of it is quite clear. Everything implied by some of those who signed the "answer," which filled the others with indignation, is here said quite openly: lack of any knowledge of the Party, lack of belief in its abilities and those of its local organizations, and, finally, the statements and steps, "unprecedented among Bolsheviks." I dare say that some members of the Politburo should be more careful when speaking about the steps and statements, "unprecedented among Bolsheviks." My statement then and now has aimed to make the TsK speed up that amendment of the course, which is inevitably arising from the entire situation we have now. By the way, there were some cases with us, when, on the eve of the decisive battles and in the course of them—it was in October 1917—some important executives deserted their posts, appealing to the Party against the TsK, in face of non-Party elements and opponents.[48] I consider that the belief and unbelief in the Party and in its creative abilities become apparent on the days of the greatest trials, through which we are at present passing in all four corners of our country. There is almost no provincial Party committee among those with which I have not had to work hand in hand during the most difficult hours of the Civil War, and among those mistakes I have made there has been no criminal distinct with regard to the creative abilities of the Party and the working class. So, I reject this accusation as a false one and deliberately insulting.

Here are my explanations to the most important points of the letter of the members of the Politburo. The least morbid and the shortest way out—I am saying it once more—may be found only by a serious and firm desire on the part of the leading group of the TsK to remove the artificial partitions within the Party; to consider more attentively the urgent demands to amend the Party course; and in doing so, to help the Party return to itself its independent actions, its activity, and its unanimity. Having taken this path, the TsK would win the most active support of an overwhelming majority of Party members, and those questions, which at present seem or are represented as private information would vanish by themselves.

L. Trotsky

October 23, 1923

RTsKhIDNI (Rossiiskii Tsentr Khraneniya
i Izucheniya Documentov Noveishei Istorii—
Russian Center of Preservation and Study of
Documents of Modern History, RCPSDMH).
f. 51, 51, op. 1, d. 21, 1. 54 ob. to 57 ob.; the
printed text, having been checked against a
typewritten copy.[49]
It was published for the first time in the journal
of *Izvestija TsK KPSS*. 1990. No. 10.
pp. 167–181.

NOTES

1. The letter was written on October 23, but it was received by the Secretariat of the TsK of the RKP(b) on October 24.

2. The answer by the members of the Politburo of the TsK, dated October 19, is presented in Document No. 17.

3. The resolution of the Tenth Congress of the RKP(b), titled "Party Unity," is meant here (refer also to note 2 to Document No. 11).

4. At the session of the Politburo of the TsK of the RKP(b), held on October 11, 1923, Trotsky's letter dated October 8 was under discussion. The extract from the minutes of the Politburo session is presented in Document No. 11. There were no stenographic records of the debates; Trotsky cited the debate speeches on the basis of his own notes made at the session. It is worthwhile to underline the position of N. I. Bukharin with respect to the necessity to develop inner-Party democracy, his position being in conformity with his suggestion expressed in his telephone message to Stalin and M. P. Tomsky on October 20, 1923 (refer to Document No. 18).

5. In his letter dated October 8 Trotsky bore in mind the fact that on the eve of the Twelfth Congress of the RKP(b), at a great number of the provincial Party conferences, the delegates to the congress were being elected on recommendations of the secretaries of the provincial committees, the secretaries, in turn, had been elected since summer 1922 on recommendations of the TsK, that is, they were virtually nominated by the Secretariat of the TsK.

6. Yet as early as in 1921 G. I. Myasnikov sent to the Party TsK a long report, where he suggested that some deep democratic reforms in the political sphere and be brought about such as abrogation of death penalties and proclamation of freedom of speech (from monarchists to anarchists), and that they be brought about with the aim to ensure civil peace in the country. In August 1921 the Orgburo (Organizatsionnoye byuro—Organization Bureau) of the TsK voted that the theses of G. I. Myasnikov were incompatible with the interests of the Party, and it obliged him not to speak about them at Party meetings. Myasnikov did not

agree with the decision of the Orgbyuro and proceed with keeping up an agitational work among the Communists and non-Party workers. In 1922 he was expelled from the RKP(b). For the "Workers' Group of the RKP" (Myasnikov was one of its leaders), refer to note 5 to Document No. 4.

7. The commission of the Politburo of the TsK was formed on September 18, 1923 with F. E. Dzerzhinsky as its leader, with the purpose of studying the economical and inner-Party situation (also refer to note 2 to Document No. 4).

8. Refer to V.I. Lenin. *Complete Collected Works*, vol. 45. pp. 349-350. Some differences (eg., in Trotsky's text the word "discrepancy" is used, while in the text of the *Complete Collected Works* the word "nonaccordance" is used) are explained by the fact that Trotsky quoted Lenin's notes, using the typewritten copies he had at that time.

9. It is quoted inexactly, but there is no distortion of the meaning. Refer to the record made on December 29, 1922, V.I. Lenin, *Complete Collected Works*, vol. 45, p. 353.

10. As to the differences of opinion in the Politburo of the TsK of the RKP(b) with regard to the question of the monopoly of foreign trade (October–December, 1922), refer to note 7 to Document No. 5, as well as to Trotsky, *Stalin's School of Falsification* (1952; Moscow: Nauka, 1990), pp. 70-75.

11. It is quoted inexactly, but there is no distortion of the meaning. Refer to V. I. Lenin, *Complete Collected Works,* vol. 54, p. 324. Lenin's letter, dated December 12, 1922 and sent by him to M .I. Frumkin and B. S. Stomonyakov, which is mentioned by him here, has not been included in the *Complete Collected Works*. The letter was published for the first time by Trotsky in 1932 in *Stalin's School of Falsification*, pp. 71-72.

12. Meant here is the Party faction that was a part of the delegates of the Congress of Soviets, and the Communist delegates were the members of the faction.

13. Meant here is the decision of the plenary meeting of the TsK of the RKP(b), dated October 6, 1922. Refer to note 7 to Document No. 5.

14. As to the differences of opinion arising in the Politburo of the TsK with regard to the question of the formation of the USSR and international relations, refer to note 8 to Document No. 5, as well as to Trotsky *Stalin's School of Falsification*, pp. 77-83.

15. Meant here is the letter dictated by Lenin on December 30-31, 1922, and titled "To the Question of Nationalities or about 'Autonomization.' " See V. I. Lenin, *Complete Collected Works,* vol. 45, pp. 356-362.

16. V. I. Lenin, *Complete Collected Works*, vol. 54, p. 329. The text of Lenin's letter is quoted by Trotsky on the basis of the typewritten copy he had, with the copy having been attested by M. A. Volodicheva, Lenin's secretary. In the *Complete Collected Works* Lenin's letter was published on the basis of the typewritten copy told the addressee over the telephone on March 5, 1923. In the text quoted by L. D. Trotsky, there is no phrase: "Even on the contrary," but the given phrase is present in the *Complete Collected Works* after the words: ". . . I cannot rely on their impartiality." In the next phrase of Lenin's letter the words ". . . his defense" are given in the reverse order of Trotsky's copy. Both texts have some discrepancies, having no effect on the meaning, when compared with the form of Lenin's letter in the book titled *Archives of Trotsky: Communist Opposition in the USSR 1923-1927*, compiled by Yu. Felshtinsky (Moscow, 1990), vol. 1, p. 34.

17. The senioren-convention is the organ the was formed two days before the opening of the Twelfth Congress of the RKP(b) according to the decision of the April (1923) ple-

nary meeting of the TsK of the RKP(b). (Refer to the *Twelfth Congress of the RKP(b). Stenographical Report*, pp. 768, 821).

18. Lenin's letter "To the Question of Nationalities or about 'Autonomization' " was published in the USSR for the first time in 1956.

19. Refer to the suggestions dictated by Lenin to the Twelfth Congress of the Party with respect of the reform of the People's Commissariat of the Workers' and Peasants' Inspection (Rabkrin) and the Central Control Commission (TSKK). *Complete Collected Works*, vol. 45, pp. 383-388. For the differences of opinion arose in the Politburo of the TsK with regard to the essence of Lenin's suggestions, as well as to the fate of his article, titled "How We Should Reorganize the Workers' and Peasants' Inspection," refer to note 9 to Document No. 5, as well as to Trotsky, *Stalin's School of Falsification*, pp. 83-85.

20. V. I. Lenin, *Complete Collected Works*, vol. 45, p. 393.

21. From March 1919 to April 1922, Stalin was the People's Commissar to the State Control (Goskontrol), and then he became the People's Commissar of the Workers' and Peasants' Inspection (RKI). In 1923 V. V. Kuibyshev became the People's Commissar of the RKI (Workers' and Peasants' Inspection).

22. After the Twelfth Party Congress Stalin (General Secretary), B. M. Molotov, and Ya. E. Rudzutak were the members of the Secretariat of the TsK of the RKP(b). Since Trotsky does not mention Rudzutak among those secretaries of the TsK who took part in the discussion, his words: "especially sharp words and flat objections were expressed by the members of the Secretariat," should be referred to Stalin and V. M. Molotov. Their position is quite understandable and explainable: the reform suggested by Lenin raises the role of the Politburo and the plenary meetings of the TsK, places the whole TsK under more effective control of the "lower strata" via the combined People's Commissariat of RKI—TSKK (Workers' and Peasants' Inspection—Central Control Commission), and thus crushes to a considerable extent the system of the secretaries' hierarchy.

23. From 1923 (after the Twelfth Party Congress) V. V. Kuibyshev was the chairman of the TSKK (Central Control Commission) and simultaneously the People's Commissar of the RKI (Workers' and Peasants' Inspection).

24. The "harmlessness" was rendered to Lenin's plan by means of a formal, purely superficial following after Lenin's suggestion made on the side of the "leading kernel," and as a result the TsK reserved for itself absolute rule.

25. As to the given episode, refer to note 48 to Document No. 17, as well as to Trotsky, *Stalin's School of Falsification*, p. 66.

26. Lenin's April Theses, the theses "On the Tasks of the Proletariat in the Present Revolution," with which V. I. Lenin addressed just after his arrival in Russia from emigration in April 1917. The main idea of the April Theses consisted in the struggle for the development of the bourgeois-democratic revolution into the Socialist revolution with the support on the proletariat and the poorest peasantry, in the establishment of their dictatorship in the form of the power of the Soviets. Trotsky bears in mind the fact that some Bolsheviks, in particular, L. B. Kamenev and A. I. Rykov, opposed Lenin's April Theses.

27. Trotsky bears in mind the period of the Civil War, when the Red Army, consisting mainly of peasants, was under formation and was gaining strength and experience.

28. As to the question of the "underestimation" of the role of the peasantry by Trot-

sky, refer also to V.I. Lenin, *Complete Collected Works*, vol. 37, p. 478, and to L. D. Trotsky, *Stalin's School of Falsifications*, pp. 48-51.

29. The Sengileievo District (uzed) Party organization was an organic part of the Simbirsk Party organization. Here it is a matter of discontent and disturbances among the peasantry in the areas located along the river Volga in autumn 1919.

30. In the previous paragraphs Trotsky quoted his letter titled "Basic Questions of Food and Land Policy," which he sent to the TsK of the RKP(b) on March 20, 1920 (and not on February 20). Besides, the measures suggested by him, which were unconditionally of a new economic policy character, Trotsky, at some points of this document, considered it possible to continue pursuing a policy of active state interference, mainly in the central provinces of Russia, brought to ruin by the war (refer to L. D. Trotsky, *Works*, vol. 17, part 2, M.-L. Publishing House, 1926, pp. 543–544). It is beyond any doubt that the realization of Trotsky's suggestions, and first and foremost, the substitution of a tax in kind for the surplus-requisitioning system, would have beaten down the tide of rising discontent among the peasants, they would have eased the acuteness of the political crisis, which took place in autumn 1921.

31. For "smychka" and "scissors" (price gap), refer to notes 8 and 19 to Document No. 4.

32. Refer to the *Twelfth Congress of the RKP(b). Stenographic Notes*, pp. 447–448.

33. Judging from the enumerated suggestions, the problem of Party guidance of the state machinery was raised by Trotsky as the problem of an organizational and administrative character; i.e., the guidance amounted to the consolidation of the functions of the Politburo of the TsK as a permanent administrative controller of the activities of the state departments, which essentially meant a strengthening of the Party machinery's dictatorship, its coalescence with the state machinery.

34. "The Declaration of the Forty-Six" is meant here.

35. *The Twelfth Congress of the RKP(b). Stenographic Notes*, p. 678.

36. Ibid.

37. Ibid, p. 679. It is quoted inexactly, but there is no distortion of the meaning.

38. For the G. N. Curzon ultimatum, refer to note 32 to Document No. 4.

39. From the moment the revolutionary events began to spread in Germany, Trotsky insisted that the TsK and Soviet government should assume a definite position in relation to Poland, concluding an agreement with her on a mutual noninterference in the events going on in Germany, and to simultaneously take, in this case, all necessary measures to prevent any war with Poland. In his talk with Mr. King, an American senator, in September 1923, Trotsky said: "First and foremost, we want peace. . . . We do not keep it a secret from anybody that our sympathies are with the German working class and its heroic struggle for its liberation. . . . But we do not want any war. . . . Only that revolution displays its viability which gains victory with its own forces, especially when a great nation's fate is in question. . . . We firmly know, that our war with Poland might mean an occurrence of pan-European conflagration which would wipe all remnants of European civilization off the face of the earth." (*Pravda*, September 30, 1923).

40. For the differences of opinion, or more exactly, the absence in principle thereof, between Trotsky and the members of the Politburo of the TsK with regard to the German revolution question, refer to note 24 to Document No. 17.

41. The article written by Trotsky and titled "Is it Possible to Make a Counter-Revolution or Revolution by a Specified Date?" was published in *Pravda* on September 23, 1923.

42. Meant here is the armed insurrection against the Bulgarian monarchist and fascist government, which took place in September 1923. The rebels managed to capture a number of towns, where a Workers' and Peasants' Power was proclaimed. The given armed insurrection was cruelly suppressed.

43. Meant here is the position of Stalin, who insisted on the necessity to create in Germany to Soviets, as the centers of the future insurrection (according to the Russian example), but it did not correspond to the situation and was erroneous. Besides, Stalin supported G. E. Zinoviev in that it was necessary to intensify the efforts aimed at an alienation of the German workers from the Social-Democracy, the influence of which among the masses was considerably widespread.

44. Meant here are the differences of opinion that existed between the TsK of the German Communist Party and the leaders of the Berlin organization with regard to the questions of Party strategics and tactics in the revolutionary events which took place in autumn 1923.

45. Refer to the *Twelfth Congress of the RKP(b). Stenographic Notes*, pp. 198-199.

46. The "MOSKUST" joint-stock company (Moscow Combined Kust), organized at the beginning of the New Economic Policy period, amalgamated the local industry enterprised (subordinated to the State authorities), located in the territory of Moscow.

47. For the works by Trotsky on the questions of literature, mode of life, and others, written and published by him in 1923, refer to note 13 to Document No. 17.

48. Here Trotsky means the position taken by G. E. Zinovyev and L. B. Kamenev, who at the beginning were against the Bolsheviks' policy of preparing for an armed insurrection in October 1917.

49. The typewritten copies of the document are available at the RTsKhIDNI (f. 17, op. 22, f. 685) and at the archives of the President of the Russian Federation.

21

From the Papers of the Joint Plenum of the TsK and the TSKK of the RKP(b)

October 25–27, 1923

I. THE ROUGH DRAFT OF L.D.TROTSKY'S AND I.V. STALIN'S CONCLUDING SPEECHES AT THE PLENARY SESSION OF OCTOBER 26, 1923[1]

Trotsky. Comrades! They quoted here my remark that there were controversies on a number of questions. But some comrades tried to interpret it, as if the Party were being torn with (disagreements) of principle. What has been quoted is the response to Comrade Kuibyshev. Kuibysbev accused me of being too energetic.

But Vairekis touched on a more general question concerning foreign policy. The latest telegrams from Poland read that Trotsky's speech at the metal workers' congress made bourgeois governments think that we are for peaceful policy. I should speak being People's Commissar of War; I should answer whether war will break out or not; I confirm that my position is absolutely right.

There are two attitudes to my letter: some say Trotsky's speech is a bolt from the blue and interpret it as Trotsky's discontent with the RVSR membership; others say Trotsky repeats what he has been saying for two years; it was the same under Lenin, too.

Comrades, it was said here that private conferences were held. Comrades, one should take a certain position. Of course, both are wrong; there is an echo of the former controversies. But there are also new controversies, and the new situation aggravated them; this happened at the end of this year; it is sheer falsehood that I did not raise them at the PB:* I did—the results. Rykov tried to convene a private conference. Nothing came of it. As there is the other PB within the PB and as there is the other TsK within the TSK, I was removed from the actual discussions of the question.

I had no opportunity to address other TsK members with the information, so this way alone was left to me. Zinoviev says that I am uncompromising, but/ this is sheer childishness; I have not seen Serebryakov for two years. When he came to me, I answered: what does this "pyatyorka"† mean? We have the PB and the TsK, haven't we? If Zinoviev is going to make normal relations, both the "troika" and "pyatyorka" should be eliminated.

Why didn't I pass it through the TSKK? They spoke much here about "the conventionalism." I won't repeat the word, though it is not out of place here.

The TSKK members know a number of instances that "the Trotskyists" are being called those who are not fighting against Trotsky. Otherwise, what can "a Trotskyist" mean? I have never washed TsK dirty linen in public. What could their being "Trotskyists" mean? "A Trotskyist"is called a person who thought that we needed not the "environment" of what Petrovsky said or of what Frunze said. I had no confidence in the TsK majority and I still do not. That is why I did not address it.

The Secretariat policy bearer was Kuibyshev (the policy being that everyone who has no active mistrust to Trotsky is "a Trotskyist"). Now Kuibyshev and Yaroslavsky are TSKK members. The TSKK Presidium discussed the question of a Party member being guilty, accusing him of /a non-Party behavior and/ they did not call him to explain himself. It is just like the TSKK, isn't it? The TSKK Presidium and the TSKK members' conference was held. Did they invite me? The TSKK should be an independent institution and it should improve the excesses and shortcomings of TSKK members.‡

I confirm that you have turned the TSKK into the TsK Secretariat's

---

*TsK Politburo. (Ed.)
†Five-man commission. (Trans.)
‡Apparently a slip of the pen. The TsK is meant. (Ed.)

weapon in this inner-Party contest. You are misinterpreting Vladimir Ilyich. I did not address the TSKK. You are accusing me of this. This is, namely, "the conventionalism", which I oppose.

On the Bonapartism. (*Kamenev*: There was no such mention.) I cannot ignore the PB members' letter, as it is recommended by Comrade Kamenev.

The letter reads: "I want to add the authority in the sphere of the VSNKh to my authority over the War Department." All the appointments in the army are carried out through the OB and PB. Personally—heads of districts . . .*

Well, they only tell about the authority in the War Department in order to deceive provincials. They say I said at the Twelfth Congress that the army was drawing together with the Party, and now I am saying the opposite. Nothing of the kind. The process is going on. I spoke on the conditions of my own work. Every person who is working or who can work with me, is immediately under suspicion as "a Trotskyist." (But I never speak on Party questions even with Sklyansky, my nearest colleague.) It is a picture of complete isolation. And they are called "unlimited authorities" in the sphere of the war department.

I could manage the VSNKh as well as many others. But I answered Bukharin that it was impossible to combine this job with a military office.

The conversation with Vladimir Ilyich (when I spoke about being a deputy etc.). My personality—my Jewish origins. On October 25 (1917), lying on the floor in the Smolny Vladimir Ilyich said: "We'll make you NKVD†; You will crush the bourgeoisie and nobility."

I opposed NKID‡ resolutely.

People's Commissar of War I opposed still more resolutely. Why, I was right. It interfered greatly. It meant nothing in my private life; it is very serious as a political moment. Vladimir Ilyich thought it to be an eccentricity on my part. Vladimir Ilyich proposed that I should be the deputy (the only one); I refused for the same reasons and Vladimir Ilyich almost agreed. Why wasn't I a member of the SNK or of the STO? Most of all I feared making the impression that Trotsky was organizing a faction.

After the Tenth Congress Vladimir Ilyich was on his guard; I visited

---

*Sic. (Ed.)
†People's Commissar for Internal Affairs. (Ed.)
‡People's Commissariat for Foreign Affairs. (Ed.)

him and said resolutely that there was nothing of the kind; I did not deceive him; I have never publicized anything that could be interpreted as controversial or as criticism of the TsK. When the controversies on economic questions aggravated (The State Planning Commission).

I think that there should be an office that should work on every question from the aspect of economic coordination before bringing it in to the decision of the supreme organs. I cannot vote at the PB if experienced people, who know the matter inside out, have not worked at these questions. If I were discharged from some work and were appointed to the State Planning Commission, I would not oppose; I confirm that all our crises are 50 or 75 or 100 percent aggravated by extemporizing approach. The State Planning Commission is our most important organ. If it is not reorganized—that is the most important question now. What shall I do in the SNK, if the State Planning Commission is not reorganized? Either I shall work at the questions, which is practically impossible, or I shall transfer the questions from the PB either to the SNK or to the STO. My working day is busy or enough. Insinuations concerning my work on the questions about my life—I did it during my sick leave.

The only way out is the reorganization of the office.

The inner-Party situation. The Ukrainians dotted the i's. Mantsev shifted them. His information meets the logic of the situation; what Frunze said does not. What Petrovsky said meets it in the part, where he speaks about "the environment." I have never been "a democrat." The uniform military doctrine is Yenchmenism in military science. But Frunze and I carried on quite friendly polemics with each other, and then edited it as a small brochure.

Arzhanov. He is as close to me as Sologub or Arens. But the thing is, he should be replaced. He is an extremely energetic person. As soon as they had decided to replace him, I agreed. They appointed Dmitriev as an assistant. He worked for three months—he is not cut out for this work. Kolegaev is ill. Oskin is fired, and was appointed to be an assistant—when he becomes familiar with the work, he will be appointed. The question of the replacement—it is monstrous to make it a disagreement on principle. As far as Voroshilov is concerned about the record on a sheet of paper, I have good memory, but I have quite forgotten about it.

I don't patent democratism. But the situation that I found after my arrival made me scrutinize the question. My records of the PB session from October 11 is the fact. One way should be chosen: either to turn to the Party democracy, or to acknowledge that it (democracy) is prospering. They say

I made it up to organize a faction. When? What moment? What for? Where? In the army? Express it in full. Call it Bonapartism.

Since I thought over and tested my impression with a dozen experienced comrades and said: Let there be less criminal investigation and more planning, you are going to condemn me.

I will speak frankly. There are comrades in the PB who are going to carry out the matter—i.e., to keep aggravating controversies, to let Party masses know about it, and to make the further work impossible.

The majority are against this. I fear that your one-sided decision is preparing ground for those who are going to eliminate conditions for further collective work.

Sometimes I find myself in very complicated circumstances. I could not oppose those who make the impression that I am fighting against Vladimir Ilyich's traditions. I was in a tragic situation. I could not explain, I could not accept battle. Who suspects me in a personal* . . . could take me for a thorough rascal and a complete madman.If you choose the way that you seem to be choosing, you will make a blunder.

Stalin. Some actual remarks concerning the delivered appeals.

1. In letter II[2] Trotsky declared that we had controversies on the national question not only in respect to the persecution of certain persons, but also the principle of the matter. I don't understand: there were no serious disagreements.[3]

2. Why the PB members doubted whether Lenin's article about the Workers' and Peasants' Inspection should be published or not.[4] Sosnovsky introduced a degree of mysticism. The matter was as follows: the article mentioned the danger of split three times. We feared that the Party could be disoriented. But there is not a hint of disagreements in the PB.We found the way out: to send the article and the notice from the PB members at the same time to "gubernia" committees that there is not a hint of a split.

3. Trotsky says that according to the resolution of the congress.,we do not need a Party commission on economic questions.[5] But it talks about occasional commissions. One cannot call the commission on salary an occasional one. A week ago the commission for the defense of the country was appointed with Trotsky as its chairman. We need them, don't we?

4. On secretarial disturbance of the RVSR organs while distributing

officers within the army. Trotsky often spoke about it. We asked Antonov-Ovseyenko. His answer was: there were no controversies.

Now to the questions, touched on by Trotsky and by the group of forty-six.

Osinsky said: "We are floating on the waves of the element";Trotsky said: "We have a crisis, we have no planning, we have not managed the element." Crises are a necessary element of the NEP. You don't understand the NEP. You have made a fuss at the first obstacle. But it is just the beginning.

About the divergence of prices. Have you set to the matter? The cause of tithe scissors"[6] is that the rates of development of industry and agriculture are different. There are few finished products,there is a lot of bread. We cannot export it, so far. By improving the State Planning Commission you will not improve the matter.

There is another aspect of "the scissors." Metallurgy and the coal industry are showing a loss.

The third case. Trusts and syndicates are monopolists: "I fix prices—if you don't buy, you will not buy anywhere." This should be improved, we should pay our attention to this.

Is anybody against improving the State Planning Commission? Trotsky often has to abstain,* because the question is not elaborated enough. And what if we also abstained? What would happen? The abstention cannot become theory. It is ridiculous to form a platform on the necessity of improving the State Planning Commission.

Sosonovsky thinks that if we "squander" agricultural machines among peasants, we shall save the situation. This is not even a drop in the ocean. We should import finished products, but we need money, and we are on the eve of war.[7]

Instead of assisting in the discussion of these serious problems, you are pestering us with platforms. I have not found a single concrete recommendation in all the speeches by the opposition members.

The TsK fulfills the decisions of congresses. The Twelfth Congress said: probation for secretaries and the approval of higher authorities.[8] This is the limitation of democracy. The purge—a half of the Party will dismiss the other half of it.[9] This is the limitation of democracy, too. They are all a system of measures for protecting the Party from NEP influence.

---

*From voting at the TsK Politbureau sessions. (Ed.)

Democrats, tell the congress that this protection from NEP influence is unnecessary. We shall see whether the congress agrees to this. But so far we are an accountable organ, carrying out the resolutions of the congress.

There is no discussion, Yakovleva says. Like a lady in a story by Chekhov*: "Give me the atmosphere." There are moments, that are not proper for discussion.

Comrades from the provinces say that now there is a multitude of economic questions for "gubernia" committees. The Party is busy with great and important work on petty questions. It is criminal to invent discussions now. It has never happened that the TsK refused, if someone addressed the TsK proposing to discuss a question.[10] The group of Forty-Six raised the question to make a noise, but they did not attempt a businesslike discussion of the question.

The TsK made no secret of all the economic questions. They are not the heart of the matter. The matter is that Comrade Trotsky and the Group of Forty-Six did not use the ways permitted by the Party and addressed Party members over the TsK.[11] They spoke here about trifles, but they said nothing about the main issue, for the sake of which we have assembled here. The thing is that, not having used legal ways for correcting TsK "mistakes," (Trotsky) addressed Party members over it.

Trotsky writes that he will consider it his duty to address any sufficiently experienced Party member.[12] If Trotsky were exhausting every legal possibility to correct TsK "mistakes," he would be right and would be obliged to address Party members over it. But he did not make these attempts, did he?[13] This is the heart of the matter over which we are gathered here. The discussion at the center is now extremely dangerous. Both peasants and workers would lose their confidence in us and our enemies would count this a weakness. We experienced such a discussion in 1921.[14] We lost a great deal then.

Trotsky, speaking over the TsK members, creates the conditions for a factional contest and takes an extremely dangerous step. The group of forty six has made a still further step.

The way out: we cannot repeat the experience of the discussion before the Tenth congress. Then Trotsky began it, having refused to carry out Lenin's recommendation for settling the matter by the trade-union commission of the congress.

---

*One of A. P. Chekhov's characters. (Ed.)

The case has repeated itself. Trotsky repeated the step that created the situation leading to the split. In this way we should evaluate Trotsky's behavior and condemn him. We should assure such order as to settle all the disagreements within the collegium and not to take them outside it.

B. Bazhanov's autograph
RTsHIDNI, f-17, op.2, d.104, 1.31–36.
First published in: *Izvestiya TsK KPSS,*
1990, No. 10, pp. 183–187.[15]

NOTES

1. According to the TsK Politburo resolution of October 18, 1923 (see Document No. 15), the TsK Secretariat made a list of big industrial Party organizations, representatives of which were invited to the united TsK and TSKK Plenum, which was held on October 25–27, 1923. The organizations of Petrograd, Moscow, Ivanovo-Voznesensk, Nizhny Novgorod, Kharkov, Donetsk, Yekaterinburg, Rostov, Baku, and Tula had registered. But, judging by the minutes of the Plenum, they were not representatives from Party organizations of industrial bodies who were invited to its sessions, but important Party officials (secretaries of "gubernia" and town Party committees and chairmen of provincial control commissions), i.e., the representatives of the apparatus secretary hierarchy, of whose "loyalty" the TsK Secretariat could be sure. The representatives of the opposition were invited to the Plenum, too: twelve persons of those who had subscribed the declaration of the group of forty six. The following items were among those discussed at the Plenum: (1) the inner-Party situation in connection with Trotsky's letter, (2) the events in Bulgaria, (3) the events in Germany, and (4) Lenin's health.

On October 25, the first day of work by the Plenum, Stalin and L. D. Trotsky spoke. The records of these reports have not survived, since prior to January 1924 Plenum sessions were not taken down in shorthand. The next day, after the debate was finished late in the evening, both opponents made concluding speeches. In the archive file the rough drafts of both speeches are kept together with the Plenum papers, made by B.V. Bazhanov, who had become the Secretary-General's assistant by that time. The rough drafts are made with ordinary (not shorthand) cursive, with typical ("student" type) abbreviations of words and sentences. The records of the speeches are published in the sequence in which they were made at the Plenum, though in the file Stalin's rough draft is the first, followed by that of Trotsky. Bazhanov is supposed to have changed the sequence of these records, probably at Stalin's order, so as to be able to decipher and to make a finished copy of Trotsky's speech immediately after the Plenum. Thus, the document appeared following the rough draft (see Document No. 21: II).

Both drafts of Trotsky's speech are identical in their essence, while the second, finished copy, has been deciphered and perfected by Bazhanov. All notes and comments refer to the second text titled "The Summary. . . ." The rough record of Stalin's speech is provided with the necessary notes.

In the published rough drafts indisputable abbreviations are written out in full. Words added by the authors of the publication are parenthesized.

2. On the controversies over the national question, read Trotsky's letters dated October 8 (Document No. 4), October 10 (Document No. 5), and October 23 (Document No. 20).

3. On the controversies within the Party leadership on the question of principles of relationships between the Soviet republics in the period of the establishment of the USSR, see note 8 to Document No. 5.

4. On the controversies within the TSK Politburo as regards Lenin's article "How We Should Reorganize the Workers' and Peasants' Inspection (Recommendation to the Twelfth Party Congress)," see note 9 to Document No.5.

5. Trotsky's letter dated October 23, 1923 (see Document No. 20) quotes the resolution of the Twelfth RKP(b) Congress "On the Industry," stating that the setting up "of various provisional and occasional commissions" is "the greatest harm to our state work" (see *Dvenadtsatyis' ezd RKP(b). Stenograficheskii otchet* [*The Twelfth RKP(b) Congress. The Stenographic Report*], p. 679).

6. "The discrepancies" in prices. See note 19 to Document No. 4.

7. The reference is to the possible war with Poland, though Stalin knew that by that time, according to Trotsky's letter dated October 23 (see Document No.20, "The Questions of the Foreign Policy"), the negotiations with Poland were being carried on over transit and mutual noninterference in the internal affairs of Germany.

8. According to the resolution of the Eleventh All-Russian RKP(b) Conference "On the Question of Reinforcing the Party's Checking Up on Its Membership" (1921), approved by the Eleventh RKP(b) Congress in 1922, secretaries of "guberniya" Party committees were to have a Pre-October membership record in the RKP(b), and "uyezd" Party secretaries were to have a three-year Party record. Also, "guberniya" and "uyezd" Party secretaries were to be approved by a higher Party authority.

9. When the civil war had finished, purges of the Party ranks were systematically held, their aim being to clear the Party of anti-Party elements, of demoralized communists, etc. As a rule, purges were executed by so-called troikas consisting presumably of worker-communists (under the supervision of local committees and control commissions). In late 1923 there began a wide-ranging purge of non-industrial Party organizations, which in 1924 took the specific form of the reprisal of the opposition.

10. Obviously demagogic declaration: rank-and-file worker-communists merely feared to criticize the inner-Party regime (there were many who remembered the case of G. I. Myasnikov, who was expelled from the Party). As far as the representatives of the higher echelon of Party authorities were concerned, the attempts of some, like E. A. Preobrazhensky, for example, in 1920 to discuss the question of the "top" and "bottom" in the TsK finished with his leaving for the opposition.

11. The attentive reader, having familiarized himself with all the previous documents of the collection, can make certain of the groundlessness of this declaration: all Trotsky's letters and the declaration of the Group of Forty Six were delivered to the TsK and TSKK for discussion of the problems raised, namely within these Party instances.

12. The reference is to the concluding paragraph of Trotsky's letter to the TsK of October 8, 1923 (Document No. 4), the meaning of which is quite clear in the context of the letter.

13. The correspondence between Trotsky and the TsK during October 1923 shows the groundlessness of this statement. Stalin used it to convince the Plenum participants, who in their majority were ignorant of the mystery of the apparatus intrigues, in Trotsky's intention to organize a faction.

14. The reference is to the all-Party discussion on the role of trade unions, which was summed up by the Tenth RKP(b) Congress in March 1921 (see note 6 to Document No. 17).

15. Besides the author of the book and comments, the deciphering of B.V. Bazhanov's rough records and preparing the document for the first publication in *Izvestiya TsK KPSS* were made also by L. P. Kosheleva, V. P. Naumov, and L. A. Rogovaya.

As the document is being published according to the original, there are small divergences in comparison with the first publication, which however, do not change the sense.

II. THE SUMMARY OF L. D.TROTSKY'S CONCLUDING SPEECH AT THE PLENARY SESSION ON OCTOBER 26, 1923[1]

Comrades! They quoted here my remark that there were controversies on a number of questions. But some comrades tried to interpret it as if I had written that the Party were torn up with disagreements of principle. I should remind you that what has been quoted is an excerpt from my response to Comrade Kuibyshev.[2] Comrade Kuibyshev accused me of being too energetic in the solution of the most serious questions and nearly reduced the whole thing to a matter of my temperament.[3] To show that it is not a matter of temperament, but a matter of deep differences in the approach to the solution of some questions, I had to enumerate these differences.

But Comrade Vareikis touched on a more general question concerning our foreign policy. I should tell you that the latest telegrams from Poland state that Trotsky's speech at the metal workers congress made bourgeois governments think that we are for peaceful policy.[4] Meanwhile the Politburo had no certain policy on the question of relationships with Poland. I made a demand for this certainty. Just imagine that I am speaking at a mass meeting. I don't speak as a mere Party member, do I? I speak as People's Commissar of War, being War Minister, whose words (and this is on the question of a possible war) are being attentively listened to by all the bour-geois governments. I am asked:Will the war break out or not? If I answer yes or no, it will have great consequences, won't it? I am asked and I should know what to answer, but to do it, the Politburo should have a cer-tain position in this respect; to do it, the question of the relationship with Poland should be clarified. I strove for that.[5] I confirm that my position was absolutely right.

There are two attitudes to my letter[6]: some say that Trotsky's speech is a bolt from the blue, something quite unexpected, which can be interpreted only as Trotsky's discontent with the membership of the Revolutionary Military Council.[7] Others say: Trotsky repeats what he has been saying for two years; nothing new has happened; it was so under Lenin, too.

Comrades, it was said here that private conferences were held for pre-liminary consideration of the question. One should take a certain position.

Of course, both of the two main opinions on my speech mentioned by me are wrong. There is an echo of the former controversies, but there are also new controversies, and the new situation aggravated them. I named both of them. When at the end of this year the actual situation proved that my opinion of the main fact of the economics of the country were right, I raised these questions again. It is sheer falsehood that I did not raise them at the Politburo. I did, here are the results. Rykov tried to convene a pri-vate conference. You have heard what came of this attempt.[8] Nothing has come of it.

And what then? As there is the other Politburo within the Politburo and as there is the other TsK within the TsK, I was removed from the actual dis-cussion of the question. But I had no opportunity to address other TsK members with the information. So only this way was left for me. Comrade Zinoviev said that I deviated from the attempt to agree, which Comrade Zi-noviev made through Serebryakov. Comrades, it is sheer childishness to put the question in this way. Just imagine. I have not seen Serebryakov for two years. Suddenly he comes to me with this suggestion. Of course, when he came to me, I answered him: "Why "pyatyorka"? Why should we in-clude Trotsky and Bukharin in the "troika"? We have the Politburo of the Central Committee, don't we? If Zinoviev is going to establish normal re-lations, both the"troika" and "pyatyorka" should be eliminated."[9]

Why didn't I pass the question through the TSKK? Comrades, they spoke a great deal here about "conventionalism." I won't repeat this word, but it is not out of place here. The TSKK members know a number of facts about the group contest of the so-called Trotskyists. The TSKK members know that "the Trotskyists" are being called those who are not fighting against Trotsky. Otherwise, what can "a Trotskyist" mean? I don't know any other interpretation. I have never washed TsK dirty linen in public, I have never told Party comrades about them, I did not try to unite them, or to organize a group or a faction. However, you know that recently there have been a number of replacements and removals of so-called Trotsky-ists.[10] Why could they be "Trotskyists"? Any groups or factions are out of the question. "The Trotskyist" is called a person who thought that we needed neither the "environment" of what Comrade Petrovsky said, nor that attitude to Trotsky in what Comrade Frunze said. The TSKK members knew about these replacements, about this attitude to "the Trotskyists," and there was no reaction by the TSKK to it. How could I, knowing all this, pass the question to the TSKK decision? I had no confidence in the TSKK majority, and I still do not. That is why I did not address the TSKK.

Some personal reasons that are of importance in this question make me treat the TSKK in this way and have made me avoid raising the question at the TSKK. Comrades, one should not forget that the Secretariat policy bearer, the policy that considered "a Trotskyist" everyone who has no ac-tive mistrust of Trotsky, was Comrade Kuibyshev. The adherent of this pol-icy was also Comrade Yaroslavsky. Now Comrades Kuibyshev and Yaroslavsky are TSKK members and direct its work. Let us see what comes of it. Let us regard some facts. The TSKK Presidium discussed the question of a Party member being guilty,[11] and this Party member was ac-cused of severe Party crimes; essential Party ethics and an impartial ap-proach to the case demand that this Party member's explanations be heard; however, they discuss the question and decide, but they do not call him to explain himself. It is natural of the TSKK, isn't it? Moreover, the TSKK Presidium and The TSKK members' conference is being held on the same question.[12] Again they discuss the question and decide. Did they invite me to this conference, did they give me the opportunity to explain myself and to clarify the facts? They did nothing of the kind.

Comrades, remember the essential idea of the TSKK establishment.[13] The TSKK should be an independent and highly impartial institution, im-proving defects and shortcomings in the work and excesses on the part of responsible Party officials.

I confirm that you have turned the TSKK into the TsK Secretariat weapon in this inner-Party contest. I confirm that you are misinterpreting

Vladimir Ilyich's idea, essential for its establishment. I did not address the TSKK., I did not pass the question raised by me for its decision. You are accusing me of that. This accusation, comrades, the accusation that I did not address the TSKK, the organ which I could not address, according to everything said above , is the very "conventionalism" that I am opposing.

Now, comrades, let us talk about the Bonapartism of which the Politburo members accuse me in their letter.[14] (*Comrade Kamenev*: "There was no such word in the letter.") Comrades, I cannot ignore the Politburo members' letter, as it is recommended by Comrade Kamenev: The members' letter says (I am quoting) that I want to add the authority in the sphere of the VSNKh to my authority in the War Department. Comrades, let us see who the "authorities" mentioned in the letter are. Of course, you all know that all the appointments in the army are carried out through the Organizational Bureau and the Politburo. All the work in the army, like everywhere, is executed by people. Just look at the personnel of the most responsible army figures. Look personally at who the heads of war districts are: Comrade Lashevich in Siberia, Comrade Voroshilov at the southeast, Comrade Frunze in the Ukraine, etc. Only in Moscow Muralov, an awful "Trotskyist," is occasionally the head of the district. Well, comrades, one can speak about my authority in the War Department in order to deceive provincials! Isn't it clear to you?

They say that I spoke at the Twelfth Congress that the army was drawing together with the Party, the links were tighter and, in general, the army was all right,[15] and now I am saying the opposite. Nothing of the kind. I spoke at the congress and I am repeating it now that this process of drawing together is going on. I don't reject any of these words. I meant a different thing, speaking about abnormalities in the army work. I spoke on the conditions of my own work. And these conditions are as follows. Every person who is working with me and who, with no group or political considerations, can work with just me, is immediately under suspicion as "a Trotskyist." But, comrades,I never speak on Party questions even with my closest colleagues, for example, Comrade Sklyansky, with whom I spoke for nearly two hours daily and see on business. I repeat, I never do this. And here comrades, is this picture in which they deprive me of the people with whom I can work, and surround me with people who are actively against me; it is the picture of complete isolation, isn't it? And this is "the unlimited authority" in the sphere of the War Department!

Now to the VSNKh. I don't refuse the work in the VSNKh. I could manage the VSNKh no worse than many other comrades. And when Comrade Bukharin told me about my work in the VSNKh, I did not tell him that I was against it; I answered that it was impossible to combine this job with the military office.

I should describe for you, comrades, my conversation with Vladimir Ilyich, when I spoke with him about my being a deputy[16] and other things. The thing is, comrades, that there is a personal element in my work, which, being of no importance in my private life, so to speak, is of great political importance in my everyday life. This is my Jewish origin. I remember quite well that on October 25, 1917, lying on the floor in the Smolny, Vladimir Ilyich said: "Comrade Trotsky! We will make you People's Commissar for Internal Affairs. You will crush the bourgeoisie and nobility." I opposed. I said that, in my opinion, one should not place such a trump card in our enemies; I thought that it would be much better if there were no Jews in the first revolutionary Soviet government. Vladimir Ilyich said, "Nonsense. Never mind!" But despite his attitude, my arguments seemed to have influenced him somehow. At any rate, I avoided the appointment to the post of People's Commissar for Internal Affairs and was appointed leader of our foreign policy,[17] though, by the way, this also I opposed no less resolutely. When it was necessary to organize our military forces, they chose me; I should say that I opposed the office of People's Commissar of War still more resolutely. Well, comrades, after all my work done in this sphere, I can tell with certainty that I was right. I won't talk about direct results of my work; you know that I fulfilled my duties and you will evaluate my work positively. But, comrades, perhaps I could have done much more, if this element did not intrude in my work and did not interfere with it. Remember what a hindrance it was in some acute moments during Yudenich's, Kolchak's, and Vrangel's offensives, how our enemies in their agitation used the fact that the Red Army was headed by a Jew. It interfered greatly. Comrades, I should repeat once again that in y private life this fact meant nothing; it is very serious as a political moment. I have never forgotten this. Vladimir Ilyich considered it to be my "eccentricity," and he often said in conversations with me and with other comrades that it was my "eccentricity." And that time, when Vladimir Ilyich proposed that I should be the Deputy of the Chairman of the Soviet of People's Commissars* (the only deputy) and I refused resolutely for the same reasons, in order not to

---

*Sovnarkom. The Chairman of the SNR was Lenin. (Ed.)

give our enemies cause for confirming that a Jew governed the country, Vladimir Ilyich almost agreed with me. To tell the truth, outwardly he did not show that and kept repeating, as usual: "Nonsense, rubbish," but I felt that he said it in a different way, that in his heart he agreed with me.

Why wasn't I a member of the SNK or of the STO? Comrades, the thing is that I feared above all making the impression that Trotsky was organizing a faction. But at one time Vladimir Ilyich feared that. After the Tenth Congress Vladimir Ilyich was on his guard. When I felt that, I visited him specially for the purpose of telling him that there was nothing of the kind. We had a long conversation, and I think I convinced him that I was not organizing any groups or factions and had no intention of doing so. Comrades, I did not deceive him. I did not publicize anything that could have been interpreted as controversial or as criticism of the actions of the Central Committee. When the controversies on the economic questions became aggravated, I had to inform the TsK members about them. Here the question of the State Planning Commission was of primary importance.

I think, comrades, that there should be an office that should work at every question from the aspect of economic planned coordination before bringing them in to the decision of the supreme Soviet and Party organs. If there is no such office, if there is no such preliminary work, how can we solve such problems? I don't understand this at all. Personally I could not vote at the Politburo, if experienced people, who know the matter inside out, did not work at these questions. I cannot base my opinion on those dull, semiconventional accompanying sheets of paper, which the delivered papers mostly are. And if I am not sure that this economic question is considered and interpreted from the aspect of plan and coordinations, I cannot vote. That is why, comrades, recently I have often abstained from voting on the most important economic questions at the Politburo.

If I were discharged from some work and were appointed to the State Planning Commission, I would not oppose. I confirm that our crises are 50 percent, 75 percent, maybe 100 percent aggravated by the nonplanned approach to the problems of our economy. The State Planning Commission is our most important organ. But you heard, comrades, that, according to Comrade Kamenev, it is "not too good." We cannot go far with the "not too good" State Planning Commission. If this "not too good" commission is not reorganized, the most important problems of our economy will be solved, as usual, occasionally and unsystematically; as usual, there will be no plan, and, as usual, both ends will not meet. Comrades, it is no exag-

geration to say that this is the most important question now. I am returning to the question: what shall I don in the SNK or in the STO, if the State
Planning Commission is not reorganized? I should either have taken the responsibility of carefully carrying out preliminary work on the questions,
which, of course, is practically impossible, or shifted this responsibility
from the Politburo to the SNK or to the STO. Here my personal attributes
should be taken into account. It is my peculiarity that I cannot subscribe
any illiterately written document, be it an order or something else, be it
merely illiterate or economically illiterate. I don't stand for inaccuracy,
thoughtlessness, or an offhand approach. Perhaps it is very bad, but, I repeat, this is my peculiarity and I cannot be a different person. Then, my
working day is always busy enough. I don't spend time in vain. Here I
should draw aside with indignation all the insinuations concerning my
work on the study of the questions concerning my private life.[18] For this
work, which, in the end, is not superfluous at all, I did not take a minute
of my working time; I carried it out during my holiday in Kislovodsk,
which was granted me for my convalescence. Thus, comrade, the only way
out of this situation that I see, is to reorganize the office and only in this
way can better working conditions be made.

I now turn to the inner-Party situation. Here the Ukrainians dotted all
the i's.[19] Comrade Mantsev moved them. His information meets the logic
of the situation. What Comrade Frunze said does not meet the logic of the
situation; it meets it only in the part about "the environment." The situation has been created, when Trotsky speaks and, what is more, he speaks
for "democratism." Comrades, you know quite well that I have never been
"a democrat." This does not mean that I did not allow a critical thought and
ignored my colleagues' opinion. Here is an example. You remember that
military circles had long talks about the uniform military doctrine, which
was enthusiastically supported by Comrade Frunze.[20] I should tell you
that I did not understand the meaning of that uniform military doctrine
then, I don't understand now, and, generally speaking, I doubt whether
there is anybody who can understand it. It is best characterized like Yenchmenism[21] in military science. But despite my negative attitude to this uniform military doctrine, Comrade Frunze and I carried on quite friendly
polemics, and when the polemics were over, we collected our articles and
edited them as a separate brochure.[22]

Here is another example. They say that despite the fact that the conference of military commanders was for the removal of Arzhanov, I don't

implement the idea and delay it. You should know that Arzhanov is not an attractive person, having a very nasty past. He is a former officer, who is said to have shot Reds in Turkestan. He is not loved and as for my attitude to him, he is as close to me, as, say Sologub or Arens. My personal sympathy for him is out of the question. But the thing is that he should be replaced. While having a number of shortcomings, this person of the adventurer type possesses the great virtue in that he is extremely energetic and he will fulfill any work assigned to him. For example, if he were ordered to transfer some millions *poods* of grain to Germany, he would fulfill the task, despite everything, and 100 percent. *A voice*: "And he would do more harm than good." Well, quite right, I don't argue. It is quite possible that he would a lot of harm doing this, but he would fulfill the task, and I am giving this example to show his great capacity for work, his energy and expedition. As soon as the conference of military commanders had decided to replace him, I agreed immediately. But he should be replaced at the post of the head of the Chief Directorate of Supplies for the Red Army. They appointed Comrade Dmitriev to be his assistant, as it is a big and complicated task and he should become familiar with it. They thought that when he became familiar with the work, they would appoint him to take Arzhanov's place. Dmitriev worked for three months. But it turned out that he was not cut out for this work. They began to look for other candidatures. They promoted Kolegaev. But this candidacy fell away, as he is ill and he could not begin to work for many months. At last, they chose Comrade Oskin, discharged him, and appointed the assistant. Now he is getting familiar with the work. When he becomes adequately familiar with it, we will appoint him. It is a matter of time. It is clear, comrades, that the essence of the matter is to offer the replacement, to find the replacement, and it is monstrous to make it a disagreement on principle.

Now about that incident with the record on a sheet of paper of Voroshilov's words about Rumania, which has been mentioned here. I have good memory, but I completely forgot about it; even if it happened, it must have been a trifle; I attached too little importance to it then, and I quite forgot about it.

Comrades, I don't patent democratism. But the situation that I found on my arrival after two months' holiday, made me scrutinize the question. The facts testify that the situation speaks for itself. Comrades, these records of the Politburo session from October 11,[23] which I read, are a fact, aren't they?

The situation demands a way out. One alternative should be chosen: either a turn to Party democracy (I won't repeat Comrade Bukharin's "a sudden turn of the helm"; no, just the turn), or to acknowledge that it is prospering. They also say that I made all this up to organize a faction. When? What moment? What for? Where? Perhaps, in the army? Express it in full, call it Bonapartism!

I repeat: When I, having come back from my holiday, found such a situation, when I thought over and tested my impressions through a dozen experienced comrades (and you know that due to my official position any other way of sounding out the Party opinion is very difficult for me), I said: let there be less criminal investigation and more planning. You are going to condemn me for this.

Comrades, I will speak frankly. There are comrades in the Politburo who are going to carry out the matter—i.e., to keep stirring up controversies—they are striving to let Party masses know about the matter and to make the further common work impossible.

I think that the TsK and Party majority don't want it. But the one-sided decision which is being prepared here and which will be proposed for your decision,[24] very probably, will be decided. I fear that it will create the ground for those who are going to eliminate conditions for further common collective work.

Comrades, before voting for it, try to think over and understand my situation. I found myself in very complicated circumstances. I could not oppose those who left the impression that I was fighting against Vladimir Ilyich's traditions. Comrades, I was in a desperate plight, in a really tragic situation. While this net was entangling me, I could not explain anything, I could not tell the truth to anybody, I could not accept the battle. But this net should have been torn up.

At that moment, perhaps the most decisive moment of the world's history, anyone who suspected me of personal motives, of the ridiculous striving to shoulder all the enormous responsibility by myself, would take me for a thorough rascal and a complete man.

Comrades, think well before your decision. If you choose the way you seem to be choosing, you will make a blunder.

B.V. Bazhanov's autograph
RTsHIDNI, f. 17, op. 2, d. 685,
1. 39-49. First published in Voprosy istorii KPSS, 1990,
No. 5, pp. 33–39.[25]

NOTES

1. The document is titled by B.V. Bazhanov. Note 1 to the previous document said that he deciphered and made a fair copy of the rough draft only of Trotsky's speech, he seems to have done it immediately after the evening session on October 26, as all the texts (rough and finished ones) are written with the same pen, and with the same (red) ink on the same paper.

    The text of the published speech could not be preserved in Trotsky's private archive, as it was spoken impromptu, being a direct and immediate response to the accusations in speeches and particularly in the draft resolution presented by A.F. Radchenko and expressing the "troika" attitude. Trotsky could not know about the existence of "the summary" of his speech, otherwise, he first would not have left it without correcting it; but the text has not a single correction. Secondly, according to a strictly followed rule, Trotsky would have had its duplicate in his archive. One can suggest with a great degree of probability that Bazhanov wrote down and rewrote Trotsky's speech on Stalin's behalf.

2. The reference is to the talk between V.V. Kuibyshev and Trotsky, after the latter left the RKP (b) TsK Plenum Session on September 25, 1923, where they examined the question of the extension of the membership of the Republic Revolutionary Military Council on account of having inducted six TsK members into it (see documents No. 2 and 5).

3. The reference is to V. V. Kuibyshev's memo to the TsK and TSKK members dating October 7, 1923 (see document No. 3).

4. On October 20, 1923, Trotsky delivered a report about the international situation and the prospects of the revolution in Germany at Moscow "guberniya" conference of the metal workers trade union, where, in particular, he said: "We should take all the measures to avoid the war, and this means first of all that we should intensify and increase tenfold our usual routine work" (*Pravda*, October 21, 1923).

5. See note 39 to document No. 20.

6. The reference is to Trotsky's letter to the TsK and TSKK members dated October 8 (see document No. 4), which had been declared by the Plenum to be a factional platform in the TsK and TSKK documents.

7. See the resolution of the RKP (b) TsK September Plenum (Document No. 1).

8. Trotsky describes the conference in his letter to the TSKK Presidium and to the TsK Politburo of October 19, 1923 (see document No. 16).

9. See note 3 to document No. 2, and also document No. 29. In this speech at the Plenum it was Trotsky who first overtly declared the existence of factional blocs within the TsK, carrying out their apparatus policy to TsK and TSKK members.

10. Apparently, Trotsky is referring to: breaking up of the Ukrainian government with Kh. G. Rakovsky at the head and the "banishment" of the latter to diplomatic work in England; the "shaking up" of *Pravda*'s editorial board by Stalin and the removal of E. A. Preobrazhensky from it, and other facts.

11. Trotsky is referring to the resolution of the RKP (b) TSKK Presidium of October 15, 1923, where the question about his letter to the RKP(b) TsK and TSKK members dated October 8 was examined (see document No. 11).

12. Trotsky is referring to the session of the TSKK Presidium of October 17, 1923,

where twenty-six members and candidates to TSKK membership present in Moscow at that time participated. They discussed V. V. Kuibyshev's and E. M. Yaroslavsky's information about Trotsky's letter. The following resolution was adopted: "Without considering each item of the TSKK Presidium resolution, the conference in general shares the evaluation of the incident made by the TSKK Presidium and its position of the question" (RTsHIDNI, f. 17, op. 2, d. 685, 1.102).

13. The Central Control Commission (TSKK). See the List of Abbreviations. It was set up, according to Lenin's recommendation, as an independent institution "responsible only to the Party congress. . . . (Lenin V. I. *Poln. sobr. soch.* [*The Complete Works*], vol. 45, p. 200). Here and in the next paragraph Trotsky refers to Lenin's recommendations set forth in his article "How We Should Reorganize the Workers's and Peasants' Inspection" (see note 9 to Document No. 5 and note 24 to Document No. 20).

14. Trotsky is referring to the Response by the Politburo members and candidates of October 19, 1923 (see Document No. 17).

15. In his concluding speech on the report on industry, Trotsky said: "Relationships between the army and the Party have changed during these years in their organizing form. There was a period when the Party formed calvary squadrons, infantry regiments in provinces, and "uyezd" and "guberniya" committees carried out this work. . . . Now our troops are organized as divisions and corps and have their own centralized organization which does not coincide with the organization of "guberniya" and "uyezd" committees. But from the political aspect of the army, the Party supremacy in it both through the Party apparatus and through the local Party committees, judging by the army's mood has never been so full, so complete, so deep, so indisputable as at the present" (*Dvenadstyi syezd RKP[b]. Stenograficheskii otchet* [*The Twelfth RKP(b) Congress. The Stenographic Report*], p. 147).

16. Deputy. The reference is to the post of Deputy of the Chairman of the SNK offered to Trotsky by Lenin. There is no documentary evidence about the precise date of this talk. In his work on Trotsky I. Deutscher dates it to April 11, 1922 (I. Deutscher *The Prophet Unarmed, Trotsky: 1921-1929*, p. 35). See also note 9 to document No. 17.

17. In the first Soviet government (SNK) Trotsky took the post of People's Commissar for Foreign Affairs, which he held until the spring of 1918. Then he was appointed People's Commissar of War and from the autumn of 1918 he was chairman of the established Revolutionary Military Council of the Republic.

18. The reference is to Trotsky's brochure "Voprosy byta. Epokha kulturnichestva i yeyo zadachi" (The Problems of the Way of Life. The Epoch of Culture-Mongering and Its Tasks). M., 1923.

19. Trotsky is referring to the draft resolution offered to the Plenum on behalf of the Ukrainian delegation by the candidate to the RKP(b) TSKK members, A. F. Radchenko.

20. In 1921 in Kharkov M.V. Frunze's brochure "Edinaya voennaya doktrina i Krasnaya Armiya" (The Uniform Military Doctrine and the Red Army) was issued.

21. Yenchmenism. A biological theory which attempted to unite the ideas of reflexology, developed by I.P. Pavlov, with Kantianism and Machism. Its founder, E. S. Yenchmen, thought that the man was "a system of organic movements" possessing physiological reactions without the participation of a psyche. These views were criticized in N. I. Bukharin's work "Yenchmeniada (K voprusu ob ideologicheskom vyrozhdenii)" (The Yenchmeniade [The Problem of Ideological Degeneration], Krasnaya Nov. 6, [1923]). In

this context, Trotsky seems to refer to a certain inherency of the formulation "the uniform military doctrine."

22. Trotsky seems to be referring to his and M.V. Frunze's polemics at the conference of military delegates of the Eleventh RKP(b) Congress in April 1922 and the book *Osnovnaya voennaya zadacha momenta. Diskussiya na temu o edinoy voennoy doktrine. Stenograficheskii otchet 2-go dnya soveshchaniya voennykh delegatov XI's ezda RKP 1 aprelya 1922 g. (The Main Military Task of the Moment. The Discussion on the Topic of the Uniform Military Doctrine. The Stenographic Report of the 2nd Day of the Conference of Military Delegates of the Eleventh RKP Congress on April 1, 1922)*. M., 1922.

23. At the session of the TsK Politburo of October 11, 1923, the question of Trotsky's letter to the RKP(b) TsK and TSKK members from October 8, 1923, was discussed (see document No. 6). In this episode the reference is to the records made by Trotsky at the Politburo session and used by him in the letter to the RKP (b) TsK and TSKK members of October 23, 1923 (see document No. 20).

24. The reference is to the resolution of the RKP (b) TsK and TSKK Plenum published below (see the next document). The basis of the resolution was the draft proposed by A. F. Radchenko, candidate to the TSKK members, and expressing the "troika" position. The remaining draft resolutions were rejected.

25. Besides being the author of the publication and the comments, V. P. Danilov (Dr. SC., History) took part in the preparation of the document for its first publication in *Voprosy istorii KPSS*.

III. THE RESOLUTION OF THE JOINT PLENUM OF THE TSK AND THE TSKK OF THE RKP(b). OCTOBER 25-27, 1923

On The Question of the Internal Party Situation, in Connection with The Letters Of Comrade Trotsky[1]

a) On the statements of Comrade Trotsky and forty six comrades (Preobrazhensky, Osinsky, Sapronov et al.).
(Adopted by: 102 for; 2 against; 10 abstentions)[2]

1. The Plenums of the TsK, TSKK, and representatives of the ten largest Party organizations (Petrograd, Moscow, Ivanovo-Vosnesensk, Nizhny Novgorod, Kharkov, Donetsk, Yekaterinburg, Rostov, Baku, and Tula), having discussed during a common session accusations put forward

by Comrade Trotsky and the forty-six against the Politburo, entirely endorse the political line and practical work of the Politburo, Orgburo, and secretariat, and regard the response of the majority of the Politburo members as in essence correct.[3]

2. The Plenums of the TsK, TSKK, and the representatives of the ten Party organizations regard the intervention of Comrade Trotsky, made at this crucial moment through which the international revolution and our Party are now passing, as a severe political mistake, especially since Comrade Trotsky's attack, directed against the Politburo, objectively took on the character of a factional fight, threatening to deal a blow to Party unity, and creating a crisis in the Party. With regret, the Plenum ascertains that Comrade Trotsky chose to raise his questions through an appeal to individual Party members, instead of the only permissible way, that of first raising these questions before the bodies of which Comrade Trotsky is a member.

The path chosen by Comrade Trotsky served as a signal for a factional grouping (The Declaration of Forty-Six).

3. The Plenums of the TsK, TSKK, and the representatives of ten Party organizations resolutely condemn the Declaration of the Forty-Six as a step in a factional-splitting policy, even if it acquired this character irrespective of the intentions of the signatories of this statement. This Declaration threatens to place all of Party life in the coming months under the sign of an internal fight, thereby weakening the Party at a moment crucial for the fate of international revolution.

4. Regarding as its self-evident duty to guarantee, in accordance with Party statutes, the right of every Party member to critically analyze the policy of the TsK, both as a whole and in its separate decisions, this gathering considers as necessary a fight against inner-Party factional groupings and their disruptive activities. This gathering expresses its confidence that the TSKK will take all measures necessary for Party unity, so that the internal fight which has already begun, will not in the future go beyond limits acceptable inside the Party in the current tense moment of discussion among comrades.

5. The Plenums of the TsK, TSKK, and representatives of the ten Party organizations consider it critically necessary to propose to Comrade Trotsky that he in the future participate more closely and directly in the practical work of all Party and Soviet organs of which he is a member.

6. The gathering realizes that in the given situation the Politburo could not ban the distribution of the letter of Comrade Trotsky and the forty-six,

which was directed precisely against the Politburo. The gathering regards the Politburo as having chosen an altogether correct path for the preservation of Party unity by rejecting the transfer of the dispute to broad discussion,[4] and calling for an immediate special Plenum. The gathering, having acquainted itself with all the materials, now takes onto itself the responsibility to stop the factional discussion that has begun. The gathering considers that we have already entered what can be described as a period of direct combat (the events in Germany, potential wars).[5] The Plenums of the TsK, TSKK, and representatives of the ten Party organizations are confident that, in forbidding factional discussion on the basis of platforms at the current moment, they are expressing the opinion of the whole Party.

7. The gathering thinks that in the coming period of crucial decisions, the Politburo should be especially concerted and undivided in its work. At the same time, the gathering considers that the revolutionary duty of all active Party workers is to provide full confidence and steadfast support for the Central Committee in this difficult time.

b) On internal Party democracy
(Passed unanimously)

The Plenums endorse completely the course to internal democracy, opportunely projected by the Politburo, as well as the suggested intensification of struggle against excesses and the corrupt influence of the NEP on certain elements in the Party.[6]

The Plenums instruct the Politburo to do all that is necessary for the acceleration of the work of the following commissions formed by the Politburo and September Plenum: (1) the commission on "scissors," (2) on wages, (3) on the internal situation.

The Politburo must work out necessary measures on these problems, start to carry them out immediately, and make a report to the next Plenum of the TsK.[7]

RTsHIDNI, f.17, op.2, d.104,
1.1–4; typewritten text. First published
in full in the journal *Izvestiya TsK KPSS*,
1990, No. 10, pp.188–189.

Notes

1. The participants of the joint Plenum of the TsK and TSKK were offered three draft resolutions for vote. The first version, adopted by the Plenum, was proposed on behalf of the Ukrainian delegation by a candidate TSKK member, A. F. Radchenko. This resolution absorbed all formulations and evaluations Trotsky's letter and of The Declaration of Forty-Six made in previous documents of the TsK and TSKK, as well as in Stalin's final speech to the Plenum. The resolution of the Plenum was not published in full until 1990.

2. Cited in the resolution, the results of the vote which on Trotsky's demand was by roll call, do not correspond to the results cited in the minutes. According to the minutes, out of 117 people who participated in the vote, seven voted for the draft proposed by N. K. Goncharov (see Document No. 21:IV) and one for the draft proposed by E. A.Preobrazhensky (see Document No. 21:V). Twelve people abstained from the vote (RTsHIDNI, f.17, op.2, d.104, 1. 25).

We should note one important circumstance. In order to provide maximum support for the resolution condemning Trotsky and the Group of forty-six, the "leading nucleus" of the TsK resorted to a straight violation of the Party rules, granting the right of decisive vote during the Plenum to the invited representatives of ten Party organizations (twenty people).

3. The October 19, 1923 reply of members and candidate members of the Politburo to Trotsky's letter of October 8 (see Document No.17).

4. Analysis of the whole complex of documents relating to the October period of the 1923 discussion testifies that the factional "leading nucleus of the TsK," headed by the "troika,"had made all possible efforts to ensure that the discussion, which started in the upper echelons of the Party power, would take an all-Party character. The resolution, adopted by the Plenum, reflected the position of the "majority" and set the tone and direction for further discussion on the documents of the opposition, switching the attention of Communists from truly pressing problems of internal Party life to the opposition's "guilt" for its "factionalism and striving to split the Party."

5. This refers to the revolutionary struggles of the German proletariat, which unfolded by the fall of 1923, and possible war with Poland "in the event of the necessity to give help to the German workers."

6. Corresponding circular of October 19, 1923.

7. The summing up of the internal discussion took place at the TsK Plenum of January 14–15, 1924 and at the Thirteenth Party Conference (January 16-18, 1924). The resolution, adopted by the joint Plenum of the TsK and TSKK on October 26, 1923, in fact determined the results of the discussion.

IV. N. K. GONCHAROV'S DRAFT RESOLUTION ON THE INTERNAL SITUATION[1]

With the beginning of the era of international revolution, the epoch of the transitional period with its extremely complex contradictions in the economy and, consequently, in social relations, is fraught with particularly sharp disagreements in the assessment of separate elements of concrete policy by leading Party activists, as well as during the solution of those extremely complicated current and new practical problems faced by the TsK RKP.

Bearing this in mind, the joint Plenum of the TsK and TSKK underlines the critical need for a very careful attitude toward the bringing to light of disagreements in the leading organs of the Party. The unity of the Party's will is more necessary at the current time than ever before.

At the same time, the Plenum underlines that during the solution of the most important questions, it is necessary to use more widely the experience and collective thinking of the most responsible Party workers. The drawing in of collective thinking for discussion of the questions faced now by the leading organs of the Party will stimulate maximum initiative of the whole Party, which is the most important condition for the victory of the revolution.

The Plenum draws Comrade Trotsky's attention to the anxiety which emerged in the Party in relation to his letter[2]; on the other hand, the Plenum proposes to the Politburo to establish a more friendly attitude toward Comrade Trotsky.

It is proposed that Comrade Trotsky participate more actively in the supreme state organs; at the same time, it is proposed that the Politburo provide Comrade Trotsky's work with the necessary attention by the cadres of those organs. The Orgburo is charged to improve the use of all Party forces, and the most important posts in the Party and state must be urgently revised in order to reinforce them with otherwise insufficiently occupied Party activists; in this work Comrade Trotsky must participate.

RTsHIDNI, f.17, op.2, d.104,
1.63; certified true typewritten copy.
Published for the first time.

NOTES

1. As we noted in note 1 to the document 21: III, seven Plenum participants voted for this draft resolution proposed by TsK RKP(b) member N. K. Goncharov. Probably, it was that part of the attendants who shared the opposition's anxiety about the state of affairs in the Party. The suggested resolution is in fact an attempt to direct the Plenum onto the path of seeking a compromise, to overcome the disagreements on the basis of constructive collaboration and to prevent a further deepening of the split at the "top."

2. Trotsky's letter of October 8, 1923 (see document No.4).

V. YE. A. PREOBRAZHENSKY'S DRAFT RESOLUTION ON THE INTERNAL SITUATION[1]

The current course of Party policy stands in manifest contradiction with those tasks which we face now in the sphere of internal work. There are objective signs of this disparity in the Party sphere: dying down of the life and initiative of organizations, particularly lower ones; virtual exclusion of the huge mass of Party members from participation in Party life and from preparation of decisions; the transfer of all work and responsibility to the narrow circle of Party functionaries; the growth of bureaucratism and carrierism; the cessation of living exchange of opinions on the questions which are most vital and current for the rank-and-file Communists; the growth of indifference toward the internal life and total silence on the one hand, and the disillusionment and bitterness of groups of discontented comrades on the other; the intensification of activity of the anti-Party organizations like "Workers Truth"[2] and the impossibility for our Party to use all available means for ideological fight against them.

As a result, the Party, while formally securing its unity, enters a period of forthcoming struggles and tests internationally with less fighting capacity than it could have in the case of the correct course of internal Party policy.

For the struggle against all these objective consequences of the current course of the Party policy, in order to fulfill resolutions of Tenth Party Congress about the Party's work[3] and for effective realization of the principle of workers' democracy in our Party life, we propose to the Plenum of the TsK and TSKK to carry out following measures:

1. The cessation of the practice by which the leaders of the Party bodies are to be appointed from above and reestablishment of the fundamental principle of the election of officials and executive bodies of Party organizations. The guarantee of real and permanent control of the work of the leading organs by members of Party organizations through reestablishment of the practice by which regional and district conferences are to be called periodically, no fewer than two times a year, and Party committees should systematically report back to the local cells and Party-wide assemblies.

2. The guarantee of the freedom of expression of opinions—individual, as well as collective—in the Party. The lifting of the virtual ban of discussions which is a basic form of internal practice, the revival of activity of Party clubs and Party press in this direction.

3. Real fulfillment of resolutions of several Party congresses about involvement of the Party periphery into active work.[4] This periphery should become not only a transmission from top bodies to the workers' masses, but also the environment in which the Party's public opinion is being worked out on the basis of a connection with the masses. The broad discussion of all questions of the Party policy and economic life in all part organizations: questions should be put up for discussion not only by recommendations of the Party committees but also by the initiative of the cells and individual comrades.

4. The cessation of the existing system of the selection of officials when it is often being carried out not according to the extent of their suitability for one or another kind of work, but rather according to the extent of their obedience of law. It breeds negative phenomena like cringing, carrierism, etc. In order to fight these undesirable phenomena it is necessary to radically change the character of the work of the attestation commissions and registration-distribution departments.

5. The revision of transfers and appointments that were done out of factional consideration and revocation of those that were and remain particularly harmful.

RTsHIDNI, f.17, op. 2, d.104,
1. 67; certified true typewritten copy.
Published for the first time.

NOTES

1. This draft resolution, which expressed opposing views on internal Party problems and was proposed by the Party veteran, prominent Party journalist and economist E. A. Preobrazhensky, received only one vote. However, it was this draft that to the greatest extent corresponded to the real state of affairs in the RKP(b), and it did not at all pose the question of the lifting of the ban on factions, of which the opposition will be accused later. The measures for making internal life more healthy, listed in the draft, coincided in essence with those recommended by the Tenth Party Congress as far back as in 1921 (see *CPSU in Resolutions*, vol. 2, pp. 329–330).

2. About the illegal group "Workers Truth," see note 5 to Document No. 4 and note 6 to Document No. 20.

3. It refers to the resolution of the Tenth Congress of the RKP(b) "On the Questions of Party Building" (see *CPSU in Resolutions*, vol.2, pp.323–334).

4. The question of the involvement of local Party organizations in active work pointed both to the resolution of the Tenth Congress "On the Questions of the Party Building" and to the resolution of the Eleventh Congress "About Strengthening of the Party and Its New Tasks" as well as in the others (see *CPSU in Resolutions*, vol. 2, pp. 329, 502 et passim).

22

N. K. Krupskaya's Letter to G.Ye. Zinovyev

October 31, 1923

Dear Gregory, after the Plenum[1] I wrote a letter to you, but you were away and the letter sat. Now on rereading it, I've decided not to send it, so sharply posed are all the questions. In the atmosphere of "loosened tongues"[2] which prevailed at the Plenum, it was appropriate and understood, after a week it sounds different.

I will explain what was written in the letter.

You understand that before the Osinskys, the Rafails and Co.,[3] I could not intervene in any other way than I did.

But in all this disgrace—you agree that the entire incident is a sheer disgrace—the blame is far from being only Trotsky's. For all that happened the blame falls also on our group: you, Stalin and Kamenev.[4] You, of course, could but didn't want to, prevent this shame. If you could *not* do it, this would prove the complete impotence of our group, its complete helplessness. No, it's not a question of impossibility but of unwillingness. We ourselves took a wrong and intolerable tone. It is wrong to create an atmosphere of such squabbling and personal accounts.

Workers—I don't mean workers like Yevdokimov or Zalutsky who are workers by birth but long ago became professionals,[5] but rather workers from plants and factories—would harshly condemn not only Trotsky, but also us. Healthy class instinct would compel them to speak out sharply against both sides, but still more sharply against our group which is *responsible* for the general tone.

That is why everybody was so afraid that all this squabble would be carried into the masses. We have to *hide* the whole incident[6] from the workers. But leaders who have something to hide from the workers (I am not speaking of purely conspiratorial affairs, that is another matter) don't dare to tell them whole truth—what does it means? This is impossible. Also absolutely intolerable was that abuse in Ilyich's name, which took place at the Plenum. I imagine how indignant he would be, if he knew about abuses in his name. Fortunately, I wasn't around when Petrovsky said that Trotsky is responsible for Ilyich's illness, I would have screamed: this is a lie, most of all, V. I. [Vladimir Ilyich—*Ed.*], worried not about Trotsky, but about the national question[7] and about the manners which have become common in our top ranks.[8] You know that V. I. saw the danger of split not only in Trotsky's personal characteristics but also in those of Stalin and others.[9] And since you know this, the references to Ilyich were insincere and impermissible. We should not have permitted them. They were hypocritical. As for me, those references brought me unbearable torment. I thought, is it worth it for him to recover when his closest comrades treat him in this way? They think so little of his opinion, they misrepresent it.

And now the main point. The moment is too serious to have a split and make Trotsky's work psychologically impossible. We should try to come to an agreement with him *in a comradely manner.* Formally the whole odium for the split is now heaped on Trotsky, but as a matter of fact, wasn't Trotsky driven to this? I don't know the details, but this is not a question of details—you often can't see the forest for the trees. The simple fact of the matter is that we should take Trotsky into account as a force in the Party, and try to create such a situation, where this force would be of maximum use for the Party.

So, now I have told you what I have in my heart.

V. I. recently read the announcement about *Zvezda* and about his article in it.[10] He wants to get it as soon as it is published. He obviously remembers this article. I would ask you very much, that the issue with Ilyich's article be sent me right after its publication.

With all my best,

N. Krupskaya.

Autograph.

Printed according to the text of the
first publication in the journal *Izvestiya TsK KPSS*,
1989, No. 2, pp. 201–202.11

NOTES

1. This refers to the joint Plenum of the TsK and TSKK RKP(b) that was held October 25-27, 1923 (see Document No. 21:1–V).

2. In the explosive, polemical atmosphere the participants of the discussion sometimes were going beyond permissible limits, permitting themselves tactless lunges such as, for example, G. I. Petrovsky's accusation that Trotsky was responsible for Lenin's disease, made at the second session of October 25. Speaking of "loosened tongues," "squabbles and personal accounts," N. K. Krupskaya perhaps meant precisely that, as well as harsh lunges against Trotsky, which she, judging by the second part of the letter, didn't endorse.

3. This refers to representatives of the former group of "democratic centralism," the most radical wing of opposition, who, together with others, signed the Declaration of Forty-Six (see also note 8 to Document No. 35).

4. Probably, in her intervention at the Plenum, N. K. Krupskaya supported the "majority." The fact that she became a participant of, as she put it, "this disgrace," tortured her and forced her to explain herself in writing to G. E. Zinoviev. Having been almost permanently by the side of the ailing Lenin, Krupskaya could not know about all the undercover apparatus intrigues staged by the "troika" around Trotsky. But she accurately guessed the "troika," having named G. E. Zinoviev, Stalin, and L. B. Kamenev and having accused them in "intolerability of tone" and of creating the atmosphere which reigned at the Plenum.

5. Professional means here a Party functionary who is devoting himself to Party work only and living on the Party's means. This expression had been in use since pre-revolutionary times.

6. The incident was a split in the Politburo and TsK, for which, in Krupskaya's opinion, the working class, if it learned about it, would condemn the Party leadership.

7. See V. I. Lenin, *K voprosu o natsionalnostyakh ili ob avtonomizatsii* (*On the Question of Nationality and about "Autonomization"*), in *Complete Works*, vol. 45, pp. 356–362. Lenin asked Trotsky to take on himself the defense of the "Georgian affair" at the Plenum of the TsK in a letter of March 5, 1923. (Ibid., pp. 485, 607)

8. As follows from Lenin's last letters and articles, he worried very much about the danger of a split in the TsK. This question was concerned first of all with the relationship between Stalin and Trotsky. In order to prevent a possible split and the danger of bureaucratization of the apparatus, Lenin proposed to carry out "a number of changes in our political system" (see V. I. Lenin, *Complete Works*, vol. 45, pp. 343–348, 383–388).

9. This given phrase of N. K. Krupskaya testifies that the Letter to the Congress (or at least parts of it, dictated December 23-25, 1923), which Lenin asked his personal secretaries to keep strictly secret while he was alive, was known to a narrow circle of Politburo

members. It was in the text dictated on December 25 that Lenin gave individual descriptions of the most prominent Party leaders, having stressed that in the personal characteristics of Stalin and Trotsky he saw the danger of split in the TsK. Hence Krupskaya's accusation of hypocrisy against the Party leaders.

10. Lenin's article "About a Caricature of Marxism and 'Imperialist Economism' " was published in the journal *Zvezda*, 1924, No. 1–2. After receiving this journal, Krupskaya read his article to Lenin.

11. G. A. Bordyugov and V. N. Stepanov took part in the preparation of the first publication of this document.

23

I. V. Stalin's Answers to the Questions Directed at Him at the Enlarged Meeting of the Party Activists of the Party Organization of the Krasnopresnensky District of Moscow[1]

December 2, 1923

(Stalin). The note that has a relation to Comrade Trotsky: "Tell me what ground the rumors about Comrade Trotsky's letter have among the Party members. What is its essence[2]? Stop making it secret. Report to me.

Comrades: With the best will in the world I cannot disclose the contents of Comrade Trotsky's letter, which was read before the October plenary meeting. There is also a letter of forty-six comrades, among whom was Comrade Stukov. I have no right to disclose the contents of these two letters because the October plenary meetings of the TsK and the TSKK decided that it is not proper to report about the contents of these letters, about demands that were set forward and about the resolution of the plenary meeting of the TsK and the TSKK in October.

(A voice: "It is not a secret to many."). I am very sorry that it is not a secret to many, but the plenary meetings of the TsK and the TSKK made a decision that it is not proper to report either about letters or about the answer of the Politburo. Besides the letters sent by Trotsky and forty-six comrades there was also an answer by members of the Politburo to these letters undersigned by Rykov, Kalinin, Stalin, Bukharin, Molotov, Zinivijev, and Kamenev.[3] Comrades Lenin and Rudzutak were absent. Comrade Rudzutak, who arrived later at the Plenary meeting, approved this answer. The Plenary meetings of the TsK and the TSKK adopted the position of the Politburo by a great majority: 102 votes in favor and two votes against with ten abstaining,[4] and condemned the behavior of Comrade Trotsky and forty-six comrades. I do not dare make a more detailed report to you. (Applause)

Stalin: Now I am going to the question about Comrade Rosenberg.[5] She said that she knows more about the TsK than the TsK itself. Do you see? She knows well what happened at the plenary meeting of the TsK and the TSKK in October. She says what is known to everyone. However, I am at my wit's end and I don't know where it has come from. She says that our system does not fit, that we choke Party thought and that the plenary meetings were allegedly against democracy and so on. I cannot understand where she had read all these things.

Rosenberg: From Comrade Kamenev's report.

Stalin: I do not know about Comrade Kamenev's report, I am not acquainted with it. But it is possible to make judgements about the system by reading the report made by one official. At the plenary meetings in October the question was raised that to transgress the normal boundary of discussion means to create a faction. To split the government means to ruin the Soviet power. The talk was just about that. They allowed debates to be conducted, but they do not bring the discussion to the formation of factions, for factions in our Party, which holds the power, lead to the incitement of internal and external enemies. On the ground of that the plenary meetings of the TsK and the TSKK condemned the comrades. At these plenary meetings they raised this question: the question was not about whether the plenary meetings had been against democracy.[6]

Printed copy.
Printed according to the text of the
first publication in the journal
Izvestija TsK KPSS, 1990,
No. 12, pp.164–165.

NOTES

1 Stalin's report "About the tasks of the Party" made at the extended meeting of the Krasnopresnensky district committee of the RKP(b) of Moscow without answers to questions was published in the *Pravda* on the December 6, 1923 (see also I. V. Stalin, *Works*, vol. 5, pp. 354–370).

2. Here and below the resolution of the joint plenary meeting of the TsK and the TSKK on October 26 is meant (see Document No. 21:III).

3. The answer of the members of the Politburo of the TsK of the RKP(b) on October 19, 1923 is meant (see Document No. 17). Stalin did not name M. P. Tomsky among those Party members who signed the document.

4. It is related to the results of voting at the plenary meeting of the TsK and the TSKK. See note 2 to Document No. 21:III.

5. Rosenberg, student of the Sverdlov Communist University, the first highest Party educational institution that taught the Party and soviet workers.

6. In the resolution of the October joint plenary meeting of the TsK and the TSKK (see Document No. 21: III) the question was not whether the formation of factions led to the split of the government and the ruin of the Soviet power.

24

Disagreements In the Subcommittee of the Three during the Preparation of the Resolution "On the Party Building"

December 5, 1923[1]

An exceptionally important and critical period in the Party's development imposes on us an obligation to do everything in our power so that the necessary and urgent changes in the Party's course can take place with minimal organizational shocks, and what is more, without factional convulsions within the framework of Party rules, and also preserving not only the Party's unity but its unanimity. It is possible to reach this result only under the condition that the Central Committee, with absolute unanimity in its own ranks be at the head of events now taking place in the Party's movement toward workers' democracy. We, the members of the subcommittee, were charged with the final formulation of the document proclaiming, on behalf of the Central Committee, the necessity of serious new steps in the economic field and a change in the course of the inner-Party policy. Within bounds of this general consideration in the subcommittee of three, it was possible to observe different trends, which were expressed in that Comrade Trotsky from his side, considered it necessary to adopt far more decisive and explicit formulation of planned new steps in order to remove any doubts about the Party in relation to the TsK's intentions to realize its proclaimed beginning. With particular persistence Comrade Trotsky underlined his fears that collective statements of sufficiently disciplined workers addressed to the Central Committee will be further considered factional, as was done at the October plenary meeting in relation to the Statement of Forty-Six which, to Comrade Trotsky's thinking, was basically correct and presented a healthy dissent by responsible workers who warned the TsK about the necessity to revise their course. That has not happened. In addition, Comrade Trotsky expressed his fear that the preservation of Party personnel, and the habit of using bureaucratic methods of administration in the Party will become the most serious obstacle to implementation of the new course; for this reason they are capable of provoking organizational shocks and the appearance of subgroups. Precisely for the purpose of timely influencing the Party personal, Comrade Trotsky insisted on more decisive, categorical, and clear formulations of different paragraphs of the document.

From the other side Comrades Kamenev and Stalin in their disagreement expressed their assurance in that Comrade Trotsky's fears are groundless, for the Politburo and later the Central Committee considered it necessary to implement the planned measures and really provide principles of Party life from top to bottom, using a firm hand supported by the Party as a whole.

Guided by characterized above intentions to take the Party from present complications to the way of full unanimity and fighting ability, three subcommittee members decided to voice in favor of the document in its present form in order to facilitate the solution of the extremely critical problem that faces the Party.

Printed text[2]
Printed according to the text of the first publication
in the journal *Izvestiya TsK KPSS*,
1990, No. 10, pp. 170-171

APPENDIX:
From the Resolution "On the Party Building."
December 5, 1923.
The Party and Workers' democracy[3]

Negative occurrences of the last months both in the life of the working class as a whole and within the Party certainly lead the Party to the conclusion that its interests in the sense of both improving its struggle against the new economic policy and of increasing its fighting ability in fields of work, demand a serious change in the implementation of a real and systematic application of principles of workers' democracy.

The workers' democracy signifies the freedom to discuss frankly among all the members all the most important principles of Party life, the freedom to debate these problems as well as an opportunity to elect the leading administrative persons and board from top to bottom. This does not mean, however, the freedom to form factional groupings which are extremely dangerous to a ruling Party, for they usually threaten to bisect or split the government and state machinery as a whole.

It is self-evident that within the Party which represents voluntary association of people on explicit ideological and practical grounds, it is not possible to tolerate groupings whose ideology is directed against the Party as a whole and against the dictatorship of the proletariat (for example, "the Rabochaya Pravda" and the "Rabochaya gruppa."[4]

Only constant, animated ideological life may preserve such a Party that was marked both before and during the revolution, by constant critical study of its past, correction of its mistakes, and collective discussion of the most important problems. Only these methods of work are able to provide effective guarantees against those episodic disagreements which are converted into the formation of factional groupings with all the above-mentioned consequences.

In order to prevent this development it is essential that Party's leading authorities heed the voice of the broad Party mass and not consider any criticism to be a manifestation of factionalism, not to seclude those honest and disciplined Party workers and thus drive them to factional activities.

Under no circumstances can the Party be considered not to be an office of an institution, but it cannot be seen as a discussion club for any and all kinds of directions either. The Tenth Congress set up the principles of the workers' democracy, but the same congress, and later the Eleventh and Twelfth Congresses, established a number of limitations on applications of principles of workers' democracy. The prohibition on the formation of factions (see the resolution of the Tenth Congress "About Party Unity," and the resolution of the Eleventh Congress: purges in the Party, limitation of admittance to membership in the Party for nonproletariat elements, establishment of the length of Party membership for some categories of officials in the Party, and approval of secretaries of the higher Party echelons (see "the Party rules").[5] In the circumstances of the New Economic Policy, considering preservation of known limitations to be inevitable later on, it is necessary at the same time on the basis of experience already gained, especially by lower organizations, to check some of these limitations, for example, the limitation on the right to approve appointments of secretaries by higher authorities. In any case, it is not allowed to permit the conversion of the right of approval of secretaries into their actual appointment.

THE NEXT MEASURES TO INTRODUCE WORKERS' DEMOCRACY

In an effort to carry on the struggle against distortion of the Party policy, to introduce real workers' democracy, and to provide the whole mass of Party members with an opportunity to influence systematically the direction of the whole Party policy, it is necessary to put into practice, in the first place, the following measures:

- To monitor the elections of all officials with the limitations that were mentioned above, to consider it inadmissable to press with adoption of these persons in spite of the will of the organization, and in particular, to keep attentive watch over the elections of secretaries of Party cells.
- To dutifully raise all substantial questions of Party policy, as long as this is not impeded by any significant circumstances; to discuss these questions by Party cells and the Party mass as a whole; to spread a network of Party discussion clubs, not to resort to incorrect references to Party discipline when the matter is relative to the right and obligations of Party members to discuss questions they are interested in and to adopt resolutions.
- The pay attention to the task of promoting Party workers from the bottom, in the first instance, from working people.
- To pay particular attention to mastering the correct Party policy by comrades who are in direct contact with the Party mass.
- To put into practice obligatory reports on Party authorities to the collectives which had elected them, and to the broad mass.
- To intensify Party and educational work, avoiding in every way possible its bureaucratic realization both among the whole Party mass and particularly among the members of the young communist league and women.

- To pay attention in exchange of experience gained by workers of different fields, to dutifully hold both at the TsK and at the regional and provincial Party committees, periodic conferences of executive officials in all fields of work.
- To give more information to members of the Party through the press and travel over all the localities by members of the TsK, the TSKK regional and provincial committees and members of boards, commissariats, and so on.
- To strengthen units devoted to Party life in periodic press.
- To come to the next Party congress with a proposal to convene provincial and all-Party conferences twice a year.

In order to enforce all the measures mentioned above and to realize workers' democracy, it is necessary to move beyond words to deeds, allowing local Party cell, district, regional and provincial Party conferences to renew systematically at the next elections the Party bodies from the bottom, promoting workers who are able to effectively keep inner-Party discipline, to important posts.

NOTES

1. The history of the appearance of published documents is as follows. As long ago as 1923, at the September Plenary meeting of the TsK of the RKP(b), the commission of the TsK on inner-Party situation under the chairmanship of V. M. Molotov was formed. The report of the commission was heard at the meeting of the Politburo of the TsK on November 29, 1923. The Politburo took decision to pass proposals made by V. M. Molotov for discussion of the newly formed commission of the Politburo consisting of Stalin, Molotov, Bukharin, Kuibyshev, Zinovyev, Trotsky, and M. P. Tomsky. The time of work of the commission of the Politburo was limited by December 3. In the resolution it was also mentioned that "In a case of unanimity the commission should be charged with adoption of document sent to it for consideration and its publication on behalf of the TsK (the RTsHIDNI, f. 17, op. 3, v. 397, pp. 5–6). For the preparation of the final edition of the resolution about Party building the subcommittee consisting of L. D. Kamenev, Stalin, and Trotsky (the subcommittee of three) was formed.

At that time Trotsky was ill, and the meetings of the Politburo and subcommittee of three were taking place at his place (see L. Trotsky, *My Life. An Attempt at an Autobiography*, [Moscow, 1991], p. 474). On December 5, the subcommittee of three presented the final text of the resolution "On Party Building" for consideration of the joint meeting of the

Politburo of the TsK and the Presidium of the TSKK. The resolution was unanimously adopted the same day (see Appendix). On December 7, it appeared on pages of *Pravda*.

The resolution "On Party Building" did not become a turning point for the new course. (The resolution will be determined in such a way in the following documents.) This was the course to develop inner-Party democracy, because for the "leading body" of the TsK it appeared to be a tactical step to temporary compromise with the opposition, which it was forced to agree with, so as to "calm" ordinary communists, particularly those who were in the chief Party organization.

It is no accident that the document "About Disagreements in the Subcommittee of Three" appeared only on December 5, the day of approval of the resolution "About Party Building." In all probability Trotsky was the author. Considering disagreements that occurred in the subcommittee of that the preparation of the resolution to be critical, he decided to set them down in writing. In favor of this supposition we should notice the existence of entire phrases that are repeated verbatim in his letter to the TsK of December 9, 1923 (see Document No. 31); there are editorial corrections in the text in Trotsky's hand and, finally, his remark: "very important. Into the folder of L. D. Trotsky." As subsequent events demonstrated, Trotsky's doubts and fears related to the readiness of the subcommittee of three to work out resolutions were well-grounded.

2. The document "About Disagreement in the Subcommittee of Three" (printed text) is presently on file in the archives of the President of the Russian Federation.

3. The term "workers' democracy" in the Party Lexicon of 1920, signified conception of "the inner-Party democracy," because the RKP(b) according to the rules was determined as a political organization of the working class.

4. See note 5 to Document No. 4 and note 6 to Document No. 20.

5. See notes 8 and 9 to Document No. 21: I.

25

L. D. Trotsky's Statement to the Politburo of the TsK of the RKP(b)

December 6, 1923

Strictly Confidential
Urgent

To the Politburo

At the latest joint plenary meeting of the TsK and the TSKK, the Politburo took a decision not to distribute and not to publish its resolution.[1] It is a great pity, because informing all the members of the Party about my letter and about the statement of the Group of Forty-Six as well as about the resolution of the plenary meeting[2] would be better than spreading rumors which had appeared. But in any case the decision had been taken. In the meantime, Comrade Stalin in his concluding remarks in the Krasnopresnensky district[3] said the following: "The plenary meetings of the TsK and the TSKK adopted by a great majority the position of the Politburo: 102 votes in favor, two votes against, eight abstaining,"[4] and condemned the behavior of Comrade Trotsky and forty-six comrades. I do not dare to report above. this." Nevertheless, in the course of his concluding remarks, Comrade Stalin stated in addition: "At the plenary meeting in October the question was raised that breaching the known limits of the discussion means a form of factionalism, a splitting of the government. To split the government means to ruin the Soviet power. On the basis of that the plenary meetings condemned the comrades. At these meetings the problem just looked like that.

211

In such a way Comrade Stalin in a way decides by himself as to what to report and what not to report, and he even does so in two different places differently.

I ask than an urgent decision by the Politburo be taken on the question whether I have a right to explain to the Party members, in answer to numerous written and oral questions to me, what was the essence of my letter, what resolution the joint plenary meetings passed, and what position this resolution is in during the current change in the Party's course.

L. Trotsky

December 6, 1923

No. 425

Printed copy with the facsimile signature.[5]
Printed according to the text of the
first publication in the journal
Izvestiya TsK KPSS, 1990,
No. 12, pp. 166-167.

NOTES

1. The resolution of the October joint plenary meeting of the TsK and TSKK of the RKP(b) is meant (see Document No. 21: III).

2. Trotsky has in mind his letter to the TsK dated October 8 (Document No. 4), the statement of Forty-Six (Document No. 12) and the resolution of the October joint plenary meeting of the TsK and the TSKK (Document No. 21: III).

3. Trotsky cites the text from answers by Stalin to the questions posed to him at the meeting of the active members of the Party organization of the Krasnopresnensky district of Moscow on December 2, 1923 (see Document No. 23). Stalin's report "About Tasks of the Party" without answers to the questions was published in *Pravda* on December 6, 1923.

4. As to the total vote on the draft resolutions at the plenary meetings of the TsK and TSKK, see note 2 to Document No. 21: III.

5. The document is presently in the archives of the President of the Russian Federation. In the RTsHIDNI there is a certified printed copy (f. 17, op. 3, v. 398, p. 4).

26

M. N. Lyadov's Memo to I. V. Stalin

December 7, 1923

To Comrade Stalin

I state to you, according to your request,[1] that I really announced in a talk with you, that it became clear at the joint bureau of the Party cell of Sverdlov University[2] and at the joint meeting of Party organization letters by Comrade Trotsky and the Group of Forty-Six were distributed among students and the majority of circles' listeners read them. I made an oral announcement to you on the 28th or 29th of November, in any case not later than the 29th of November.

M. Lyadov

December 7, 1923

The autograph

Printed by the text of the first publication in the journal *Izvestiya TsK KPSS*, 1990, No. 12, p. 168.

NOTES

1. Because in his speech at the meeting of active members of the Krasnopresnensky district Stalin in essence disclosed the content of the resolution of the October joint plenary meeting of the TsK and the TSKK, he added what had not been in the resolution (see Document No. 23). He wanted, in return for the violation of the prohibition imposed on the disclosure of the resolution, written evidences of the distribution of the opposition documents among Moscow Communists. This was the reason for his request addressed to the rector of the Sverdlov Communist University (the higher educational institution) to M. N. Lyadov, appointed to his post by the Secretariat of the TsK in May 1923.

2. In the Sverdlov Communist University the Party organization and its elected bureau were united; they included teachers and students who were members of the RKP(b).

27

I. V. Stalin's Statement to the Politburo of the TsK of the RKP(b)

December 8, 1923

To the Politburo of the TsK

Citing below the extracts from the shorthand record of my report in the district of Presnya* about Party building,[1] I consider it necessary to declare the following:

1. Comrade Trotsky acted by making his statement[2] incorrectly taking citations from the shorthand record of my report, which I had not looked through, with all the blanks and inaccuracies usually in shorthand records that have not been proofread by the authors.[3]

2. I admit that, having reported to the meeting of the Presnya district about the real situation with the *resolutions of the* plenary meetings of the TsK and the TSKK on the question of statements by Comrade Trotsky and the Group of Forty-Six, I went against the resolution of the plenary meetings about the secrecy of the resolution. However, I was literally obliged to act in such a way under the pressure of false rumors undermining the prestige of the TsK and the TSKK, which were widely spread among members of the Party, by its evil-wishers, its destroyers. Among members of the Party there are some rumors that reports about Comrade Trotsky's illness do not correspond to the facts[4] that Comrade Trotsky was put under house arrest by the

---

*Krasnopresnensky district of Moscow (Krasnaya Presnya). (Ed.)

215

Politburo because at the October plenary meetings he demanded the introduction of democracy into the Party. (My statement made during my report
in answer to a note saying that Comrade Trotsky is ill was met with ironic
giggles and exclamations of doubt from the entire number of participants in
the meeting). Sverdlovsk inhabitant Comrade Rosenberg[5] in her speech directly stated that the letters by Comrade Trotsky and the Group of Forty-Six
are no secret and that Comrade Trotsky suffered because of his attitude to
democracy against which the October plenary meeting of the TsK and the
TSKK objected. These absurd rumors find their root in the following:

1. The documents by Comrade Trotsky and the Group of Forty-Six, in
spite of their prohibition by the TsK, are extensively distributed among
Party members. In the meantime the answer of the Politburo members[6] to
these documents, and to the resolution of the plenary meetings itself, are
kept in the strictest secret according to the decision of the TsK of the Party.

2. The supporters of the forty six do not take measures to quell these
absurd rumors and they distribute the documents by Comrade Trotsky and
the Group of Forty-Six among members of the Party, although, certainly,
they could take effective measures against distribution of these documents,
for the distribution itself is initiated by the Group of Forty-Six.

3. The representatives of the TsK at the discussion meetings do not
wish to violate the resolution of the plenary meeting related to the secrecy
of the known resolution. They are obliged to answer with silence a number of questions related to the work of the plenary meetings of the TsK and
the TSKK. That complicates matters more and creates false impressions
that representatives of the TsK are afraid to tell the truth and that their conscience is guilty.

All this leads and cannot help but lead to undermining the prestige of
the TsK and the TSKK, in the opinion of Party members, to please disor-
ganizers and destroyers of the Party.

I do not know any other remedy against lies and slander than truth.
Therefore, I see no other way to protect the TsK and the TSKK from slander and lies except to tell the truth about the resolution of the plenary
meetings of the TsK and the TSKK.

                                                      I. Stalin

December 8, 1923

                                        Manual text with Stalin's
                                        remarks and his signature.[7]

Printed by the text of the first publication
in the journal *Izvestiya TsK KPSS*, No. 12,
1990, pp. 167–168.

NOTES

1. See the extract from the shorthand report of Stalin's report (the answers to the questions) at the meeting of active members of the Party organization of the Krasnopresnensky district of Moscow (see Document No. 23).

2. Trotsky's statement to the Politburo on the 6th of December (see Document No. 25).

3. Stalin's text cited by Trotsky in his statement is kept in the corrected shorthand record as well (see Document No. 23).

4. Trotsky was really ill during November and December in 1923, having caught a cold (see L. Trotsky, *My Life* [*Moya zhizh*], p. 42.

5. The hearer of the Sverdlov Communist University.

6. Stalin means an answer of members of the Politburo of the TsK on the 23rd of October to Comrade Trotsky's letter dated October 8, 1923 (see Document No. 17).

7. The document is presently filed in the archives of the President of the Russian Federation. There is a printed copy of the document in the RTsHIDNI (f. 17, op. 3, v. 398, p. 5-6).

28

The Extract from the Minutes No. 50 of the Politburo of the TsK of the RKP(b) Session

December 8, 1923

Strictly Confidential

1. The statements by Comrades Trotsky and Stalin. (see Appendix)*

More and more information is coming to the TsK saying that Comrade Trotsky's letter and the letter of the Forty-Six, rejected by plenary meetings of the TsK and TSKK[1] as acts of factionalism, are more widespread (for example in the army in the Ukraine[2] according to the statement made by the representative of the TSKK, and in Moscow in the Sverdlov University, according to Comrade Lyadov's statement,[3] these letters are intensively read). The statement of the joint plenary meetings about keeping all the information about incidents among members of the TsK and the TSKK, is not interpreted by fractious elements as a step dictated not by the interests of the Party but by inner-Party diplomacy. In this connection in the circles of the Party the absurd rumors are spread in order to undermine the prestige of the TsK.

Comrade Stalin's statement made at the meeting of the Krasnopresnensky district[4] was provoked only with the intent to properly illuminate

---

*The statements by Trotsky on December 6, 1923, and by Stalin on December 8, 1923, are added to the resolution of the Politburo of the TsK of the RKP(b). See Documents Nos. 25 and 27. (Ed.)

the real motives of the plenary meeting of the TsK and the TSKK and by this to bring about a healthy atmosphere in the Party in Moscow.

In the meantime the Politburo considers that Comrade Stalin incorrectly cited the document reporting to the meeting the contents of the resolution of the plenary meeting of the TsK and TSKK, because by this the direct resolution of the TsK and the TSKK was violated.

The Politburo has no right and does not consider it expedient in interests of the Party to cancel further discussion of letters by the Group of Forty-Six and Comrade Trotsky and the resolution of the October plenary meetings. It is only the joint plenary meeting that is allowed to cancel that resolution.

The Politburo believes that subsequently all the members of the TsK should strictly observe the resolution of the joint plenary meeting and to avoid any worsening during the discussion on problems of workers' democracy, particularly after the resolution on the workers' democracy was unanimously adopted by the Politburo and the Presidium of the TsK and the TSKK.[5]

The RTsHIDNI, f 17, p. 3,
v. 398, p 1. Printed copy.
First publication was in the journal
Izvestiya TsK KPSS, 1990, No. 12, pp. 165–166.

NOTES

1. The letter by Trotsky of October 8 (Document No. 4), the statement of the Group of Forty-Six (Document No. 12) and the resolution of the October joint plenary meeting of the Tsk and TSKK in 1923 (Document No. 21: III are meant.

2. In the note of the secretary of the TsK of the Ukrainian Communist Party, D. Z. Lebed, dated December 4, 1923, to the TsK of the RKP(b) and addressed to I. V. Stalin, it was said, for example, that "the information coming from Moscow in roundabout ways is intercepted here and used."

3. M. N. Lyadov's note of December 7, 1923, directed to Stalin, is meant. See Document No. 26.

4. See the extract from the shorthand record of Stalin's report at the broadened meeting of the Krasnopresnensky district of Moscow (answers to questions), Document No. 23.

5. The resolution "On Party Building" adopted unanimously on December 5, 1923, at the joint meeting of the Politburo of the TsK and the Presidium of the TSKK (see note 1 to Document No. 24) is meant.

29

G.Ye. Zinovyev's Memo Addressed to I. V. Stalin, L. B. Kamenev, A. I. Rykov, and M. P. Tomsky at the Meeting of the Politburo of the TsK of the RKP(b)

December 8, 1923

They are acting in accordance with all the rules of factional art. If we fail immediately to create our own extremely unified faction, everything will be doomed.[1]

I put forward a proposal to come to this conclusion at the first opportunity. I suggest getting together especially in order to discuss this question, probably at Comrade Stalin's place in the country or at my place.

Delay may mean death.
G. Zinovyev.

December 8, 1923

Adopted. St.* Sehr gut.† Agreed. M. Tomsky
Only not earlier than at seven o'clock in the evening L. K.‡ agreed, but I should prefer to go to "the show."§
A. I. Rykov

Autographs by G. E. Zinovyev and by those who signed the document. Printed by the text of the first

---

*Stalin (Ed.)
†Very good (German) (Ed.)
‡Leo Kamenev. (Ed.)
§The theater performance is probably meant. (Ed.)

220

publication in the journal *Izvestiya TsK KPSS*,
1990, No. 12, p. 168.

NOTE

1. The document published here may be considered to be an initial, starting step of expansion of "the group of three" and the formation of the group of seven consisting of the Party leadership which would head the factional "leading collective body," the body that was parallel to the TsK of RKP(b). Its final legislation would take place in August 1924. The group of seven included N. I. Bukharin, A. I. Rykov, M. P. Tomsky, and V. V. Kuiybishev in addition to G. E. Zinovyev, L. B. Kamenev, and Stalin.

30

L. D. Trotsky. The New Course*
(A Letter Addressed to the
Party Meetings)¹

December 8, 1923

Dear Comrades!

I firmly believed that today or tomorrow I would be able to take part in the discussion of the inner--Party situation and new tasks. But my illness came at an inopportune time, more aggressive than ever and lasting longer than the doctors had earlier thought. I have nothing but to give my opinion in this letter.

The resolution to the Politburo on the question of Party building² is a document of exceptional importance. It underlines the fact that the Party has approached the turning point on its historic way. As was pointed out at many meetings, it is necessary to observe care at this turn, but side by side with care we need firmness and decisiveness. A temporizing, amorphous policy would be the worst form of rashness.

Some of those who are conservatively oriented, and therefore inclined to overestimate the role of the staff and to underestimate independent actions of the Party, speak critically of the *resolution* of the Politburo. They say that the TsK assumes obligations that it cannot fulfill that the resolution will only seed false hopes and will lead to negative results. It is clear that such an approach to the problem is permeated with bureaucratic mistrust of

---

*Published with minor abridgements. (Ed.)

the army. The new course proclaimed in the resolution of the TsK consists, namely, in that the center of gravity which was incorrectly shifted toward the apparatus in the old course, should under the new course be redirected towards activity, critical independent activity, self-control in the Party which is considered to be an organized vanguard of the proletariat. The new course does not at all mean that the Party's personnel is charged with the task to proclaim, create, or establish a regime of democracy during some time. No. The Party itself is able to set up this regime. In short, the task may be formulated in the following manner: the Party should place its staff under its own command while it remains the centralized organization.

In debates and articles it was often pointed out for the last time that "clean," "large-scale," "ideal" democracy is impracticable and that democracy is not at all the end in itself for us. This fact is completely indisputable. But with the same right and ground it is possible to say that pure and absolute centralism is impractical and is incompatible with the nature of the Party mass, and that neither centralism nor the Party staff is an end in itself in any way. Centralism and democracy represent two sides in a process of Party building. The task lies in those two sides' being balanced more correctly, i.e., by the manner that is the most sensible to the situation. For the last time such a balance was not present. The center of gravity was incorrectly moved to the staff. The independent action of the Party was minimized. This allowed the introduction of skills and methods that radically contradicted the spirit of the revolutionary Party of the proletariat. The excessive strengthening of the staff's centralism at the expense of independent action by the Party provoked the feeling of an indisposition. This fact found extremely sick expression at the edge, right up to the formation of illegal groupings in the Party under the leadership of elements that are clearly hostile to Communism.[3] At the same time throughout the Party a critical attitude to bureaucratic methods of solving problems has increased. An understanding or at least a feeling that the Party's bureaucratism was threatening to bring the Party to a halt, became almost universal. Warning voices were raised. The first official and, to be sure, the most important expression of the turning point that has occurred in the Party is the resolution of the New Course. It is being put into practice to the extent in which the Party, i.e., its 400,000 members, will wish or be able to realize the resolution.

By killing an independent activity, bureaucratism hinders the improvement of the general level of the Party. This is its major fault. Because the Party staff inevitably includes more experienced and distinguished persons, the bureaucratism of the staff influences more heavily the ideological and political growth of the younger generations in the Party. It illustrates how the youth is the most faithful barometer of the Party, as it sharply reacts to the bureaucratism within the Party.

It would be incorrect to think that the extreme bureaucratic methods of solving Party problems occur without leaving any trace for the older generation which is an incarnation of the political experience of the Party and its revolutionary traditions. No, the danger is high at this pole as well. It is not necessary to speak about the greatest significance (not only in Russia but also in the whole world) of the older generation in our Party. It is a well-known and universally recognized fact. But it would be the gravest mistake to judge this significance as if it were self-sufficient. Only the permanent interaction of older and younger generations within a framework of Party democracy can save the older guard as a revolutionary factor. Otherwise the old men may ossify and become the most complete expression of the bureaucratism in the staff.

The regeneration of the old guard has been noted in history more than once. Let us take the most recent and illustrious historic example: the leaders of the Second International.[4] We do know that Wilhelm Libknecht, Bebel, Victor Adler, Kautsky, Bernstein, Lafarg, Ged, and many others were strict students of Marx and Engels. However, we know that all these leaders, one of them partly, and the others completely, turned in the direction of opportunism under circumstances of parliamentary reforms and the sufficient growth of the Party and professional personnel.[5] We see, especially clearly on the eve of the imperialistic war, how the powerful social-democratic staff, overshadowed by the authorities of the older generation, became the greatest deterrent to revolutionary development. And we must say that we, the old men, believe that our generation, naturally playing the leading role in the Party, does not include any sufficient guarantee against gradual and imperceptible weakening of the proletariat and its revolutionary spirit if it is admitted that the Party experienced further growth and strengthening of staff and bureaucratic methods of policy which turn the younger generation into passive material for training and inevitably settle estrangement between the staff and the masses. There is no other remedy against this certain danger but a serious, profound, radical change in the course in the direction of the Party democracy, with ever stronger involvements in the Party of the proletarian who stands at the lathe.[6]

In the Party press lately, many examples were given that characterized the bureaucratic regeneration of Party customs and relations. In response to the voice of criticism they say: "Show us your Party membership card." Before the TsK resolution about the new course was published, the bureaucratic representatives of the staff considered any mention of the necessity of a change in inner-Party policy to be heresy, factionalism, and a breakdown in discipline. Now they are also formally prepared to take a new course into consideration, i.e., to reduce it to nothing by bureaucratic means. The renewal of the Party staff (certainly within clear guidelines of the Party rules) must be carried out in order to replace old bureaucrats with fresh ones who are closely connected with the life of the collective and able to provide this connection. First of all, it is necessary to remove from Party posts those elements who, at the first sign of criticism, objections, or protests, are inclined to demand to see the Party membership card for the purpose of repression. The new course should begin at the moment when everyone from the staff, from top to bottom, feels that nobody can terrorize the Party.

It is not enough for the youth merely to repeat our formulae. The youth must acquire revolutionary formulae by force, put them into practice, develop in their own mind and appearance, and be able to defend their own views with courage that comes easily with silence, conviction, and independence of character. Passive obedience, mechanical alignment with leaders, lack of initiative, subservience, and self-seeking have no business in the Party. The bolshevik is not only a man of discipline, but one who, by looking deeply within himself, works out his own firm opinion in every case and independently, and with fortitude defends it not only in battle against enemies but inside his own organization. Today he will find himself in the minority in his own organization. He obey because it is his Party. But surely it does not always mean that he is not right. Probably, he saw or understood the new task and necessity of turning earlier than the others did. He persistently raises questions for the second, the third, the tenth time. By this he renders the Party a service, helps it to face the new task fully armed or to undergo necessary changes without organizational shocks and factional convulsions.

Yes, our Party was not able to perform its historic mission, as it split into factional groupings. It should not be so, it is impossible. The Party will prevent this development itself, as a self-governing collective. But the Party can overcome the danger of factionalism successfully only by means of developing and strengthening the course toward the workers' democracy. It is the staff's bureaucratism that is one of the chief sources of factionalism. It suppresses criticism and breeds dissatisfaction. It tends to pin a factional label on every individual or collective voice of criticism or warning. Mechanical centralism is inevitably supplemented by factionalism which is a wicked caricature of Party democracy and represents a terrible political danger at the same time.

In a clear understanding of the entire situation the Party will make the necessary adjustment with all the firmness and decisiveness necessary for the extent of the tasks facing us. By this the Party will place its revolutionary unity on a higher level, as a pledge that it will meet economic and international tasks of immeasurable significance.

I have not exhausted the question in any sense. I consciously refused to consider a lot of its significant aspects out of fear of taking too much time from you. But I hope that I'll soon cope with malaria, which, as I myself judge, is in explicit opposition to the new course of the Party and then in more free speech I am going to try to supplement and to specify what I did not accomplish in this letter.

P.S. Seeing that the letter is not appearing in *Pravda* for two days, I want to make some additional remarks.

It was reported, as if at the announcement of my letter, that at the district meeting some comrades expressed fear that my considerations related to interrelations of the "old guard" and the younger generations may be used to pit the youth against the older men. We may rightly assume that such a thought occurs only to those comrades who could not face the question of the necessity to change our course two or three months ago. In any case bringing such fears to the fore in this situation at this moment may be the result of an incorrect estimate of the real dangers and their order. The present mood of the youth, which, as should be clear to any thinking member of the Party, is an acute symptom of the situation, was begotten by the same methods of "the calm,"[7] the condemnation of which represents the unanimously adopted resolution of the Politburo. In other words, it is "the calm" that included the danger of growing estrangement between the leaders of the Party and its younger members, i.e., the great majority. The Party staff has a tendency to think and take decisions instead of the Party. This tendency leads in its development to the intentional strengthening only of the prestige of the leading Party circles in accordance with tradition. The respect for Party tradition is indisputably the most required component of Party education and

Party unity; but this component can be vital and firm only when it is constantly fed and strengthened by an active and self-regulating check on Party tradition by means of collective generation of the present Party policy. Without this activity and self-regulation respect for tradition may degenerate into bureaucratic romanticism or the direct creation of bureaucracy, i.e., a form without substance. First of all it is necessary to create preconditions so that Party tradition is not concentrated in the staff but flourishes and is renewed in the living experience of the Party. By this it is impossible to avoid another danger: splitting the oldest generation into staff elements, i.e., suitable for supporting "the calm," and nonstaff elements. It goes without saying that Party staff, i.e., its organizational body, will lose all reticence and will not become weaker but grow stronger. But there must not be two opinions in the Party about the need for a powerful centralized staff.

Perhaps it is possible to put forward more objections to that the reference to the reincarnation of the social democracy incorrect in view of deep differences of eras: the former stagnant reformist era and the present revolutionary era. It is self-evident that the example is only an example, not an identity. However, this groundless comparison does not clarify anything by itself. It is not without reason that we point out the dangers of the New Economic Policy, closely connected with the protracted character of the international revolution. Our everyday state and practical work that is more detailed and specialized, hides, as was pointed out in the resolution of the TsK, the dangers of narrowing our horizons, i.e., opportunistic reincarnation . It is perfectly clear that these dangers become more serious the more Party leadership is replaced by reserved "secretarian" command. We would be bad revolutionaries if we hoped that the revolutionary character of "the epoch" would help us to overcome all the difficulties, first of all, internal ones. It is necessary to help "the epoch" to implement correctly the new Party course, proclaimed unanimously by the Politburo of the TsK.

Pravda, December 11, 1923

NOTES

1. On December 8, 1923, Trotsky did not receive the permission of the Politburo of

the TsK to speak at the meeting of the Communists in order to explain his position (see Documents Nos. 26 and 28). He considered that it was necessary to make such an explanation because Stalin, in his speech of December 2, accused the opposition of all out intending to "split the government and to ruin the Soviet power." Trotsky, still being ill, made the decision to address the Party organizations directly through *Pravda*. On the same day he wrote a letter to the Party meetings (i.e., conferences of the Party organizations) under the title "The New Course." Because the publication of this letter was delayed and it had already spread among the Party organizations of Moscow Trotsky wrote a supplement to them (the "Postscript"). In this form it was published in *Pravda* on December 11, 1923. Later Trotsky collected his articles written between December 1923 and January 1924, in a volume under the general title of *The New Course*. It was issued on the eve of the opening of the Thirteenth Party Conference (January 16 to 18, 1924) and was not published in the USSR again.

2. The resolution of the TsK and the TSKK "On Party Building" is meant (see appendix to Document No. 24).

3. Illegal groups of "the Rabochaya pravda" and "the Rabochaya gruppa of the RKP" are meant. See note 5 to Document No. 4 and note 6 to Document No. 20.

4. The Second International, the international amalgamation of socialist parties, was founded in Paris in 1889. It was created with Engels's participation. It assisted in the spread of Marxism in workers' movement, in order to establish ties among workers' parties. At the beginning of the First World War (1914) a number of the leaders of the Second International defended the policy of their governments ("obbronshectvo"). It meant in fact the ideological and political bankruptcy of the Second International.

5. See the remarks made by Trotsky in the Postscript about this comparison.

6. The workers involved directly in industrial production are meant.

7. The term "the calm," relating to inner-Party life, was used for the first time by G. E. Zinovyev in his article "The New Task of the Party" published in *Pravda* on November 7, 1923.

31

L. D. Trotsky's Letter to the TsK of the RKP(b)

December 9, 1923

TO THE TSK OF THE RKP*

Strictly confidential

In the commission of the Politburo which was working out the resolution on Party building,[1] I pointed out that I would be able to vote for that resolution only bearing in mind serious reservations that I intend to introduce into the TsK without their publication, in order not to create superfluous difficulties caused by my speech.

I made a statement of such a sort during the joint session of the Politburo and the Presidium of the TSKK, where the text of the resolution worked out by us was approved. The present document reflects my statement in a written form related to the voting that took place.

1. The major contradiction in the resolution adopted is that it is expressed in a form that is successfully tied with the resolution of the October plenary session. In fact *the October Plenary session[2] became the high-*

---

*In the original there are some remarks made in Stalin's hand: "To be urgently distributed. Stalin." The document was sent out to the members of the Politburo of the TsK of the RKP(b).

229

est expression of staff's bureaucratic course*: now subjected to the radical changes. The October plenary session condemned principles that now, two months later, the Politburo found it necessary to adopt.

2. The Party staff is still mechanically going by that way, the brightest expression of which the resolution of the October plenary session has become. Not only does very numerous and influential grouping in the Party staff (essentially factional grouping) resist the turn toward a new course, but it will undoubtedly judge the resolution of the TsK as a maneuver that doesn't bring essential changes to the Party. That is precisely why I insisted on incomparably more distinct, sharp, and clear condemnation of the elements of the Party staff that have become formal and bureaucratic.[3]

3. It is the *purely formal attitude*† of the members of the Politburo on the issue of groupings and factional formations that fills me with anxiety. It goes without saying that we have no disagreements on the issues of harmful influence, extraordinary political danger, and the inadmissibility of factional formations within the Party. But there are some contradictions related to those methods and approaches that could help us to protect the Party against factional splitting. Factions and groupings revealed recently in the Party, did not grow from misuse of the regime of workers' democracy; on the contrary, they appeared under the influence of a purely bureaucratic regime. In order to undermine the factionalism it is necessary to deliver a blow to the bureaucracy. In the meanwhile the Party is still under the impression that it is condemning "for factionalism" irreproachable Party members who had warned the TsK beforehand about erroneous Party course."[4] If methods of such a kind were transferred into "a new course," they would undermine that course at the root

4. In the same manner the attitude of some members of the Politburo toward the economic crisis which we are undergoing, toward its meaning, its reason, and its perspective, arouses anxiety. We heard statements in some responsible speeches that the crisis proved to be "a tempest in a teacup," that the September movement was "only an episode."[5] If the Party was filled with such views it would not find in itself sufficient means of overcoming economic difficulties and problems.

Thus, because of its belated appearance, the adopted resolution seems

---

*Stalin's emphasis (Ed.)
†Stalin's emphasis (Ed.)

to be insufficient and badly designed. At the same time the resolution undoubtedly represents a serious step away from the dominating bureaucratic course toward a more healthy Party regime. Under the conditions created during the voting I had made a choice between abstention from voting and voting "in favor," with the following motivation.

> *In view of the fact that in the subcommittee Comrades Kamenev and Stalin persistently spoke about a firm decision by the Politburo to provide real implementation of a new course, I made up my mind to vote for the resolution in those forms in order to facilitate the serious and profound turning for the Central Committee in every possible way, avoiding organizational shocks and factional convulsions.**

However, I consider it to be my duty to point out with all my energy that any attempt to use the unanimous adoption of the resolution in order to provide unanimity in the Party by means of *bureaucratic measures*† would lead to results directly opposite to those we are all striving for. That is, because the serious and prolonged economic problems lie at the very heart of the difficulties the Party faces, it is necessary to provide a clear and firm policy of the TsK in that direction, the first stage of which is traced by the unanimously adopted resolution of the Politburo.

9/XII.23

No. 430.T. L. Trotsky

The original.[6]
Printed according to the text of the first publication
in the journal *Izvestiya TsK KPSS*, 1990
No. 12, pp. 169–170.

NOTES

1. About the committee and subcommittee of the Politburo of the TsK working out of the resolution "On the Party construction," see note 4 to Document No. 24

2. For papers of the October joint plenary session of the TsK and the TSKK RKP(b), see documents No. 21: I–V.

3. See Document No. 24.

---

*Stalin's emphasis. (Ed.)
†Author's emphasis. (Ed.)

4. Trotsky has in mind the "condemnation for factionalism" of the Communists who had signed the Statement of the Forty-Six (see Document No. 12).

5. The strike movement that took place in the industrial regions of the country during the summer and the autumn of 1923 are meant.

6. The document is now in the archives of the President of the Russian Federation.

32

Ye. M. Yaroslavsky's Letter to the Members of the Politburo of the TsK and to the Members and Candidate Members of the TSKK of the RKP(b)

December 11, 1923

Strictly confidential
Copy No.19, p. l*
To Comrade Kamenev
December 11, 1923

TO ALL THE MEMBERS OF THE POLITBURO OF THE TsK OF
THE RKP AND TO ALL THE MEMBERS AND THE CANDIDATE
MEMBERS OF THE TSKK

The developing discussion about the inner-Party situation caught me
on my way to the Donbass region. There the discussion is just beginning
to develop. What made me address the members of the Politburo of the TsK
is that at the very first meeting which I had to attend, I heard a speech by
a representative of one of the military units, who stated literally the following. (The speaker was no more than twenty):

---

*This letter was sent to the members of the Politburo and to the members and candi-
date members of the TSKK of the RKP(b). The document is published according to a copy
belonging to L. V. Kamenev. The letter was delivered to the secretariat of L. B. Kamenev
on December 12, 1923. (Ed.)

We, military men, have a grudge against the TsK, too; we are going to demonstrate that we shall be able to do away with the conventionalism and we shall be able to ban "naznachenstvo."*

Attending two debates (in the economic department and at FON's† department of foreign relations of the First Moscow University, I got the impression that both the issue about "naznachenstvo"[1] and the question about comparing young Communists to the old guard assume nearly the same character on some speakers' lips. Trotsky's letter of December 8[2] to the Party meeting, taking into account all the reservations, did not dispel that danger, and I shall not be surprised if the evolution of the discussion in a direction set by individual comrades and groups of comrades will lead to demands for appointments by election of not only political workers, to remove "naznachenstvo," but can go further to making demands for appointments by election of all the officers in political units of armies.[3]

I consider to be my communist's responsibility to warn about that danger.

With communist regards,

Ye. Yaroslavsky
and facsimile signature[4]

Printed according to the text of
the first publication in the journal *Izvestiya TsK KPSS*,
1990, No. 12, pp. 171–172

Notes

1. The abbreviation of "naznachenchestvo," i.e., the practice of appointment of pleasing people to elective Party posts; these appointments are usually made by direct orders from above.

2. Trotsky's letter "New course" (Novyi kurs) written on December 8 and published in *Pravda* on December 11, 1923 (see Document No. 30).

3. Political departments are the Party bodies in the Red Army and in the fleet. They

---

*Author's emphasis. (Ed.)
†FON—The Faculty of Social Services. (Ed.)

were created in 1918 in order to perform ideological and political work among the servicemen. They were headed by the Central Political administration ("Glavpur"). The chief of the Glavpur in 1923 was V. A. Antonov-Ovseenko.

4. Presently the document is filed in the archives of the President of the Russian Federation.

33

L. D. Trotsky's Letter to the Politburo of the TsK and the Presidium of the TSKK of the RKP(b)

December 13, 1923

To the politburo of the TsK
To the Presidium of the TSKK

Dear comrades!

Today's leading article in newspaper *Pravda*,[1] as well as speeches by some members of the Politburo of the TsK and the Presidium of the TSKK, especially Comrade Stalin's speech in the TsK of Youth,[2] have the same character, as if these comrades were proceeding from the frustration of our unanimity at the vote on the resolution about Party building,[3] or frustration of such a sort.

As a cause for speeches of such a kind, they point to my letter printed in *Pravda*.[4] From a formal point of view, the essence of the matter is that if the Politburo or the TSKK considered that my letter contradicted the unanimously adopted resolution, they were obliged to demand from me something in explanation of my conduct and delay the publication of my letter. So, when I came to know the content Comrade Stalin's speech in the Krasnopresnensky district, I demanded an explanation from the Politburo.[5] I believe that this is the only correct way.

I do not intend here to go into an appraisal of the interpretation which the *Pravda* article attempts to give to my letter, because the article was clearly dictated not by a desire to point at one or another, real or imaginary mistake or flawed perspective in my letter, but by a desire to present my article as a cause for frustration of the unanimously adopted resolution on whose grounds I am standing.

I ask the Politburo to tell me whether it considered the issue about my article and gave respective instructions to *Pravda*. If it considered the issue and gave instructions, then when did it? Why did it without my participation? I cannot suppose by any means that *Pravda* or individual members of the Politburo are acting in this extraordinarily important question on their own responsibility.

Exactly the same questions are related to the Presidium of the TSKK. I put these questions, to be sure, not for formal motives which have their own weight and meaning, but indeed because I consider it necessary, as I considered during the commission's working, to do everything on my part that can help the Party go forth from its present difficulties without organizational shocks and factional convulsions.

With communist regards,
L. Trotsky

No. 431/+
Printed copy with facsimile signature.[6]
Printed according to the text of the first publication
in the journal *Izvestiya TsK KPSS*, 1990, No.12, pp. 172–173

NOTES

1. On December 13, 1923 the newspaper *Pravda* was issued with a leading article titled "Our Party and Opportunism" ("Nasha partiya i opportunism"). The author of the article was N. I. Buharin, the editor-in-chief of *Pravda* and an alternate member of the Politburo of the TsK. All his gifts of publicity and controversy were used to publicly declare Trotsky a political bankrupt. For this purpose, there were hints about Trotsky's non-Bolshevik past, on the connection of the past and the present. They also used biased interpretation of the letter "New Course" (Novyi kurs") and reminders about Bolsheviks' irreconcilability to opportunism. Trotsky and the opposition perceived yet more proof of the impossibility and undesirability of compromise for the "leading body."

2. On December 11, 1923 Stalin addressed the session of the TsK of the RKSM (The Russian Communist Youth Union) with information about inner-Party discussion.

3. For the resolution "On Party Building," see the appendix to Document No. 24.

4. The letter to the Party's meeting "New Course"("Novyi kurs"), published in *Pravda* on December 11, 1923, is meant.

5. See Trotsky's statement in the Politburo of the TsK on December 6, 1923 (Document No. 25).

6. Presently the document is filed in the archives of the President of the Russian Federation.

34

N. I. Bukharin's Statement to the Politburo of the TsK and the Presidium of the TSKK of the RKP(b)

No Earlier than December 13, 1923

To all the members of the Politburo
and the Presidium of the TSKK.
I ask the secretariat to distribute the document.
N. Bukharin.

To the Politburo of the TsK.
To the Presidium of the TSKK.

Dear comrades!

Apropos Comrade Trotsky's letter of December 13, 1923,[1] I consider it necessary to declare the following.

The issue of Comrade Trotsky's[2] article was not discussed and the article was delayed by two days only because I was summoned to the Krasnopresnenski district before I had enough time to read it to the end. And because the article written by me excited the feelings of the deepest amazement and was understood as a declaration of war, I asked to delay the article until I should be able to read in as a whole. The following day was a holiday. Hence the two days' delay occurred.

I am the one who wrote the leading article for *Pravda*, and I wrote it on my own responsibility. The article was a response to Comrade Trotsky's

239

letter, and because I had absolutely no doubt that the article expressed the TsK's line, I did not show it to any of the members of the TsK and, consequently, to any of the members of the Politburo.

Probably, the essence of my mistake lay there. But you see that Comrade Trotsky did not send his article either to the Politburo or to the TSKK, but he sent his letter *directly** to the districts' meetings (the letter was announced even on Saturday). In such a way the Politburo had no real opportunity to detain the article, even if the Politburo (or its individual members) wanted to, thus any opportunity to delay publication of the article no longer existed. I essentially considered it necessary to declare the following.

Because we discuss the issue of disagreements inside the TsK, I consider it my responsibility to smooth over differences of opinion in any way I can. But from a good many talks and observations related to Party life for the last days, I came to the conviction that Comrade Trotsky's *letter plays* a directly harmful role. The effect excited by it (particularly in places† about Bernstein,[3] Party staff and youth) greatly surpasses even the effect that would probably be desirable to Comrade Trotsky himself. Having that in mind, I considered it necessary to write absolutely and definitively in protest against this letter. It is possible to criticize the entire Party and its highest offices, but it is not allowed to shake the main foundations of our Party even under the pretense of criticizing traditions.

With friendly regards,
Bukharin

Attested printed copy and autograph.[4]
printed according to the text of the first
publication in the journal *Izvestiya TsK KPSS,*
1990, No. 12, pp. 173–174.

---

*Emphasis on the original. (Ed.)
†As in the text, if probably should read "places." (Ed.)

NOTES

1. Trotsky's letter to the Politburo of the TsK and to the Presidium of the TSKK, December 13, 1923. See Document No. 33.

2. The article "New Course. The Letter to the Party's Meetings" ("Novyi kurs Pismok partiinym soveschaniyam").

3. The part of Trotsky's letter where he hypothetically admitted the possibility of regeneration of the Party's leaders, as had happened to some leaders of the Second International.

4. The document is presently filed in the archives of the President of the Russian Federation.

35

From the Statement of Eight Members and Candidate Members of the Politburo of the Tsk of the RKP(b)

December 14, 1923

The resolution of the Central Committee and the TSKK about the workers' democracy[1] means the immediate setting up of complicated tasks for the Party.

During the discussion of the resolution of the TSK in the committee and in the subcommittee,[2] Comrade Trotsky introduced a great many amendments that threatened, we firmly believe, to imbue the transitional period* with a painful and dangerous character. With the help of all these amendments Comrade Trotsky strove to impart the document of the Central Committee an air of condemnation of all previous work of not only the Central Committee, but Party personnel as a. whole. At the same time Comrade Trotsky did not absolutely agree on a clear and outright condemnation of so-called grouping inside the Party when working out the Central Committee's resolution itself.

Both in the Committee of the Politburo and in the Subcommittee we strove in every way possible to persuade Comrade Trotsky to abandon the part of his amendments that threatened to convert the resolution about workers' democracy from a weapon of inner-Party peace into one of inner-Party struggle and the undermining of the authority of the leading bodies within the Party.

---

*To inner-Party democracy. (Ed.)

Comrade Trotsky withdrew a number of his amendments and, by doing so, created the possibility of the unanimous adoption of the resolution.

However, at this time we must draw the attention of the Central Committee to Trotsky's actions, which are extraordinarily disquieting from the point of view of the unanimous implementation of the adopted resolution. The day after* the adoption of the resolution. Comrade Trotsky addressed, over the heads of the TsK, the districts' meetings in Moscow, and then published his article "New Course" (Novyi kurs) in *Pravda*.[3] In our opinion the article in its essence represents the frustration of the unanimous decision which could take place only as a result of the abandoning of some amendments by Comrade Trotsky.

A significant part of the article lies in (1) setting one part of the Party against the other, (2) setting the Party youth against the major kernel of the Party, and (3) discrediting the central administrative kernel in the Party.

The crowning achievement of Comrade Trotsky was his statement in a letter to the TsK of the RKP that "the October plenary session became the highest expression of staff's bureaucratic course."[4] It is perfectly clear to us that Comrade Trotsky constructed his address to the Party, devoted to the problem of Party staff, in such a way as to hint at his real thought, i.e., that the Central Committee itself and now acting Party staff as a whole are "bureaucratic groupings which do not deserve the Party's trust."

We cannot consider such a. statement made the day after the unanimous adoption of the resolution of the Central Committee as nothing but an attempt to frustrate the unanimous implementation of the resolution of the TsK and TSKK.

In his statement to the TsK RKP, Comrade Trotsky said: "The October plenary session condemned what now, two months later, the Politburo found it necessary to adopt." That is the most thorough distortion of facts that we will be obliged to remedy.†

In the subsequent text Comrade Trotsky opens up his attack,[5] pitting the youth against the "older generation," personifying practical experience of the Party and its "revolutionary traditions." It is theoretically incorrect that the young people are the most accurate barometer of the Party. It is also

---

*The resolution "On Party Building" was adopted on December 5. Trotsky's article "New Course" (Novyi kurs) is dated by December 8. (Ed.)

†The abstracts of the answer of the Politburo's members of October 19 and the resolution of joint October plenary session of the TsK and the TSKK of the RKP(b). (Documents Nos. 17 and 21: III). (Ed.)

incorrect that the youth gathered by us within precincts of "rab faks"[6] and institutes of higher education* may be considered to be the Party's group from which the Central Committee must take direction using the youth as a barometer. For the TsK and the Party as a whole, such a group is not and must not be the Party's group placed under very specific conditions and undergoing specific processes, but the main proletarian part of our Party. However, this theoretically wrong construction was used by Comrade Trotsky only in order to undermine the Party center's authority, which can "unwittingly become the most complete expression of staff bureaucracy" by means of opposing the major center of the Party to the younger generation at a later stage.

An unambiguous hint at "Marx's pupils," who "regenerated in a direction of the opportunism," is certainly being made in order to additionally undermine the authority of the central bodies of the Party, in which a great majority belongs to Lenin's own pupils. Comrade Trotsky may not like the structure of these bodies, but we cannot help but think that similar analogies and hints at the opportunistic regeneration of the major Bolshevik cadres which grew up and got stronger in a struggle against opportunism, are irrelevant in every way because they were made by Comrade Trotsky,[7] who fought closely together with opportunists against Bolshevism for many years.

In his address to the Party Comrade Trotsky doesn't touch upon the question of such groupings. In the meantime we are well informed that the question of freedom for groupings within the Party became the focus of disagreements when we worked out the resolution at the Central Committee. Naturally it inevitably became a major point debated in all the Party meetings lately. Of course, the former faction of "democratic centralism"[8] tirelessly and absolutely declares its complete solidarity with Comrade Trotsky's views on the inner-Party problems. From the other side, during the meeting of the Politburo Comrade Trotsky announced his full solidarity with the Group of Forty-Six and repeated it in another form in his written statement to the Central Committee.[9] Thus in this point Comrade Trotsky took a position which opens up the possibility to the former group of "democratic centralists," forming the kernel of the forty-six,[10] to consider itself headed by Comrade Trotsky.

The system of views on Party building, which was developed by Com-

---

*Colleges. (Ed.)

rade Trotsky and especially visually expressed in his attitude to Party staff, the major Party center, and freedom for groupings, clearly deviates from the organizational principles on which our Party has been built for many years, and undoubtedly includes elements which we are accustomed to see on the pages of newspapers, which for a number of years systematically criticized "Bolshevik Centralism," "bolshevik komitetchina," "bolshevik bureaucracy."[11]

Thus, the Central Committee is faced with the fact that the day after unanimous adoption of the resolution Comrade Trotsky addressed to the Party. an article which really presents the frustration of unanimous implementation of unanimously adopted resolution, and which is able to lead to factional shocks and convulsions at the transition to the new track mentioned by Comrade Trotsky, we would like to avoid in every possible way. We do not put the issue of Comrade Trotsky's statement on the agenda of the Politburo's meeting only because of the anxiety that immediate discussion of this statement in the present circumstances may create difficulties in Party implementation of the resolution of the TsK and the TSKK. But we considered it to be our duty to inform members of the TsK and the TSKK, that we consider Comrade Trotsky's statement his address to the Party to be (1) theoretically wrong, (2) incorrectly orienting the Party in a matter of implementation of workers' democracy and dangerous for planned realization of the Party's principles, and (3) undermining the unanimity which was reached at the Central Committee's meeting and which is a main guarantee of the most painless realization of inner-Party democracy.

We are not going to abandon the hope that Comrade Trotsky will offer corrections and changes in his subsequent statements which place his position nearer to that of the Central Committee of the Party.

Buharin
Zinoviev
Kalinin
Kamenev
Molotov
Rykov
Stalin
Tomsky

RTSHIDNI, f. 51, op.1, d. 21,
pp. 62–63; typographic text,
Originally printed in the journal
Izvestiya TsK KPSS, 1990, No.12, pp. 174–179.

NOTES

1. The resolution "On Party Building" see the appendix to Document No. 24.

2. About the committee of the TsK on the inner-Party situation and about the sub-committee of the Politburo of the TsK, which worked at the final text of the resolution "On Party Building," See note 1 to Document No. 24.

3. The article "New course" ("Novyi kurs.") The "letter to the Party's Meetings" (Pismok partiynym soveshjaniyam") was written on December 8 and published in *Pravda* on the December 11,1923 (see Document No. 30).

4. Trotsky's letter of the December 9, 1923 to the TsK RKP(b) is meant (see Document No. 31).

5. In this and the.following extract Trotsky's article "New Course." "Letter to the Party's Meeting" (Pismo k partiinym soveshchaniyam) is meant.

6. Workers' faculties ("rabfaks") were general education schools for preparation of youth for the colleges. They were set up in the institutes of higher education, and there were daytime and evening classes. Based on a Bolshevik conception of class approach to the formation of the education system, the youth from workers' families were chiefly admitted to "rabfaks."

7. This extract almost literally repeats the text from N. I. Buharin's article, "Our Party and Opportunism" (Nasha partiya i opportunism), published in *Pravda* on December 13, 1923. As a whole, taking into account the style and argument presented, it may be supposed that the author of the published document was N. I. Bukharin.

8. The group of "democratic centralism" proclaimed its separate platform on the issues of Party and Soviet construction at the Eighth, Ninth, and Tenth Congresses of the RKP(b). After the Tenth Congress (1921) it ceased existence as an organized group. However even at the following congresses (Eleventh and Twelfth) the most active leaders of the group (I.V. Sapronov and N. Osinsky) sharply criticized the inner-Party regime. In the spring of 1923, on the eve of the Twelfth Congress of the RKP(b), they secretly spread the document under the title of "The Present Situation in the RKP and the Tasks of the proletarian Communist Vanguard" in the Party organization. The document, according to the version of G. E. Zinoviev, was written by the leaders of the group of "democratic centralism." The document's authors pointed to the growing trend toward the bureaucratic regeneration of the RKP(b); put forward the proposal to destroy the Communists' monopoly on administrative posts; and demanded the dismissal of G. E. Zinoviev, Stalin, and L. B. Kamenev who, in their opinion, did the most to promote under the cover of hypocritical phrases, the decay of the Party and the growth of bureaucracy out of the Party leadership.

9. Probably the meeting of the Politburo of the TsK on October 18 and Trotsky's letter of December 9 to the TsK (see Document No. 31, paragraph 3) are meant.

10. The representatives of the former group of "democratic centralism" numbered not more than ten persons in the Group of Forty-Six who had signed the statement to the TsK of the RKP(b) of October 15.

11. The criticism of organizational principles of the Bolshevik Party, which the opponents of Lenin provided from the very beginning, since the Congress of The Russian Social Democratic Labor Party. The opponents were from the Menshevik faction, who considered rigid centralism in the construction of the Party to be a reason for the buildup of bureaucracy.

36

Materials of the Discussion Meeting concerning Courses for Secretaries of District Committees of the RKP(b)[1]

December 14, 1923

I. N. I. BUKHARIN'S REPORT

Comrades!

I must begin today's report with a somewhat unusual statement which nevertheless is the result of the course of discussion in districts and of those undesirable considerations that are spreading in connection with our inner-Party struggle, which is rather desperate now.

You see, comrades, the situation in our country is that we have, if it can so be expressed, a single-Party system, and that all other parties or their embryos, or groups hostile to us, hostile to the dictatorship of the proletariat, are all defeated and exist underground. Thus, our Party is the only one. It goes without saying that this single-Party system, as this regime can conditionally be referred to, entails a series of consequences, the chief consequence being that various classes and social groups, as well as various political entities, find themselves definite channels and come to being inside the Party, where under different circumstances they would exist outside our Party.

We can see this manifested in some crude and undesirable ways, for instance, in the form of so-called rumors, gossip, unproved facts, and so on.

Simply by virtue of our having a single-Party system our Party being a universal one while being a workers' Party, those narrow-minded gossips, who heretofore would have sprung from the ranks of Mensheviks, social-ist-revolutionaries,[2] and others, tend now to come from our own Party. Our inner-Party discussion awakens a series of monstrous rumors and gossip. I am speaking here about such things which I can speak about only at inner-Party meetings.[3] It is said that Trotsky did not inspect a military parade[4] be-cause he was kept from inspecting a parade, that he is under arrest, and that the malaria which he writes about is a fig leaf. Other, similar things are whispered, and Party members are engaged in this gossip.

Just recently a rumor was set in motion, in connection with our dis-cussion, which very often generate other rumors, the latter at time break-ing away at our Party meetings, that discussion is supposedly proceeding about whether or not Comrade Trotsky should be turned out of the Central Committee or even out of the Party.

I am empowered to state here, on behalf of like-minded members of the Party, that all these rumors being spread are absolute lies and slander. Such an incredible thought that a place is being prepared for Comrade Trot-sky outside our Party or our Politburo has not occurred to any members of the Politburo or the Central Committee.[5] And just because our Party is a united one, the only proletarian Party, there should be an end put to this. If we continue to carry on a discussion that feeds on such gossips and to lis-ten such speeches we shall indeed bring about the disintegration of our Party in a very short time. To burden our inner-Party discussion with such things is, without a doubt, a morbid phenomenon.

The following events are noted: in a district an old worker, under the spell of rumors said that the Central Committee fabricated Curson's ulti-matum[6] out of considerations of inner-Party policy and was deeply con-cerned with this original fabrication of Curson's not with respect to Soviet Russia.

. . . I repeat once again that despite the existing disagreements with Comrade Trotsky and other comrades, the stories being put into circula-tion[7] have not come from any member of the Politburo of the Central Committee, and should be decisively rejected.

A canard is making the rounds[8] that Comrade Trotsky has been ex-pelled from Politburo membership, and that Lenin died three months ago and the Central Committee is hiding this.

I repeat that such foolishnesses helps nobody but our apparent enemies and that an end should be put to it at last.

Most members of the Politburo are, on the contrary, very satisfied with the existing unanimity among themselves; as you know, the Central Committee's resolution, which was adopted at the united session of the members of the Politburo and the Presidium of the Central Control Commission was done so unanimously.[9] The session was held in Comrade Trotsky's apartment[10] and Comrade Trotsky voted for this resolution.

We esteem the unanimity of this decision. The fact that most members of the Politburo tried to get the resolution on at all times as well as the resolution itself adopted unanimously proves that all gossip circulating through other channels and making an impression on some Party members should be dismissed.

One can shake one's fists and say: See, they do not provide Comrade Trotsky with the opportunity to work and want to turn him out of the Central Committee. By doing this one can shock the ill-informed public and make them prick up their ears. But I should categorically warn against such a tactic; it is not serious.[11] The policy must be serious, and a serious Communist, being a Marxist, is obliged, even in personal disagreements taking place within or outside the Party, to look not for a personal squabble but a certain political trend. If the question tends to be focused on individuals, it has to do with political disagreement and political trends.

This is the first remark which I am obliged to make so that any objections to be raised along these lines can be omitted beforehand.

Let me pass to the heart of the matter.

The Central Committee unanimously adopted the resolution which I mentioned above. We firmly hope that it will become a basis for all of us, for all members of the Central Committee, for all comrades thinking about the fortune of the Party, and that this resolution will be carried as amicably as possible. What was the signal that forced the Central Committee to change course? What was to a certain extent the warning voice that caused the Politburo and the Presidium of the Central Control Commission to pay particular attention to the inner-Party situation?

Comrades who come out against the Central Committee very often ascribe the initiative to themselves in this case. They say: We were condemned at one time for what is now being adopted; we set the fashion for the Party, we forced the Central Committee to pay attention to pursue the irregular policy and the serious inner-Party situation and in so doing we promoted settling the matter properly. And they considered that not a drop but the whole tun of honey belonged to them.[12]

Comrades, there can be no denying that both resolutions and opposition groups[13] had certain importance, but all should be assigned under distinct headings so that the question can be considered in essence.

The principal resolution that began to track down and uncover this illness was the September resolution of the Politburo, which resolved to establish a series of commissions, including a commission on inner-Party life.[14] It was adopted because there were a series of symptoms revealing that the illness was both outside and within the Party. Among these symptoms were a variety of large strikes, including those in Sormovo, Donbass, and Kharkov.[15] There was a rather disturbing meeting of railwaymen which was Kronstadt-like in character[16]—perhaps it was not, but in any case, attending comrades regarded it so.

It is self-evident that there were profound reasons for these events in our economic life: dissatisfaction on the part of a major portion of the workforce in a variety of industrial centers, being of high strategic importance, and discussions at transport. These events, needless to say, were that socio-political background against which such groups as the "Rabochaya Pravda" (Workers' Truth) and "Rabochaya gruppa" (Workers' Group) headed by Myasnikov,[17] who was expelled from the Party, could arise and come to the surface.

That was the principal fact which struck the Central Committee in the face and forced it to pay attention to the necessity of some reforms, sometimes quite substantial ones. There follows a need therefore to form a diversity of commissions of the TsK (Tsentralny Komitet—Central Committee): the activity of the commission on "price scissors"[18] has led to price reduction, and to the policy of reducing trade prices and changing the price policy of our syndicates. Further [as the result of work of the Tsk's commission on wages] a number of resolutions regarding wages were adopted and circulars were sent around that put the responsibility for paying wages on time upon our provincial committees.

A commission on inner-Party building was formed.[19] It is reasonable that hesitations which generally arose had to affect our Party and force it to take a closer look at these questions. Because of this, a commission on inner-Party questions was formed which directed the source to inner-Party democracy, which was then approved by the October plenum[20] and, later on, was reflected in the resolution which is known as the resolution unanimously adopted by the Politburo and so on.

All these events, the succession of events, forced us to pay quite serious attention to the state of our Party machinery because other things were often hidden from view under the guise of talk about the machinery.

At present there is nobody who would not take a profound interest in substantial shortcomings in our Party machinery. In the course of discussion it is common for the opposition to assume the exclusive right to speak about the shortcomings of this machinery while others, including members of the Politburo, do not supposedly see these shortcomings. Here I can, for a whole hour or two, or even three hours, speak on and on about the evils of our Party machinery, about our defenders, members of Party cells very often "trembling" before non-Party people and once again being afraid of saying the least word: they cannot find a real connection with non-Party workers, cannot find the proper words, and merely try to somehow hush up sore subjects; and how, by virtue of the members of our organizations being incapable of standing a discussion, incapable of explaining, engaging, forcing themselves to listen, and so on, our organizations turn into purely bureaucratic institutions.

One can, I repeat, very eloquently and very truthfully represent the shortcomings of our machinery and all this will to a large measure be right, but our task is much more profound: it is to find the ways, the methods which we want to use for settling the present situation.

If we pay attention to our discussion and ask ourselves: What are we discussing now, what is going on with us, what are we disputing, then what does it turn out? the opposition says that it recognizes the resolution of the Central Committee. And we say that we, who wrote this TsK's resolution, recognize it, too. The opposition says: We demand that the discussion be guaranteed. But you know, discussion is going on everywhere: these discussions are allowed far and wide. Are they forbidden? No, they are not. (Voice from the floor: "Except the pages of *Pravda*"). We shall talk about this later on. In this regard, with us it came down to the fact that someone, whose article was rejected based on some other considerations, asks: Where is the right of Party members to freely discuss their questions? But I shall return to the question later on.

Thus, I ask: have we the guarantee for discussions which take place everywhere: Do we have them or not? We have before us the fact that discussion is going on, and this is the best proof that the resolution of the Central Committee is being put into practice.[21]

I repeat my question: what are we discussing? If we raise the question in this way, it is amply clear that we are discussing quite another thing and not only that which the resolution says. The discussion deals with a variety of questions that are very large; they should be considered, considered in detail. The first question is of the correlation between our Party machinery and we can imaging two modes of treatment: the first says: Our machinery is bad and we must approach it carefully and take all measures so as to treat it. How can we do this? Available to us are a certain cadre of machinery workers.

The other way is merely to say: away with all machinery workers. But if we thros out all the machinery workers, nothing will remain of our Party organization. If we throw out even three-fourths of them, we shall thereby force our machinery's disintegration.

If we winnow and sort out by a new, i.e., through democratic elections from lower strata in such a manner that in each stage of development an uninterruptedly functioning machinery will be provided, we shall only gain by it.

Any statement, any discussion of a question, has its positive and negative aspects. If in our Party organization we create condition for the persecution of those holding Party posts, we shall thereby only weaken the machinery but not treat it. Everyone will be ashamed to be elected to this machinery and will consider the label "machinery worker" as a definite stigma, for they will be afraid of being considered, if an official and bureaucrat, as a second-quality and dishonorable element from the Communist standpoint.

When we see some comrades criticizing the machinery's work we say, certainly, that one can make his run and avoid our interference. But then, at some time, we will regret having done this due to a misunderstanding of the qualitative aspect of the matter. I offer an example. At one meeting I said that I can undertake "to incite" any factory and carry on the resolution of mistrust of the Soviet power there. I can do it at any factory, any plant, and for this very simple reason: one has only to summarize all the existing disgraceful practices (irregular payment of wages and many similar transgression). Do you really believe that after this it will be difficult to carry on the resolution of mistrust of our machinery? Even Ilyich,* a member of the Central Committee, speaks of it as being czarist and bureaucratic.[22]

But no Communist does it because we would thereby bring on a situation that would mean disaster for us. The voicing of such a question would mean causing our state machinery to crumble, not treating it.

---

*V. I. Lenin (Ed.).

To even greater extent this relates to our Party machinery because, if our state machinery is covered with sores, we can and must treat it through our Party machinery. How can we improve the state of our economy? Through our Department of Registration and Distribution.[23] And as we have an urgent need for a healthy Party machinery we say: Keep within limits, comrades, do not provoke a hatred for "machinery workers"; keep in mind that very honored comrades are among these machinery workers who hold high posts and do not betray your machinery which has rendered such great services to you. Treat it, take stern measures, but do not cause it to crumble.

Now let me speak about the statement of the question about "the old" versus the youth which at present is being hotly discussed. Our discussion, which at the beginning rested only on inner-Party questions, then went beyond these limits and turned into organizational questions in connection with Comrade Trotsky's letter.[24] Thereafter the discussion began in districts, too. That was a certain small step in the direction of discussing questions somewhat political in character. When the question is of the "old" and the youth, it is quite natural that we are faced with a great political problem. In this regard our situation, and the problem of correlation between "the old" and the youth, is acute. The seriousness of the situation is explained by the circumstance that the difference between "the old" and the youth is that of age, not merely that of feeling and temper; here we have something greater which results from our having for the first time to set about the formation of a new stratum within the cadre of workers and peasants. This stratum is now entering the store of life. How to qualify this new stratum and how to compare it with the old guard?

It is a misconception for someone to say that they are the younger generation, small fry, that they have not been Party members long enough and need to learn. Conceivably such a conservative standpoint is not right. It is irregular for the simple reason that the living movement, the living Party must continuously keep up the succession between generations, continuously have somebody in reserve so that from this reserve there might be people to hold executive posts in our Party. It is the wide latitude given to choose and re-elect people that renders the transition period good. But, on the other hand, comrades, we should see quite clearly that this is a stratum that can more than any other be captured by the wave of regeneration for the simple reason that there ideology did not pass through that school which the old guard passed through. There are strata which have not the experience of the civil war and they are promoted to definite leading posts.

These are not merely factory workers* but rather a new cadre of intelligentsia and, naturally, because of its youth, it is perhaps to a greater extent subject to the influence of strata alien to us. This danger is present and we should recognize it.

One cannot say at the meeting that the youth is in danger of regenerating into Bernsteins.[25] This is a definite untruth, this is irregular both politically and theoretically, for our principal cadre are workers and our task with respect to the youth is not to allow the connection between new intelligentsia and workers, between new intelligentsia and our Bolshevik guard to be severed.

Now I must speak about "the old." There is such an estimated of the "old" and the youth in the letter of Lev Davidovich†: our *Pravda* says‡ that the most honored comrades the closest Lenin disciples are at the head; but Marx also had close disciples who regenerated into opportunists and traitors, we are faced with the prospect of regeneration. When in the course of discussion some comrades accuse the Central Committee and say that Lenin's disciples can take on irregular course, it becomes dangerous and important in character, it is not a theory, an abstraction; it has a definite political sense. And it is just this sense that is dangerous for our Party.

As for the question at issue, we perhaps shall positively regenerate in historical prospects but there are wits who say that to raise the question in such a manner is a touch stone. But this touchstone is the attention to the events in Germany.[26] All the members of the Politburo and all the members of the Central Committee, and not these alone, know that we reconstituted our military budget so that everything can be oriented to the war. You know that part of our regiment was sent to the western frontier; all know that we took the last means and gave it for the war. Is it possible to make a charge with such accusations? Where is the logic here? Are there any reasonable political arguments? One cannot trifle with an accusation in such a manner, and one can not so raise a question, too. Lenin was absent for only a year, and in this year we so regenerated that we were ready to sacrifice all to the German revolution. Is there at least a drop of the actual, true objective analysis? If we say this to Lenin's closest disciples, and to the rest of the youth we just say without giving them notice that this is the whole

---

*Engaged immediately in industrial production. (Ed.).

†L. D. Trotsky. (Ed.).

‡*Sic.* Apparently it should be "our Party says." (Ed.).

point, then, rashly comparing one or another assertion relative to "the old" and the youth. There follows from this a definite political line which one can roughly speak about: away with the old Central Committee consisting of "the old," orient yourself to these new strata. If we lose Lenin's traditions we shall entangle ourselves. Comrades, such statements are definitely too political in nature, I consider them theoretically irregular, logically false, and politically harmful.

The same can be said relative to the freedom of criticism. We are for freedom of inner-Party discussion. But if we approach comrades and say, "Your task is to persist in your opinion[27] and not to add a word to it," we shall thereby make a political mistake. We must be for full freedom of criticism inside our organizations and among the youth, but we have currents which, I imagine, have nothing in common with Marxism. I consider that we have non-Marxist groups and I believe that if this danger were rightly understood, there would be no one who would think that this is Marxist ideology.

As our youth is subject to various influences, if you tell it about freedom of discussion and firmness of convictions, but, knowing the current state of youth, do not add that there are limits beyond which one enters into non-Marxist ideology, you are making a mistake. You merely flatter this youth, which is inadmissable on the part of a man who pretends to Party leadership. This question is connected with the previous one of "the old" and so on.

Finally, disagreements refer to [the question of] factions and factional groups. This, comrades, is a disagreement, but very often it is slurred and very often one fashions it into a harmless form. In such cases they say that the factional group is nonsense, the bugaboo with which one wants to frighten in order to stop discussion. I do not know what this bugaboo must frighten comrades who want to discuss the question. Referred to as factional groups are those that have a political platform, have their own discipline, distribute their forces, and work up public opinion. We are against such groups as well as against the abolition of the Tenth Congress's decisions.[28]

Here many comrades have a grudge against my referring, as an argument, to the times of the Brest peace[29] because during the Brest peace the freedom of factions existed. I presented a reference for which some comrades hold a grudge against me. I said at one Party meeting that then there was a sharpened struggle, that leftist socialist-revolutionaries offered a collaboration with us. I did not say that we agreed with this but I said that

I was a culprit in the struggle against leftist socialist-revolutionaries. offered a collaboration with us. I did not say that we, agreed with this but I said that I was a culprit in the struggle against leftist socialist-revolutionaries. We did not put leftist socialist-revolutionaries under lock and key for this. Owing to this sharpened factual situation we frankly thought among ourselves that we should have to form a cabinet together with the leftist socialist-revolutionaries with Lenin being made to resign.[30]

One accuses me: why have you been silent about this for six years and why are you speaking about this only now? I do not look at it from the standpoint of moral appraisal. But when I see that we have at least some danger of dissidence I am obliged to use all arguments that can mollify this situation. Then I say that one cannot appeal to the experience of Brest because then we were within a hairsbreadth of the death of the proletarian revolution

I spoke about it at all the meetings. One tries to tease me: why repent now? Repented of the national question, repented of one thing and another and now you repent again. But what to do, God bless me? We are debating a question and for this we need to learn lessons from our experience. How to learn lessons when we are silent about this experience?

Now again we have a critical situation in the Party, a profound Party crisis one more. Many do not even understand the depth of the crisis and each has the right to think about all circumstances related to this crisis. I am afraid that it will be the most profound crisis we have faced yet. Perhaps, I am making a mistake. History will show whether it is so or not.

This is what we must consider: you can criticize the Central Committee and discuss any question excluding the military and activities; but the discussion of groups and platforms is of particular danger for us because we are the ruling Party and this can cause splits and disruptions and, as a consequence, disruptions and, as a consequence, disorganization of all machinery. With us it is particularly dangerous because any discussion on platforms and any factional discrepancy are headed by such outstanding persons that this further increases the danger. For this reason this dissidence can become more profound.

We had the only man, Lenin, who had an indisputable authority. Now he has left us and this circumstance should be taken into account as well. Why Comrade Lenin foresee and why was he anxious about possible dissidence? Because he foresaw this thread of events beforehand when we did not see it. He imagined this possibility of dissidence just as it is occurring now.[31] (Preobrazhensky's voice from the floor: "It is not true.")

Bukharin: Quite so, Comrade Preobrazhensky. It was right, and I affirm and shall say in my concluding remarks that it is right; but if it is not right, you must think over Lenin's last articles which he considers as a kind of testament: there he expresses anxiety about the fortune of our Party, about the dissidence being possible. Now when some time passed and our Party began to "be shaken," a number of the Politburo members and the TsK became anxious and this anxiety grows more and more. You should think this over so as to take Sapronov[32] and comrades of great value in hand. There is another nuance which is difficult to formulate but which, nevertheless, I am trying to describe by several phrases.

This nuance, if it can be so expressed, resides in some difference [in opinions] about the state and role of the Central Committee of the Party. In your opinion,* the TsK must be merely a registrar of what occurs in the Party. There exist Party masses, there exist transmission links between these masses and the TsK, and there exists the TsK, which connects the masses, which discusses problems and the masses carry them out. In this case the TsK is not quite a quintessence of our Party machinery. The Central Committee was not merely a registrar of events but a leading Party organ in all instances. Always it was the true strategist and in this resides in its difference from the Second Internationale.[33] Our Party features the role, the authority, and the function which were assumed by the Central Committee. We should never forget this and there are no reasons for changing this inner organization state. From here follows a series of misunderstandings based on a failure to understand the role of the Central Committee. Must the Central Committee direct the process of reorganization? Is it obliged to do this, has it the right to do this? I believe that it has the right that it is obliged to do so, and that it would not be a Bolshevik Central Committee if it did not do this.

Here I have formulated the disagreement between us and comrades belonging to the opposition. The present stage of our discussion is characterized by comrades from the opposition who adduce a number of sins which they attribute to the Central Committee. All these sins can be categorized as follows: the TsK did not take measures in economic and Party spheres, it did not take measures to linking† the working class and peasantry in the proper time. One conclusion follows from this: such a TsK

---

*That is, in the opinion of the opposition. (Ed.).
†Reinforcement of the economic union. (Ed.).

should be sent to the devil because the TsK that has led the country to its fall is worthy of but one thing: to be swept out of existence and driven out.

Initially, an impression grew in all that the matter comes down to this. But can I go to non-Party workers and tell them: "The Soviet power has led the country to the edge of disaster" and then say: "Cry hurrah for the Soviet power." If I say that the government has led the country to the brink the inevitable conclusion is: away with this government. Some comrades say that they "did not call for overthrowing the Soviet power at all." But why say this when the conclusion suggests itself?[34] At present they begin to step back and no longer bring forward such accusations. But now we should keep them in mind, for this is the question we are in essence discussing now, that is, the question of trust or distrust of the Central Committee.

As for our enemies, in their opposition speeches they say that they cannot carry on the resolution with the expression of distrust of the Central Committee and so they carry the resolution with the expression of trust in the Central Committee, but in essence this Central Committee is fit for nothing. Exactly here resides the retreat. Such a statement of the question is quite erroneous. We must openly and definitely answer the question: is our TsK trustworthy or not?

After evaluating the last two years, during one of which our Party existed without the chief, Vladimir Ilyich, we have the right to say that our Central Committee has passed an examination even without Vladimir Ilyich. If the question is one of trust or distrust of the Central Committee, without any diplomatic reservations, as I imagine, we shall unconditionally vote for trusting our leading organ which has led this country to a much wider road than it was two years ago. (Applause)

RTsKhIDNI, f. 17, op. 84, d. 476, l. 2-21.
Published for the first time.

NOTES

1. In accordance with the decision of the Twelfth Congress, in Moscow the Central Committee of the RKP(b) (Rossiiskaya Kommunisticheskaya Partiya [bolshevikov]— Russian Communist Party of Bolsheviks, RKP[b]), conducted courses on training and teaching secretaries of district committees of the Party, the local and mass links of the Party

structure. At meetings secretaries and machinery workers of the TsK RKP(b), heads of state and economic administrations gave lectures and reports. Forming Party opinion in district organizations in many respects depended on what information secretaries of district committees received at these courses.

2. On Mensheviks and socialist-revolutionaries see not 39 to Document No. 17.

3. The question is one of closed, inner-Party information for the members of the RKP(b) only.

4. By tradition, military parades in honor of the next anniversary of the October Revolution in Red Square in Moscow inspected the people's commissar of military and marine affairs (the minister of war).

5. In three days, on December 17, 1923, the Politburo of the TsK RKP(b) adopted the decision (see Document No. 38) which repeated these words of Bukharin almost verbatim. Indeed, it was too early to turn Trotsky our of the TsK and Politburo, for his authority in the Party, the army, and among the youth was still too high. In addition, Lenin was still alive and to judge from the note of M. I. Ulyanova and N. K. Krupskaya to the TsK (see Document No. 42), he followed the discussion through the newspapers. But nevertheless both N. I. Bukharin's statement here and the Politburo's decision were a fraud for Party masses. As G.Ye. Zinovyev would recognize later (in 1926), both the "team of three" and the factional "team of seven" were formed as part of the TsK's leadership with the aim of politically discrediting Trotsky, isolating him, excommunicating from the old guard, and "surrounding" him with people welcome to the "leading kernel" of the TsK. As for Bukharin's positive statements as well as the adoption and publication of the Politburo's decision of December 17, they required to "calm" Party masses; many resolutions adopted at discussion meetings in Party organizations demanding that the TsK guard Trotsky from personal attacks.

6. On Curson's ultimatum see note 32 for Document No. 4.

7. On expelling Trotsky from membership in the Politburo of the TsK RKP(b).

8. To set a canard in motion means to spread rumors and gossip.

9. It means the resolution of the Politburo of the TsK and the Presidium of the TSKK (Tsentralnaya Kontrolnaya Komissiya—Central Control Commission, TSKK) "On Party Building" (see Appendix 2).

10. See note 1 to Document No. 24. On these sessions at L. Trotsky's apartment see: L. Trotsky, *My Life. An Attempt at an Autobiography*, (Moscow, 1991), p. 474.

11. N. K. Krupskaya wrote in her letter to G.Ye. Zinovyev, just after the October united plenum of the TsK and TSKK, about the forming of conditions in the Politburo which excluded the possibility for Trotsky to work jointly and amicably and the responsibility of the "team of three" for this. (see Document No. 22).

12. This is a lame use of the metaphorical expression "a spoon of tar in a tum of honey" (analogous to the English saying "a fly in the ointment").

13. Bukharin means that both the fact of an existing opposition and its documents definitely affected the activity of the TsK RKP(b).

14. On the TsK's commission on the inner-Party situation see note 2 to Document No. 4.

15. The question is of workers' strikes, which in the summer and autumn of 1923 enveloped large industrial regions of the country.

16. In the present case it means the characteristic of being sharp and anti-government.

The Kronstadt mutiny emanated from the garrison of Kronstadt (a port in the Gulf of Finland, 30 km. from Petrograd) and crews of some ships of the Baltic navy in March 1921. The mutiny which went on under the slogan "Power to Soviets but not to Parties," reflected the dissatisfaction among wide strata of the peasant and working classes with a policy of war communism and was an immediate consequence of delaying the transition to a new economic policy after the termination of the civil war. "Economics of the spring of 1921 has turned into policy: Kronstadt," wrote Lenin (see *Complete Works*, vol. 43, p. 387). On March 18 the mutiny was suppressed by troops under the command of M. N. Tukhachevsky.

17. On the illegal groups "Rabochaya pravda" and "Rabochaya gruppa RKP" see note 5 to Document No. 4 and note 6 to Document No. 20.

18. The September plenum of the TsK of 1923 formed a commission for settling price policy and regulating payment of wages to workers (RTsKhIDNI, f. 17, op. 2, d. 103, 1. 6–9).

19. On the Tsk's Committee and Politburo's Subcommittee for working out proposals and on the resolution "On Party Building" see note 2 to Document No. 4 and note 1 to Document No. 24.

20. It means the October united plenum of the TsK and TSKK (see Document No. 20: I-II).

21. This is a very discrepant and demagogic argument. Following Bukharin's logic, widespread discussion would guarantee putting the resolution "On Party Building" into practice. However, on the same day, December 14, he signed and perhaps wrote himself the statement of members and alternate members of the Politburo, in which the opposition was accused of violating Party discipline by spreading the debate (see Document No. 34).

22. In his last works Lenin repeatedly emphasized this thought: "In essence, we took the old machinery from the czar and bourgeoisie." it "represents to a greater extent the survivals of the past . . . it is slightly altered on the outside but otherwise it is the most typical czarist leftover of our state machinery" (see V. I. Lenin, *Complete Works*, vol. 45, pp. 347, 383).

23. The TsK RKP(b)'s Department of Registration and Distribution was in charge of the registration and distribution of Party and Soviet executives. It was immediately subordinated to the TsK's secretariat.

24. This refers to Trotsky's article "New Course (The Letter to Party Meetings)" (see Document No. 30).

25. Bukharin means that passage in the article "New course" where Trotsky speaks hypothetically about possible machinery and bureaucratic regeneration of Party leaders but not about the youth (see Document No. 30).

Taken out of context and incorrectly interpreted, the topic on "regeneration," in consequence of demagogic eccentricities, would be represented in public speeches and newspaper articles by Stalin, G. Ye. Zinovyev, and L. B. Kamenev, as well as in Bukharin's report here, as Trotsky's attempt to raise the question of mistrust of the Bolsheviks' TsK, which would merely become a principal political accusation against him. Trotsky's main opponents were in a great hurry to give their "leading and directing" interpretation of his article in order to steer the TsK clear of possible criticism from the side of the Party mass in the course of the discussion.

26. The question is of revolutionary actions of the German proletariat, whose peak was observed in late 1923.

27. This refers to the passage of Trotsky's article "New Course" where it is said that the youth must critically relate to revolutionary traditions, work out its own opinion, and so on.

28. This refers to the resolution of the Tenth Congress of the RKP(b) "On the Unity of the Party," which forbade forming factions and groups.

29. As is known, during the First World War (1914-1918) two state coalitions were battling one another: the Entente (France, Great Britain, and Russia) and the Four-state union (Germany, Austro-Hungary, Bulgaria, and Turkey). In April 1917 the United States entered the war on the side of the Entente. After the October revolution of 1917, Lenin, proclaiming Soviet power in Russia on behalf of the Soviet government, appealed to the governments of the belligerent states to make peace without annexations and contributions.

Lenin, as head of the government, and Trotsky, the foreign minister, understood equally well that the Russian army could not and did not want to continue the war. Peace or at least peacetime respite was necessary for a Russia exhausted by war, and for its soldiers who were hurrying home in order to receive landed estates turned over to peasants. The continuation of the war and the further offensive of the German troops threatened the very existence of the Bolsheviks' power. However, reiterated peace overtures by the Soviet government to Entente states (before diplomatic contacts and during them) to sit down at the bargaining table with Germany met with no response. Under these conditions Soviet Russia began separate negotiations. On December 2 (15),* 1917, in Brest-Litovsk (the name of Brest until 1939) an armistice was concluded and in a week peace negotiations were started.

The three-month period of these negotiations was full of dramatic collisions and serious trials for Bolsheviks' power. First, the Brest peace significantly complicated the international situation for Soviet Russia, since the pro-German policy of its government turned its former Entente allies into potential enemies. Second, in political circles of Russia itself and inside the block of the two parties (Bolsheviks and leftist socialist-revolutionaries) there was by no means a unanimous policy toward the Brest negotiations.

Lenin was the most consistent and unswerving defender of the conclusion of peace negotiations though his position came in conflict with the Marxist doctrine of world revolution. Within the Party Lenin met with resistance from the leftist opposition ("leftist communists") headed by N. I. Bukharin. Being the adherents of revolutionary war, "leftist communists" believed an agreement with capitalist states to be impossible and considered a declaration of peace as treachery against both the proletarian revolution and the interests of the working masses in both Germany itself and Russia's regions occupied by the German army. Also counting on the proletarian revolution in Germany and Austro-Hungary was Trotsky, who believed that in the case of its development German troops would not continue a full-scale offensive (conditions in these countries fed similar illusions). From here followed his position aimed at every king of delaying negotiation, expressed by the formula "neither peace nor was" meaning not to sign the peace treaty, to stop the war.

As a result of bitter controversies, culminating in Lenin's ultimatum that he would resign, in which eventually a new German offensive (after Trotsky's declaration to stop the war and not sign the peace treaty) became the main argument, on the night of February 24, 1918, the VTsIK.

---

*I.e., December 2 in the Old Russian calendar, which was two weeks behind the Western calendar. (Ed.).

(Vserossiisky Tsentralny Ispolnitelny Komitet—All-Russian Central Executive Committee, ACEC) and the SNK (Sovet Narodnykh Komissarov—Soviet of People's Commissars, SPC) of the RSFSR (Rossiiskaya Sovietskaya Federatinaya Sotsialisticheskaya Respulika—Russian Soviet Federal Socialist Republic), informed the German government that they would accept new peace terms. On March 3 the annexation treaty, humiliating for Russia, was signed. The price that Russia paid for this peace and the supposed respite, which turned out to be very short, was most high. According to the terms of the treaty, Russia lost about a third of the territory of the former Russian empire, whose approximately 56 million inhabitants comprised a significant production potential. The economic, military, and political terms of the treaty were also severe. On November 13, 1918, after the German monarchy had been disposed, the VTsIK of the RSFSR declared the treaty to be void.

30. On the Party of the leftist socialist-revolutionaries see note 30 to Document No. 17. At the beginning of the Brest negotiations, when the Soviet delegation proposed signing a democratic peace without annexations and contributions, the leadership of the leftist socialist-revolutionary Party supported the idea. But after clearing up the annexation policy of the German government, leftist socialist-revolutionaries took a stand to continue the revolutionary war. The Brest peace having been signed, leftist socialist-revolutionaries left the government. Bukharin appears to mean the moment of ratification of the Brest peace by the Fourth Extraordinary Congress of Soviets on March 15, 1918. The episode, as told by Bukharin fifteen years later during the political trials for so-called Rightists would become one of the items in the charge against him of collusion with Trotskyites and leftist socialist-revolutionaries with the aim of wrecking the Brest peace, killing Lenin, Stalin, and Ya. M. Sverdlov, and forming a new government. As for Trotsky's position on the course of negotiations and the signing of the Brest peace it was misrepresented already in the course of the inner-Party struggle and the discussion of 1923, in which Bukharin also played a not inconsiderable part.

31. Bukharin appears to mean the "Letter to the Congress" where Lenin speaks about the danger of dissidence in the upper echelons of Party authority residing in interrelations of Stalin and Trotsky.

32. Bukharin recommended "taking in hand" G.V. Sapronov, one of the leaders of the former group of "democratic centralists" who came out at discussion meetings, in particular at the meeting of Moscow Party activists on December 11, 1923, with strongly worded criticism of the TsK and the inner-Party regime as a whole.

33. On the Second Internationale see note 4 to Document No. 3.

34. In none of the documents of Trotsky or the opposition was there the question of overthrowing the Soviet power. Identifying the TsK of the Party with the Soviet power and guarding it from any criticism, the representatives of the "leading kernel" and in the present case, Bukharin, in particular, resorted to evident falsification of the opposition's opinions. Beginning with the discussion of 1923 Stalin would use political labeling and the identifying of any criticism of the TsK with anti-Soviet activity as a means in the struggle for power.

II. YE. A. PREOBRAZHENSKY'S REPORT*

Comrades, Comrade Bukharin differs from the other members of the Central Committee by his being very liberal in supporting the TsK, and in this regard it is enjoyable to listen to him most of all for those who do not want to make the discussion excessively keen. I am one of them. I enjoyed Comrade Bukharin's speech. But it had one shortcoming: the elucidation of most questions made by him did not conform with reality. I shall give you proof of this in my report with, as it seems to me, full objectivity.

First of all, on trust and distrust of our Central Committee with respect to the line of inner-Party policy.

You know what methods of inner-Party work and inner-Party life were like during the war. You know that since [the moment of] seizing power and the beginning of the "war communism,"[1] the change in inner-Party methods of our work started. We began to adapt our inner-Party work to those conditions under which the Party and the country found themselves, that is, to the circumstance of the war. We had to carry out the centralization of our partisan armies by bringing them together into the united Red Army. . . .

. . . We had to carry out the strictest centralization of supplies through the line of the "narcomprod,"† of organization of our national economy, and primarily in the field of our army centralization. But it turned out that our directing bodies, focused as they were on forming local authorities, were not fitted for fulfilling the task, and the Party alone was able to accomplish this centralization. The Party was the father and the mother of our centralized state machinery. Subsequently, some perversions were brought into it; but, in any event, our Party kept on that centralization which was formed in the war period and which helped us to rout our enemies.

All peculiarities of the military sphere, characterized by tasks being clear and concrete and imposing a certain responsibility on everybody—all these methods were automatically extended to the whole of the industry. If we look at our industry in the past, we will see our state proletariat in the form of a commune of beggars which waged war under terribly severe conditions. We had to count up our resources and to carry the war

---

*Published with some abridgement. (Ed.).

†Through the people's commissariat of food supply.

through with the greatest economy. It is self-evident that this had an impact on our inner-Party work in that we stepped aside from the democratism of the 1917–1918 time period.

However, these military methods transferred to our work proved their justification and sense in that we were waging a civil war. The same war established its limits and known restrictions on our methods. The civil war resulted in our political departments in the army[2] being built differently than civil organizations.* Here other peculiarities took place: oversimplification of methods of work and administration, unitary work not only at the front but also inside the country. The correlation of forces was clear, the enemy was present in thousands of persons, and this led to the simplification of our administration. This, comrades, was characteristic, but it should be noted that this was characteristic *of that period* only.† We had need of unlimited centralization, of a certain participation of the machinery which began to form under the war conditions themselves.

In 1918 other demands were imposed on us. We were expecting strikes at factories and we had to speak at meetings and persuade workers not to lose hope once and for all. In that period we mobilized our executives and they were in constant contact with the masses. We had to share our impressions and to discuss the emergent situations, and, in so doing, our Party had to accomplish somewhat more centralization. But at the same time, this centralism and bureaucratism were limited by the Party's being forced to inwardly study the experience of the civil war, it was the civil war then, which resulted in the centralization and which limited it at the same time.

It was begun with my and Zinoviev's raising the question of changing this course, the question of "lower" and "upper" strata,[3] and the resolution[4] was adopted that outlined the basis of the regime with a certain indication that the regime should be changed. This was my proposal for the Tenth Party Congress in March 1921. This deviation from old methods and the attempt to pass from the "war communism" to new peaceful conditions had to lead to changing methods of inner-Party work, to revising our inner-Party course.

This revision was begun and virtually completed in 1921 at the Tenth Party Congress. Here the series of events occurred. On the one hand, the

---

*By this is meant Party organizations. (Ed.)

†Emphasis in the original. (Ed.)

Party had to adopt the efficient and well-developed resolution regarding the inner-Party democracy[5] on the report of Bukharin who reported the current situation. But at the same congress, after adopting the resolution, we were to reflect the new epoch as well. There was the Kronstsdt mutiny,[6] and at the same congress, after the trade-union discussion[7] that shook the Party, we had to adopt the resolution against any factional groups[8] because the moment was desperate, because only full and absolute Party unity could give us all chances that the Party had missed.

In order to find a way out, we adopted two resolutions at this congress which contradict one another inwardly. So long as the question is of the groups that are not the groups within the working class, and we are talking about collective discussion of the questions, about what was going on in the Party, what is and what will be, that is, about matters that the Party will not refuse if it does not cease to be a Party in general. If we don't talk about embryos of new parties inside our Party (which is always possible and took place in all parties), if we don't talk about these groups—and these were precisely the groups that were banned (the resolution of the Tenth Congress does not point out what kinds of groups are mainly meant)—if we don't talk about these groups, there was a profound contradiction here.

This resolution completed the transition to a new track. We had to pass to the NEP (Novaya Economicheskaya Politika—New Economic Policy)[9] and had to do what was necessary for our Party.

We made this transition with the most unanimity that could be expected and that could not be expected even after the trade union discussion. We did not spill any milk* if not counting a few suicides among our youth which were justified by the fact that our youth after having received Marxist education, considered the transition to the NEP to be a betrayal of Marxism, and therefore those not willing to soil their hands, passed away. But this uncertainty did not last long and the suicides were not numerous. Our part made this transition harmoniously. This transition required from us an extremely high level of discipline and centralization; and this resolution concerning factional groupings should have been adopted in case such groupings emerged, and this resolution would have been expedient.

But, comrades, we were done with this transition in about one year and during the NEP we were able to finish the main regrouping of the forces.

---

*A reference to the saying "It is no use crying over spilt milk." (Ed.)

During that period, when we had to appoint economic planners to important positions and also re-arrange all the forces under NEP, we could not make use of our democracy due to the above mentioned circumstances.

Finally, we cannot forget the fact that during the war period we lost many thousands of our Party's best members who were killed. Unfortunately, we don't have the statistical data neither in the TsK, nor in the RevVoenSovet, as to how many Party members were lost. I believe the number was eighty thousand. In Ural alone, when there were twenty thousand Party members before the Czechoslovakians,[10] after the fall of Perm, during this period we lost ten thousand people, i.e., half of the Ural Party organization. Some of these people joined the Party even before the war, some of them became its members in 1917. We lost very many [communists] in Ural, many of them were executed by the white guards, many were taken from our underground organizations and executed in Siberia under Denikin, and in Ural under Vrangel,[11] etc.

This circumstance resulted in lowering qualifications inside our Party. It should not be forgotten that at that.time we went through a period of death of Party executives. The situation arose in which we lost a significant part of our old and experienced Party members; we received lots of new members who by their quantity and quality were the actual representatives of the proletariat as a class, but who had neither sufficient political experience nor sufficient revolutionary length of service.

Under these conditions, maintaining the dictatorship of revolutionary Marxism was a most difficult task. This could be accomplished only as the result of stability in the ranks of the Party and at such a member ratio that old Party members were arranged in such a manner that they combined their Party authority with functions that gave them executive posts in the leadership of our state machinery. Thus, our Party had in its leadership 10 to 15 thousand old Communists and the "tail-end" of young members who had joined the Party, only between one and two years before. Such a situation existed over the war period and at the period of transition to the NEP.

When the transition to the NEP was completed, when declassing merit of the proletariat came to an end, a new period came in spite of the Tenth Congress's resolution.* The proletariat began to be concentrated in towns, declassing ceased, and gathering the proletariat started, when our factories began to operate again, approximately a year after the transition to the NEP. At the same time we did a lot in the sense of Party schooling.

---

*Meant here is the resolution "On Party Unity." (Ed.)

And that was the moment when we should have raised this question without expecting it to have been raised spontaneously, because we were the Party, because we were leaders of the Party and should have raised the question ourselves without waiting to be hit on the back of the head. War conditions elapsed, they no longer exist. We are living under peaceful conditions when there is no acute danger and the possibility exists to debate, to discuss, to search for something new. Now we can return to the normal conditions of life that existed in 1917 when we did not fall into such a dead thing as happened in 1923. We should have raised the question about one and a half years ago of changing the course. If we did not raise the question, I personally consider it to be a mistake on my part and that of the Central Committee that the question was not raised when we had an opportunity to raise it, approximately a year after the Tenth Congress.

An unbelievable noise was made against me in view of my having said that for two years the Party had been pursuing an erroneous policy in inner-Party work.[12] Recently, Comrade Zinoviev said that a year had passed since the proletariat had begun to move. Perhaps, he made a faulty calculation: it was not one but two years. A year after March 21 we could enter the new phase; at that time conditions changed radically and we should have changed our inner-Party policy as one of the functions of the dictatorship of the proletariat under new conditions.

At that time I spoke mildly because Comrade Lenin and many executives constrained me. Many kept silence then though they could have said many things. In any case, the fact remains.

Comrade Bukharin raised the question of who was the first to forewarn. If we want to be objective, if we take old protocols, we shall see that Comrade Kosior[13] was then the most resounding, his voice was the most loud. At the Tenth Congress the question should have been raised but so as not to offer the possibility of using this abroad. It should not be spoken as sharply as was done by Comrade Osinsky. Maybe this was a mistake. If we had spoken about it at the Tenth Congress we would now have a normal Party life; but instead, we have now entered a period of some Party crisis, and we must find a way out.before properly setting about inner-Party construction.

I think we can regard our action highly, though I nevertheless think that we were late. It is said in the resolution o the Politburo[14] that such a policy can lead to lots of troubles if it goes on in this way. There were comrades at the TsK's plenum[15] who exposed all our deadly sins. . . . The arguments that they present against us constitute only legally formal accusation: why did we apply to Dzerzhinsky's commission which was specially intended for Party questions[16] rather than go straight to the Politburo? But the chairman* himself declared at the sitting of the TSKK (Tsentralnaya Kontrolnaya Komissiya—Central Control Committee, TSKK): "We have too entangled ourselves, we have deviated too early from war methods.[17]

In any event, we applied to the Politburo demanding the *transition to be made*. And it would, certainly, make no sense, it would actually be the height of foolishness (I do not want to reproach the TSKK and its policy), but I cannot imagine that blame would be expressed to comrades who applied demanding the workers' democracy. One cannot reproach us with our applying collectively, with our applying as a group rather than Preobrazhensky, Serebriakov, and Piatakov separately because that would not be so authoritative. There were also comrades who did not belong to any group; for example, Comrade Muralov signed, too. This was done in order to show that we were many. We simply wanted the Central Committee to raise this question. But here I must declare that we raised it late, we should have raised it much earlier.

Many reproach us with dread, but here I must declare that we considered Vladimir Ilyich's illness to be an obstacle. Many considered that this was so but now I think it was not. If not just follow the legal, formal point of view but to consider the matter in essence, then it can be seen that we were blamed for doing this. They† should have said: We ourselves are shifting to democracy and we are going to make a certain decision in this regard; we subscribe to your proposal and will even realize it within the TsK. We suggested that the Central Committee itself should raise this question on its own initiative so as not to suggest either the Party Congress or anything else. That is the way it was.

That this document‡ had some impact, I have no doubt, and that strikes[18] also had some impact is certain. Also important was the fact that they did not let Comrade Zinovyev speak for fifteen minutes[19] as well as the fact that other comrades were aware of the sentiments of our Party masses in Moscow, which Comrade Stalin sensed at one of the meetings.[20] But all this comes down not to who was the first to forewarn and what

---

*This is a reference to F. E. Dzerzhinsky. (Ed.)
†The TsK or the Politburo of the TsK. (Ed.).
‡Here is meant the Declaration of Forty-Six.

words were said but what must be done.

We proceed to discussion of inner-Party democracy. The wording that is published* points right to it. It can be said that there are some wishes, rather cautiously expressed, to change the Party statutes, namely those items which were inserted by the conference (on calling of conferences annually and so on)[21] and amendments which resulted in the bureaucratic course in the Party and which appeared in the Party statutes, I hope, not for long, and these bureaucratic items will undoubtedly be excluded. I think this decision is substantiously right, and on the basis of this decision we can pass to the course of workers' democracy.

At the moment we cannot say that we clearly see the desire to make this transition.

Subsequently, I shall speak about the Central organ of our Party.† What we observe today is a downright outrage. I do not know whether Comrade Bukharin is the editor of *Pravda* and if it it is so it would be interesting to hear him out. Now several "commissars" are appointed there and I do not know whether he remained the editor or these "commissars.[22]

In order that the regime of the workers' democracy be realized it is necessary that, first, the freedom of discussions should exist. . . . We are not democrats only by profession, which is quite natural only for bourgeoisie. For us the democracy is a means for attaining the objective, and the democratic centralism is a means for a attaining a definite objective, and the fact that at some moment, we make a transition to the centralism through the democracy and at other moments we make a transition to the democratism through the centralism, is a means of accomplishing political aims for the Party that is pursuing class objectives.

I regard this discussion in the same manner. In order for me to renounce it, at first demonstrate for me that this discussion is needless. We disagree in that after being silent for two years the Party should be made to speak, it is necessary to change rules of holding Party meetings, to pass to a system of drawing new workmen into our Party work and to reeducate our youth, which we consider as necessary and which Comrade Bukharin spoke about and which must be carried out later on.

All this will be all right if after the Politburo's resolution some com-

---

*Hereinafter the question is of the resolution of the Politburo of the TsK and the Presidium of the TSKK "On Party Building." (Ed.)

†This is a reference to the newspaper *Pravda*. (Ed.)

rades do not speak at meetings and call for help. I heard this call for help in the speech of Comrade Zinoviev who,with his inherent woman's logic, said one thing in the beginning of his speech and quite different thing at the end.[23] At first he says that we are revolutionaries and our Central Committee is the elective organ of the Party; and everybody is welcome to criticize and so on, in short, it is this verbal democratism that is well learned by Comrade Zinovyev. . . . Then he says it is impossible to criticize in such a manner as Comrade Preobrazhensky does.

First of all: whether we have the right to criticize? Yes, we do. Why then to jeer at democracy? At the period of workers' democracy the Central Committee must not be criticized in such a manner that this criticism be concerning only with two or three items with this and that. But such things takes place and I consider it to be the mockery at the workers' democracy and the violation of the resolution a day after its signing.

There should be one thing, comrades: either we have seriously and for long passed to the new course or this document is fated to play quite different role in our inner-Party life.

We have the right to criticize the Central Committee and must criticize it; the Party which does not criticize and fears to criticize, I do not know, whether such a Party can exist as the Party of proletariat. During the construction when we face such important tasks and every member of the Party must be involved in accomplishing the tasks, the criticism is a primary necessary condition. To criticize the TsK is hot a privilege of only the opposition but the TsK's supporters must also criticize it in cases when it makes mistakes.

Comrade Bukharin says that at first an attack was carried out against the Central Committee, then a retreat. During the discussion Comrade Lenin said: who takes somebody at his word is a perfect fool.[24] Because of this, when we hear about the opposition attacks, documents should be used. And what documents do you have that the Central Committee drove the country into downfall? The sharpest word in the document of the Forty-Six group was that the further TsK's policy can drive the country into lots of troubles. This is the strongest expression throughout the document.[25]

If we consider my resolution which I proposed in Zamoskvorechye* and which was not published in *Pravda* (it was also accepted by other

---

*This is a reference to the discussion meeting of the Party organization of the Zamoskvorechye district of Moscow. (Ed.)

newspapers but was not published under the regime of the "workers' democracy" which exists in *Pravda*), in this resolution, which I myself wrote, I pointed out the mistakes in political and economic fields and in the inner-Party policy. We did not speak about the economy, we really had a long talk at the stage of discussion due to the Central Committee's fault exclusively, and because of this we could not pass to principal economic questions where disagreements can come to light. This is in the resolution. This is my resolution which criticizes the Central Committee for definite erroneous aspects of its policy.

Comrade Bukharin says that the question is of whether to trust or not trust the Central Committee, and of expressing trust or distrust in it. Comrade Bukharin represents us like this: at first we criticize, and then we do not say that the Central Committee should be removed. We, comrades, are the old revolutionaries and never allowed our Central Committees, and we never permitted ourselves to say that the Central Committee must be thrown off. Then we would have to be considered as politicians. But the Party must have the good majority and the good-quality opposition which plays a role as a revolutionary.

Comrade Bukharin presents us not only in ridiculous but in humiliating air. He ventures on casting aspersions of comrades who have 20-year length of service.*

Being revolutionaries, they will never permit themselves to criticize the Central Committee in such a manner that it would lead to its full replacement. We did not say so and we at no occasion proposed the Central Committee to be fully replaced.

The main body of the Central Committee that defines its policy, I'd say, the majority of the TsK, is the best which our Party was able to select during decades. To think of disbanding this body would be folly and it can be blamed on the opposition in order to gain argumentation in struggle against the opposition. But so long as at the present time we propose certain measures and say that we consider the majority of the Central Committee as quite efficient and being worthy of full Party confidence, which should characterize its future composition, we should be trusted. I consider it to be a polemical attack because we are imputed by what we did not say while simultaneously knowing that we don't even think so.

Comrade Bukharin knows well that what I say here is what I think.

---

*Length of Party membership. (Ed.)

Comrade Bukharin adduces another argument. He says: yes, from the outset you sat that you do not propose to disband the Central Committee and
you do well, but quite contrary conclusions follow from your speeches.
This is wrong.

Here we come to another question, the question of groups. But I shall
touch on this question in the end. I state quite categorically that the Central Committee was the first to sabotage the realization of the Politburo's
resolution. Comrades who speak on the side of the Central Committee react
on criticism so that one should refuse to criticize the Central Committee in
order not to intimidate the Party masses that have just now woken up and
attend meetings.

I accuse the Central Committee of non executing the Politburo's resolution. The Central Committee, if it wants us to have a real regime of the
workers' democracy that would be somewhat close to life, should not convert all its organs into purely factional organs which provide with a definite line,* and do not allow to defend one's own point of view to those who
have it and allowing only a mechanical way of stating this opinion.

I hold the point of view that since the Central Committee is the Organ
of the leading Party so it is not a statistical bureau and not a recorder of
events but their active participant and leader. It has the right to advocate
through its organs the line which it considered as being right, through its
Central organ it also has the right to.advocate the line which it considers as
being right and gave the major part of its Central organ for advocating the
line. It is a statute that follows from functions of the Central Committee.

But we are against TsK restoring to that methods which suppress contrary criticism when it advocates its line and opinion to be approved by the
Congress.When the MK† assembles to advocate a definite line it deliberately does not invite that comrades who hold different point of view.[26] It
can forbid us to come out on behalf of the MK but we can persist in our
opinion personally, if we find it necessary, but it does not do so.

As for *Pravda*, impossible and outrageous things take place there
against which the whole of the Party must protest. I shall present one fact:
in Baumann district the resolution is adopted against Kamenev's report on
my co-report. All the meeting votes were for my resolution excluding six
people while the resolution proposed by the district committee on

---

*Apparently, it means "dictating its line." (Ed.)
†Moscovskii Komitet—Moscow Party Committee, MPC. (Ed.)

Kamenev's report collects only six votes of which five are the members of the district committee. But it is printed in *Pravda* that the resolution is adopted just on Kamenev's report whereas it is not printed that Kamenev's resolution was not adopted. It is outrageous and shameful. At the Zamoskvorechye the resolution proposed by Kamenev and Zinoviev is turned down. Both join Ryazanov's resolution. A fourth of the meeting votes for my resolution and the others vote for the joint Comrade Riazanov's resolution. But it is not reported in *Pravda* that Kamenev's resolution was not adopted by the meeting.[27]

Then, comrades, you read in Comrade Kamenev's statement that Moscow uttered its opinion.[28] But what Moscow? They gathered the executive machinery, gathered secretaries, gathered in the hall accommodating only 2.5 thousand while it would be for 5 to 6 thousand and we know that comrades who hold different points of view received no entrance tickets there. They gathered only their "own" Party organization, a definite resolution was adopted, and in order to falsify his opinion before the whole of the Party, Comrade Kamenev says that this the voice of Moscow whereas Moscow is raising its voice just now. More than six thousand votes were given for the opposition's resolution, that is, three times as much as those for the official line, but Comrade Kamenev states before the whole of the Republic that Party Moscow uttered its word.[29]

Comrades, that is disgraceful, and *Pravda* turned into the organ for the dissemination of untruth among the members of the Party. You, comrades, know the following truth: wherever I speak at the meeting, a resolution on my report was adopted almost always. It was adopted in 24 Party cells and, in addition, in 10 workers' cells of Baumann district. In these 34 cells, of which 24 to 25 are workers' cells, our resolutions were adopted but none of them was published in *Pravda*. They all are sent to *Pravda* but only resolutions in the spirit of bureaucratic confidence are printed.

The resolution of the Mossukno No. 1 factory is printed but the last resolution of the Mossukno No. 2 factory that was sent earlier is not printed. Maybe it comes about by virtue of the copy of the resolution being mislaid in Comrade Zinoviev's briefcase, he wanted to read it but it got mislaid. Party people want to express their opinion, send their resolutions to *Pravda* with agitation, then these resolutions are lost. We have a scandalous fact of sorting out resolutions in the spirit of the chosen line, while *Pravda* is closed for comrades who want to express their point of view.[30]

It is a scandalous fact which is taking place in the editorial staff of

Pravda. We have a picture where they do not allow the opposition not only to express itself through articles but even to say that there-and-there we had adopted such-and-such resolution. We see the picture where the method of exerting mechanical pressure upon living thought is put in practice. What is it?

And we see all this several days after the resolution on workers' democracy has been adopted. Is that really the implementation of what the Politburo says in its resolution? Isn't it whether nothing but flout at the resolution and the scorn for the Party? And every politically conscious person should speak about it. So long as I see such facts, so long as I see that the members of the Central Committee tremble from a slight criticism which we began in economic and political fields, when wee see this, a doubt creeps into my mind which I did not have before and of which Comrade Bukharin tried to persuade me during our private talk.

I had a belief that it is inconceivable that the Central Committee would decide not to execute its own resolution. When we know about facts that took place at Schreder's plant, in Zamoskvorechie where oppositional resolutions were adopted and then every measure was taken on the side of directors, secretaries in order that within two or three days contrary resolutions be adopted. And we say that this is dangerous, this can lead to the aggravation of the situation which is the expression of the policy of pressure pursued during two years and in connection with which the Party life started standing still. We, comrades, must categorically protest against this fact.

On pages of *Pravda*, you, comrades, saw attacks and you understand clearly who these attacks are targeted at, that is, at Comrade Trotsky.[31] He, as turned out, is guilty of opportunism, of inclination to Menshevism and so on. Comrades, he is guilty of too many things. If Comrade Trotsky's letter* which Comrade Bukharin criticized here is considered by the Politburo as harmful, they must object to him [Trotsky] in the same tone as that of the letter. But why do we need these things at which the white guard press will jeer, why to print such things in editorials of *Pravda*?

When a front-rank worker reads this he will think that YOU shift your personal misunderstandings from a definite narrow circle to the wide Party arena, the misunderstandings accumulated by you, your personal spite which arises in close atmosphere of the Central Committee and in the

---

*This is a reference to the article "New Course (the Letter to Party Meetings)" published in *Pravda* on December 11, 1923. (Ed.)

Party. If you disagree with Comrade Trotsky come out openly, but if open statements against him are on the questions which we are discussing, these statements will be unfriendly in nature and will contain hints, teases, mockeries and as a result, our enemies abroad will jeer at us. I am sure that the polemics directed against Comrade Trotsky will not be carried out in a friendly spirit.

When I mentioned this at meetings not in such an excited tone as I do here, every meeting adopted a resolution with the protest against such an editorial. Why would they need Comrade Bukharin with his pious speeches when such things can take place? We, members of the Party, must call the Central Committee to order. We, comrades, have the right to criticize the Central Committee and must demand it not to be capricious and not to send in its resignation. What kind of workers' democracy is it? It must hear out the criticism. We trust it s main line and it should remain.Why to be nervous, why to regard any criticism as a nervous young lady would, and to allow quite intolerable things to occur when as the result of the criticism, which has started just now, we see that our hostility has grown to such an extent that it becomes a European scandal.

I accuse *Pravda* and Comrade Bukharin as the editor of that outrageous editorial which was published. If Comrade Trotsky stated his difference of opinion you should show him your disagreement in the same tone as Comrade Trotsky did. We see quite intolerable hints in the editorial and I am sure that we shall have the same articles in *Pravda* later on.[32] Owing to the criticism of this sort we shall pose as a laughing stock and we shall wreck the transition to workers' democracy. Comrade Bukharin should have protested against it: either he should have sent in his resignation as the editor of *Pravda* or he should have upheld the honor of both the Central Committee and the [printing] organ of the Central Committee.

This is, comrades, the way it is.

Further, I shall speak about the last issue, about groups. Comrade Bukharin should agree that this question must be considered with a certain social analysis. What is the group? The group can represent an embryo of different class inside our Party as it was when we brought off with Mensheviks, when it turned out that they were the part of a different class,[33] then, of course, we must put an end with those groups and the quicker the better.

But there are other groups for example, when before the Congress people struggle for majority at the Party Congress. Have you ever seen the country which knows sure ways of socialism construction? We do not know those ways but judge them on the basis of lots of definite conclusions; here we shall have disagreement in: whether the pressure on the NEP must be greater or lesser; how shall we act with regard to foreign trade. We shall always have such questions which concern the general situation on the one hand and are of practical importance on the other.

Due to all this, we shall always have groups. We have always had groups because we have been a living Party. We have such groups and, I repeat, we shall have them. As an attempt is being made to formulate definite opinion [by some group], and it struggles for the majority in the Party. Everybody has the right to persuade the Party for the majority to follow him and to persuade the majority of that. This is the right of every member of the Party. When the struggle for definite measures and for change of the policy takes place, this is a legal right of every member of the Party. The Party needs such groups, and without them the Party would die as a living organism. They confuse us with groups which are forerunners of new parties. They being us under one rubric. These are, comrades, unconscientious methods, for the unwillingness to understand us is manifested here. . . . It is so senseless and everybody sees to what extent it is made up, and socialist supports invented by Comrade Bukharin for this story is a misuse of his sociological talent that should not have been compromised here.

Can the regeneration happen with us? Yes, it can. I do not agree with Comrade Trotsky who gave the example concerning the German Social Democracy but then he did not develop the idea,[34] that the question is of such an apparatus regeneration which would take the apparatus to a different social base.[35] That is what the question is about. Comrade Bukharin says: the youth is in opposition and it should be furnished with a psychological basis so that it be for the NEP. Generally speaking, the regeneration may happen to us, and I thought that if power would be seized without civil war here, it would mean that the October Revolution had been not proletarian but bourgeois revolution under a socialist cover as all Mensheviks appraise this revolution. But that, comrades, I say among other things.

I want to say here that the regeneration is possible, that "the old" can regenerate since they lost touch with the workers' mass, meanwhile inside the working class, whose power must be absorbed by the Party, the construction of different organizations begins which go against the line projected before. Here a gap between leadership and worker members of the

Party may occur. I do not think that this will happen with us but such a danger can exist under known conditions. The regime of workers' democracy cannot guarantee against it.

Further, the same [the regeneration] may also occur through the youth when with time the working youth take the same positions now held by executive communists who cut off from the lower strata. Then it will run the same danger plus it has not gone through the course of Marxism. From this standpoint I consider Comrade Bukharin a one-sided man.

... I wish the discussion that took such a keen from would not result in a trade-union discussion,[36] but, first of all, we must demand the Central Committee not to forget the state of health of our Party and to be more composed. If members of the Central Committee violate it more than oppositional orators, we must protest against it.

RTsKhIDNI, f.18, op.84, d. 476,
1. 22-41.
Published for the first time.

NOTES

1. This is a reference to the period of civil war and military intervention (1918-1920) when the Soviet state pursued the economic policy of "war communism," main features of which were: nationalization of the whole of large-scale and middle-scale industry as well as most of small enterprises; strict planned centralization of production and distribution; expropriation of paysantry of all surplus products on the basis of food appointment; full prohibition of private trade; universal labor conscription; equalization in renumeration of labor.

At present, several standpoints exist in Russian historiography relative to chronological framework of the period of "war communism." Following the Menshevist historian N. N. Sukhanov, some researcher are prone to consider its beginning to be the introduction of state grain monopoly immediately after the February Revolution of 1917; others, analyzing the policy of "war communism" as a long-term process, find its quality parameters since the beginning of the first world war, when Russian economy was being put on a war footing.

2. Political departments (politotdely) are Party organs in armed forces. See also note on Document No. 32.

3. Ye. A. Preobrazhensky refers to the summer–autumn of 1920. At that time, when he was the secretary of the TsK and dealt with complaints and conflicts in the Party, he prepared a letter for the next Party Congress in which he raised the question of "upper" and "lower" strata and proposed to take measures of restoring normal political life in the Party (RTsKhIDNI, f. op. 86, d. 203, 1.3). The result of raising this question was a circular letter

of September 4, 1920, by which the Central Committee appealed to Party organizations. In it, specifically, the division of the Party into "upper" and "lower" strata, into workmen of central and local organs was treated as unwholesome phenomenon in Party life.

4. This is a reference to the Ninth All-Russian Conference of the RKP(b) Russian Communist Party (of Bolsheviks), RKP(b), which took place on September 20, 1920 and which adopted the resolution "On immediate tasks of Party construction." In it the course was chosen for democratization of inner-Party life, development of the criticism, overcoming such abnormal phenomena as the division into "upper" and "lower" strata, into intellectuals and workers and so on (see KPSS in resolutions, v. 2, pp. 297-303).

Hereinafter Ye. A. Preobrazhensky advocates and develops his opinion on questions of Party construction which he has begun to raise in the TsK since the summer of 1920. In effect, the question was of what characteristics of the Party should have under conditions of the transitional period. Expressing the opinion of many representatives of the "old guard," Ye. A. Preobrazhensky considered it to be necessary to return to that, in his opinion, relatively democratic Party model which existed in the 1917 to 1918 time period when every important question of its policy was widely discussed in Party organizations, and where there was freedom of opinion and the possibility of persisting in one's opinion existed even in organizations of oppositional groups.

5. This is a reference to the resolution "On Questions of Party Building," adopted by the Tenth Congress of the RKP(b) (see KPSS in resolutions, v. 2, pp. 323–334).

6. Kronstadt mutiny, see Note 16 on the preceding document.

7. The discussion of 1920-1921 on the role and purposes of trade unions, see Note 6 on Document No. 17.

8. This is a reference to the resolution "On Party Unity" adopted by the Tenth Congress of the RKP(b) (see KPSS in resolution, v. 2, pp. 334-337).

9. On the new economic policy see Note 8 on Document No. 4.

10. Czecho-Slovak corps was formed in Russia during the first world war from prisoners of war of the Austria-Hungarian army and Russian subjects of Czech nationality. On March 26, 1918, the Soviet government signed an agreement with the Czech national council, which the corps was to follow, on its evacuation through Vladivostok. But on May 25, 1918, troops of the Czechoslovak corps began the counter-revolutionary mutiny in Povolzhi Siberia and in the Ural. One of the reasons for the mutiny was Trotsky's order to immediately disarm the corps.

Perm was seized by Kolchak's troops on the night of December 24 1918. It was won back by the Red Army on July 1, 1919.

11. Ye. A. Preobrazhensky points out the most severe period of the civil war for the Soviet power: establishment of the military dictatorship of the white-guard admiral Kolchak in Siberia and Ural (beginning with 1918), the offensive of A. I. Denikin's Voluntary army in the south of the country (summer-autumn of 1919), then (after the crushing of Denikin's army) the offensive from the Crimea by the white-guard army of P. N. Wrangel who was proclaimed to be the ruler of the south of Russia.

According to official statistics, more than 50 thousand communists were killed during the civil war.

12. In the article "On Our Inner-Party Situation," published in *Pravda* on November

28, 1923, Ye. A. Preobrazhensky wrote, "In my opinion, that for the last two years the Party has pursued a basically erroneous line in inner-Party policy. This policy turned out to be in conflict with the tasks that the NEP puts before us."

13. Hereinafter the question is of speeches of V. V. Kosior and N. Osinsky (V. V. Obolensky) at the Eleventh (1922) and Twelfth Congress of the RKP(b). In his speech at the Twelfth Congress, V. V. Kosior, the editor of the newspaper *Trud,* said that the leading body of the TsK pursued a "group policy," especially in personnel issues, which was not in convergence with the Party interests. He emphasized that the resolution of the Tenth Congress "On Party Unity" adopted under extraordinary conditions of spring of 1921, became "the exceptional law" in the Party's hands elevated to the system of ruling the Party, that in those conditions every criticism addressed to the TsK was brought under factionalism and clannishness (see the Twelfth Congress of the RKP(b). Stenographical record, pp. 101-105, 130-134).

14. This is a reference to the resolution of the Politburo of the TsK and the Presidium of the TSKK "On Party Building" (see the supplement to Document No. 24).

15. The question is of the October united plenum of the TsK and TSKK of 1923 (see Documents No. 21: I-V).

16. On F. E. Dzerzhinsky's commission on questions of the inner-Party situation see note 2 on Document No. 4. Hereinafter the question is of Declaration of Forty-Six group, sent to the Politburo of the TsK (see Document No. 12).

17. M N. Pokrovsky, the known Russian historian, characterizing Party leaders of those times, emphasized that they all "were war communists," Really, a major part of Party and Soviet as well as economic leadership featured a certain idealization of the policy of "war communism" with its united centralized planning, system of commanding, etc. The leadership did experience rather strong anti-NEP sentiments existed in working class and Party apparatus.

18. In the summer-autumn of 1923 main industrial regions of the country were enveloped by workers' strikes.

19. This is a reference to G. E. Zinoyev's speech at the meeting of the bureau of cells and activists of Moscow organization on December 11, 1923. The report on behalf of the TSKK at this meeting was given by L. B. Kamenev and the co-report on behalf of the opposition was given by T. V. Sapronov (*Pravda* of December 13 to 16, 1923).

20. This is a reference to I. V. Stalin's speech at the broadened meeting of Party activists of the Krasnopresnensky region of Moscow on December 2, 1923 (see Document No. 23).

21. This is a reference to those items of Party statutes which were introduced by the Twelfth Party conference (August 1922). Among them are: change in periodicity of calling Party conferences (once every year, every three months—in former statutes); obligatory pre-October experience of Party membership for secretaries of governor's committee and three-year length of Party membership for secretaries of district's committee, as well as that all the secretaries had to be approved by higher instance, that is, the actual preservation of appointment practice and reinforcement of secretary hierarchy.

22. The event of sending "commissars to the *Pravda*" occurred as follows. After publishing, G. E. Zinoviev's article "New Tasks of the Party" in *Pravda* on November 7,

1923, which opened the inner-Party discussion, the editorial staff received lots of responses, notes, articles, and resolutions of Party meetings. Since in November there was not yet strict TsK control over these materials, they were published by the Party life department of *Pravda* as they were received by the editorial staff.

However, published material which reported the life of Party masses served as an impressive argument in favor of opposition rightness: the facts which were discussed in Trotsky's letter and in the letter of the Forty-Six group to the TsK, showed up on pages of the Central organ of the Party. On November 28 *Pravda* printed Ye. A. Preobrazhensky's article with the sharp criticism of the inner-Party policy of the Party. The next day, according to I. V. Stalin's proposal, the Politburo of the TsK adopted the resolution where it suggested to the editorial staff of *Pravda* to send *through the TsK's secretariat* all, or at least, the most important articles which were not published but were waiting in the paper case of the editorial staff concerning questions of the Party construction. (RTsKhIDNI, f. 17, op. 3, d. 397, 1. 5).

Within a few days more than a hundred debatable materials were laid on the table of G. E. Zinovyev as the member of the Politburo and the author of the article which was getting responses. He chose four articles for urgent publishing. The tendentious choice of these articles and the strict control established by the TsK over work of Party life department of *Pravda* gave rise to the indignation of all its employees which resulted in the chief of the department and its deputy leaving the editorial staff of the newspaper. To their positions were appointed "commissars" about whom Ye. A. Preobrazhensky says: G. E. Zinoviev sent G. I. Safarov, the editor of *Petrogradskaya pravda*, I. V. Stalin sent A. M. Nazaretyan, the manager of the Bureau of the TsK's secretariat and his assistant. From that moment on the character of materials which were published in *Pravda* changed sharply. See Document No. 40 on how the resolutions pleasing to the TsK were prepared. Moreover, in order to organize "the convincing support of the TsK," A. M. Nazaretyan used direct forgery and falsification of received resolutions (see Document No. 45).

23. See Note 19 of the present document.

24. This is a reference to the inner-Party discussion of 1920-1921 on the role and purposes of trade unions under conditions of peaceful construction. In the article "Crisis of the Party" V. I. Lenin wrote that if disagreements came into existence, it is necessary that *all* communists should understand their essence and size up the course and development of the inner-Party struggle but only on the basis of documents: "Who takes somebody at his word is a hopeless idiot who is given up as lost." (V. I. Lenin. *Complete Works,* vol. 42, pp. 234–35).

25. Declaration of Forty-Six group, see Document No. 12.

26. The question is of the already mentioned meeting of cell bureaus and activists of Moscow Party organization on December 11, 1923 (see Note 19).

27. On the same see Document No. 45.

28. This is a reference to L. B. Kamenev's note "Word of Moscow" published in *Pravda* on December 12, 1923 (on results of the meeting of Moscow Party activists on December 11); Ye. A. Preobrazhensky talks further about the same meeting.

29. According to the official information, which provokes natural distrust even in the context of facts told by Ye. A. Preobrazhensky, the opposition was supported by 40 to 50 thousand communists of the whole of the RKP(b). The largest number of the opposition's supporters were in Moscow; about 40 percent of all communists voted for the opposition

there.

30. For example, on December 29, 1923 the Politburo of the TsK forbad the publication of the articles of G. L. Piatakov, V. M. Smirnov and T. V. Sapronov as "those which can inevitably provoke replies in the form of personal attacks" (RTsKhIDNI, f. 17, op. 3, d. 406,1. 10).

31. Hereinafter the question is of the editorial of *Pravda* on December 13, 1923, "Our Party and Opportunism." Apparently, Ye. A. Preobrazhensky did not know that the author of the article was N. I. Bukharin.

32. Ye. A. Preobrazhensky turned out to be right: after the editorial of N. I. Bukharin mentioned above, the articles of I. V. Stalin, G. Safarov, Ye. M. Yaroslavsky, and others written in the same spirit were published.

33. Up to April 1917 Bolsheviks and Mensheviks within the united Russian social-democratic labor Party (RSDRP, Rossiiskaya Sitsial-Demokraticheskaya Rabochaya Partiya), had a common Party statute and a common Party program. In the course of political struggle for power, Bolsheviks accused Mensheviks of opportunism and treachery of working class interests. In this connection a myth on Menshvism as a petty-bourgeois opportunist trend in Russian social democracy has settled over Soviet historiography for many years (see also Note 39 on Document No. 17).

34. This is a reference to "New Course (The Letter to Party Meetings)" by L. D. Trotsky (see Document No. 30).

35. Hereinafter the sociological talent of Ye. A. Preobrazhensky himself allowed to foresee the consequences of machinery-bureaucratic regeneration of the Party, i.e., the formation of the stratum of Party-state nomenclature with its own psychology and narrow corporative interests which were quite far from needs and aspirations of those on whose behalf priests of this case would constantly come out.

36. See Note 24 of the present document and Note 6 of Document No. 17.

37

I. M. Vareikis' Letter to I.V. Stalin

December 16, 1923

Kiev

Comrade Stalin!

This is to inform you briefly of the situation in the Kiev organization,[1] especially since a nest of Trotskyism has been grouping here.

The Party meetings are being held in a better way than I expected. The Resolution of the TsK[2] was discussed by almost all cells (some of them went over those three times). Three regional meetings (general) have been held, resolutions of approval have been passed. At the general meeting of the Podolsk region (1,230 Party members) the resolution of approval of the TsK line was passed unanimously. The meeting in the (R)akov region was rather heated, it has not yet finished, where the Trotskyists decided to "give battle," a member of the gubkom Comrade Golubenko criticized sharply the TsK line. Tomorrow it is going to continue. I am sure, they will get one and a half dozen of votes at most.

The majority is ensured. In the okrugs the course of the discussion does not have any political importance.

In general in Kiev "Trotskyism" is strong, it has been cultivated systematically for the last two years. Drobnis was here, as I learned, the purposely "explored" the ground. The gubkom is unanimous in its decision (with the exception of Comrade Golubenko).

So the "main Ukrainian citadel" has dissolved.

The press is wholly in our hands. I'll present the subsequent development of the discussion in my next letter.

With communist regards.

I. Vareikis

   16. XII. Kiev

The autograph.[3]

Published according to the text of the first publication in the magazine *Izvestia TsK KPSS,* 1991, No. 3, pp. 201–202.

NOTES

1. In 1923 I. M. Vareikis was the secretary of the Party organization of the Kiev guberniya.

2. This is a reference to the resolution "O partstroitelstve" (On the Party Building) (see Supplement 2).

3. At present the document is kept in the archives of the President of the Russian Federation.

38

The Resolution of the Politburo of the TsK of the RKP(b)

December 17, 1923

AGAINST THE AGGRAVATION OF THE INNER-PARTY STRUGGLE [1]

Trotsky's appearance the day after the unanimous adoption of the resolution of the Politburo and Presidium of the TSKK[2] with his article "Novy i kurs,"[3] which was sent directly to the Party meetings for its proclamation before any attempt on the part of Comrade Trotsky to come to a preliminary agreement with the TsK, undoubtedly, hampered the unanimous adoption of the above resolution. That article of Comrade Trotsky has been undoubtedly used by the opposition to aggravate the inner-Party struggle.

This appearance of Comrade Trotsky could not help but provoke resolute objections both on the part of the central organ of the Party (*Pravda*)[4] and of individual members of the TsK (the article of Comrade Stalin).[5]

Those forced objections in defense of the Party line are maliciously interpreted as a desire of the Politburo to hamper Comrade Trotsky's joint and concerted work in the governing bodies of the Party and of the state power.

Not agreeing with Comrade Trotsky in some of the points, at the same time the Politburo sweeps aside as a malicious invention the supposition that allegedly in the TsK of the Party or in its Politburo there is at least a single comrade who can imagine the work of the Politburo, the TsK and the bodies of state power without the most active participation of Comrade Trotsky.[6] Such ideas are being spread only for evidently factional reasons and are intended only for the aggravation of the discords and the inner-Party struggle, which should be avoided at any cost. There were discords in the TsK of the Party more than once both at the time when Comrade Lenin directly guided the work of the TsK and during his illness. Divergencies between individual members of the TsK were the most various. Nevertheless, the unity and the concerted work of the TsK in the matter of the guidance of the Party has been always in the foreground.

Considering the concerted and joint work with Comrade Trotsky quite necessary for all governing establishments of the Party and state power, the Politburo considers it its duty to do everything possible to ensure the concerted work in the future as well.

Pravda, 1923, December 18

NOTES

1. The decision of the Politburo of the TsK was passed on December 17, published in *Pravda* on December 18, 1923. The heading of the decision was apparently given by the editorial board of *Pravda*, since the decisions of the Politburo, as a rule, did not have any headings. In the same issue of *Pravda* there was published a letter-address of the Petrograd Party organization to the members of the RKP(b). In its appraisals and arguments it is absolutely identical to the decision of the Politburo of the TsK. It is possible that the text of both documents was prepared by G. E. Zinoviev, who was at the time both a member of the Politburo and the Chairman of the Petrograd Soviet.

2. This is a reference to the resolution "O partstroitelstve" (On the Party Building) (see Supplement to Document No. 24).

3. The article "Novyi kurs" (Pismo k partiinym soveschaniyam) ("The New Course: Letter to the Party Meetings" of L. D. Trotsky (see Document No. 30).

4. This is a reference to that article of N.I. Bukharin "Nasha partiia i opportunizm" ("Our Party and Opportunism") published in *Pravda* as the editorial on December 13, 1923.

5. This is a reference to the article of I.V. Stalin "O diskussii, o tov.Rafaile, o statiakh tt. Preobrazhenskogo i Sapronova i o pisme tov. Trotskogo" (On the discussion, on comrade Rafail, on the articles of Comrades Preobrazhensky and Sapronov and on the letter of Comrade Trotsky) published in *Pravda* on December 15, 1923.

6. See comments 5 and 11 to Document No. 36: I.

39

L. D. Trotsky's Letter to Pravda and the Postscript of the Editorial Board

December 17, 1923

LETTER OF COMRADE TROTSKY

(In reply to inquiries)
Dear Comrades,

I will not reply to some specific articles[1] which have been published lately in Pravda since I believe that this will coincide more with the interests of the Party and, in particular, with the discussion on the new course which is currently being held.

L. Trotsky

December 17, 1923

On behalf of the editorial board. The editorial board, as a body of the TsK, was bound to publish in reply to the letter of Comrade Trotsky "Novyi kurs" the articles received by *Pravda* in defense of the line of the TsK. Of course, the editorial board is ready at any moment to offer the pages of *Pravda* to Comrade Trotsky for his reply.[2]

Pravda, December 18, 1923

287

NOTES

1. L. D. Trotsky refers to the articles of N. I. Bukharin, "Nasha partiia i opportunizm" (Our Party and Opportunism) and to I. V. Stalin's "O diskussii, o tov.Rafile, o statiakh tt. Preobrazhenskogo i Sapronova i o pisme tov. Trotskogo" (On the discussion on Comrade Rafail, on the articles of comrades Preobrajensky and Sapronov and on the letter of comrade Trotsky) (*Pravda,* December 13 and 15, 1923).

2. In the second half of December, 1923, and the beginning of January, 1924, L. D. Trotsky published in *Pravda* the article "Gruppirovki i fraktsionnye obrazovaniya" (Groupings and Factional Formations), "Vopros o partiinyh pokoleniyah" (The Question on the Party Generations), "Obschestvennyi sostav partii" (Public Composition of the Party), and others which were the explanation of the author's position on a number of questions raised by him in the article "Novyi kurs" (The New Course), and concerning which the main political accusations were made against him.

40

I.V. Stalin's Letter to S.M. Kirov

December 17, 1923

To Comrade Kirov[1]

The discussion in Moscow for the last days has acquired an unpleasant character of a squabble accentuated not so much around certain principled theses as around individuals, especially around Comrade Trotsky, Preobrazhensky, Radek, and others having lost the battle on the principled ground are trying now to prove in their speeches that the question is in fact not about democracy but about the kicking of Comrade Trotsky out of the TsK. Hence, the Politburo published a resolution,[2] in which it rejects the malicious rumors about the kicking-out of Comrade Trotsky and suggests the organizations should not shift from the principled ground of the discussion given in the resolution of the TsK and TSKK on the inner-Party democracy.[3]

At the same time the Peter organization* published in *Pravda* its statement in which it, criticizing the well-known letter of Comrade Trotsky ("Novyi kurs"),[4] in essence, at the same time states that the active work of Comrade Trotsky in the governing bodies of the Party is absolutely necessary (see the enclosed statement of the Peter organization).[5]

We think that our largest organizations such as the Kharkov, Ekateri-

---

*The Petrograd Party organization. (Ed.)

289

noslav, Donbass, Rostov, Baku, Tifliss, Nizhegorodsk, Ivanovo-Voznesensk, and others—should not dare to reply. In our opinion, the statement of the Peter organizations should become a model to follow, be carried through, in a slightly changed form, *shortened, softened, and so on,** at a broad meeting of cells' buro or the buro of active workers and the resolution should be sent immediately to *Pravda* and to the TsK.[6] All this should be done promptly. The propaganda started following the example of Comrade Trotsky against the main cadres of our Party (see the article of Trotsky: "Novyi kurs") cannot remain without reply and rebuff on the part of our largest organizations.

I. Stalin

Regards!
17. XII

P.S. The statement of the inhabitants of Petrograd will appear in *Pravda* tomorrow.[7] Tell Sergo[8] to pass through a similar statement in the Tifliss organization.

I.St.†

The manuscript is an unknown handwriting.
The postscript and the signature—the autograph
of I. V. Stalin.[9] Published according to the text
of the first publication in the magazine *Izvestia*
TsK KPSS, 1991, No. 3, pp. 202–203.

NOTES

1. The published document is an obvious sample of how the secretarial hierarchy headed by the General Secretary was functioning.

The addressee, S. M. Kirov, was in 1921 the secretary of the TsK KP(b) of Azerbaidzhan. I. V. Stalin sent similar letters also to the first secretary of the TsK KP(b) of Ukraine E. I. Kviring, to the secretary of the Northern-Caucasian regional committee of the

---

*The italicized words are handwritten by I. V. Stalin. (Ed.)
†Stalin. (Ed.)

Party, A. I. Mikoyan, to the Chairman of the All-Ukrainian military group K. E. Voroshilov, and to others. All of them were members of the TsK RKP(b).

Such impetuous organizational activity on the part of I. V. Stalin was accounted for by the fact that in the Moscow Party organization a considerable part of organizations of institutes of higher education, institutional and military organizations had adopted the oppositional resolutions and sent them for publication in *Pravda*. A prompt and powerful counterbalance to those resolutions was necessary.

2. This is a reference to the decision of the Politburo of the TsK RKP(b) December 17 (see Document No. 38).

3. The resolution "O partstroitelstve" (On the Party Building) (see Supplement to Document No. 24).

4. This is a reference to the article of L. D. Trotsky "Novyi Kurs (Pismo k partiinym sovescaniiam)" (The New Course: Letter to the Party Meetings) (see Document No. 30).

5. Appendix to the letter (The statement of the Petrograd organization to the members of our Party) is missing in the archives, since, probably, it was supposed to be published in *Pravda*.

6. Formerly, when this document was not open to the researchers they were surprised by the extraordinary resemblance of the resolutions supporting the TsK. The document reveals the mechanics of how the "necessary" resolutions, pleasing to the TsK, were fabricated through the secretarial hierarchy.

S. M. Kirov carried out the instructions of the General secretary: on December 21, 1923, the Party activists of the Baku organization adopted the resolution supporting the TsK and condemning the factional actions of the opposition.

7. "The statement of the Petrograd organization to the members of our Party" was passed at the all-city meeting on December 15. About 3,000 persons were present there. Five voted against and seven abstained. The statement was published in *Pravda* on December 18, 1923.

8. This is a reference to G. K. Ordzhonikidze, then the first secretary of the Transcaucasian regional committee of the RKP(b). On December 23 the resolution of which I.V. Stalin had requested, was also adopted by the broadened meeting of the Transcaucasian regional committee plenum jointly with the TsK of the communist parties of Azerbaijan, Georgia, and Armenia.

9. At present the document is kept in the archives of the President of the Russian Federation.

41

The Cipher Telegram from the High-Level Officials of Ukraine to the TsK of the RKP(b) to I. V. Stalin

December 17, 1923

Kharkov* 17 hrs., 56 min.†

Top Secret
Copying is forbidden

Moscow TsK RKP to Comrade Stalin
The Party demands the information on the last Plenum.[1]
The rank-and-file workers inform the meetings from hearsay.
We insist on the solution of the problem by cable poll. We suggest charging the Politburo with determining the form, limits of information.

Kviring, Lebed, Chubar, Frunze,
Manuilsky, Petrovsky
The original[2]

Published according to the text of the
first publication in the magazine *Izvestiya*
TsK KPSS, 1991, No. 3, p. 203

---

*Until 1934 Kharkov was the capital of the Ukrainian SSR.
†The time of sending from Kharkov. Received in Moscow on December 17, 1923, at 9:25 P.M. (Ed.)

NOTES

1. This is a reference to the October united Plenum of the TsK and RKP(b) (see Document No. 21: I-V).

2. At present the document is kept in the archives of President of the Russian Federation.

42

M. I. Ulyanova and N. K. Krupskaya's Memo to the TsK of the RKP(b)

December 21, 1923

To TsK RKP
Dear Comrades!

In view of the fact that the discussion in the newspaper troubles V. I.,*
and can worsen his state, and we cannot give him newspapers—we would
request transferring discussion articles to Diskussionnyi Listok (the Discussion Leaflet).

With communist regards

N. Krupskaya
M. Ulyanova

P.S. Of course, if the TsK considers it convenient from the general political of view.[1]
21/XII.23

The autograph of M.I. Ulyanova, the
postscript is written by N.K. Krupskaya.[2]

---

*Vladimir Ilyich (Ed.).

Published according to the text of the
first publication in magazine *Izvestia
Tsk KPSS*, 1991, No. 3, p. 204.

NOTES

1. In accordance with the request by N. K. Krupskaya and M. I. Ulyanova the Politburo of the TsK adopted the following resolution on December 22, 1923:

a) To decide beforehand the transfer of the discussion from the pages of *Pravda* to the pages of the Discussion Leaflet.

b) To make the Plenum of the Tsk responsible for establishing the dates of this transfer.

c) Pending this transfer, to confirm once more the necessity of conducting the discussion in a more calm and objective tone excluding any aggravation.

d) To inform the editorial board of *Pravda* and to the other Party bodies on which pages the discussion is being conducted about this resolution (*Izvestia Tsk KPSS*, 1991, No. 3, p. 204).

However, the adopted resolution proved to be a formal reply. Till the end of the discussion, i.e., till the Thirteenth Conference of RKB(b), which closed three days before the death of V. I. Lenin, its materials were published on the pages of *Pravda*.

2. At present the document is being kept in the archives of President of the Russian Federation.

43

L. D. Trotsky's Letter to the Party Cell of the Railroad-Yard of the Moscow Section of the Oktyabrskaya Railroad

December 22, 1923

Urgent.

Dear Comrades!

It goes without saying that those openly anti-Party conclusions which some members of the Party try to draw from my article on the new course[1] are a monstrous misrepresentation of my thought. Anyone who will read the article calmly and conscientiously will understand its real thought consisting in that the *bureaucracy** in the Party represents the greatest danger both to the governing apparatus and to the mass of the rank-and-file members. Our Party school is the best Lenin revolutionary school in the world. But it would be basically erroneous if one would rely on the old capital only. With the bureaucratic regime in the Party this old capital can be spent imperceptibly, without new Party capital being acquired. This is the main idea of my article. I have no doubt that the Party will understand it exactly this way.

If I have not so far refuted the false interpretations it is because I wanted to do it in a serious, thorough article, but my real state at present is such that it allows me to work not more than an hour or two a day. Never-

---

*Underlined by the author. (Ed.).

theless, I hope to complete the article explaining the main questions raised by the discussion in the nearest two or three days and then I shall publish them.[2]

I hope also that I shall get the better of the inopportune sickness and then I shall be able to make a speech as well.

With communist regards.

L. Trotsky

December 22, 1923

The machine-typed copy with the facsimile signature.[3]
Published according to the text of the first publication in the magazine *Izvestia TsK KPSS*, 1991, No. 3, pp. 204, 206.

NOTES

1. This is a reference to the article of L.D. Trotsky, "Novyi kurs (pismo k partiinym soveshchaniam)" (The New Course: Letter to the Party Meetings), published in *Pravda* on December 11, 1923.

2. On December 28 and 29, 1923, L. D. Trotsky published in *Pravda* the articles:"Gruppirovki i fraktsionnye obrazovaniya" (Groupings and Factional Formations), "Vopros o partiinykh pokoleniyah" (The Question on the Party Generations), and "Obsheshtvennyi sostav partii" (Social Composition of the Party).

3. At present the document is kept in the archives of the President of the Russian Federation.

44

Two Letters of V. A. Antonov-Ovseyenko

I. The Letter to the Presidium of the TSKK and the Politburo of the TsK RKP(b) December 27, 1923

To the Presidium of the TSKK and Politburo of the TsK RKP(b)[1]

The discussion assumes a character that worries more and more every time many comrades, especially those working in the army.

At all meetings and especially at the meetings of the "military" communists the official representatives of the TsK spend considerable, sometimes, exclusive, time on the analysis of the political biography of Comrade Trotsky, emphasize strongly the fact that Comrade Trotsky by no means can be reckoned among "the old guard of the Bolsheviks," that he has always fought with the Bolshevism, that he is a secret Menshevik who reveals his Menshevism even now in his entire political line.

And this is not a Moscow phenomenon only.

A certain comrade, unknown to me, a military political worker,[2] writes to me in a private letter from Kharkov:

"The discussion developed on the questions of the Party construction

298

and those forms which it assumes, in particular with us in Kharkov, make me write you this letter. The question is that the discussion assumes a character of sharp personal attacks on the part of the leading Party comrades against Comrade Trotsky and others, who allegedly are members of his faction. The secretary of the Ukranian TsK Comrade Kviring speaking at the city meeting of the cells of the Kharkov Party organization three days ago, declared that 'Comrade Trotsky is splitting the Party and violating its unity.' Yesterday at the regional Party meeting of the the Petinsk region the speaker on the question of the Party construction Comrade G. I. Petrovsky (Chairman of the VUTsIK)* in an embittered tone declared that 'Comrade Trotsky has always been fighting against our Party, only in 1917 he joined the RKP, that his political line has been incorrect and harmful during all his revolutionary activity.' This is provoked on the part of the military part of the meeting spontaneous cries: 'Long live Comrade Trotsky,' 'Down with the speaker,' and so on. Comrade Makar—a member of the TSKK of Ukraine, who took part in the debate, declared that 'Trotsky has always been a political bankrupt,' and started to enumerate all his 'blunders'— permanent revolution, Brest, trade unions and so on.[3]

"They did not let the reporter speak, they made a noise in the hall, cries 'Long live Trotsky' and so on.

"I believe that this is very dangerous. Among the military communists there are already talks that it is necessary that one and all should support Comrade Trotsky. . . ."

I consider it my duty to note that you are facing danger. I am not at all under a self-delusion. The political meaning of the well-known article of Comrade Stalin[4] and of the leading articles of *Pravda*[5] is clear to me. It is exactly those articles that set the fashion to the whole campaign, the meaning of which is to blindly mobilize a support of the line of the majority of the Politburo, all forces of "the old guard of Bolsheviks," all best traditions and the most nasty prejudices, derived by the Bolsheviks from the old prerevolutionary fights,[6] in order to isolate Comrade Trotsky from the old Bolsheviks, to deprive him of a serious Party support in the realization of his views.

The whole apparatus of the Party is set in a certain motion for this purpose (isolating Trotsky), with all their forces they try to make Trotsky a banner of everything "non-Leninist" in our Party and, abusing the im-

---

*The All-Ukranian Central Executive Committee of the Soviets. (Ed.).

mense prestige of Leninism, to supress any criticism of the political line of the current majority of the Tsk.

It is my strong conviction that this is an extremely dangerous undertaking. In the provinces this is believed to be a direct disruption of the course for the working democracy* proclaimed in your unanimously adopted resolution of December 5 and adoption of the line toward a split of the Party organization.

And outside the Party limits, those reckless attacks devoid of principles and ideas, on somebody who in the eyes of the broadest masses is an undisputable leader—the organizer and inspirer of the victories of the revolution—cause a painful alarm, discord, and uncertainty. The essence of the differences inside the TsK is utterly unclear either to the Party or or to the non-Party masses, the Party is unable to weigh the seriousness of those differences and to settle them easily. The Party and the entire country, instead of a serious analysis of serious questions, are being fed by personal attacks, suspicions, bilious slanders, and that method is made a system as if the widely proclaimed new course consists exactly of that. It is clear where it leads to.

To the deepest demoralization of both the Party, and the army, and the working masses, and to the undermining of the influence of our Party in the Comintern,[7] to the weakening of the firmness and steadfastness of the Comintern line.

Only an extreme narrowing of the political views, under the influence of the factional passion, can explain the fact that such serious leaders of our Party are carrying it away to such a wrong road.

I know that this warning voice of mine will not make the slightest impression on those who have hardened with regards to their own infallibility of the leaders selected by history.

But know, this voice is symptomatic. It expresses the indignation of those who by all their life have proved their utter devotion to the interests of the Party as a whole, to the interests of the Communist revolution. Those Party taciturn members raise their voice only when they understand a real danger to the whole Party. They will never be "Moltchalins,"[8] courtiers of the Party hierarchy. And their voice will some day call to order the presumptuous "leaders"[9] in such a way that they will hear it even in spite of their extreme factional deafness.

Antonov-Ovseyenko

---

*The resolution "On the Party Construction" (Ed.).

December 27, 1923.

The original.[10]

Published according to the text of the first publication in the
magazine *Izvestia TsK KPSS*, 1991, No. 3, pp. 206-208.

NOTES

1. V. A. Antonov-Ovseyenko, from 1922 Chief of the Political Department of
Revvoensovet of the Republic (PUR) (Revolutionary War Council), was one of those who
signed the Statement of the Forty-Six. Just this fact was enough to receive from the Stalinist grouping a lifelong brand of a Trotskyist. And his direct attempt to defend the honor and
dignity of L. D. Trotsky, after having called in a published letter all things by their names
cost him his official career in a fortnight, and in fifteen years—his own life. As a matter of
fact, from that man, from his shameful political public dishonor, the "leading kernel" of the
TsK will start the violence against the opposition which will especially develop in 1924.

2. This is a reference to a worker of the political department (politotdel—a body of
the Party in the Red Army).

3. For the first time the idea of the permanent (continuous) revolution was advanced
by K. Marx and F. Engels in the middle of the past century. They believed that the proletartiat which came out on the proscenium of history because of its social state becomes
hegemon of the revolutionary movement and will be able to make the revolution continuous, having accomplished the transaction from the burgeois-democratic revolution to a socialist revolution, right up to the attainment of state power. Continuity was understood as
a consecutive change of stages of the revolutionary process.

The permanent revolution theory was added to the armory of the Russian revolutionary Social Democracy, although both Bolsheviks and Mensheviks believed that its application to the concrete conditions of the Russian revolutionary movement would require new
theoretic and political elaborations. From the very first days of the first Russian revolution
(1905-1907) the problem of the development of the burgeois-democratic revolution and the
determination of the hegemon of the revolution at its democratic stage (liberal burgeoisie
or the proletariat) gave rise to serious differences between Bolsheviks and Mensheviks
which were caused by the dissimiliarity in the evaluations of the specific features of the development of Russia (the assessment of the Russian capitalism, the burgeoisie, the proletariat and its allies, etc.).

At that period L. D. Trotsky jointly with a well-known at that time leader of the Russian and German Social Democracy Parvus (A. L. Gelfman) gave his own interpretation of
the Marxist permanent revolution theory as applied to the specific conditions of Russia. In
brief, the essence of the views of L. D. Trotsky consisted of the following. He believed that
due to the lagging of Russia behind Western Europe and in the presence of a powerful brake
on progress in the autocracy the conditions of the development of the burgeoisie in the coun-

try were extremely unfavorable. Not seeing in Russia a revolutionary burgeois democracy capable of liquidating the monarchist regime and the remnants of serfdom, L. D. Trotsky assigned the part of the main revolutionary force to the proletariat. He believed that in case of victory of the democratic revolution in Russia there will be established the dictatorship of the proletariat, a workers' government will be formed (hence the well-known slogan of Parvus without tsar, but the government of workers). Having come to power, as L. D. Trotsky believed, the proletartiat cannot limit itself to democratic tasks only, and the logic of the class struggle will push it to socialist transformations. Since he did not see inside the country such forces which would support the proletariat, he considered a socialist revolution in Europe to be the only guarantee of its retention of power and the victory of the revolution.

During the first Russian revolution some theses of the "permanent revolution" theory of L. D. Trotsky were close to the views of V. I. Lenin, therefore there were no polemics between them on the questions of the development of the burgeois-democratic revolution into a socialist revolution. Criticism would start later which was promoted to some degree by the extreme aggravation of the inner-Party struggle in the RSDRP. After the October Revolution both V. I. Lenin and L. D. Trotsky himself considered the former theoretic disputes and differences as settled by the active part of L. D. Trotsky in the preparation and realization of the October coup of 1917.

As regards the position of L. D. Trotsky during the Brest negotiations see note 29 to Document No. 36:I. As regards the discussion on the role and tasks of the trade unions and the position of L. D. Trotsky in same see note 6 to Document No. 17.

4. This is a reference to the article of I.V. Stalin "O diskussii, o tov. Rafaile, o statiah tt. Preobrajenskogo i Sapronova i o pisme tov.Trotskog" (On the discussion, on comrade Rafail, on the articles of Comrades Petrovsky and Sapronov and on the letter of Comrade Trotsky) published in *Pravda* on December 15, 1923.

5. This is a reference to the editorial articles of *Pravda* "Nasha partiya i opportunizm" (Our Party and Opportunism) (December 13, 1923), "O klevete i spletne" (On Slander and Gossip) (December 19), and others, containing sharp criticism of L. D. Trotsky and the opposition.

6. V. A. Antonov-Ovseyenko means the struggle between the Bolsheviks and the Mensheviks in the RSDRP which took place before 1917, when in the course of the polemics on the theoretical and political questions of the revolutionary development did not spare each other, using a killing irony and extremely sharp expressions.

7. Comintern—see List of Abbreviations.

8. Moltchalin—a personage of the comedy of A. S. Griboyedov "Gore ot uma" (Misfortune Because of Intellect). As a collective image means toadying, careerism, time-serving.

9. I. V. Stalin in his closing speech at the Thirteenth Conference of the RKP(b) on January 18, 1924, among the reasons which had led to the release of V. A. Antonov-Ovseenko from the post of Chief of Politupravlenie of Revvoensovet (Political Department of the Revolutionary War Council) adduced also the fact that the letter "sent to the TsK and the TSKK absolutely indecent by the tone and absolutely inadmissable by the contents letter with a threat against the TsK and the TSKK to call to orders the "presumptuous leaders" (see Stalin, *Complete Works,* vol. 6, p. 43).

10. At present the original documents are kept in the archives of President of the Russian Federation. In RTsHIDNI there is a typewritten certified copy (f. 76, op. 3, d. 314, l. 14–16).

II. The Letter to I.V. Stalin January 2, 1924

Dear Comrade Stalin!

I am writing to you, in copy only to Comrade Dzerzhinsky,[1] as a friend.

There was no need for you to exaggerate that story with the Party conference of the Higher M(ilitary) Ed(ucational) establishments.[2]

It was a regular conference.

It was ventured long before the "discussion."

Both its membership and the agenda were carried through the Orgburo. The Orgburo was informed of the necessity to postpone it as long ago as on December 4, and there were no objections. The only thing which is not going on well is that the circular about it was not sent to the TsK.

Why did you need—not giving me an opportunity to come furnished with the documents—to reprimand me without any warning?

It is clear—why? Because of the general discontent with my work, and because of such discontent those particular questions, in their real concrete definition, were dissolved in it.

This was said at the meeting of the Orgburo[3] in a number of the additional remarks of some of its members and, especially, in your remarks, Comrade Stalin.

I have a right to request to make things absolutely clear.

What is the matter? Are you in earnest thinking that I transform the PUR into the "headquarters of the faction?" That I am mobilizing the public opinion of the Red Army "against the TsK"?

Or simply—it seems to you intolerable that one of the important departments of the TsK[4] is headed by such an independently thinking Party member who dares to express (even if at the authorized pre-congress discussion) his discontent with the inner-Party policy of the majority of the Politburo?

I affirm that for the doubts of the first order you do not have any grounds. And you yourselves told me recently that it was nothing.

As for the second. You need to appoint to the leading posts absolutely "law-abiding" people.

I do not belong to such a type as this. Then you should raise the question openly. There is no need to adjust the material to prove my inability to conduct the work with which I have been entrusted and the desire to "conspire" against the TsK.[5]

Nothing will come out of it. Under my control, the work in the PUR, in all branches, has started energetically as never before. This was recognized unanimously by the recent All-Union assembly of the political workers as well.[6]

I have never carried on diplomacy with the TsK. I have spoken and I am speaking openly what I think to be correct.

With communist regards,

Antonov-Ovseyenko

January 2, 1924.

Small addition

Nachposekr* EVA (of the united military academy) is Comrade N. Kuzmin, who fully shares the position of the majority of the Politburo. You should not fear "EVA" under such an Adam. He informed me that out of eight academies in two only had the oppositional resolutions been adopted.

It is Comrade Kuzmin who should have coordinated everything with the TsK; it is he who drew up the order, some words of which you considered "undemocratic."

Antonov-Ovseyenko

NOTES

1. The document is published according to the copy sent to F. E. Dzerzhinsky with whom V. A. Antonov-Ovseyenko was connected not only by the team work in the Narkomat Truda (People's Commissariat for Labor), but also by a warm human friendship of almost twenty years. In spite of this, when at the Plenum of the TsK on January 15, 1924, the question concerning V. A. Antonov-Ovseyenko was settled, F. E. Dzerzhinsky "in the name

*Chief of the secret department. (Ed.).

of unity of the Party" voted for his dismissal from the post of Chief of the Political Department of the Revolutionary War Council.

2. The question is about the third Party conference of the military academies and the higher military schools. The same day, on January 2, 1924, when the letters to I.V. Stalin and F.E. Dzerzhinsky were sent, V.A. Antonov-Ovseyenko sent a letter to the Orgburo of the TsK RKP(b) as well, in which he showed with the help of documents that all dates, members of the conference and reporters had been agreed upon with the Orgburo and personally with V. M. Molotov. Thus, "the story with the Party conference" was actually "exaggerated"—I. V. Stalin needed an occasion to dismiss the chief of the PUR.

3. The question of the third Party conference of the higher military educational establishments was discussed at the meeting of the Orgburo of the TsK on December 31, 1923, at which V. A. Antonov-Ovseyenko as the chief of the PUR was censured for the terms and the composition of the conference supposedly not agreed upon with the TsK. V. A. Antonov-Ovseyenko's reply to that decision were his letters dated January 2, 1924— one letter to I. V. Stalin (in a copy to F. E. Dzerzhinsky) and the second letter—to the Orgburo of the TsK.

4. The Political Department of the Revvoensovet (PUR) (Revolutionary War Council, RWC) as a leading body of the Party in the Red Army. According to its status it functioned as a department of the TsK RKP(b).

5. The story of the release of V.A. Antonov-Ovseyenko from the post of Chief of the PUR (RWC) is an obvious example of how the leading "trio" of the Politburo (G. Ye. Zinoviev, L. B. Kamenev, I. V. Stalin) deprived L. D. Trotsky supporters and surrounded the chairman of the Revvoensovet (Revolutionary War Council) with "their" people. The story with the Party conference of the military educational establishments whipped up by the Orgburo of the TsK was evidently insufficient as a material compromising the chief of the PUR (RWC). Therefore the letter of V.A. Antonov-Ovseyenko dated December 27 was officially set going through the Central Control Commission of the RKP(b) obedient to the "troika."

On January 4, 1924, the Secretariat of the Presidium of the TSKK appointed a commission for checking up the PUR (RWC) of which V. A. Antonov-Ovseyenko was not even informed. In a week, on January 12, 1924, the commission presented at the meeting of the Orgburo of the TsK new "evidences" of the alleged attempt of V. A. Antonov-Ovseyenko to take the PUR out of control of the TsK and to turn it into the headquarters of the factional struggle. Now the question was about the circular letter of the PUR No. 200 dated December 24, 1923. Written in the spirit of the resolution "O partstroitelstve" (On the Party Building) the circular suggested that the Party members of the army organizations should discuss the problems of the inner-Party life. And although the main theses of the circular had been preliminarily discussed with the secretary of the TsK V. M. Molotov, at the Orgburo on January 12 it was recognized that the circular had not been agreed upon with the TsK.

The cavils at the circular letter No. 200 were not at all directed at its contents but were purely bureaucratic: according to the established practice circulars of the PUR signed by its chief only, they did not have to be agreed upon with the Orgburo of the TsK. Only the circulars bearing two signatures—that of the secretary of the TsK and the chief of the PUR— had to be agreed upon. Therefore the main accusatory document against V. A. Antonov-

Ovseyenko was his own letter to the TsK and the TSKK dated December 27 (see the preceding document), which would be called by I. V. Stalin at the Plenum of the TsK of January 15, 1924, a riot, a revolt against the TsK. On January 12, the Orgburo passed the decision to relieve V. A. Antonov-Ovseyenko of the post of chief of the PUR and to remove him from the Revvoensovet of the USSR. On January 14 that decision was approved by the Politburo, and on January 15, by the Plenum of the TsK. In 1924 V. A. Antonov-Ovseyenko would be assigned to a diplomatic service, and his post would be taken up by a "law-abiding" A. S. Bubnov.

6. The All-Union Assembly of the army political workers was held at the end of October 1923.

45

The Declaration of L. D. Trotsky, G. L. Pyatakov, and K. B. Radek to the Politburo of the TsK of the RKP(b)

December 29, 1923

To the Politburo of the TsK RKP(b)
Declaration

We, the undersigned, members of the Tsk, have been following lately with the greatest anxiety the character which the Party information has assumed in *Pravda*. The rumors about the incorrectness of that information, about the intended delays in publishing the resolutions, etc. were coming from everywhere.[1] Some facts, known to us personally, confirmed these rumors. Nevertheless, we have been until recently very far from the real idea of the methods and ways with the help of which *Pravda* informs the public opinion of the Party. The information known to us at the present moment no longer leaves any room for doubts that the staff appointed specially to the editorial board of *Pravda* to be in charge of the Party department,[2] are using the methods which cannot be called anything but falsification and forgery. The information delivered to us evidences that the main part of those forgeries belongs to Comrade Nazaretian and that Comrade Safarov is quite aware of what Comrade Nazaretian is doing. This time the question is not about any one-sided selection of articles and not even about advancing some resolutions and delaying the publication of others, *but about the*

deliberate and ill-intentioned distortion of text of official documents with the
purpose of imparting to them the meaning, sometimes *quite contrary to that
which was given to those resolutions by those who voted for them.**

To characterize all that work that embraces dozens of cases we shall
cite an example, the most simple and striking. The telegram of the ROST†
from Kiev dated December 22 informing of the meeting of the Petchora region, reads as follows: "The meeting protests categorically against the inadmissable accusations put forward against Trotsky in the opportunist deviations and Menshevism." In the text of the ROST telegram several words
were written in the hand of Comrade Nazaretyan, as a result of which the
phrase reads as follows: "The meeting protests categorically against the inadmissable accusations *brought by Comrade Trotsky against the kernel of
the Party*‡ in the opportunist deviations and Menshevism." All other alterations and distortions although less striking by appearance, were in general similar to the one just cited. The aims of those methods and ways are
quite evident: to deceive the public opinion of the Party relative to what is
going on among its members. As Comrade Nazaretyan is the secretary of
the meetings of the Politburo,[3] assistant to Comrade Stalin, and was appointed extraordinarily into *Pravda*'s staff for management of the Party department, then the crimes committed by them assume quite exceptional
meaning.

We demand an investigation of the conduct of Comrade Nazaretyan
and those persons who assisted him in this. Such investigation must give
every guarantee of impartiality. The guilty persons must be punished according to the crimes committed by them against the Party.

It is too obvious, that if the practice of forgeries reigning now at the
Party department of *Pravda* is not stopped immediately, it will surely
strike the Party with terrible blows of the disgusting actions which are
being carried out against it, although on its behalf. It is no use talking about
the Party democracy, if an unpunished forgery substitutes the Party information. The Party will not allow this. And recognizing our responsibility
toward the Party we propose:

1) To entrust a commission, whose impartiality would not arouse anybody's doubts to carry out the investigation. In view of the extreme sim-

---

*Underlined by the authors. (Ed.).
†The Russian Telegraph Agency (Ed.).
‡Underlined by the authors. (Ed.).

plicity of the question, to give the commission a short period of time, twenty-four hours at most.[4]

2) To discharge Comrades Nazaretyan and Safarov of the work in *Pravda* for the term of the investigation.[5]

3) To declare categorically that none of the comrades who furnish that commission with the necessary information will fall a victim to the Party or any other repression.

4) To charge *Pravda* to furnish the investigation commission with all necessary materials.

5) To entrust the guidance of the Party department of *Pravda* to a collegium of absolutely conscientious and responsible comrades, charging them with the review of all materials already published and with the publication in *Pravda* of all necessary amendments and additions.[6]

In conclusion we consider it necessary to mention that this episode has a colossal symptomatic meaning, evidencing those truly tragic dangers which the Party is meeting using these methods of struggle, one of the expressions of which are the above-cited facts. We believe that there should be an end put to it at any cost and that it has to be done today as every day makes the situation more and more dangerous to the Party.

L. Trotsky.
Piatakov.
K. Radek.

29. XII—1923.

RTsHIDNI, F. 17, op. 3, d. 407,
1. 7-9; the attested typewritten copy.
Published for the first time.

NOTES

1. E. A. Preobrazhensky also spoke about similar facts (see document No. 36:II).

2. About the mission of A. M. Nazaretyan in *Pravda* see note 22 to Document No. 36:II.

3. A. M. Nazaretyan was at the time manager of the Bureau of the Secretariat of the TsK and assistant to I. V. Stalin. Apparently, he performed the duties of the technical secretary of the Politburo of the TsK as well.

4. About the committee of inquiry of the TSKK RKP(b) on the question see note 2 to Document No. 46.

5. After the scandalous story of the forgeries in *Pravda* I.V. Stalin removed A. M. Nazaretyan from the newspaper, but he did not return him to the apparatus of the TsK either. Probably A. M. Nazaretyan himself did not want to return. From 1924 he was the secretary of the Transcaucasian territorial Party committee, and in 1937 he was repressed.

6. No additions or explanations, and all the more excuses to the readers, as one is supposed to do in such cases, were published by *Pravda*.

46

The Resolution of the Politburo of the TsK of the RKP(b) on the Declaration of L. D. Trotsky, G. L. Piatakov, and K. B. Radek of December 29, 1923

December 31, 1923

From the minutes of the meeting of the Politburo of the TsK RKP(b) of December 31, 1923:

Decision of the Politburo in connection with the declaration of comrades Trotsky, Piatakov, and Radek of December 29, 1923.[1]

Expressing firm confidence in that the unheard and unfounded accusations of comrades Trotsky, Piatakov and Radek at the editorial board of *Pravda* of the the "regime of forgeries" allegedly established by the latter will not be confirmed, nevertheless the Politburo has requested the TSKK to urgently check up those accusations.[2]

During the announcement of Comrades Trotsky, Piatakov, and Radek's declaration to the Politburo, the members of the TsK pointed out on the spot a number of cases of the incorrect transmission of the results of the discussion right to the detriment of the line of the majority of the TsK (the resolutions in favor of the TsK were published as the resolutions against the Tsk; the resolution of the Sormov workers in favor of the TsK was published only after a thrice-repeated reminder on the part of the Nizhny-Novgorod gubkob; in the speech of Comrade Zinoviev[3] and in the article "Ot redaktsii" against Comrade Trotsky[4] there were essential distortions to the detriment of the line of the TsK, etc.)—which is obviously accounted for by haste and overwork.

The Politburo will still revert to the application of comrades Trotsky, Piatakov and Radek after the inquiry which will be carried out by the Cen-

312 The Struggle for Power

tral Control Commission and which will have to ascertain if there were abuses in the department of the Party life of *Pravda*. But irrespective of the results of the inquiry of the TSKK as regards the above, the Politburo considers it necessary to give just now the Party political assessment of the application of comrades Trotsky, Radek, and Piatakov in general.

Of course, every member of the TsK, if he learns about the abuses in the Party body, has a right and is obliged to apply to his Central Committee with the proposal to inquire into the matter, and to punish the guilty persons. But the form in which it was done by the above-named three comrades, is quite unheard of among the Bolsheviks. Comrades Trotsky, Piatakov, and Radek write: "The rumors about the incorrectness of that information, about the intended delays in publishing the resolutions, etc., were going from every quarter." The Politburo ascertains that no such declaration has been made either by the above-named three comrades or by any member of the Party in general to the Politburo or the Presidium of the Central Control Commission.[5] The Politburo ascertains that the Presidium of the TSKK published a special invitation to all members of the Party to inform the TSKK of the eventual abuses and that in reply to that decision of the TSKK no application has been received.[6]

Comrades Trotsky, Piatakov, and Radek, citing a certain, but even not confirmed example, speak about "the methods which cannot be called otherwise but falsification and forgery," about the "deliberate and ill-intentioned distortion of the text of the official documents for the purpose of imparting to them the meaning sometimes quite contrary to that which was put into those resolutions by those who voted for them," about "the crimes which assume exceptional meaning," about "the regime of forgeries reigning now at the Party department of *Pravda,* and so on. On the grounds of the unconfirmed facts the above-named three comrades demand that Comrades Nazaretyan and Safarov should be removed from their posts. Moreover. The above-named three comrades suggest that the TsK of the Party should "declare categorically that none of the comrades who will furnish that commission with the necessary information will fall victim to the Party or any other repression." In other words, the above-named three comrades, members of the TsK, suppose that the TsK of our Party can bring down the Party or even any "other" repression on the people who will help to disclose falsification and forgery. Only the people who feel that they are an independent faction and not members of the united TsK of the Party can raise the question in such a way.

The application of Comrades Trotsky, Piatakov and Radek has not only a factional character but is evidence of that the above-named comrades consider the TsK of the Party and the TsO a hostile force against which one can fight by the methods so far admitted by the embittered political adversaries of our Party only.

The whole of the application of Comrades Trotsky, Piatakov, and Radek has a rudely defiant character. As in the past when the most secret documents and statements directed against the TsK (for instance, the letter of forty-six, the letter of Trotsky[7] and so on) became immediately known to the broad circles of the Party members and even of the non-Party people and of the Army, and widespread, it is evident that the present defiant application will be put into circulation in order to undermine confidence in the TsK of our Party and in its TsO.

The Politburo declares categorically that such speeches having a typical character of a squabble indeed threaten to create an atmosphere of a split fraught with the most serious consequences.

Secretary of the TsK I. Stalin

31. XII. 1923.

RTsHIDNI, f.17, op. 3, d. 407,
1. 2-4; the attested typewritten copy.
Published for the first time.

NOTES

1. The declaration of L. D. Trotsky, G. L. Pyatakov, and K. B. Radek of December 29 (see the previous document) was considered that same day at the meeting of the Politburo of the TsK which by its decision obliged the TSKK to investigate the accusations directed against A. M. Nazaretyan and G. I. Safarov and to give the general appraisal of the application of the troika. N. I. Bukharin was entrusted with the drafting of the decision of the Politburo. Yet before the termination of the work of the inquiry committee of the TsK on that question, the Politburo at its meeting of December 31 discussed and approved of the wording of the decision drafted by N. I. Bukharin, published here.

2. The Presidium of the TSKK RKP(b) appointed an inquiry committee which worked for almost a week. On January 4, 1924, and the Presidium of the TSKK approved of the conclusion of the inquiry committee. The conclusion in general rejected the accusations brought against the department of the Party life of *Pravda* of the "regime of forgeries" existing in same. As regards the concrete fact, and namely, the falsification committed by

A. M. Nazaretyan in respect to the published resolution of the Pechora region of the city of Kiev, the conclusion of the committee was that it was "a blunder, absolutely inadmissable, but not ill-intentioned, and a quite conscientious mistake." The Presidium of the TSKK in its decision warned L. D. Trotsky, G. L. Pyatakov, and K. B. Radek against the continuation of "the opposition to the Central Committee which is dangerous for the unity of the Party" and reproved them for "the inadmissibility of the methods of the inner-Party struggle used by them" (RTsHIDNI f. 613, op. 1, d, 14, 1.12; f. 51; op. 1, d. 21, 1. 20 ob.–22).

3. Apparently, this is a reference to the report of G. E. Zinioviev at the meeting of the Party activists of the Petrograd organization published in *Pravda* on December 21, 1923, under the headline "O borbe za partiiu" (On the Struggle for the Party).

4. Beginning on December 13, from the leading article "Nasha partiya i opportunism" (Our Party and Opportunism) written by N. I. Bukharin, *Pravda* appeared time and again with the editorials against L. D. Trotsky and the opposition: "O klevete i spletne" (On slander and Gossip) on December 19, "Partiinaia diskussiia i moskovskaia organizatsiia" (The Party Discussion and the Moscow Organization) on December 25, and others.

5. It is possible that no written applications of such kind were received by the TsK and the TSKK, but at the discussion meetings, as, for instance, in the speech of E. A. Preobrazhensky (see Document No. 36: II) such facts were cited.

6. This is a reference to the information of the TSKK RKP(b) about the conflict in the editorial board of *Pravda* published on December 23, 1923.

7. For the letter of L. D. Trotsky dated October 8, 1923, see Document No. 4; for Zaiavlenie 46-ti (Statement of the Forty-Six), see Document No. 12.

47

The Reply by Nine Members and Candidate Members of the Politburo of the TsK of the RKP(b) to L. D.Trotsky's Letter of October 23, 1923

December 31, 1923

Strictly Confidential

To Members and Candidates of TsK and TSKK*
Reply of Members (And Candidates) of Politburo
To Comrade Trotsky's Letter of October 24, 1923[1]

The undersigned have not yet given a reply to Comrade Trotsky's letter of October 24, so far because we believed that the decision of joint Plenums of TsK and TSKK[2] would put an end to the conflict. We see now we were mistaken in this respect. Comrade Trotsky and his faction, on the contrary, are doing their utmost to aggravate the conflict. Comrade Trotsky demanded his letter of October 24 be again sent out to all members of TsK and TSKK.[3] With this in view we have to look into this document by Comrade Trotsky as well.

---

*The document has been slightly abridged. (Ed.)

CHAPTER I. COMRADE TROTSKY'S LETTER AS A WEAPON OF FACTIONAL STRUGGLE

We were puzzled for a long time: why does Comrade Trotsky write so many letters and declarations to TsK? The purpose of these documents has become totally clear to us only in connection with recent events.

The letter of Comrade Trotsky's Forty-Six advocates[4] as well as his own letter addressed to the Central Committee members[5] have gotten wide attention, although joint Plenums of TsK and TSKK unanimously decided to leave both these documents and the resolution of the joint Plenums within the Central Committee. One should not be a prophet to foresee that these documents will soon appear in the foreign Menshevist or Socialist-revolutionary press.[6]

Disseminating these documents Comrade Trotsky's advocates conceal from the members of the Party that there is a reply of Politburo[7] to letters by Comrade Trotsky and the Forty-Six, that in October this year Plenums of TsK and TSKK considered Comrade Trotsky's declaration and that of the Forty-Six, and they condemned Comrade Trotsky's and the Forty-Six's action as factional by 102 votes against 2 with 10 abstaining. Comrade Trotsky's faction used this method to lead the youth into error and partially reached its purpose.

Who was engaged in disseminating these documents? Comrade Trotsky's factions. Why did they need to disseminate them? In order to sow mistrust among the majority of the Central Committee whose hands were tied by its own resolution that the entire conflict with Comrade Trotsky was to remain within the Central Committee.

These factional methods remind us of the most fierce factional battle within the united (with Menshevists) Central Committee.[8] Such methods were understandable in those days. Nowadays our Party is not likely to allow Comrade Trotsky and his faction to carry on with these methods for a long time.

CHAPTER 2. "LEGEND" ABOUT COMRADE TROTSKY'S "PSEUDO" ANTI-LENINIST LINE

In his letter of October 24, Comrade Trotsky is trying to allege that "the majority of the Central Committee makes up 'malicious legends' about my (i.e., Comrade Trotsky's) nearly anti-Leninist line."*

Yes, we declare openly that the problem involves following Comrade Lenin's policy on the part of the majority of the Politburo, on the one hand, and Comrade Trotsky's struggle against this policy, on the other. In different periods Comrade Trotsky's struggle against Comrade Lenin's general line takes on different forms. But the fact remains the fact. What is considered to be a specific feature of Comrade Trotsky and his faction is totally hostile to Leninism. And this is a secret to nobody.

What is the reason for our discord? What are Comrade Trotsky's deviations from the main line of Lenin's Bolshevism?

We quite agree with our Central Organ† when they give the following answer to these questions[9]:

"After October our Party went through three main crises: the Brest crisis,[10] the trade-union crisis[11] and the present one. Comrade Trotsky made mistakes on all stages of the Party development. We should take a composed and thoughtful attitude to the subject and try to understand the *root-cause*‡ of these mistakes. Only if we find this root-cause will we be able to duly *correct* the deviations which are an inevitable followup of the previous ones.

"*The Brest Peace.* What was Comrade Trotsky's (and left communists') error? They were carried away by the revolutionary phrase, by the drawing, by the beautiful *paper plan.* The Brest peace opponents had such a drawing but they failed to see the damned reality which Lenin's genius saw so clearly. And first of all they failed to see our peasants who did not want, did not intend, and were not able to fight.

"Trade-unions . . . During the trade-union discussion the country demanded removal of military communism's yoke which restrained the growth of production forces and the trade-unions suggested tightening our

---

*This is a loose wording of Trotsky's words. See Document No. 20. (Ed.)
†This is a reference to *Pravda.* (Ed.)
‡Emphasis in the original. (Ed.)

belts. Therefore the question was again about misunderstanding *reality* and, first of all, not taking the mass psychology of *the peasants* into consideration. However, the proletariat is not able to rule this country without considering this psychology.

Our present contradictions with Comrade Trotsky have the same basis. These contradictions existed when Comrade Lenin headed the activities of TsK, they existed after that as well. Comrade Trotsky put all the blame on the lack of planned work. In Comrade Trotsky's opinion it is this lack that led all the country to "disaster." This is what Comrade Trotsky kept accusing TsK of, repeatedly and systematically.

. . . But TsK thought that Comrade Trotsky made a terrible *excess* in this issue. TsK believed that the plan of our economic policy should be worked out very carefully in order not to be only on paper but to be real, not to share the fate of Order N1042[13] but to live. TsK believed that contrary to Comrade Trotsky we cannot speak about the "dictatorship of industry" but we will have, as Lenin has taught us, to ride a peasant's skinny horse for a long time and that will be the *only* way to save our industry and to *create a profound basis for the* dictatorship of the proletariat.*

"This is the root-cause of our *current* differences. We may ask ourselves: could it be the same mistake but in a new form?

"Of course, it is so. And here we see a hypertrophy of the plan without making this plan suitable enough for reality. And here again the *reason* is underestimating the peasants' reality.

"This very basis of Comrade Trotsky's errors is a deviation from Leninism."

"In our current discussion as well as from Comrade Trotsky's recent article[15] we clearly see that in the issues of inter-Party politics the faction of Comrades Trotsky, Sapronov, and Preobrazhensky willy-nilly *deviate from Leninism.*

What was the general *organizational principle* of the Bolshevist Party? This Party, our Party, has always been notable for its unity and cohesion. There has always been a clear distinction between our Party and its organizational structure, on the one hand, and opportunist parties, on the other.

---

*Com. Trotsky's reference to Com. Lenin's propaganda article,[14] where the latter denounced "the landlords' lies," about differences with Com. Trotsky concerning the fact that Com.Trotsky is allegedly against the peasants, is sure to be very far-fetched because the problem is different. The fact is that while making up his plans Com.Trotsky leaves the peasants out of his sight; he undermines the role of the peasants. Authors of the reply.

Our Party grew and matured in the fights with opportunism as a Party made out of rock. Our Party *has never been and, we hope, will never be a federation of collaborating groups, small groups, factions and "trends."* On the contrary, Mensheviks, Socialist-revolutionaries, and other "soft" ones[16] as opposed to "intolerant," "steadfast" Bolsheviks, cultivated extreme "freedom of opinion," "freedom of small groups," "freedom of trends." Not long ago at the trial of Socialist revolutionaries[17] the accused bragged about their "tolerance": they had had a wing openly supporting the White, they had had an "Administrative Center," they had had the left, they had had centrists, etc.; in short, what did they have? The same may be said about Mensheviks. But our Party managed *to destroy* our enemies partly because it was a united "steadfast cohort" of fighters, it fulfilled and embodied the greatest unity of wish, it was arranged so that all the shades of opinion melded into the *united flow*, but did not split the Party into fighting factions which only weaken each other.

"And if now a number of comrades, with Comrade Trotsky at the head, deviate from the organizational tradition they deviate from the organizational *tradition of Leninism*[18] in this case . . .

"Bolshevism has always highly appreciated and still highly appreciates the *Party apparatus*. It does not mean that Bolshevism must suffer or is suffering from night blindness toward the *diseases* of the apparatus (including its bureaucratization).

"One may and should be a fiery fighter against the diseases of the apparatus which reflect the disease of the Party, but to *set the Party off* against its apparatus means exactly to *deviate from Leninism*."*

The position Comrade Trotsky occupied on the eve of the Tenth Congress of the Party and the position he occupies now, shortly before the Thirteenth Congress of the Party[19] seem drastically different on the surface. As for the question about democracy Comrade Trotsky seems to have made a ninety-degree turn. However, if you consider all Comrade Trotsky's speeches made both on the eve of the Tenth Congress of the Party and after it they have, no doubt, their *own inner logic*. Before the Tenth Congress of our Party Comrade Trotsky spoke against Leninism by putting forward a bureaucratic slogan of shaking up the Leninist main body of professionalists†

---

*This is the end of the quote from the article "Doloi Franktsionnost" (Away with Factionism) from the *Pravda* of December 28, 1923, by Bukharin. (Ed.)

†Trade-union workers. (Ed.)

from above and perpetuating the military methods of Party control. Now, before the Thirteenth Congress of our Party Comrade Trotsky sets forth slogans of "genuine" democracy according to the principle of shaking up "from above" the same Lenin's main cadres of the Party apparatus and Party members in general. Quite recently between the Twelfth and Thirteenth Party Congresses when it seemed to Comrade Trotsky that serious differences might appear in the *national question* he did not hesitate to use the opening hole as well.[20] . . . In short, all occasions, all opportunities, all platforms are good for Comrade Trotsky if they can shake the basis of the Bolshevik Party, all main cadres of the RKP. In the end Comrade Trotsky's present attempt is again aimed at turning our Party youth, and first of all students, against the same main cadres of the Party. . . .

CHAPTER 3. ECONOMIC ISSUES

In his letter of October 24, Comrade Trotsky refers to a "rather huge correspondence with Comrade Lenin" on some issues. This *"huge* correspondence" boils down to two to three notes by Comrade Lenin.[21] Each People's Commissar might have written a number of such notes. If the undersigned had found it necessary to present all letters and notes where Comrade Lenin shared their opinion in this or that issue or those articles, and notes where Comrade Lenin dissociated himself from Comrade Trotsky it would have been much more than a couple of pages. Comrade Trotsky must be referring to this "huge correspondence" because he himself is thinking of the cases when Comrade Lenin, as an exception, shared his opinion as outstanding.[22]

As to the possibility of involving Comrade Trotsky in economic work Comrade Lenin was always totally uncompromising. It was he who believed that Comrade Trotsky could not be entrusted with the economic work of the Republic. And we agreed with Comrade Lenin. Notorious order number 1042 initiated by Comrade Trotsky when he was Narcomput* clearly reflected an overestimation of the paper—"plan beginning" and was an amateurist order. Nobody was so concerned about the fate of railroads in Russia as Comrade Lenin when these railroads were in Com-

---

*People's Commissar of Railways. (Ed.)

rade Trotsky's hands, and nobody showed so much initiative to get Comrade Trotsky away from railroad operations as Comrade Lenin. Even when Comrade Trotsky tried to set up for himself a substitute of the notorious Moskust[23] Comrade Lenin spent months struggling even against this small "economic idea" of Comrade Trotsky. In Comrade Trotsky's presence and in his absence Comrade Lenin many times proved in detail that Comrade Trotsky's approach to economic problems may only ruin the economy.

Comrade Lenin totally disagreed with Comrade Trotsky on the issue of Gosplan. In his letter of May 6, 1922, to Politburo members Comrade Lenin wrote[24]:

". . . As for Gosplan Comrade Trotsky is not only completely wrong in this question but he is surprisingly ill-informed about the things he speaks of Gosplan's shortcoming is not academism, but, on the contrary, it is overloaded with everyday routine "noodles." . . .

The second document by Comrade Trotsky of April 23, 1922, contains, firstly, very excited but entirely wrong "criticisms" of the Politburo resolution about setting up a financial troika* . . . as a brake between the Small and the Large Sovnarkom. Sending this criticism to deputies† does not comply with any planned or, in general, organizational state work.

Secondly, this document contains the same totally wrong accusations of Gosplan in academism which is not true at all. . . ."

This is how Comrade Lenin assessed Comrade Trotsky's wrong views of Gosplan.

Basically these differences also boil down to Comrade Trotsky's wrong understanding of the role of the peasants and peasant farm in our country. Comrade Trotsky insists on a "complete plan" as a hollow abstraction. His "plan" has but a "small" disadvantage: it is *built on sand*, as it was the case with Comrade Trotsky's notorious "planned" order number 1042. As for Comrade Lenin and us, his close supporters, we believed and still believe that a real plan can be built only if the great part played by agriculture in our country is taken into account. Up to 1923, i.e., before improving finances, creating the basis for the budget, and accumulating maneuver funds the question about the "maneuver" planned work was in the air to some extent. Only recently there appeared preconditions for increasing the real role of Gosplan. And Politburo immediately made an appropriate decision.

---

*People's Commissar of Finance and his two deputies. (Ed.)
†People's Commissar's deputies. (Ed.)

As is known in his next letters Comrade Lenin agreed to make a concession to Comrade Trotsky in the issue of Gosplan's administrative rights.[25] But this last question is of very little importance. In general Comrade Lenin by no means made and could make a concession on this question for a very simple reason: Comrade Trotsky's ignoring the role of the peasants again deviated and deviates from the fundamentals of Bolshevism. In our opinion it accounts for the fact that when Comrade Trotsky's candidacy for the Gosplan's chairman was under discussion Comrade Lenin, in his note dictated in December 27, 1922, was definitely *against* this candidacy. Everybody knows that when saying we should not "appoint any eminent political leaders or Chairman of VSNH, etc, as Chairman of Gosplan"[26] Lenin meant Comrade Trotsky. During V. I.'s* illness some comrades were inclined to nominate Comrade Trotsky for economic work to improve the relations inside TsK. After what we have seen in the last months we come to the conclusion that those of us who agreed to such attempts were wrong and Comrade Lenin was completely right on this question.

CHAPTER 4. MONOPOLY OF FOREIGN TRADE

This question was, in fact, made clear at the Twelfth Congress of the Party. But since Comrade Trotsky and his faction keep returning to this question we have to dwell on it too. In December 1922, in Comrade Lenin's absence, the plenum of TsK[27] took some decisions on foreign trade which Comrade Lenin disagreed to. The question was, by no means, about abolition of foreign trade monopoly. This idea never came to the plenum of TsK. The TsK plenum just wanted to make an experiment of opening one or two ports for the free import of some absolutely necessary staples for some period of time as it was done previously for Batumi, and especially to speed up the transportation of the Kuban grain surplus. Having learned about this decision Comrade Lenin argued about it and managed to convince us that this decision should be reconsidered, which was done unanimously by the next plenum.[28] The note quoted by Comrade Trotsky was written in the period

---

‡Vladimir Ilyich. (Ed.)
*People's Commissariat of Foreign Trade. (Ed.)

between these two plenums, at the moment when it might seem to Comrade Lenin that this question would really bring about serious differences.[29]

There have been no differences on the questions of foreign trade monopoly in the Politburo since then and the policy carried out by TsK in this sphere has brought very good results.While planning distribution of work within the Politburo we entrusted Comrade Trotsky with supervising Vneshtorg* and did it on purpose but Comrade Trotsky did absolutely nothing to carry out this mission of the Politburo.

CHAPTER 5. THE NATIONAL QUESTION

When a most difficult transition to the formation of the Union of Socialist Republics was taking place and the national question was put forward again there were really some differences among our Bolshevist main body members.[30] At first each question connected with this transition underwent wide discussions with Comrade Lenin, in particular, between Comrades Lenin and Stalin. There is no doubt that if Vladimir Ilyich's illness had not hampered us we would have come to a 100 percent agreement. But the situation when it became impossible to contact Comrade Lenin personally and later in writing, led to the fact that some misunderstanding remained, mainly, on the question of assessing the well-known conflict in the Georgian Communist Party. All this together gave rise to a well-known letter by Comrade Lenin.[31] The draft of the resolution on the national question (its author was Comrade Stalin) was approved by TsK unanimously.[32] The resolution of the well-known national conference[33] was also approved by TsK unanimously. Comrade Trotsky voted *for* these resolutions. At the Twelfth Congress Comrade Trotsky did not put forward any objections. What for, then, to arouse arguments over unanimously approved resolutions claiming that there were fundamental differences over this question. It is done only for *fuctional reasons*. There is no other issue where Comrade Trotsky beats himself the way he does in the national question. Comrade Trotsky and his faction claim that we, their political opponents,[34] settle questions in some circle-like manner while all the Party witnessed us settle the national question. In reality at the Twelfth Congress of RKP we never concealed shades of our opinions in this question from the entire Party. Surely we made

Comrade Lenin's letter known to all the members of the Congress.[35] At the Congress some of the undersigned had an open and keen discussion among themselves.[36] The decision of the Twelfth Congress was adopted fully in the spirit of Comrade Lenin. Nobody has dared to dispute it so far. Shortly after the Twelfth Congress, at Comrade Stalin's initiative, the Politburo convened a meeting of Communist-nationals which performed much work and ensured putting Lenin's ideas for the national question into life, not in words but in reality. The conflict in Georgia was overcome long ago. The right course on the national question in Georgia has been ensured fully and completely.[37] But Comrade Trotsky still goes on stirring up a conflict in this question. Let the Party judge who is engaged in circle-like acting here.

CHAPTER 6. COMRADE LENIN'S ARTICLES ABOUT REORGANIZATION OF RKI AND TSKK[38]

In his letter of October 24, Comrade Trotsky tries to invent a legend that only thanks to him Lenin's article became known. This is all very thin. Comrade Lenin's first articles on this subject was, by mistake, addressed to the Presidium of the congress of the Soviets which was held in Moscow at the moment.[39] This address evidently left the Politburo members puzzled. Comrade Kuibyshev, in particular, has already explained at the Plenum of TsK and TSKK that a wish to pigeonhole Comrade Lenin's article attributed to him by Comrade Trotsky is really a malicious legend. We confirm it fully. As soon as it was found out that Comrade Lenin addresses his articles not to the Presidium of the Congress of the Soviets but to the TsK of the Party and, in fact, wants them to be published it was, of course, decided immediately to have these articles published. However when some weeks later a question about putting Comrade Lenin's plan into life virtually was set forth at the Plenum of the TsK no one else but Comrade Trotsky stepped forward with a completely anti-Leninist draft of creating a two-center system in the Party (TsK and Party Council).[40] And none other than Comrade Trotsky began firing at reorganized TSKK and RKI during the first stages of their activity as soon as Comrade Trotsky realized they would not defend his factional action.

CHAPTER 7. FOREIGN POLICY

We expressed our reproach to Comrade Trotsky because: (1) in connection with Kerzon's ultimatum he drove the Politburo to the policy of adventure which could lead to the rupture with England, and (2) in connection with the Polish government's reluctance to recognize the USSR and in connection with the development of events in Germany Comrade Trotsky more actively drove the Politburo to some reckless steps which could lead to the rupture and even military clash with Poland earlier than serious events would have started in Germany.[42]

These accusations are still fully in force. The situation does not change because of the fact that after his proposals on the English question were turned down by the Politburo Comrade Trotsky took the mst active part in the work of the Politburo to formulate* those counter notes which were sent to Kerzon. As to the Polish conflict the Politburo had to hold up the draft order on the army which has already been prepared by Comrade Trotsky. The consistent policy of the Politburo led to the Polish government giving up its attempts not to recognize the USSR and getting into a difficult situation in connection with the proposals handed to him by Comrade Kopp by the instructions of the Politburo.

CHAPTER 8. COMRADE TROTSKY'S WORK IN THE ARMY

The comrades remember Comrade Trotsky's reaction during the September Plenum of the TsK when the TsK plenum in view of the war threat who decided to strengthen the Revolutionary Military Council of the Republic and to introduce a few experienced military men—members of the TsK.[43] Comrade Trotsky just left the Plenum. The TsK Plenum had to send a special delegation to Comrade Trotsky with the proposal to return to the Plenum meeting. Despite this Comrade Trotsky refused to return to the Plenum.

---

*Quote from the original. Could possibly mean—on formulating or preparing those counter notes. (Ed.)

This proved again and again that in this sphere Comrade Trotsky is far from putting basic interests above side motives. . . .

We have to insist vigorously that Comrade Trotsky does not, in fact, attach enough attention to the work in the army. As much Comrade Trotsky's work was useful when the primary task was the task of revolutionary propaganda on the fronts as dissatisfactory his work in army has become now when there is an urgent need for everyday scrupulous work. Each military man knows only too well that the procurement in the army is extremely poor, that the present Central group of the Revolutionary Military Council headed by Comrade Sklyansky does not carry out any systematic, businesslike, scrupulous or satisfactory work. But, nevertheless, each member of the TsK and TSKK knows that any slightest attempt of the TsK to strengthen the present Revvoensovet of the Republic gets a hostile reception from Comrade Trotsky and is nearly considered a reason for breakup.

CHAPTER 9. DISTRUST OF THE PARTY AND POOR KNOWLEDGE OF IT

When we reproach Comrade Trotsky that he does not believe in the creative possibilities of the Party and its local organizations, Comrade Trotsky replies he had to work with all the gubkoms (provincial committees) in the hard times of the civil war. Nobody would think of denying Comrade Trotsky's great services during the civil war. But one cannot deny the fact that the Red Army was guided by the TsK of the Party as a unit.

Comrade Trotsky neither believes in the creative possibilities of our Party nor does he know them; or he probably does not believe in them because he does not know them. . . .

CHAPTER 10. A FACTION OF NON-FACTIONISTS

Comrade Trotsky still considers that the decision of joint plenums of the TsK and TSKK which condemned Comrade Trotsky's behavior for setting forth a factional platform and attempting to found a faction is wrong. In his letter of October 24, Comrade Trotsky refers to a number of statements by members and candidates of the Politburo (Comrade Bukharin, Molotov) to the effect that it is necessary to make a sharp turn to working democracy "and that he" (Comrade Trotsky) would have expressed himself more carefully.[44] But these quotations are fully against Comrade Trotsky. They confirm the well-known fact that the Politburo itself considered the turn to working democracy necessary as far back as September of this year and it refutes the legend created by Comrade Trotsky and the Forty-Six that it is only due to their pressure that the Politburo decided to take a turn to working democracy. The joint plenums of the TsK and the TSKK (October 1923) condemned Comrade Trotsky and his faction of Forty-Six not because they suggested (like the majority of the Politburo members) turning to working democracy but because they put forward a factional platform, invented "crises" which do not exist and started organizing their own faction. For factionalism, i.e., for the aggravation of the Party split threat—that is what the joint Plenums condemned Comrade Trotsky and his group of Forty-Six for.[45]

During the joint Plenums of the TsK and TSKK it was already clear that there was a simple division of labor between Comrade Trotsky and the Forty-Six. In the course of the joint Plenums Comrade Trotsky kept silence on the issue of his attitude to the letter of the Forty-Six. But later Comrade Trotsky made an official statement to the Politburo that he would assume full responsibility for the letter of the Forty-Six. This division of labor is still in effect. Sapronov, Rafail, Preobrazhensky, Smirnov,[46] and others come forward as a faction more or less openly. Comrade Trotsky calls himself "nonfactional" but he *fully supports* the above-mentioned statement, refers to these factionaries as "ideal Party members," etc. We have known this division of labor for a long time. At one time Comrade Trotsky hesitated between different extremes and now, at last, he found his place at the faction of "democratic centralism,[47] which he now virtually heads.

Comrade Trotsky's faction began a struggle in our Moscow organization unprecedented in the history of our Party. It virtually organized its factional center. One of the organs of Revvoensovet of the Republic—PUR— has been turned into an executive factional center. Such collectives as the Kremlin guard students and the core of General Headquarters are approached with proposals to express non-confidence to the Central Committee of the Party. The *same proposals* are brought to the 1500-person GPU. What it means in the conditions when the Party rules the country is clear to everybody. One of this faction's supporters, Comrade Radek, does his utmost and even more to move the fight against the TsK of the Party into Comintern. In short, a factional fight against the Party is in full swing.

In his letter of October 24, Comrade Trotsky complained that there were personal issues in inter-Party disputes. But as the present discussion in Moscow is under way we may state that we have never witnessed so much personal badgering , slander and rumors concerning the majority of TsK and Politburo members as it is practiced now in Moscow at the initiative of Comrade Trotsky's allies.

. . . Thus, the behavior of Comrade Trotsky and his close allies has fully confirmed the instructions of the joint Plenums concerning Comrade Trotsky's factional action. Comrade Trotsky's article published in the *Pravda* of December 28,[48] contains a direct confession of Comrade Trotsky that he, in fact, set up a faction. It is clear to each experienced politician from Comrade Trotsky's article. Comrade Trotsky and his close allies now go further on. They are trying not only to set up their faction but to legalize it within the Party. We think our Party will not allow and should not allow any of these actions.

N. Bukharin

G. Zinoviev

M. Kalinin

L. Kamenev

V. Molotov

Y. Rudzutak

A. Rykov

I. Stalin

M. Tomsky

December 31, 1923

RTsHIDNI, f. 51, op.I, d. 21, 1. 58ob.–61;
Printed text. First published in the journal
Izvestia TsK KPSS , 1991, No. 3, pp 208–218

NOTES

1. L. D.Trotsky's letter was written on October 23, 1923; it came to the Secretariat of the TsK (Tsentralny Komitet, Central Committee, TsK) on October 24 (See Document No. 20).

2. For the resolution of the October joint Plenum TsK and TsK RKP(b) (Tsentralny Komitet Rossiiskoy Kommunisticheskoy partii bolshevikov—Central Committee of the Russian Communist Party of Bolsheviks, TsK RKPB), see Document No. 21:III.

3. L. D.Trotsky's note to the TsK Secretariat of December 17, 1923, said: "Secretariat of the TsK sent to members of TsK and TSKK (Tsentralny Komitet Kominterna, Central Committee of Comintern, TSKK) my reservation to the vote of the resolution on the Party construction (which I did not ask about but which I do not object to). At the same time the Secretariat sent a new statement to members and candidates of the TsK and TSKK and in the form of supplements No. 1 and No. 2 it sent a previous reply of the Politburo members and candidates and the decision of the joint Plenums.

"With this in view I ask to arrange the sending immediately to all members of the TsK and TSKK of my reply of October 24, to the letter of the Politburo members. L. Trotsky."

The note makes reference to the following documents: L. D.Trotsky's reservation to the vote offer the resolution "O partstroitelstve" (On the Party Building) of December 9—see Document No. 31; L. D.Trotsky's new statement for the TsK and TSKK members of December 13—see Document No. 33; previous reply of the Politburo members of October 19—see Document No. 17; resolution of the October joint Plenum of the TsK and TSKK of October 26—see Document No. 21:III.

Judging by the note the TsK Secretariat did not acquaint TsK and TSKK members with L. D.Trotsky's reply of October 23 (see Document No. 20) which caused his request to send this document round.

4. Statement of the Forty-Six, see document No. 12.

5. Reference is made to L. D.Trotsky's letter of October 8, 1923 (See Document No. 4).

6. Extracts from L. D. Trotsky's letter of October 8, were first published in the journal *Sotsialistichskyi Vestnik* (Berlin), 1924, No. II (81) of May 24.

7. For the reply of the Politburo members of October 19, 1923, to L. D. Trotsky's letter of October 8, see Document No. 17.

8. Reference is to sharp differences between factions of Bolsheviks and Mensheviks in the united RSDRP (Rossiyskaya Sotsial Demokraticheskaya Rabochaya Partiya, Russian Social Democratic Workers Party, RSDWP), on the eve of and during the First Russian revolution in 1905–1907.

9. Reference is meant to the editorial of *Pravda* written by N. Bukharin and published under the title "Doloi fraktsionnost" (Away with Factionalism) (A reply of the Central organ to L. D.Trotsky) in *Pravda* issues of December 28, 29, 30, 1923, and January 1, 4, 1924. The article under the same title was shortly thereafter published as a brochure. The text quotes *Pravda* of December 28, 1923.

10. Reference is made. to differences in the Party leadership while negotiating and signing the Brest peace treaty with Germany (see note 29 to Document No. 36:I).

11. Reference is made to the discussion launched in the Party at the end of 1920–beginning of 1921 on the role and tasks of trade-unions (see note 6 to Document No. 17).

12. The left oppositional group in the RKP(b) led by N. I. Bukharin existed in the period of Soviet-German peace negotiations signing and ratifying the Brest peace (see note 29 to Document 1–136–1).

13. Reference is made to the order for the People's Commissariat of Railways issued by L. D. Trotsky in May, 1920 (see note 17 to Document No. 17).

14. Authors of the reply refer to V. I. Lenin's article "Otvet na zapros krestyanina" (A Reply to a Peasant's Inquiry) published in *Pravda* and *Izvestia VTsIK* of February 15, 1919, in which V. I. Lenin confirmed L. D. Trotsky's statement (*Izvestia VTsIK* of February 7, 1919) that they have no differences over the question of their attitude to the middle peasants (see V. I. Lenin, *Complete Works,* vol. 37, p. 478).

15. Reference is made to L. D. Trotsky's article "Novyi kurs. Gruppirovki i fraktsionnye obrazovaniya" (New Course: Groupings and Factional Formations) published in *Pravda,* December 28, 1923.

16. See note 39 to Document No. 17 about Mensheviks and Socialist revolutionaries.

17. A trial of left Socialist revolutionaries leaders took place in the summer of 1922.

18. Bolshevist orientation towards steadfastness and wholiness based on absolutism of the class approach and intolerance toward political opponents which was to some extent reasonable during the years of Party's underground activities did not allow any dissidence in the ranks of the Party later, during NEP which contradicted the real political situation and the necessity to establish civil peace. Therefore the Party leadership manipulating prerevolutionary traditions so easily went beyond the limits of political accusations claiming any shades of meanings and positions to be factious, anti-Party, anti-Leninist.

19. The Thirteenth Congress of RKP(b) took place in May 1924.

20. See notes to section "Chapter 5. The National Question" of the present document.

21. As for this episode see note 48 to Document No. 17.

22. V. I. Lenin's notes mentioned by L.D. Trotsky in his letter of October 23 refer to foreign trade monopoly, "Georgian incident" and the national question (see Document No. 20), i.e., basic problems which V. I. Lenin was very much concerned about and to which he attached a lot of importance. In the fervor of a factional fight with L. D. Trotsky the authors of the reply allow a direct falsification and play down the importance of Lenin's notes.

23. See note 46 to Document No. 20.

24. Reference is made to "Otvet na zamechaniya, kasayutchiesya raboty zamov samestitelei predsedatelya SNK" (A reply to remarks concerning the work of the deputies of the People's Commissars Council Chairman) written by V. I. Lenin on May 5, 1922 (and not May 6). The letter is quoted with some deletions not marked by ellipses in the text (V. I. Lenin, *Complete Works,* vol. 45, pp. 181-182).

25. Reference is made to V. I. Lenin's notes dictated December 27-29, 1922, under the title "O pridanii zakonodatelnykh funktsii Gosplanu" (On Giving Legislative Functions to Gosplan) where he suggested raising Gosplan's role as a commission of scientific experts, where "administrative force . . . should be, in fact, auxiliary" (see V. I. Lenin, *Complete Works,* vol. 45, pp. 349–353). Besides in the first version of "Pismo k siezdu" (Letter to the Congress) of December 23, 1922, which was known to the Poliburo members in spite of its being highly confidential, V. I. Lenin proposed to the Twelfth Congress of the Party to the imparting of a legislative character . . . to Gosplan's decisions meeting Comrade Trotsky's request to *some extent and on certain conditions* (ibid., p. 343). The interests of inter-

Party fighting made the authors of the reply not only treat V. I. Lenin's proposals as "of less than secondary importance" but also undertake direct falsification of the document: the words italicized in the quotation are absent in the first manuscript (see Y. A. Buranov, "K istorii leninskogo politicheskogo zavechaniya" [1922-1923]) (The Background of Lenin's "Political Will) in the journal *Voprosy istorii KPSS,* 1991, No. 4, pp. 47–56).

26. The quotation is not exact (See V. I. Lenin, *Complete Works,* vol. 45, p. 350).

27. The text erroneously mentions the December TsK Plenum. Reference is made to the decision taken at the TsK Plenum of October 6, 1922 (see V. I. Lenin, *Complete Works,* vol. 45, pp. 220–223, 561–563).

28. Reference is made to the Plenum which took place on December 18, 1922.

29. As for differences in the Politburo of TsK RKP(b) on the issue of foreign trade monopoly see note 7 to Document 5 as well as: L. D. Trotsky, "Stalinskaya shkola falsifikatsii" (Stalin's School of Falsification), pp. 70-85.

30. As for differences in the Politburo of TsK RKP(b) on the issue of the USSR formation and inter-ethnic relations see note 8 to Document No. 5 as well as: L. D. Trotsky, "Stalinskaya shkola falsifikatsii" (Stalin's School of Falsification), pp. 77–83.

31. Reference is made to V. I. Lenin's article "K voprosu o natsionalnostyakh ili ob 'autonomization' ") ("On the question of nationalities or about "autonomization") (see V. I. Lenin, *Complete Works,* vol. 45, pp. 356-362).

32. At the February (1923) Plenum of TsK the draft was adopted only as a basis.

33. Here and in the next paragraph reference is made to the fourth meeting of TsK RKP(b) with senior officials of national republics and regions which took place in Moscow on June 9–12, 1923. In fact, the meeting reconsidered the decisions of the Twelfth Congress of the Party on the national question based on Lenin's guidelines.

34. Neither L. D. Trotsky's letters to TsK nor the Statement of the Forty-Six refers to members of the Party leadership as political enemies.

35. V. I. Lenin's article "K voprosu o natsionalnostyakh ili ob 'avtonomizatsii' " (On the question of nationalities or about "autonomization") was made known at the seniorenconvention of the Twelfth Congress of RKP(b).

36. At the Twelfth Congress N. I. Bukharin made a fiery and emotional speech defending Lenin's position in the national question (see *Dvenadtsaty siezd RKP[b]. Stenografichesky otchet.*) (*The Twelfth Congress of the RKP[b].) Shorthand report*).

37. The followup to the "Georgian conflict" which was not settled in respect to the questions put forward by a group of Georgian leaders (inter-ethnic relations, the correlation between the center and the republics, etc.) was the peasants' revolt in Georgia at the end of 1924.

38. Reference is made to V. I. Lenin's articles "Kak nam reorganizovat Rabkrin (Predolzheniye Dvenadtsatomu siezdu partii)" (How we should reorganize Rabkrin—Workers' and Peasants' inspection. A proposal to the Twelfth Congress of the Party) and "Luchshe menshe, da luchshe" (It is better less, but better) (see V. I. Lenin, *Complete Works,* vol. 45, pp. 383–406). As for the background to the first article's publication see note 9 to Document No. 5 as well as: L. D. Trotsky, "Stalinskaya shkola falsifikatsii" (Stalin's School of Falsification), pp. 83–85.

39. We may say it is vice versa—the explanation of the authors of the reply is "very thin." The first Congress of USSR Soviets took place on December 30, 1922, and V. I. Lenin

started working on the article about Rabkrin at the beginning of January 1923, and completed it on January 23, having given the article the title and the subtitle "A Proposal to the Twelfth Congress."

40. Reference is made to L. D. Trotsky's proposals on the organizational issue at the TsK February Plenum (1923). They were aimed at implementing Lenin's idea for more effective control over TsK RKP(b) activities from below.

41. As for J. N. Curson's ultimatum, see note 32 to Document No. 4.

42. See note 23 to Document No. 17 and note 39 to Document No. 20.

43. As for the decision of TsK September Plenum see Document No. 1, as for successive events see Documents Nos. 2–4.

44. See Document No. 20, section 1, item 2.

45. For the resolution of the united October Plenum of TsK and TSKK RKP(b), see Document No. 21: III.

46. The statement of the Forty-Six was signed by V. M. Smirnov and I. N. Smirnov. In this case reference is made to V. M. Smirnov.

47. For the group of "democratic centralism," see note 49 to Document No. 17.

48. Reference is made to L. D. Trotsky's above-mentioned article "Novyi kurs. Gruppirovki i fraktsionnye obrazovaniya" (New Course: Groupings and Factional Formations) where he stressed that since RKP(b) was the only ruling Party in the country it would always face differences, shades of opinions on various issues which could be overcome only be means of democratic disputes and discussions but not by registering dissidents as anti-Party factions.

48

The TsK of the RKP(b) Plenum Materials[1]

January 14–15, 1924

FROM I. V. STALIN'S REPORT

Stalin. It is clear that I will not have to report on the substance of the resolution.* Its principles are well known to everybody. I'd just like to point out the facts, how the resolution emerged, in order that the comrades, TsK and TSKK Plenum members (Central Committee and Central Control Commission) understand how we created this document; how in spite of the fact that it was adopted unanimously, there was a fight that brought about negative facts. I think that all this should be mentioned.

You know that at TsK and TSKK Plenary Sessions (October),[2] there had been taken a decision that all Politburo members should be invited to pursue the work together after settling the questions of the Plenums. To execute the point we, the Politburo majority of eight men,[3] those who signed the certain papers, appealed to Comrade Trotsky, and had held a separate meeting twice[4] to unofficially arrange about the arrangeable matters. It had been done, in the first place, to implement the newly mentioned resolution of TsK and TSKK; in the second place, to prevent the emergence of facts able to lead to any kind of misunderstandings in the future. The first separate meet-

---

*The Resolution "About Party Development" of December 5, 1923. (Ed.)

333

ing with Comrade Trotsky resulted in promising the possibility of all embracing and concerted work in the framework of the Politburo.We were talking about Gosplan (State Plan), i.e., about the very acute question that had
been raised by Comrade Trotsky in his supplementary report and concluding remarks at Plenary Sessions of TsK and TSKK.[5] We were talking about
the necessity to lift Gosplan up according to its position and what kind of
workers it was to be filled with. Completing PESC (People's Economy
Supreme Council) with new top collaborators was the next question; and
democracy and inner-Party situation question was touched on shortly. . . .

As you see, comrades, the work had been going on rather smoothly.
Later on, a question of resolution on inner Party situation was raised after
solving the questions of the Politburo at one of its meetings.

It is known that a very extensive draft of the resolution was presented
by the commission that bad been elected as far back as the Plenary Session
in September. Afterward we agreed on the idea that it would be better to
set up a subcommittee to push the affair ahead and to possibly achieve mutual understanding if everyone failed to be of one voice.[6] It was made by
three persons: Comrade Trotsky, Comrade Kamenev, and Comrade Stalin.
I would not say that in this subcommittee we were unanimous at once.
There was a sort of fight, but after all we got the meaning of each other and
it resulted in adoption and publication of the draft.[7]

The subcommittee didn't approve Trotsky's two amendments eight out
of ten. The first one proposed not only to refresh our local bodies but also
to dismiss the people who were deaf to the spreading of democracy. Here,
there had been added an element of penalty against workers who might
seem to subordinate organization by those who deliberately hampered the
dissemination of democratic ideas. We didn't accept this, flatly refusing to
punish anybody and talking about our difficulties and the complicated situation and futility of complete democratic policy. Comrade Trotsky began
to object, then he gave in and the point passed as it had acceptably appeared
in the resolution.

The groups and factions amendment was the second one that we rejected at first, then it was softened and accepted. Comrade Trotsky insisted
on the retaining of the faction prohibition amendment but stood against
group prohibition. We were against it for it opened a chink to Myasnikovsky-minded people,[8] because they may talk about theirs being not a
faction but a group that will make it possible to have a kind of legal framework to set up faction.

Comrade Trotsky objected to it and afterward we agreed to make reference to the Tenth Congress Resolution about Groups and Factions.[9]

During its work the subcommittee had the advantage of circumstances that had made it possible to adopt the published resolution unanimously at the Politburo and TSKK joint conference and to pass it subsequently.

I must stress that the facts I informed you about were considered to be a characteristic of the first stage of our work concerning democratic matters under discussion. Here it is necessary to say that Comrade Trotsky, by his vote for the resolution, at the same time intended to send his application to TsK archives, dealing with his anxiety to some extent with his groundless belief that the resolution would be passed and some (according to him) conservative Party elements would interpret the resolution in their own way and would virtually keep the previous order.[10]

However, after unanimous adoption of the resolution, one or, at most, two days later, we got to know that Trotsky had written and sent his appeal to regional conferences[11] and it had been read in the regions, and workers had been informed of it. And it was done without TsK's knowledge and any attempts to inform TsK.

We learned that one copy of the document had been received by *Pravda*; one day later Comrade Trotsky had had a phone conversation with me and had been indignant at *Pravda*'s opposing the letter and not being in a hurry to publish it. He was suspicious of our intention to hush up his article. I say this because of rumors that TsK might have suppressed the publication of this document; to its mind, the article would have aggravated the situation and intensified the discussion.

But you see yourself that TsK couldn't simply ban the publication of Trotsky's article since it had been sent neither to TsK nor to TSKK, and since TsK and TSKK were faced with the fact of regional publication of this letter. So, the attempt not to publish the letter known to the workers was unthinkable. At this rate they could tell us we were silencing them and they would cry loudly about yesterday's so-called attempt to shelve Lenin's article[12] and now the attempt to do the same with Trotsky's letter.

I dwell on this question for after it the discussion of the paper absolutely changed its course in an undesirable way. This document turned out to be an initial point of class-struggle aggravation.[13] One would think the resolution had been adopted unanimously. If you don't want it—don't vote for it, nobody forces you to do it. We know that Comrade Trotsky is very popular with opposition elements. This very opposition, one or two days after the letter's publication, acted more calmly: it no longer has any motive to attack TsK, and the case could have been closed with no shocks because of the lack of differences, at least serious differences.[14] However, since Comrade Trotsky's letter, which represents a perfectly new platform shifting the center of the fight to a different plane, and talks about staff degeneration and of faction groups, everything has changed, and the discussion has taken a completely new turn.

How should we evaluate the actions of a TsK member who votes for the resolution and tomorrow comes out with a new platform that in fact opposes the TsK resolution that has been adopted by the author of a new platform?

What should we think of it? I gather that if one TsK member opposes TsK, the others are allowed to do the same. That means that we don't have an original TsK, i.e., a real TsK whose decisions are obligatory to TsK members—we don't have all this. In other words, there is a superman instead of TsK, staying above TsK, i.e., a superman who is a legal lawbreaker. The workers say not without reason: why do you with your Party discipline poke your nose into our affairs? If one of your TsK members doesn't abide by the law, then we have the right to do the same; don't interfere with your Party discipline in our affairs. If the superman staying above TsK[15] spits on TsK laws with pleasure, then the rest of the Party members have the right to do everything they want. The aforesaid made our discussion a strained one.

Let's not examine the new platform given by Comrade Trotsky in his letter, since we don't examine the matter on its merits. I'd only like to stress that if there hadn't been the letter then there wouldn't have been the new platform and our inner-Party struggle would have gone down, because the opposition wouldn't have had any substantial differences.

Comrades, I consider the inner-Party struggle's hardest moment, an especially difficult and especially dangerous one, to be the fact I'm going to inform you about, i.e., the fact that all secret Politburo decisions are evidently being openly announced by opposition TsK members.[16] Being a TsK member you speak at a meeting whose members shout at you: You tell us about such-and-such a Politburo decision, there is nothing to cover; it is all the same—we know about it.[17]

Comrades, this is the most dangerous fact in our discussion.

You know that recently three TsK members (Comrades Trotsky, Radek, and Pyatakov) sent their statement to the Politburo of TsK concerning "a forgery regime" in *Pravda*'s editorial staff.[18] At the same time, we said that we were sure that before solving the matter and taking certain measures "sverdlovtsy"* and other Party members would get to know about the decision, i.e., those who were not to know of all the decisions and who were not to discuss them if they hadn't been settled yet in the TsK. That time Comrade Pyatakov told us that this document was a duplicate of one of kept by the Politburo and the other by Comrade Trotsky's secretariat. However, it is commonly known that the document has been circulating in localities.

Pyatakov. None of the documents.

Stalin. Comrade Pyatakov can't vouch for Comrade Serebryakov's methods of struggle.[19]

Rudzutak. I assert that the next day Sapronov and Shlyapnikov became aware of it.

Stalin. I don't even mention that the very next day the worst opposition members but not the best ones, i.e., Sapronov and the others, were talking about the facts mentioned in the letter which dealt with forgery and soon at all meetings, they discussed this matter before the TSKK discussed it. On the basis of what one of the TSKK members told me, I inform you[20] that the paper was recently found by him outside of Moscow. Maybe this TsK member will confirm it himself. The method of divulging all the Politburo's actual or nonexistent decisions, all solved or to-be-solved problems, is the most harmful, for it is the source of reckless gossip. The papers[21] banned from publication by TsK are being spread by the opposition; whole bunches of these documents are being brought to the TsK from everywhere. Young people, because of their age, who don't look for profit but the truth, constantly surround TsK members at the meetings, wanting them to clarify the documents banned from publication and secret decisions. What could be a TsK member's reply except that the documents are not to be revealed and that they don't see any way of explaining why? However, it can make the youth feel that TsK covers up the truth and is afraid of it, and it means there is something dark in the TsK. Nevertheless, since lies and gossip can be attacked only by the facts, then many TsK members are sometimes forced to publish original documents.[22]

What comes of it? People on the street become aware of our secret documents; and as you know it does harm to our affairs, Soviet power, the whole state, for we are and will be surrounded by enemies for a long time.

---

*This is a reference to Sverdlov Communist University students. This university was the higher Party instructional institution whose students actively supported the opposition. (Ed.)

This is a lethal oppositional method of struggle which consists of gossip being created around the TsK in general and its members in particular; this specific method of Comrade Serebryakov is to be outlawed, if we want to make the atmosphere healthy.

There can be only one conclusion. Obviously, at the meeting we'll have to conclude the discussion and work out a special resolution able to make the Party free from quakes and poison emerging in the rage of discussion.[23] This way, I suggest, together with the resolution on democracy,* a special resolution be included in conference agendas connected with the discussion results, in order to discuss there the platform of Comrade Trotsky concerning Party establishment, groups, and so on,[24] and calling off the practical measures—I'm not talking about repressive measures, but those measures that could serve as Party safeguards against future upheavals.[25]

NOTES

1. Before 1924 TsK RKP(b) Plenary Sessions were not taken down in shorthand. There were only short protocol records and later on they were translated into protocols. For the first time TsK Plenum meetings (January 14–15, 1924) were taken down in shorthand although not entirely. There are three texts of stenographic reports in Plenum's archive file: text without corrections retyped right after its decoding, text corrected by the speakers, themselves and typescript that had been made from corrected shorthand report. It is necessary to stress that the shorthand report of the January Plenum had been sent to be published on February 15, 1924; i.e., the speakers were already engaged in completing their work on the texts after Thirteenth Party conference held January 16–8, 1924. The comparing of texts showed that I. V. Stalin's speech was the one that had the most corrections and it not only reflects the editing that has been done to it, but had also been coordinated in a certain way with conference resolutions primarily the resolution "About discussion results and petty bourgeois deviation in the Party."

In contrast to all others, Stalin's speech had been removed from shorthand reports (where corrections were inserted by the speakers themselves), edited accordingly, retyped with another typewriter on paper of a different quality and size, and turn reinserted in the rest of the shorthand report.

It was planned that on the TsK Plenary Session (January) the matters submitted to the RKP(b) Thirteenth All-Party conference (January 16) would be discussed. There were eight questions on Plenum's official agenda: the immediate tasks of economic policy and

---

*The resolution "About Party Development." (Ed.)

Party development, international environment problems, discussion results, credits to the military department, etc.

However, I. V. Stalin, although being the main speaker on Party development and economic policy questions (because of A. I. Rykov's sickness), didn't touch upon these the most important problems in his speech. TsK members also didn't begin to discuss Pyatakov's amendments to the Politburo resolution on economic questions (published as far back as December 1923). The Plenary Session confined itself to recommending both resolutions (Party development of December 5 and economic questions) to be discussed and approved at the forthcoming Party conference.

As a matter of fact, as you can see from Plenary Sessions papers, the main thing worrying the session participants was the question of power. Both the results of the discussion and the role of the opposition in it were discussed within the context and in light of this problem.

The speakers fairly mentioned that workers and peasants, after a long dry spell, had come back to political life, and both intellectuals and the newly emerging NEP bourgeoisie called for the deepening of political democracy. Opposition feelings increased in the Party and the country, creating a real threat to RKP(b) dictatorship. Under these conditions, keeping the Party monopoly in power and ensuring secretary hierarchy dictatorship within the Party became the main goal of the TsK "main ruling body." To overcome discrepancies with the opposition by democratic methods was out of the question. Political and organizational defeat of the opposition had been decided in advance.

2. Resolution of joint TsK and TSKK Plenum (October), see Document No. 21:III.

3. This is a reference to the TsK Politburo members and candidates: N. I. Bukharin, G. I. Zinovyev, M. I. Kalinin, L. B. Kamenev, V. M. Molotov, A. I. Rykov, and M. P. Tomsky who signed the replies of October 19 and December 31, 1923 (see Documents Nos. 17 and 47). Also the second paper is signed by Y. E. Rudzutak.

4. The reference is to the conferences in L. D. Trotsky's apartment during his sickness in November 1923.

5. L. D. Trotsky's concluding speech, summary at TsK and TSKK Rally Session (October), see Document No. 21:I, II.

6. About subcommittees of three, see note of Document No. 24.

7. The reference is to the "About Party development" resolution carried by the TsK Politburo and the TSKK RKP(b) Presidium on December 5.

8. For G. I. Myasnikov's "Workers' Group," see note 5 of Document No. 4 and note 6 of Document No. 20.

9. In the verbatim record that was not corrected the phrase was written as the following: "Trotsky offered a weak objection, and we finally agreed that in the famous Party on groups and factions we would make a reference to the Tenth Congress resolution on factions. He agreed to it."

10. L. D. Trotsky sent the statement like that: see Document No. 31.

In the uncorrected verbatim record there was the word "body" between the words "Party elements" at the end of the phrase.

11. The reference is to "New Course (a Letter to Party Conferences)" (see Document No. 30).

12. The fact is V. I. Lenin's article "How We Should Reorganize the Workers' and

Peasants' Inspection" (Proposals to Twelfth Party Conference). The history of its publication is in note 9 of Document No. 5.

13. There was no such phrase in the original stenographic entry.

14. I. V. Stalin doesn't speak of the important issue: there remained differences on the question whether the Politburo would exist and whether, first of all, the ruling "three" resolution "About Party development" would be put into practice or not. From the very beginning L. D. Trotsky had doubts about the sincerity of its members' assurances. The event of the first week of December 1923 (I. V. Stalin's speech in the Krasnopresnensky region and his publishing of TsK and TSKK October Plenary Session resolution, the TsK Politburo conference and decision concerning the question) proved that the TsK "main ruling body" did not intend to make any change in inner-Party democracy and that the resolution "About Party Building" turned out to be a paper and formal concession to the opposition.

15. The uncorrected verbatim record reads "belonging to TsK" instead of "staying above TsK."

16. The words "evidently by opposition TsK members" do not appear in the verbatim record.

17. I. V. Stalin refers to his own speech at the Moscow Krasnopresnensky region Party activists conference of December 2 , 1923 (see Document No. 23).

18. The statement of L. D. Trotsky, G. L. Pyatakov and K. B. Radek of December 29, 1923, in connection with *Pravda*: see Document No. 45.

19. In the report at the Thirteenth Party Conference I. V. Stalin announced that the opposition had held a meeting of the Bureau led by L. Serebryakov in Moscow. There has not been found any other documentary evidence of this fact.

20. Between the words "I inform" and "There can be only one conclusion" on the next page in the uncorrected verbatim record there was the following text: "that the document had been recently found by him. This TSKK member might confirm it himself. This method of submitting all existing and nonexisting resolutions, all solved problems and problems to be solved, and discussing them at the Party congress was specially destructive. We were being told at the meeting: "You crucified Trotsky." I wasn't entitled to publish the papers, I hadn't any possibility of objecting to it. The papers are spreading by leaps and bounds and they are being brought to the TsK from everywhere. And it happens in all regions of our big country, in the Caucasus—anywhere you want. As for the young Party members, they are looking for the truth, they are speaking at meetings: "We know how the Politburo, TsK, and TSKK solve their matters. You crucified Comrade Trotsky." How we can answer it, not having the right to make reference to the documents? The TsK members just say it is wrong, and they can say nothing more than this. The resulting impression is that "the TsK members lie, they are afraid of the truth, while Preobrazhensky, for instance, came and wasn't afraid to tell the truth. Unlike them he said the truth; when they were driven into a corner, when I, "sverdlovets" pressed him, he had nothing to say." Then I was forced to violate the TsK resolution and to say that it was not correct, my dear comrades, that this was the fight for the faction and so on.

What does it imply? If it continues like this, if all decisions and resolutions are kept published, we will be forced to publish everything. How else could it be if Bitker Wolks is saying everywhere that TsK entrusted him and Kontsesky (Concession Committee, Ed.) to sell Russia? Here you are, but sell for more, and so we are engaged in selling it. But we cannot say to the Party members that this is wrong. We don't possess any secret documents; otherwise there will be rumors and gossip around these statements, for our Party has a rather great number of absolutely narrow-minded persons, who prefer to deal with gossip and rumors, and, thus, TsK has to turn into an open yard where it is impossible to store any kind of documents. This is an insincere method of preventing TsK from doing the work and it was mastered by some of the opposition members that brought the Politburo to the boiling point, since we had to publish all documents in order not to be named among the liars. It was an especially destructive thing. Thus, Comrade Trotsky's letter has emerged—and this is a specific method of Comrade Serebryakov (I know it) to set Party members against the Politburo by saying that they are criminals who sell Russia and so on."

21. The reference is to the papers whose spread had been banned by the joint TsK and TSKK Plenary Session (October): L. D. Trotsky's letter of October 3, the Statement of the Forty-Six, Politburo members' replies of October 19, and resolution of the very same October Plenum.

22. Naturally, no one of the faction "main ruling body" was interested in Party members' getting to know of Party machinery backstairs intrigues around L. D. Trotsky. In this case, I. V. Stalin named TsK and TSKK Joint Plenary Session resolution (October) to be the original documents, i.e., the resolution accusing L. D. Trotsky and the opposition of splitting. Since, in reality, "the troika" wanted Party members to be aware of the resolution, the phrase of I. V. Stalin, like all other discussions concerning this matter, are looking hypocritical and demagogic.

23. To prepare the resolution concerning discussion results there had been elected a commission: I. V. Stalin, N. B. Bukharin, V. V. Kuibyshev, L. B. Kamenev, N. A. Uglanov, A. I. Mikoyan, M. V. Frunze, and others.

24. By this is meant "New Course (Letter to Party Conferences)" and other L. D. Trotsky articles published from December 1923 through January 1924 in *Pravda* commonly titled "New Course."

25. The Thirteenth Joint Party Conference passed the resolution "About results of the discussion and petty-bourgeois deviation in the Party," where it had been stressed that the opposition Party "not only made an attempt to revise Bolshevism to deviate from Leninism, but also represented a marked petty-bourgeois deviation." At that time, these were considered to be the most dreadful labels used by the Stalin-Zinovyev group to politically discredit L. D. Trotsky and the opposition. As for repressions of the opposition and its supporters, they would be out in different forms in 1924 (but for the time being through staff transfers, discharges, etc.).

A.I. MIKOYAN'S REPORT

Mikoyan. It seems to me that Comrade Kamenev is not right when he says that because the TsK was under fire during the discussion, now it is to sit twiddling its thumbs and say to the conference: we don't know what has happened.[1] It would mean that the TsK refuses to be at the head of our

Party. The discussion had very deep roots; here mistakes not only in work and in Party development but also in the alignment of classes had played their role. How can TsK (in view of being one of the sides in the struggle) say nothing about the political results of the discussion? This way of putting the problem is erroneous.

I have to say that the discussion, along with all its negative sides, turned out to be extremely useful for the ideological unity of the Party all the same. In accordance with my observations, I have to say that after the discussion we have gotten much stronger in our ideological-Bolshevik respect. After being under fire, the main Party body developed an ideological link with a grown-up and enormous layer of Party members with neither experience in revolutionary Bolshevik struggle, nor information about the internal struggle of the past. Afterward, the discussion showed that the TsK's intention to remove the differences in the narrow circle for the sake of unity and therefore to hide things from the vast Party masses had had a negative effect on the link of TsK with the Party and on the revolutionary and Bolshevik education of Party members. Probably, larger circle of Party members should have been informed about the gist of the differences and this could have been done in a timely way, but in December everything had toppled on us simultaneously, i.e., everything that had been piled up for several years and intensified the fight in a stormy way.

Among other reasons, the students followed the opposition also because the opposition was the first to show to the masses all prohibited documents. It seemed to the part of the youth who were under opposition influence, that we hide our documents not for the sake of unity of interests but because of fear and our guilty conscience. It produced a very unfavorable impression in regard to TsK authority before the Party. We will have to take it into account in a number of questions, and to bring TsK work to the notice of the larger circle of Party members. It seems that it was at the Twelfth Congress that we decided that all TsK Plenary Sessions should be held at wide local Party meetings,[2] but it had not been always put into practice. It is necessary that TsK activities be more available to Party masses; also it will promote the creation of the ideological link between the masses and TsK.

Further, the discussion showed that we had young Party layers who not only had never been Mensheviks but did not have any knowledge of Menshevism because of their late birth either politically or physically. They know nothing of the many differences that existed in the past. Now they often in their discussion very sincerely champion the principles, Menshevist in fact, that had been rejected by Bolshevism a long time ago.[3] There were attempts to inculculate the principles of formal democracy, formally equality, and so on within our Party.

Smenovekhov. Followers[4] one day wrote in their newspaper that the essence of the discussion consists in the fact that the Russian intelligentsia declared its right to national government for the first time. If this is true then it may be linked with the growing young intellectuals in the Party, students, i.e., these future "red spetsy"* and public figures.

As for the peasantry, the discussion has just penetrated there, and newspapers are just beginning to be received. The country people will understand the discussion a little bit, but will start talking in their own interests, and if they keep silent it will not be better. We'll have to think of the peasants ourselves. None of the organizations tried to use the democracy for peasants and to map out necessary restrictions. Here, big threats are hidden. Peasants need democracy to root out people from the Soviets and to fill them with their own people who are mostly well-to-do and minded against workers; as for poor country layers, they are weak politically and not active.

As for workers, they are often shutting themselves up in the framework of the Party, also forgetting the existence of the working class. A non-Party worker expresses his opinion in the following way: why is it necessary to give the worker's democracy to all communists, even to those who are not workers, and not to give anything to the non-Party worker? There is a logic in this. It is necessary that inner-Party democracy, inevitably coming out of the Party, should be applied among non-Party people with some restriction, and not be allowed to grow among the peasantry and intellectuals without strong and rigid restrictions. Of course, the application of democracy outside the Party, even with restrictions, is fraught with the greatest danger. There is a new wave among workers; among newly grown workers there is a newly raised question connected with "spetsy,"[5] drawing workers in industry management. We'll still have to work out the form of such enlisting of non-Party workers. We need to review the methods of work of the trade unions and cooperative societies from this point of view.

The discussion follows that we must come as closely as possible to the working class to create economic link with peasants; otherwise the greatest difficulties would emerge.

---

*Specialists. (Ed.)

NOTES

1. A. I. Mikoyan did not entirely understand L. B. Kamenev's proposal when the question on prohibited documents had been under consideration. L. B. Kamenev on behalf of the Politburo proposed to distribute the secret documents among the Thirteenth Party Conference delegates. "Our proposal doesn't go any further," he emphasized, taking into account the conference delegates who were to be aware of it.

2. The Twelfth Congress of RKP(b) in April 1923 carried a majority resolution "About the questions of propaganda, press, and agitation"; however, there wasn't such a point in it. At the same time, the request to send TsK activity reports every two months to the provincial committees by TsK had been a standard rule since 1919.

3. As a matter of fact, the discussion meeting demands brought up by Party youth were considered to be the standard of democratic Party internal life. Some of the standards are: the possibility of free discussion of inner-Party life problems, to unite in non-faction groups to propagate and defend one's own position, to guarantee nonpunishment for criticism of higher authorities, to ease bureaucratic centralism and Party machinery pressure, etc. But for the Bolshevik Party, where the monolithic directive unity had been a fetish and the greatest value, these demands had been considered anti-Party and Menshevik.

4. Smenovekhstvo, a social and political trend of Russian, mainly emigrant, intellectuals of the 1920s, reflected to a certain extent the ideology of a new NEP bourgeoisie. The term comes from the *Smena Vekh* (*The Changing of Landmarks*) collection published in the summer of 1921 in Prague by a group of prominent emigrant publicists. Smenovekhstvo ideologists believed that after the introduction of NEP Russia would come back to the groove of natural bourgeois-democratic development, and therefore it was possible to recognize the Soviet power and to cooperate with it. L. D. Trotsky considered "smenovekhtsy" would come to Soviet power "through the gates of patriotism"; I. V. Stalin pointed out at the Twelfth Conference that they praised Bolsheviks for their restoration of a united and indivisible Russia.

5. The question of "spetsy" (about their attitude to bourgeois special lists) is a rather painful problem that Bolsheviks faced immediately after the revolution. Without employing the old technical intellectuals the economy was not able to function, but the working class educated by the Bolshevik Party on the basis of class ideology had an extremely negative attitude toward the old specialists and created a serious social tension in bodies of workers.

N.A. UGLANOV'S REPORT

Uglanov. To my mind the Party and the TsK are facing a whole number of organizational tasks. And what do we observe? After Stalin's strongly worded article,[1] opposition ranks are confused; Stalin's word were strong and correct. Not knowing what to do, the narrow-minded Party members had been rushing about. When the worker, like a proletarian battering-ram, followed TsK firmly and calmly in one direction, one part of the confusion-makers came to their senses and followed the majority, and the number of whimperers went down. Such a tone had been given from the very beginning. If you want a discussion, let it be a discussion, fight to the finish, let it be a real one. I think our deeds were right. All sore spots had been eliminated. What do workers say about democracy? They say the following: it is good we have moved, we have to rock ourselves a little bit but without losing our consciousness. At the same time, a Sormovo engineer praised Trotsky profusely[2] in return. He says that it is right not only for workers to take part in the work of the Soviets and State development, but for us to do it as well. Muzhik is not like he used to be in the past, he does not have a shaped consciousness. He says that it is bad or incorrect if a new Party should be set up.

That is why the organizational arrangements are to be the following. Since the youth had been a pioneer of narrow-minded Party member riot, they were to take the following measures. It is necessary to radically revise our Party history teaching methods. There is no use in binding Comrade Trotskys and Mensheviks who joined our Party role in the past when we teach growing generations; first of all, Agitprop* and Comrade Bubnov must deal with it. Until this is done, you will not succeed in enlisting people for Party work in Moscow, you will not get the workmen. Further, the following conclusion follows from it. To bridge the emerging gaps, undoubtedly, it is necessary to draw workers into the Party and the congress is to adhere to Zinovyev's idea of organizational regulation of a Party. It is necessary to carry this idea through in order to "perform the regulation"; fifty thousand Party members might be expelled from the Party[3] and 150 thousand workers admitted to the Party. Maybe it is necessary to begin more widely and fully to put TsK resolutions of organizational and economic matters into practice.

I think that after adopting the decision of the Plenary Session and conference we need to take a whole number of organizational measures and concrete declarations on behalf of TsK to develop the resolution that we

---

*This is a reference to the Agitation and Propaganda Department then headed by A. S. Bubnov. (Ed.)

declared:[4] At once, to radically put the entire Party on a different footing and knock the demagogy weapon out of the hands on the opposition that has been using it up to now. To develop concrete measures on behalf of TsK and to publish a concrete manifesto. Further, on the issue of discipline: I think that there should be discipline. I visited Sverdlov University and stayed overnight with Comrade Lyadov.[5] What does it look like? The senior students gather together, invite a lecturer of economic problems without letting the Party cell and others know. I don't know who was there (Voice: Preobrazhensky was). It should be seriously punished. Democracy is democracy, but organizational forms are organizational forms and Party rules are Party rules. Here it is necessary to take action.

We have to radically change our attitude to the members of Komsomol (Young Communist League). We need to stop pulling them into meetings of workers so that they give their voice, we need to give up the tradition of five of Sverdlovtsy's people attending the meetings with their Party I.D. cards and bringing with them another hundred people. It was shameful and a regular disgrace, when at the Moscow Party Conference nearby the delegates were Sverdlovtsy's who had no right to participate in the meetings. Its disgraceful, Comrade Bubnov, you must correct it. Don't go where you were not invited.

NOTES

1. This is a reference to I. V. Stalin's article "About discussion, about Comrade Rafayl, about Comrade Preobrazhensky and Comrade Sapronov's articles and about Comrade Trotsky's letter" published in *Pravda* on December 15, 1923.

2. N. A. Uglanov states the fact that during discussion the opposition had actively been supported by intellectuals.

3. At the Plenum, the speech of secretary of the Nizhegorodsky local Party committee, N. A. Uglanov, was in its form and content symptomatic: as a matter of fact, on behalf of the secretary hierarchy he blessed TsK and gave the go-ahead to give short shrift to the opposition. N. A. Uglanov's speech evidently made an impression on I. V. Stalin—in 1924 the general secretary would "transfer" him to Moscow and appoint him to be secretary of the Moscow Party Committee.

4. This is a reference to the "About Party development" resolution (see appendix of Document No. 24).

5. This is a reference to the Y. M. Sverdlov Communist University higher Party educational institution, headed by M. N. Lyadov.

K. B. RADEK'S REPORT

Radek. It is difficult to say in ten minutes everything that would express my attitude toward the opposition, the more so, since it showed its face insufficiently. Here the same is taking place as in the debates on trade unions, where only many months later the whole Party realized that while debating about joining the trade unions with economic bodies, it was in fact discussing the possibility of further conducting the policy of military communism.[1] I can distinguish three main questions in this debate: those of the economic situation, the developments of Party masses and Party guidance.

I'll start with the economic situation. You blame Trotsky's statement of October 8 and the one by the "Forty-Six" of October 15[2] for their prodigiously pessimistic assessment of the economic situation and negative appreciation of the shortcomings of the TsK economic policy. However, let me read some extracts from the speech of TsK member Sokolnikov who, as Narkomfin,* belongs to the leaders of our economic policy announced at the VTsIk faction (All-Russia Central Executive Committee) conference.[3] It was published as a typescript together with Comrade Krzhizhanovsky's report on "scissors."[4] Here is Comrade Sokolnikov's speech:

"General peasant strike against trusts and cooperation and peasant's refusal to put the production according to its prices is the situation we are facing now. And I'm saying: tell me who is right, the peasantry or the Soviet State? I answer that the peasantry is right. We must confess that we've been entangled. If you want, I put any part of the blame for this on myself. But I must say that we were the ones who brought our affair to a position running counter to our Party policy" (p. 71).

... "This is our injurious, destructive attitude toward the peasant economy coming out of huge pressures from all directions. We are to restrain our needs. Our needs are undoubtedly legal but they are to be calculated in time and space. This is not the last year of our existence. We could postpone some things for two or three years. Don't break off the unity with the peasants. Don't bring matters to a position where the peasantry would look at the Authority as an Authority and a Party that doesn't fulfill their promises . . ." (p. 75).

---

*People's Commissar of Finances.

". . . I think that our practice in state industry, state trade bodies and co-operation has been distorted by capitalism. This is how it should be said. I met this formulation when I set out to make a retail trademan reduce his prices by importing foreign goods much cheaper than ours and selling them inside the country at lower prices. It is necessary to reduce the whole-sale prices of our trust adopted by Komvnutorg* and government. According to Comrade Krzhizhanovsky, the retail prices are exorbitantly rising. To reduce it we need to increase the supply in the market. Let's suppose that we are importing the goods from abroad. What will the co-operation and Gostorg (State Trade) do? They will start selling the imported goods at as high a price as possible to worker, peasant, and general small mass consumer . . ." (p. 80).

I could cite a number of extracts of the speech proving that Comrade Sokolnikov's assessment of the economic situation is not any less sharp than that of the opposition's, but you can read it in the original. I won't dwell upon these quotations' establishing Comrade Sokolnikov as a father of goods intervention for following which Pyatakov was labeled Mlado-Eser. I will not turn to the short conclusions on the evaluation of our economic situation. Comrade Lenin warned against rushing from a poor peasant horse to an industry trotter which we lack. But it has been proved by the developments that if our industry is not able to provide the peasantry with reasonable prices, then the peasant horse will bristle. What's the solution to the problem? I see it, on the one hand, in the enforcement of the planning element in our economy that will restrain the leakage of national riches in the hands of NEP men, and make the reduction of production costs possible and, on the other hand, in helping to sign concessionary deals that will provide us with the capital to enforce the state industry.

The second question (one of our Party construction) is closely connected with NEP. The Central Committee knew all the dangers that accompanied our Party transition to the inner-Party democratic system. He was aware that we were a Party of dictatorship in a petty-bourgeois country, he knew of our Party petty-bourgeois majority; nevertheless, on December 5 TsK decided to turn to a worker democracy system.[5] Maybe some of the comrades thought about a possibility of clasping the Party tightly in hand after that once again. However, it is impossible. If some of the oppo-

---

*Commissariat of Internal Trade of the SNK of the USSR (more precisely: People's Commissariat, Narkomat). (Ed.)

sition members want TsK to ensure against this, then they don't understand that these are in line with the reasons that led to the change. Comrade Stalin pointed out the reasons: unforeseen strikes[6] had shown the isolation of our bodies from the working mass; the appearance of illegal groups[7] within the Party had proved that while existing contradictions caused by the NEP filling keenly by working mass, it was impossible to pursue the Party line from above only; local Party organizations were to be given a possibility of taking part in the debate on our Party course. If this is the way it is, then there is no reason to tell about the recurrence of Menshevik views on organizational questions among the opposition. I myself have never been a Menshevik, neither have I participated in the work of the Bolshevik faction, for then I was engaged in the Polish and German movement. However, I thoughtfully learned the history of the organizational policy of Bolshevism. This policy passed through a whole number of stages depending on the changing general situation: in 1903 it was one, in 1905 it was another; it was during the victory of the counterrevolution and another after the events in the Lena region.[8]

Kamenev. It consisted of one thing; we have always been the organization of professional revolutionaries.

Radek. Yes. But we've always been striving for our goal, the creation of a Party carrying through its own will, one course using the methods which depend on the general situation. At one time the Party was socially united; now our Party has only 60 thousand bench lather workers,* which is why the old goal cannot be reached by the old means.

There are threats to the transition to the inner-Party democracy. There we've made a lot of mistakes in the course of debate, and I'm ready to bear any kind of responsibility for the ones I made personally. But how come you want the Party to shift to an inner-Party democracy system without making any mistakes after three years of silence? While rejecting repressions, you recognized the necessity of these mistakes yourselves. You cannot say that you gave them up because of Stalin's gentleness. Because of disagreement in views there may emerge factions. It is necessary to avoid this danger at any price, the minority are to obey the Congress decisions. However, it depends on you, comrades, whether conditions for the creation of factions are there. You received a huge majority in the Party and that is why you must keep yourselves from abusing your victory. You shouldn't

---

*This is a reference to workers directly engaged in industrial production.

dismiss the question of a planning element, replacing it with jokes and anecdotes.

Dzerzhinsky. What plan do you propose?

Radek. You, Comrade Dzerzhinsky, are yourself raising the question of a bloc of transportation, coal and iron.[9] You propose a plan. Why, then, are you talking against the planning element? If you think that Comrade Trotsky will not be able to actually implant the planning element in economic bodies, then don't appoint him to any economic posts. But don't brush the planning question aside; otherwise you'll set up factions.

I proceed to the third question—the issue of TsK structure and Party guidance. It was said that I wanted nothing but to defend Trotsky. Comrade Zinoviev in his speeches proves that Trotsky is an old Menshevik, who doesn't know workers and peasants; however, the Politburo will work with him jointly. What does this all mean? The premises contradict the conclusions, but there the conclusion is that there is a necessity to work together with Trotsky; it demonstrates that the matter concerning Trotsky is not a personal question, and, therefore, I raise the question although nothing connected me with Trotsky in the past. Either you have to openly raise the question of the impossibility of working with Trotsky as a Menshevik in the TsK and the Politburo, or you should keep him in the Politburo for his sweet sake and accept him the way he is, with all his advantages and disadvantages. It is clear from the papers that Comrade Stalin proposed him to be in charge of the industry. Then what are all today's stories about? Trotsky introduced an individual shade in the history of our Party and retained many of his special views. However, when he was with the Mensheviks on the central question of the revolution of 1905, on the question of a coalition with the bourgeoisie—he followed us, but not the Mensheviks.[10] The allegation of his underestimating the peasantry is wide open to criticism. It was not you but Trotsky who raised the question of "scissors."[11]

I proceed to the threats of teeth-crushing policy in respect to the opposition members. If you prove that Antonov-Ovseeknoe, as a chief of the Political Agency of the Revolutionary Military Council, directed the opposition against TsK, then you have the right to dismiss him (the State bodies are to pursue TsK course); however, nobody has proved it. There is no use either in clinging to organizational mistakes.[12] The way in which Trotsky, Pyatakov, and I appealed to TsK was a wrong one,[13] but we proved that Comrade Nazaretyan had informed TsK in an inadmissible way: I am not even referring to forgeries; they are not very important to me except the directive that he gave in order to divide the Party into a workers and non-workers parts.[14] Neither am I referring to my speech before the red professorate[15]—I admit that it was not necessary to raise the Germany question at the Party meeting before its discussion in TsK.[16] But the question that the Party faces, is that either the discussion should be ended with repressions or an atmosphere should be created which would push both sides to even more mistakes. The debate has upset the Party's situation. We should be able to stop it. There are elements of crisis in the country and in the Party. It is necessary to strive for TsK's common front now. Then the debate will turn out to be useful in the long run, for it has stirred the Party's brain up. One Polish worker noticed correctly that the Party came closer to workers from the moment when they had newly taken part in the decision of the questions vital for the Party.

Kamenev. Do you consider the formulation that appears in the Forty-Six's statement to be a mistake?

Radek. They piled it on, but it was done in the face of the economic crisis in order to make the shift toward inner-Party democracy a necessary one.

RTsKhDNI: 17, 2, 109
p. 4-6 (I. V. Stalin's speech);
p. 11 (A. I. Mikoyan's speech);
p. 13 (N. A. Uglanov's speech);
pp. 17-18 (N. I. Bukharin's speech);
pp. 18-19 (K. B. Radek's speech).
All speeches are published for
the first time.

NOTES

1. K. B. Radek was right in that the all-Party discussion of late 1920 and early 1921 of the role and missions of trade union in the conditions of peaceful construction, in fact, reflected the "military communism" policy crisis (also see note 5 of Document No. 17).

2. For L. D. Trotsky's letter of October 8, 1923, see Document No. 4; for the Statement of "Forty-Six" of October 15, see Document No. 12.

3. This is a reference to the Bolshevik faction of the All-Russian Central Executive Committee of Soviets (BTsIK).

4. The "scissors" of prices—see note 19 of Document No. 4.

5. The reference is to the resolution of TsK and TSKK "About Party Building" (see note of Document No. 24).

6. In the summer and fall of 1923, big industry centers of the country were on strike.

7. About the illegal groups "Rabochaya Pravda" (Workers' Truth) and "Rabochaya Gruppa" (Workers' Group), see note 5 of Document No. 4 and note 6 of Document No. 20.

8. K. B. Radek names the most important landmarks in the history of the Bolshevik Party, when depending on concrete conditions of the revolutionary and workers' movement there were changes in forms and methods of Party organizational work: the year 1903 was a period when Russian social democracy had taken shape, a time of its statutes and Program development; 1905 was the beginning of the First Russian Revolution, when the situation required joint efforts and actions of Bolshevik and Menshevik factions. After the revolution's defeat there was a period of ideological crisis and trials to combine legal and illegal forms of struggle. There were the events of the Lena region—shooting down a peaceful march of workers on strike in the Lensky gold mines, April 1912, by czarist troops that initiated the upsurge of the workers' movement.

9. K. B. Radek speaks of F. E. Dzerzhinsky's speech at the Plenary Session: he, in fact, supported the idea of the necessary planning combination of different economic branches. However, his speech was withdrawn from the printed text. In the copy of the Plenum shorthand record where the speakers made their corrections and from which the printed text was copied, F. E. Dzerzhinsky's speech was crossed out, probably by one of the members of the editorial commission.

10. Stalin's assessment of L. D. Trotsky's personality and his political activity prevailed in Soviet historiography for a long time. Stalin's propaganda and obliging historical science gave him, among the others, the following labels: an agent of Menshevism, the worst enemy of Leninism and Bolshevism, people's enemy. By the way, L. D. Trotsky, who had never been in the Bolshevik faction of RSDRP (he was admitted to the Bolshevik Party only in the summer of 1917), was neither a loyal Menshevik. According to his mentality and inclination to decisive actions he was nearer to the Bolsheviks; on the questions of Party development he was closer to the Mensheviks. In the decade preceding 1917 he took a centrist position, trying to unite all factions, groups, and trends in Russian social democracy. The October Revolution of 1917 was the triumphant hour for L. D. Trotsky's life and political career as well as for V. I. Lenin.

11. In fact, L. D. Trotsky in his report of "About industry" at the Twelfth Congress of RKP (b) did begin a serious conversation about the danger of the sharp divergence of industrial and farm product prices.

12. About this, see Document No. 44 (I-II).

13. For L. D. Trotsky, G. L. Pyatakov, and K.B. Radek's statement in TsK, see Document No. 45.

14. K. B. Radek refers to the tendentiousness of selection of information about the discussion (published in *Pravda*) showing the intention to stress the idea that the opposition was mainly supported by the nonproletarian, intellectual part of the Party, and its proletarian main body had followed TsK.

15. This is a reference to the Institute of the Red Professorate (IRP)—a special higher educational institution that trained the teachers of social sciences, employees of science—research institutions of the humanitarian type. It was set up in 1921. From 1923 to 1932 its rector was M. N. Pokrovsky.

16. By the German question are meant the revolutionary events in the summer and fall of 1923, whose culmination was the Hamburg uprising led by German communists. After putting down the uprising, the Presidium of the Komintern and TsK RKP (b) had a stormy discussion over the results and the lessons of these events. At the TsK Plenum of January 15, after G. E. Zinovyev's report on the international situation, there was adopted a decision blaming "the incorrect behavior of K. B. Radek on the German question."

N. I. BUKHARIN'S REPORT

Bukharin. Comrades, after the analysis made by the previous speakers I cannot develop this idea a lot. I think we must pay attention to the conduct of our political opponents that emerged from our Party. In the first place, I mean the "Workers' Group."[1] How do they assess our opposition? Do they have anything in common with our opposition? The white press[2] asks the question in a very clear manner; the very regime you watch in the Soviet Republic is the regime of a dictator's pressure and it should be untied from the very tight little knot represented by the Politburo of the TsK. In one white newspaper I've read that freedom of speech within the Party was nothing but freedom of speech within the country. And it goes without saying, if our political opponents are oriented toward their wish to unbind knots inside our Party and they gradually are getting up to uniting the system of proletarian dictatorship, it warns us of the all-political and democratic threat we face, and, thus, we are to appreciate the environment we have. Let's consider the creation of Panyshkin's worker-peasant group and Myasnikov's[3] group in the past.

If you compare a whole number of things with Myasnikov's platform, on the one hand, and look at all notes of the "Workers' Group," on the other, you'll see they have a great common ground. All this development of the inner-Party relations, at first, within the Party, then within the working class, in general, and then Myasnikov's ideas ("we, the working class, must have freedom of speech, assembly, and press"[4])—all that comes from this is going too far—whether the comrades want it or not. If we do not put a certain bridle on this or define the bounds, it goes to a non-Party peasant, and, thus, it leads toward the all-political democracy. It seems to me that the outlines of what is being built behind all this fuss and commotion, have already become distinct. These outlines comprise a whole number of social layers who have been knocking at the door of the all-political democracy.

As to the existence of this thing in the Party, it is perfectly clear. Comrade Kamenev tells the truth by pointing out the heterogeneity of the opposition. There is a peasant wing and the comrades use it in the inter-factional struggle. We have a bloc of factional groups that are united on the negative platform against TsK. We see that the mechanics are very simple. The various social groups and social shades are forming groups among each other. There is a growing generation striving for more activity and that has been restricted in the past by the previous regime and the Party machinery. This is a sound reaction used by the elements who are striking socially.

If we pass a question about the differences between the correct course and the opposition's course from the point of view of the tasks we face, then, it seems to me, the difference may be formulated as follows. Our task is to distinguish the two dangers. First of all, the danger, coming from the centralization of our machinery. And secondly, the danger of the political democracy that may come out if all the democracy goes too far.[5] We must see both of these dangers. As to the opposition, it sees one danger. It sees the danger of bureaucratism of our machinery, and it doesn't care about the other dangers. Behind the bureaucracy it doesn't distinguish the danger of political democracy. This is their so-called Menshevism as a certain deviation.[6] They don't see that in order to support the proletarian dictatorship we need to support the dictatorship of the Party that is unthinkable without a dictatorship of the old guard that, in its turn, is unthinkable without the leading role of the TsK as an organization of power.[7]

From the point of view of inner organizational matters, the difference may be formulated as follows: the specific thing that makes us, Bolsheviks, different from Mensheviks and Eser (the Party of socialists and revolutionaries)-minded persons is that we never championed the point of view of the formal democracy that shows the Party to be a kind of conglomerate of forces of equal value, where everyone has equal rights, etc. We are aware of the fact that the working class is not homogeneous, the Party is not homogeneous, it has layers; we are to organize our Party so that its more conscious part could tow the less conscious one and the latter could tow the following one and so on. They approach the affair with perfectly empty and abstract formulas. They don't see the concrete hooks of the inner Party mechanics. When they discuss in this direction, the wind of the non-Bolshevik camp blows. Formal democracy in our Party organization is perfectly strange to us. It seems to me that the common task we face is: the workers expressing the sound tendency are to be isolated from the leaders of the opposition. As to the groups and leaders, it is necessary that one part of them is to be assimilated (those who are able to do it), the other part—to be disciplined.

Then I asked to pay attention to the other side of the affair that to my mind is extremely important: I am afraid that with all the perfectly and correctly calculated struggle (according to all rules of art) against the deviations, we should not forget those positive tasks that Party faces, because, really, a whole number of tasks planned by us are to be put totally and wholly, into practice. It seems to me that in the very near future we will face a whole number of matters that are out of the framework of our Party. For instance, I'm sure that tomorrow a trade union question will arise. (Voice: They have already arisen.) Yes, partly. To be sure, here our Party has to start thinking. Comrade Uglanov is perfectly right that a number of business-like measures resulting from the development of TsK and TSKK resolutions, putting them into practice and their publication in the press etc., will be the best trump card in our hands. Until now, we have been complete fools: Everything that is wrong, all shortcomings we had—we had been publishing them, we had written about them, and we had almost never written about good things undertaken by TsK, etc. And these good things began to show themselves only later, for instance, the revolution salary question that became known a year and a half later. Our mistake consisted in not publishing right away our Politburo resolutions on its course toward workers' democracy.[8] Nor did we publish the October Plenum resolution[9] confirming this course. Then, it seems to me, we have to take care of transferring a considerable number of the comrades into a specific Party work. To implement our course without it, is an unthinkable thing. We have to transfer a certain number of comrades into agitation and propaganda, and other kinds of Party-specific work. The directives to integrate work among the youth are correct. We need to create a special literature, as well as that of Party history, strategy, and tasks; it seems to me, in this connection we are to pay attention to non-Party members' operations behind our inner-Party tasks. If behind the inner-Party things we forget about work-

356   The Struggle for Power

ing on non-Party workers, we run the risk that the opposition will rebound and begin to revive. It is necessary to revive the customs we have lost the habit of—that is, some kind of obligatory Friday meetings, strengthening of non-Party conferences in services, etc. This is one of the ways to indirectly liquidate the opposition which in another case will be regenerated. Consequently, it is necessary to make it Agitprop* and other TsK bodies' duty to energize a positive strategy of positive work along the line of the new course implement.

Next I want to talk about workers' admission to the Party. Actually, it is necessary to increase the admission to the Party to a very great extent. This should be done in accordance with a perfectly defined and well-calculated plan. It is difficult for us to digest such a huge mass. One of the reasons for a specific Party crisis may be formulated in that we didn't digest a considerable quantity of our Party. I have to say that since this percentage, this coefficient, is not digested, it will grow greatly and we will wring our hands. The admission of workers to the Party is to be implemented in accordance with a certain plan. Perhaps those who have a considerable length of service are to be admitted in the first place or to make some kind of proviso, to fix the admission (in large centers) of the most qualified workers, on the basis of their length of service, in batches.[10] Here is approximately what I wanted to say.

NOTES

1. About the "Workers' Group" which was headed by G. I. Myasnikov among others, see note 5 of Document No. 4 and note 6 of Document No. 20.
2. This is a reference to the emigrant press (Menshevik, Eser).
3. V. L. Panyushkin group—a small group that emerged long before Tenth Party Congress (March 1921) that had made a decision to cross over to the NEP. The appearance of a group whose goal was to create a new "worker and peasant social Party," had been a consequence of the rather widespread assessment in RKP (b) at that time of NEP as exclusively a retreat back to capitalism, as a betrayal of workmen's interests.
4. N. I. Bukharin formulated in general form the essence of the platform of G. I. Myasnikov interpreted by him in his report to TsK and in the "Sound Questions" article (1921).
5. In an almost panicky speech N. I. Bukharin, who more than once repeated the dan-

---

*Agitation and propaganda department of TsK. (Ed.)

gers of all political democracy, rather convincingly testifies to the fact that the Bolshevik leaders precisely realized an objective necessity to bring the political superstructure into line with the pluralistic NEP basis. However, the broadening of the political democracy meant that the Party power monopoly would be weakened or even lost; and Bolshevik orthodoxy couldn't afford to agree to it and Stalin's group in RKP (b) leadership which rushed to power in order to usurp it.

6. Neither L. D. Trotsky nor other opposition leaders surpassed the limits of the Bolshevik doctrine. There was a request in the opposition paper for the broadening of political democracy. While blaming the opposition of Menshevism and petty bourgeois deviation at that time, there was a sure reliance on the "main leading body" in the inner-Party struggle against L. D. Trotsky and the left-wing opposition.

7. If N. I. Bukharin's phrase is to end logically, then it would be about the Supreme Dictator who topped the pyramid of power constructed by N. I. Bukharin.

8. This is probably a reference to the Politburo conference of October 1923 where L. D. Trotsky's letter of October 8 was discussed. At the meeting N. I. Bukharin convinced Politburo members of the necessity "to sharply turn the helm" in the direction of inner-Party democracy.

9. For the October united TsK and TSKK of the RKP(b) Plenum resolution (1923), see the Document No. 21:III.

10. According to N. I. Bukharin, the admission of workers to the Party "in batches" had already been carried out in large industrial "centers" (Petrograd, Moscow) in the fall of 1923, the sixth anniversary of the October revolution. The Thirteenth Party Conference would adopt a resolution on admitting to RKP (b) 100,000 industrial workers during 1924. During this period of time, nonproletarian elements refused to become Party members.